Pauline Scudamore han family for several years the Scudamore antiquarian d whilst they were bringi o worked part-time for a ly surgeries. She has a BA Hons in politics, history and English from Thames Polytechnic. She lives in Chelsea. This is her first book.

PAULINE SCUDAMORE

Spike Milligan

A Biography

GRAFTON BOOKS

A Division of the Collins Publishing Group

LONDON GLASGOW
TORONTO SYDNEY AUCKLAND

Grafton Books
A Division of the Collins Publishing Group
8 Grafton Street, London W1X 3LA

Published by Grafton Books 1987

First published in Great Britain by
Granada Publishing 1985

ISBN 0-586-06067-7

Printed and bound in Great Britain by
Collins, Glasgow

Set in Caledonia

Contents

6 *Contents*

For
Laura, Sean, Silé and Jane

Preface

Curiosity more than anything else led me towards writing this book. To me, Spike Milligan was an enigma, an extraordinary and baffling man who sometimes appeared close up, making us fall about with laughter, and at other times seemed remote and isolated, at a great distance. After the curiosity to learn more about him came the determination to put down something of what I had learned, to consolidate, to extricate the fact from the fiction and to show something of the man behind the myth.

Biographical material has been readily available, and the advantage of an early biography has not been lost by any restrictions placed on the writer by the subject. Spike has answered every question I have put to him with the total candour of a man who sees no point in lying. He has allowed me access to all his family, friends and acquaintances, and to his manuscripts, poems, diaries, letters and private papers. He has refused to look at what I have written; on one occasion when I tried to show him something of a preliminary draft of this book he waved it away firmly, smiled and said 'Surprise me.' I have been struck by the fact that after all the taped interviews I have had with him over four years he has never rescinded a single word, back-pedalled, said 'Don't use that' or wanted to read the subsequent typescripts.

Perhaps the fact that I was never a Goon fan may have helped rather than hindered this book. I have not been unmindful of what Milligan owes to the *Goon Show*, or what the development of British comedy owes to Milligan. But the Goon period has received due recognition in this book and no more, for it was the non-Goon Milligan that first attracted me.

I needed to delve at length into areas of his extraordinary life that have not as yet been touched on. The hazards of writing a biography of Milligan are great, not because he is a difficult man (of course he is) but because his mind is so fertile, so absorbent and so totally preoccupied with whatever is catching and firing his imagination at the moment that it would seem impossible to regulate and steer such an articulate man into conventional channels of orderly discussion. Yet Milligan is no fly-by-night quick talker. He is a man of intellect, capable of serious and conclusive thought. There is no lack of discipline when he is deeply interested or committed, and his observations are often both profound and devastatingly simple. Only his emotions betray him.

Because I have come to know Spike well, it has not always been easy to detach myself from the uncritical admirers and remain objective, but my overriding ambition has been to be honest. I have not tried to gloss over all the imperfections that are part of this strange and wayward man, for Milligan is too important to be flattered or patronized. I believe that people with such acutely perceptive minds as his should be recognized and heeded.

More than anything in this book I am aware of omissions. Some of these are glaring. His work for television alone is deserving of a profound study, for a more sharply defined case of extremes would be hard to find. The richness and the poverty march together; surreal brilliance contrasts with ordinary old chestnuts. Milligan is a master of spontaneity and a victim of the rehearsal room. Overall, my conclusion was that attempting to encapsulate his rare gifts for the small screen is like trying to chase and bottle a rainbow.

He has failed to be taken seriously as a writer and not a

small part of the blame must rest with him, for no one has denigrated his achievements with deadlier marksmanship than himself. The titles of his first few books have the tongue-in-cheek self-disparagement of a man who seems to have insulated himself against the humiliation and despair of rejection – for to Milligan, rejection is tormenting and grievous. For him, it holds nothing of the spur which has driven other writers forward. Milligan is bereft, as it were, of the means to harness this particular sort of adversity for his own eventual good.

Most people are unaware of his poetry. This is sad, for many of Milligan's poems, true to no style save his own, have a curious, indelible capacity to touch the conscience of the reader. And when a conscience is touched, views can alter and an outlook can change.

It is probably my own experience with Spike's destructive and painful illness that has equipped me to write about him with, I hope, a degree of lucidity and insight, just as I believe that being a manic-depressive has, for him, been a challenge of such magnitude that merely to surmount the downs and override the ups he has needed a physical and mental tenacity that can only have been arrived at with considerable courage. Although his achievements may have been to some extent a harnessing of the positive elements of this illness, we cannot assume that the results have been achieved without pressures and pain, nor that these achievements have been arrived at without penalty to the fragile, often agonizing relationships which Spike maintains with people he cares about. It is no exaggeration to say that he is a skin short; there are times when it seems that he could be virtually skinless. Sometimes it seems as if he is a shuddering carcass flayed raw by the agonies of daily living. A highly complex personality, he is nevertheless transparently honest and he is obviously possessed of considerable insight and some self-knowledge. I have heard him say with more anger than self-pity, 'I feel like a tortoise without its shell.'

Learning about Spike has been a long, painful, and fascinating process, and it only struck me after two years of working on the book that perhaps he needed not one but rather a team of biographers, and then they would not of necessity have got it right. His wife, his family, his friends, his children; their help and good wishes have been most supportive and encouraging and my thanks go out to them.

Most of all, however, I thank Spike for his patience and tolerance, for his understanding and his kindness. I feel that I have learned a lot, and not only about my subject. I hope that I have done him justice and that there will be a glimpse of the real man who is almost totally dissimilar to the zany TV personality we have been bludgeoned into accepting.

Author's Note

When not otherwise identified, either in the text or by source notes, all indented passages in the book are drawn from conversations between Spike Milligan and myself.

Many hours have been given to these conversations. We have talked when he has been on form and when he has been tired, when he has been well and happy and when he has been ill and wretched. We have talked when he has been working and when he has been relaxing. We have talked most often in his room at Monkenhurst, sometimes with his phones ringing and sometimes with his phones silenced. We have talked in his office, in dressing-rooms at studios and theatres, in museums, in bookshops, in clubs, in restaurants, on farms, in hardware stores, on Galley Hill at Bexhill where, as a soldier, he was once stationed, and on Hadley Common in Hertfordshire, close to where he now lives with his family. We have talked in Sheffield, Southsea, Leeds, Ipswich, Oxford, Cambridge, Bristol, Dublin and Australia. We have talked in cars, helicopters, planes and even on horseback.

Acknowledgements

I have to acknowledge the help of many people who have given their time willingly and unstintingly during the preparation of this book. First, I endorse my thanks to Spike for his unfailing patience and courtesy. Shelagh (Spike's wife and my friend) who never ceased to help and encourage me. The four young Milligans and Nanna who have all welcomed me and talked to me on so many occasions. Eileen McIntyre (Spike's aunt) who gave me a long interview and another aunt, the late Kathleen Thurgar, with whom I had many telephone conversations. Terry and Jane Thurgar (Spike's cousins) who invited me to their old home in Catford.

I am grateful to my own family who have borne with my preoccupations, especially my husband who has untangled and typed my drafts with unending patience. My friends Freddy and Connie Gore who not only encouraged me but shared their dinner with me whenever I happened to walk round the block of an evening in search of support and sustenance. I owe thanks to Miss Valerie Pitt from Thames Poly who gave me the confidence to get going, and to Mick Ryan who bolstered my spirits when they flagged. I am grateful to Beryl and Robert Graves who gave me much help and access to correspondence, and to Roger McGough who helped me with my understanding of Spike's poetry. Bernard Shaw from Canterbury who gave his time for some very helpful research. Peter Eton's widow, Squirrel, who invited me to her home in Rye and let me go through Peter's old scripts and papers.

Emma Leaman, Graham Leaman's daughter, for lending

me her excellent thesis 'Theatre Under Arms'. Alan Bell of the BBC who was most generous in allowing me access to the studios and locations during the making of 'There's a Lot of It About'.

Jackie Kavanagh and Geoffrey Waldon of BBC Archives at Caversham, also Kevin Johnson, and the staff of Programme Index, Reference Library and News Information at BBC, London. Library of Independent Broadcasting Authority, London.

Over the Goon Period I have looked closely at work published by Roger Wilmut, Jimmy Grafton and Alfred Draper. Both of the first two writers have also given me helpful interviews.

I am particularly grateful to Sir Harry Secombe and Michael Bentine, who both gave me long interviews, also to Lady Secombe who has a splendid memory and a kind heart to go with it. The book was not started until after Peter Sellers' death, so I am especially grateful to his first wife Anne (now Mrs Ted Levy) who was able to talk to me about the early days that they all shared.

I must also thank the London Branch of the 'Goon Show Preservation Society', their chairman Bob Bray, and George Brown who has helped me with his extensive and meticulously kept records and collections.

Very special thanks are due to the members of Spike's old Battery, the 56th Heavy Regiment of the Royal Artillery, for inviting me to their reunions at Bexhill.

Patrick Gillepsie, Nuffield Trust. Brigadier Lewendon, Old Royal Military Academy, Woolwich. Warrant Officer Len Harvey, formerly of (02E), for the loan of his manuscript 'Chairborne Warrior'.

I am also grateful to many people who have talked to me and sent me details of the work Spike has done in a wide cross-section of conservation and animal rights movements, in particular The Finchley Society and Friends of the Earth.

In Australia I have first of all a debt of gratitude to Spike's mother, now aged 90, a most remarkable old lady who made me welcome at her home in Woy Woy, even producing a magnificent side-table of assorted sandwiches whilst nursing a broken wrist. Spike's brother Desmond, who found time to talk to me at length on several occasions.

Dr Clement Semmler and his wife in Bowral. Margaret Deakin and Miss Pat Kelly of the Archive Department of the Australian Broadcasting Company. Phillip Adams of the Australian Film Commission. John Clegg of the Anthropology Department at the University of Sydney.

Bruce Webber, Bruce Rogerson, Bobby Limb, who all worked professionally with Spike, and actors David Nettheim and John Bluthal who worked with him both in Australia and England. Noelle McCracken of the Australian Puffin Club. Wilton Morley who was responsible for some of Spike's early Australian appearances. Blair Edmunds and Patricia Barraclough.

I thank Patrick and Yvonne O'Neill for letting me stay at their lovely farm in the Hunter Valley, and Michael Beatty (son of Robert) for inviting me to Brisbane where I saw Spike's one-man show at the University.

The following people have all given willing help, mostly by personal interviews, or in some cases by letter or telephone:

Raymond Agoult; John Antrobus; Reg Barrett; Robert Beatty; Danny Black; Louisa Bowen, Curator of Manuscripts, Southern Illinois, USA; Nigel Brown; Lord Justice Cantley; Alan Clare; Francis Coleman; Ruth Conti; John Counsel; Professor Bernard Crick; Carol Crowther; Tanis Davies; J. S. Dearden, Curator, Ruskin Galleries, Bembridge, Isle of Wight; Barry Duncan; Dipper Dye; Jan Eccles, National Trust, Downhill, Ulster; Geoffrey Edgington; Father Dan Eiffe; David Elis-Williams; Harold Fagg; Norma Farnes; Ann Farrar; Ian Flintoff; Michael Foot;

Renée Forsyth; Louise Furse; Lily Gibbs; John Goldschmidt; Mrs Digby Gordon; Sidney Gotlieb; Joan Greenwood; Ron Guariento; Nina Hall; Lionel Hamilton; Tina Hammond; Leslie Hardy; Renée Helman; Jack Hobbs; Derek Hudson; F. J. E. Hurst, Librarian, University of Ulster; Torsten Jungstedt; Doug Kidgell; Graham Leaman; Richard Lester; Oscar Lowenstein; Gordon Macdonald; Campbell McMurray, Department of Printed Books, National Maritime Museum, Greenwich; Beverley Mathias, Children's Books Officer, National Book League; Charles Meinardi; Lord (Bernard) Miles; John Miles; Johnny Mulgrew; Bill Nunn; Jenny and David O'List; Michael Parkinson; Maria Pontani; John Quinn of RTE, Dublin; Julie Randall; Robb (*Daily Express*); Dr Joe Robson; Alan Samson; Ronnie Scott; Dr Martin Scurr; Neil Shand; Anne Shelton; Bill Shields; Joanna Simons; Geoffrey Smith; Beryl Southby; Graham Stark; Honor Thackrah; Jill Thornton; Clifford Thornton; Andrew Timothy; Valerie Van Ost; Norman Vaughan; Beryl Vertue; Michael Waring; Ed Welch; John Wells.

I am deeply indebted to my friend Paul Joyce whose photograph of Spike appears on the cover.

I would also like to thank Michael Horniman and Caradoc King for their valuable help and advice, and Richard Johnson of Granada who has helped me a lot without imposing in the least.

Finally, I remember with especial love and gratitude my son Simon who often persuaded me to read chunks of the manuscript aloud to him and who never failed to boost my hopes that I was doing a fair job.

1

India: The Child

O are you the boy
    Who would wait on the quay
With the silver penny
    And the apricot tree?

        Charles Causley

On 16 April 1918, the Great War still raged furiously over the battlefields of France. *The Times* carried news of Lloyd George's impassioned speech in the House of Commons on the necessity for conscription in Ireland. The British 'roll of honour' for that day showed 487 officers wounded and 105 reported dead in the battles of the Somme. *The Playboy of the Western World* and *Chu Chin Chow* were running in London. Harrods food bureau gave a lecture on 'Appetizing ways with potatoes' and advertised the sale of ladies' three-button French kid gloves at four shillings and elevenpence per pair. A London charwoman was sent to prison for six months, with hard labour, for having stolen finery from the titled lady who employed her.

In the Province of Bombay, halfway across the world, the Indian Raj seemed not to be greatly interrupted by the long-drawn-out war in Europe, and Mrs Leo Milligan, *née* Kettleband, in labour with her first child, made the last four miles of her journey to hospital by bullock cart. At 3.30 P.M., just as the shifts in Ahmednagar Military Hospital were changing, she was delivered of a male child. The boy had a mop of dark golden hair and piercing blue eyes. He looked angry, and wailed discordantly. His mother, exhausted and proud, thought him beautiful. He was named Terence Alan, but by the time he reached full manhood these names were almost forgotten and he was known simply as 'Spike'.

Flo Milligan's confinement had not been easy. In later years she was to tell her son how she had resented the offhand attitude of the nurses and doctors who put her in a labour ward and told her to pull on a twisted wet towel 'to concentrate her mind' when the pains were severe. When a medical orderly put his head round the door and called out 'Are you all right, memsahib?' Flo swore at him with some spirit. This at least produced a visit from the doctor, who received the same treatment. 'Don't swear at me, I'm not responsible,' he said sulkily, promptly disappearing down the corridor. Only one person had really helped her, said Flo – a black Indian ayah who sat with her, bathing her face in cool water and comforting her. 'Memsahib be soon good. Soon come little master or missy baba.'

Thus, even during the trauma of birth, the imperial foundation of those early years was clearly defined. 'I always accepted that we were supposed to be superior,' says Spike. 'It was emphasized by every facet of our lives.' During the evenings of great heat, the white children were carried in their beds and put to sleep on the tennis courts or balconies of their homes. Shrouded in mosquito netting, the cool air still reached them and the nights could be magical:

> I remember lying out in my bed and looking at the vast, quiet sky. Right up above my head there were three stars in a row, and I remember thinking, well, I'll have those three stars all my life, and wherever I am they will be. They are my stars, and they belong to me.

Leo Alphonso Milligan, Spike's father, was the sixth child of William Patrick Milligan and Elizabeth Higgins. He was born in Sligo in Ireland, and his impressive names were bestowed upon him not by his parents (who wanted to christen him Percy Marmaduke) but by the priest at Sligo Cathedral where he was baptized, who, at the last moment, persuaded William and Elizabeth to call him after the Pope of that time.

Leo Milligan had a neat, elegant bone structure and a sensitive, masculine beauty. Physically, Spike and in due course Spike's son Sean were to be cast in the same mould. It seems to be a pattern that wears uncommonly well, for Leo retained a smart, athletic, light-stepping poise well into middle age; right up to his death in 1969 he looked quite capable of launching into the 'buck and wing dance' which drew enthusiastic acclaim in the Indian Army concerts of the 'twenties.

The only picture in existence of Spike's great-grand-father, the earliest Milligan to be traced in the direct line, suggests that he too might have been lithe and fine-boned. Michael Milligan was born in Donegal in 1816. At the age of twenty, he left the poverty of his Irish boyhood behind him by joining the Royal Artillery, thereby establishing a family tradition, for in due course his son William, his grandson Leo Alphonso and his great-grandson Terence Alan (Spike) were also to become Royal Artillery gunners. At the time of enlisting in the British Army, Michael was a labourer by trade, and he was illiterate. He was posted to Canada (listed as Newfoundland in the records) and in order to communicate with his family back home taught himself to read and write. 'And no one,' says his wrathful great-grandson today, 'had the slightest feeling for this achievement. No letter survives. Not one. Everything thrown away.' Spike (an archivist at heart) is perplexed that his ancestors did not see fit to preserve any of the letters which must have been written with such painstaking determination by his forebear.

You would think that someone, somewhere along the line,
would have realized how great it was that this man, so
deprived, had taught himself. What it must have meant to
him! Does nobody ever care?

William Milligan retired from the army and brought his
large family to London in 1885. He had been a cabinetmaker before joining the Royal Artillery and a wheelwright
with the regiment. Now he found a job as scenery manager
at the Queen's Palace of Variety at Poplar, East London.
He was an enterprising man and speedily managed to get
a second job for himself as a caretaker at Grosvenor
Buildings, the block of flats in which the family lived in
Deptford. More importantly, perhaps, he was also able to
get occasional work as 'supers' at the Palace (a kind of
stage extra) for four of his five sons. The boys did a
considerable amount of theatrical work while still at school,
appearing with a troupe of youngsters dancing, tumbling
and acting with Fred Karno, acrobat and juggler, called
Fred Karno's Knock-about Kids. Also performing at the
theatre were a then little-known artist Charles Chaplin
and his brother Sidney. Leo became infatuated with the
theatre but was not encouraged to think of it as a profession. Nevertheless, he earned enough as a sixteen-year-
old to pay for lessons at Steadman's Dancing Academy.
Here he became a close friend of another ambitious South
London child, Hilda Munnings. Born in Wanstead in 1896,
Hilda was the daughter of a publican who became Lord
Mayor. Her career developed and she became a prima
ballerina. She danced with Nijinsky in Diaghilev's company
and changed her name to Lydia Sokolova. She corresponded with Leo Milligan for many years, long after he
had reluctantly (but only partially) laid aside his own
theatrical ambitions and joined the army, thereby pleasing
his father and following a family tradition.

* * *

One Sunday in the summer of 1913, as Leo, now a corporal, was attending service at the Roman Catholic church in Kirkee just north of Poona, Florence Kettleband was playing the organ and singing. Leo heard a clear contralto voice rising above the anthems and choir solos. He listened with great enjoyment, and in later years was to tell his sons how he fell in love with their mother before he ever saw her. On the following Sunday, he again heard the beautiful contralto tones filling the nave of the church and determined to meet the singer. Flo was enchanted with her handsome and talented admirer. Leo was not only a fine dancer, he was also a gifted musician, singer and actor. When he discussed the possibility of her appearing in one of the concerts he was arranging, she was flattered and delighted.

The Kettlebands had been established in India for as long as the Milligans, and the liaison between Florence and Leo was looked upon with pleasure by both families. The Kettlebands, like the Milligans, were colourful people. Flo and her younger sister Eileen were gifted and attractive young women who danced and sang and commanded a good deal of attention. Flo was an accomplished pianist and her younger brother Hughie, an ace army motorcyclist, played the ukulele and the banjo. They took part in numerous concerts for the army in India, and the soldiers, isolated as they were from the entertainments of their homeland, received them rapturously. Eileen had won a beauty competition and was acclaimed the loveliest girl in India, and Grandmother Kettleband, an exquisite seamstress as befitted a former ladies' maid, made beautiful gowns for the girls to wear. This was just as well, for the concerts in which the girls appeared were basically amateur, and funds were not forthcoming. 'Nobody thought our stage clobber cost us anything,' Leo wrote in a letter to Spike many years later. 'We always had to finance our own shows.' The other notable member of the Kettleband family was Grandfather Kettleband, a former trumpeter sergeant in the army who, as an old man, lay stiffly in bed with a moustache cup on a cabinet beside him. 'He wore striped pyjamas,' recalls Spike, 'and even in bed he almost laid to attention.'

Flo and Leo were married in September, 1914. The war in Europe seemed distant, but the possibility of European service was always present and this perhaps lent an air of urgency to the match. Their first marriage was a civil one in Poona; a year later they had a religious ceremony, leaving the church under crossed swords.

Not long after, Florence joined Leo in one of his relatively few professional appearances. They performed together in the Bombay Palace Theatre of Varieties under the names Gwen Gorden and Leo Gann. The show ran for a week, and played twice nightly. Leo had contrived a comedy duo with vocals and dance called 'Fun Round the Sentry Box'. This was extremely successful and remained in the repertoire for some time. It seems that Leo was given some fairly generous army leave from time to time to enable him to seek such short-term professional contracts. No doubt the assumption was that the experience he gained would reflect well in the already highly successful army shows which he mounted from time to time.

Years later, Leo explained to Spike why he had called himself 'Leo Gann'. It was a device to ensure good billing. 'You can't print a long name in large letters on a narrow playbill,' said Leo. 'A short name just has to get big billing.'

When the show was over, Leo and Florence returned to the Regimental Headquarters at Poona, where Leo continued to give all his spare time to the entertainments committee and arranged most of the concerts. Terence Alan did not make his appearance for four years.

* * *

The news of Terence Alan's birth was brought by urgent war telegraph to Leo. Immediately he called for his horse and a bouquet of flowers, and was on the point of leaving for the cantonment hospital when one of the Catholic fathers came racing up to him. His intention was to accompany Leo on his journey and lay a first blessing on the new baby. There was, however, one difficulty – Father Rudden had no mount. Leo was in no mood to delay his departure, so they set off – Leo astride his horse and a mildly aggrieved Father Rudden following on a bicycle.

Writing to his son in 1967, Leo remembered the occasion:

The 16th April will be your birthday, you will be 49 years old, and in your 50th year the next day. How time flies, it doesn't seem all that long that I watched Father Rudden give you his blessing and pin a wee gold cross on you the day you were born. I made my way on horseback to the hospital and Father Rudden followed on a bicycle, wishing all the time he had a horse.[1]

For much of Terence's early life his father was absent, away on tours of duty. His mother was left in charge in Poona, and although she was ably supported by servants and had the company of her own mother and sister Eileen it seems probable that she found the responsibility debilitating and lonely.

After her marriage their life had centred on the regular shows which highlighted the regiment's off-duty hours, and when she became pregnant in 1917 it hardly curtailed her theatrical performances. Florence says proudly that after the birth of her eldest son she used to have his bassinet in the wings, run off between acts to feed him and then return to the stage to finish the show.

Concern was caused in high places by Flo's refusal to depart for the hills with the other wives and children when the hot weather came. Many years later Leo wrote to Spike: 'Your mother always refused to be parted from me during the hot weather and insisted on staying behind to take her place in the Friday night concerts – which were, of course, a great success.'[2]

The shows were very well received indeed, and the army hierarchy was torn between the need to bolster morale during the tedious and exhausting days of the hot weather and the embarrassment of having a vociferous young woman break away from hitherto unquestioned military procedures. The conflict was eventually settled when a crisis was reached. Flo Milligan grew thinner and thinner, whilst the infant Terence wilted and screamed almost without pause. 'I think,' says Spike rather vaguely, 'that there was something wrong with the feeding.'

Whatever was wrong, it is on record that senior army matrons and nurses went in force to the colonel to voice their anxieties about Flo and baby Terence; this resulted in their being sent, rather against Flo's wishes, to Coonor in the Nilgari hills in the south-west. There was no improvement, so the decision was taken to send the family on hospital leave to England, an idea that was greeted with enthusiasm.

They embarked in the British India steamer *Erinpura* in June 1919. Terence was just fourteen months old. Their passage was smooth until the ship went off course in the narrow mouth of the Red Sea. Why this happened has always been a matter of conjecture. The rocky coasts are about twenty miles apart, and Milligan family mythology supports the theory that the captain was drunk: whether this was in fact true is now difficult to say, but the 5,000-ton vessel did run aground on a reef off Perim, a small island two miles long on the Aden side. Two of the holds were flooded, and the pumps proved inadequate. Assistance had to be called for, the ship was abandoned

and the passengers were rescued by HMS *Topaz*, a
destroyer from Aden. The *Erinpura* was irreparably dam-
aged. The Milligan family, along with the other passengers,
were taken to Alexandria and rested for a while in a
military hospital. They were then transferred to the
Château Aygulard near Marseilles. A picture exists of a
rather dismal little group which includes a pale-looking
young Terence staring wistfully at the camera. Finally they
were taken by cattle truck ('unless my father exaggerated,'
says Spike) to the coast and thence to London.

Once in London, Terence was cared for partly by his
father's sister Kathleen and partly by his grandmother's
sister in Sittingbourne. Flo was still ill, and at one stage
went blind and was put into hospital. After a few months
Leo was recalled to India, to Rawalpindi, and eventually
Flo recovered sufficiently (after being treated by a faith
healer) for her and Terence to join him. At this stage Leo
received promotion to Quarter Master Sergeant and the
little family moved to Kirkee. 'I think that life sort of
stabilized then,' says Spike. 'My first gleamings of remem-
brance begin.'

> I suppose I was four or five. I remember being given a *chota
> hazri* – that's Indian for small breakfast – on a tennis court
> where our beds had been taken out at night because of the
> great heat. And I remember the toys my father gave me, he
> had them carved out of wood for me by his Indian carpenter –
> but I had one toy I really loved, he was called Mickey, a huge
> donkey – a caricature of a donkey – who used to sit up at the
> front whenever we all went for a ride in a *gharry*, or a Victoria,
> or a tonga. I don't know what happened to him. My parents
> always threw everything out, gave everything away. I'm sur-
> prised they never threw me away. That's why I've always
> kept my children's things. My parents had no feelings for
> belongings.

Harry Secombe, always a compassionate and generous
friend to Milligan, remembers their dredging up these

childhood memories during their early days together, and
turning them to mirthful ridicule.

> We used to talk a lot about India, but there was a lot of
> conflict there. He wasn't allowed to play with officers' children
> – all that sort of stuff. It bedevilled him, in a way. And all that
> being taught to clap your hands for a servant to come – well, if
> you did that sort of thing at Catford [where Spike lived on the
> family's return to England] you'd get a clap round the ear-
> hole![3]

Nevertheless for Spike life at number 5, Climo Road,
Poona, was to become his first tangible memory, and it
was a secure, not unhappy time. Later he was to say that it
always seemed to have a sort of glamour about it.

> My father was a soldier, which meant that he was a warrior,
> which meant that he was important. My mother rode a horse
> and sang in the Governor-General's band, so that made her
> important as well.

His mother's younger sister, the beautiful, prize-winning
Eileen, was a star in her own right, and her presence in
the house was a sure guarantee that there would be a
constant stream of young army officers who were
sufficiently intoxicated by her beauty to discard the traditions of hierarchy and rank and present themselves as
would-be suitors. Leo Milligan's household – the home of
a non-commissioned officer – was consequently elevated in
the eyes of both the servants and the occupants. It was
Terence's first glimmering of class structure.

> I would see the whole family getting in a flap because Captain
> So-and-so was calling; the officers and majors came all the
> time. I noticed that Captain Parker of the Royal Army Medical
> Corps called himself Keptin Parkah and for the first time I
> realized that they had a different accent from me and I thought

Ah! That man's higher than us, but I'm bigger than those beneath, those beneath me.

Was the British Raj implanting seeds of complacent white superiority in the young Terence? Did the constant attentions of deferential native servants, and the awareness of their almost eager subjectivity to their masters affect him? Spike's own words on the matter are illuminating:

India at that time seemed to be the heart of the Empire. I wasn't a historian, I was a child, and I observed it all as a child which was observing in the purest sense, untrammelled by any political, historical or social interpretations. And my father being a soldier, every time I saw soldiers marching – well, I thought, my father's that, and these soldiers were always looking magnificent. And I thought they were powerful, they were all-powerful. I knew that they were an elite in India. Whatever they said went. And compared to the natives they always looked so stunningly smart and efficient. And organized. So this picture was of a Roman Empire of its own; in retrospect it was like a Roman Empire transplanted to India. Because they did all the things the Romans did; they made the roads, they built their forts every so often on the roads, they had their legions guarding the North-West Frontier – the Hindu Kush where Alexander came through and all that – and they supplanted the Moguls who were a great warrior race, and the whole atmosphere was one of glorious history in the making, and I felt a part of it.

Terence would watch his grandfather's horse being brought to the door every morning by a groom:

My grandfather would hit the syce [groom] sometimes. I remember that his name was Pushrum, and my grandfather would hit him with a cane if the horse wasn't properly turned out. I hated that. But it was implanted in me that I came from a different class – an elevated class. I was cushioned by servants. I don't remember doing anything for myself. I only played and went to school.

The school that Terence attended did nothing to offset the implications of these early days. In a class which included Anglo-Indians and Parsees, he was inevitably conditioned to accept his 'superior' status: 'I suppose it was a combination of being male, white and a good-looking boy. I was indoctrinated, really, to believe I was superior.'

Years later Milligan published a poem that epitomized these years. The man in his maturity explored the anxieties that the child had perhaps been too nervous to question.

India! India!

As a boy
I watched India through fresh Empirical eyes.
Inside my young khaki head
I grew not knowing any other world.
My father was a great warrior
My mother was beautiful
    and never washed dishes,
    other people did that,
I was only 4, I remember
    they cleaned my shoes,
    made my bed.
'Ither ow'
'Kom Kurrow'
Yet, in time I found them gentler
    than the khaki people.
They smiled in their poverty
After dark, when the khaki people
    were drunk in the mess
I could hear Minema and
    her family praying in their godown.
In the bazaar the khaki men
    are brawling.
No wonder they asked us to leave.

There were days when Terence drifted aimlessly about the house, incurring first his mother's delight and then her wrath:

She was always either hugging me close and loving me to death or hating me and screaming at me. I couldn't understand it. I didn't understand the extremes of temperament. I couldn't cope with it at all.

He was intermittently anxious about his father's long absences and in his maturity he recalled the distress of constant bedwetting:

I don't know what it was all about. I believe I wished my father was with me more. I think that I somehow wanted extra attention. I remember it was very awful lying there all wet, and then I remember being picked up and dried and powder put on and clean pyjamas, and then being tucked up again in fresh sheets, and it was a very wonderful thing indeed to be put back to sleep again, clean and dry and warm.

Milligan remembers what he refers to as 'a very religious childhood'. There was always a profusion of crucifixes, plaster saints, lighted candles and bowls of holy water. Prayers were said every night.

I seem to remember it was mostly my grandmother who listened to them, but I remember that my mother was very devout – there was a man once who walked into his girl-friend's bedroom and shot her whilst she sat at her dressing table doing her hair – straight through the head. Awful. Of course he was sentenced to death by hanging and my grandmother wrote to him and asked him to become a Catholic before he died, and he did.

His memories of his mother are both clouded and anxious, sharp and muted by turns. What was actual and what was hearsay are difficult now to determine.

When I was small, no native servant was allowed to touch me. She doted on me, insisted on Pear's soap when I was a baby, all that sort of thing. She was a good mother, but she was neurotic. She never had a breakdown, but she could be violent. Not in a cruel way, but in a hitting sort of way. She was always hitting me around the head. I used to hate that. She was given to these extremes of emotion. She was neurotic. No doubt about it. She won't admit it now, says 'I never hit you.' But she did, you know. I've told her – and I wonder about that bedwetting – what made me wet the bed so much? I'd like to know why.

During these early years, Leo came and went on tours of duty and shooting trips. Grandmother Kettleband sewed diligently at costumes for Flo and Eileen to wear in their concerts. In the evenings, Terence would be bathed by his ayah, arrayed in pyjamas and allowed to sit with the family. Occasionally, Eileen would lie on the floor wearing silk cami-knickers, doing exercises. The oil lamps, large and yellow, were lit. There was often a background of music. Flo would play the piano and both she and Eileen would sing. They had deep contralto voices and were trained singers. Spike has memories of how his mother's singing used to bring him to tears.

I remember once, she used to sing a song called 'If I Had the Lamp of Aladdin'. It was beautiful. I'd be lying in my bed upstairs and I'd just start crying. I don't know why.

When Terence was about six years old, his young Uncle Hughie produced a ukulele one evening to add to the cacophony. Terence regarded it with awe, and hoped that he might, one day, be allowed to play it.

It was, on the whole, a life of ease and privilege, but the young Terence knew periods of uncertainty and anxiety linked with his father's absences, and the growing unease of what was probably a dawning social conscience. He knew that most Indian young never received the sort of indulgent care that was lavished on the white children, and this puzzled him. He, for instance, was bathed by his ayah in the house, notwithstanding the fact that water had to be laboriously carried inside by the servants. The ayah's own child, however, would be bathed under the pump in the yard.

Terence played with his ayah's child, but by the policies implicit to the elders of both races the Indian child never won. In 'Cowboy' games it was always the Indian children who were vanquished and lay as dead. The Milligan photograph albums contain posed photographs taken by Leo which show the culmination of some of these games – the triumphant, proud little white 'Cowboys' holding their guns and the recumbent 'corpses' of the native boys. Spike remembers, however, a young Indian boy who could outrun him: 'I remember that it annoyed me quite a lot. It seemed wrong that he could outrun me and leave me behind. I was annoyed that he was faster than me.'

Games of 'let's pretend' were probably played with greater zest in the Milligan household than in others, for Leo Milligan had more than a touch of the Walter Mitty about him and spent hours of his own life in a virtual dreamworld of gun law and sharp-shooting. He dressed up in impressively realistic cowboy clothes, with chaps, saddle-bags, guns and holsters. The photograph album shows a handsome, sensitive face, dark luminous eyes with perhaps a trace of anxiety in them. The army backcloth to the Indian Raj, however, was to endow his children with a sense of comfortable security that had been absent from his own boyhood in Sligo. In later years Spike would remember this with a flash of rare tolerance when he recalled the hunting and shooting expeditions.

He'd been so poor, you see. They had nothing. Everything had been out of his reach, so when the opportunity came, everything he had the chance to do he did. He got the chance to shoot buck so he went out shooting buck. He shot it for

romantic reasons – he wanted to be a great hunter. He was a
man released from the penury of poverty-stricken Irish childhood and suddenly everything was available to him. He had
access to fire-arms, free government bungalows, servants,
shooting trips – eating steaks every night sitting in front of log
fires. He was able to pull strings, get army trucks and drivers
and go off on these expeditions. It must have been a wonderful
new life for him.

One clear memory Spike has is of an occasion when he and
his mother were allowed to accompany Leo on a tour of
duty. The year was 1924 and Terence was just six years
old when he and Florence joined Leo on a journey to
Hyderabad, a city in the Sind District of Bombay.

The train journey was memorable and young Terence
was enthralled with the majestic and powerful steam
engine. But when they arrived at the base, which was
almost at sea level, the heat was immense, unusually hot
even by Indian standards. The monsoon was long overdue,
and Terence wilted visibly:

I remember, I was ill when I was there. The married quarters
were a long line of conjoined terraced single-floor homes. I
can remember, I think before I got ill, that there was school in
a tent. This seemed very exciting. The lessons were given by
an army sergeant, I don't think they were all that sharply
defined, but I do remember that when the near monsoon
winds blew across the desert we all had to jump on the tent
pegs and weigh them down. Then, I think I got very ill in the
great heat. I remember there was no grass anywhere – only
sandy, rocky soil. And oil lamps at night.

Inevitably, the medical authorities became anxious, and
Terence and his mother were sent back. He did not see
his father again until his next leave, which was not for
several months.

2

India: The Boy

What happened to the boy I was?
Why did he run away?

Spike Milligan

Terence went to a girls' school first, the Convent of Jesus
and Mary in Poona. His early school reports show a pattern
of haphazard achievement. He could be top of the form
one day and placed well down the next. On his reports
'Needlework' had been altered to 'Handwork' but the nuns
in charge of the convent school did not, apparently, feel it
necessary to alter the form of address and consequently at
the foot it is Miss Milligan who is instructed to return on a
certain date.

> I think my mother chose the girls' school in one of her early
> attempts to protect me from the realities of life. I didn't really
> worry about the preponderance of girls. I was aware that some
> of the sisters – they were all nuns – genuinely seemed to
> appreciate me because I was a male. 'Thank God you're
> different,' one of them used to say. 'You're with me today,'
> and I'd be swept along as her partner on some excursion or
> other. I remember that I used to feel very pleased and proud
> and valued. Some of the sisters were wonderful. But there was
> one Mother Superior, I hated her more than I can say – she
> was wicked to me, wicked and vile.

It seems that one day, during break, he had slipped in
the playground and covered his legs and trousers with
mud. Deeply embarrassed and distressed by this incident,
he baulked at the thought of going back to school in such
disrepair and, unable to think of any other solution, called
a tonga and went home. For this deviation from custom he

was threatened with expulsion and publicly denounced by the Mother Superior at school assembly the following day:

> She had me up in front of the whole school and shouted at me, screeched and raged – I can hear her now – I was petrified and humiliated. And I was so young and in front of all those girls. Oh – it was dreadful. I was so young and so innocent. Do you know how I feel about her, to this day, if I think about her? I wish nothing better for her than to have been raped and murdered by a crazed terrorist. I've never forgotten it.

Never, indeed. Rarely does Spike demonstrate such a potential for savage revenge, and the humiliation of this day stayed with him all his life. In 1981 he published a new collection of children's poems under the title of *Unspun Socks from a Chicken's Laundry*. *Unspun Socks* includes a highly irreverent poem about a cloister of exploding nuns. It is not, however, a violent poem. The nuns' demise is not allowed to seem brutal, only ridiculous.

> The convent rang with explosions all day
> As nun after nun was exploded away.
> 'Something really must be done,'
> Said an unexploded nun.
> 'With such a very fragile exterior
> We'll have to armour the Mother Superior.'
> So Mother Fabian was covered in steel,
> They asked her, 'Mother, how does it feel?'
> She whispered as she lit a taper,
> 'Heavier but much, much safer!'
> But against the odds, Oh! cruel fate!
> She exploded that night at ten to eight.
> All over the church her bits were scattered,
> She was gone and that's what mattered.
> Said Sister O'Brien, 'Begad and Begob,
> It must have been an inside job.'
> Who would want to explode a nun?
> It wasn't their idea of fun.
> The mystery was solved by Sister Murry:

Of course, this week we've been eating CURRY!
So peace and quiet returned to the Cloisters.
But no more Curry, Guinness and Oysters.

Terence was not the only young boy at the convent.
There were several others, and they congregated in the
playground, finding strength and superiority in their mas-
culinity. The girls were not considered very important;
even the holy sisters were regarded somewhat dismissively:

> I always remember the helplessness of the nuns. There was
> this boy who'd gone to the toilet and couldn't wipe his bottom.
> A nun came hurrying into the classroom, whispered to the
> mother in charge of my class, and she came over to me and
> whispered in the best terms she could manage that it was my
> duty as his friend to go and wipe his bottom – could you
> believe that? I suppose they were incapable of doing it because
> it was something sexual.

The convent was, nevertheless, the scene of what Spike
refers to as 'the first voyage into sex'. There was Poppy
Stanton, a young Anglo-Indian girl of great beauty, who
had some custodial and teaching duties with the young
scholars. Terence discovered that if he stationed himself at
the foot of a certain circular iron staircase when Poppy was
about to come down, and raised his eyes at the appropriate
moment, he could look straight up her skirts and see her
knickers. Poppy was not naïve, however. 'Don't look up,
Terry, now – don't you dare look up,' she would admonish
sternly as she descended.

'Terrible if I'd been really affected,' says Spike with a
wicked grin. 'Imagine it if you could only get turned on by
a circular iron staircase? And then you'd have to say "Oh,
excuse me, I mustn't look at those staircases, I'll get turned
on, and at the moment it would be rather inconvenient."'

It was whilst he was at the Convent of Jesus and Mary
in Poona that Terence made his first stage appearance.

The annual school concert took place at the end of the Christmas term. It was 1924, Terence was six years old. He was a restless, active child and no doubt the nuns showed some wisdom by dressing him in a clown costume and delegating him to keep the audience amused during the scene changes. We don't know whether Terence minded not being included in the usual routines, recitations and sing-songs. We do know that he remembers his face was painted blue, and that the audience laughed when he appeared. He liked the laughter, and sought to prolong it by jumping up and down. The audience laughed some more, and some of them applauded. The final scene of the concert showed the nativity, with the Virgin and Child and the usual gathering of wise men, kings and animals round the crib. Terence had been firmly ordered to stay off-stage for this event but his adrenalin was running high after his success and he dismissed this order as unworthy of the nuns who gave it.

I saw everyone else going on stage and gathering round the crib and I felt that I belonged there too. I felt that the clown had a place in life, so I went in and stood there with all of them. I remember I took my hat off. I didn't intend to be impolite, I just felt that I had the right to be there.

Almost sixty years later, Milligan was appearing in a TV one-man show about his life. He recalled this story with a certain mock-humility. 'Well, I suppose I was a little performer, even then. Jesus came second that day!'

During the long hot summers of his childhood, one great excitement for Terence was being taken to the river to bathe. Sometimes picnic parties were arranged and several members of the family might go along. The Indian cook boy would have prepared some suitable food and there would be flasks of cold lime-juice or hot tea. The river, known as the 'Bund', wound through the parched

woodlands, and there were places where trees and foliage
grew close to the river bank making a green and luscious
little paradise. Under the watchful eye of grandmother,
aunt or mother, Terence would munch his food and then
lie down to rest before he was allowed to go into the
water. One particularly hot day when the river looked
especially inviting, a blow fell; Terence's bathing trunks
had been left behind. He listened anxiously as the adults
discussed the situation – did this mean that he would not
be allowed to bathe? Not at all. The consensus of opinion
opted that Terence should be allowed in the water without
his trunks, but in the interests of propriety it was decreed
that he must wear a vest. He was relieved, but uncertain:

> I felt a bit upset about going in the water like that, so I
> got hold of a safety-pin from my grandmother's sewing or
> somewhere and caught the front and back of my vest together,
> pinning it between my legs. I remember it was uncomfortable,
> but that was the only way I felt I could go in the river that
> day.

On one of the occasions that Leo Milligan was at home,
Terence remembers watching a small procession from the
balcony of their home in Climo Road. It was an unusual
sight. A number of armed Indian police were walking
slowly along in the wake of a police vehicle, which curiously
appeared to have no prisoner inside. Apart from the Indian
police there were four armed white policemen also on
foot. In the centre, a small figure in a white dhoti walked,
bare-foot, his head bent. Bringing up the rear was an army
police vehicle, driven by an Indian corporal. Two armed
police officers were the passengers. Terence watched this
scene with interest and asked his father what was
happening.

> I remember Dad said, 'Well, son – he's a troublemaker, that's
> all, just a troublemaker. He's on his way to Yeravda Gaol.

He'll be in prison for some time. He's insisting on walking although they allow a prisoner to ride in the van.'

Spike recalls the wonder with which he gazed at Mahatma Gandhi.

The man looked so frail, and so harmless and all in white with no weapons – and he was surrounded by all these men who carried guns and looked violent and I thought, well, who is making the trouble? He looked like a peaceful man to me, compared to all the others.

Terence's spiritual needs were not neglected. He received a good deal of religious instruction during those early days in India. He seems to have accepted the teaching of the nuns in his Poona convent school with a hint of the reservations that were to grow more apparent with age. In later years he pokes gentle fun at the nuns who – in one incident – allowed dangerous electrical wiring to present a perpetual safety hazard in an area of the school playground.

'The nuns were vague about the dangers of this world,' he says, 'even though they were eternally vigilant and oppressed with their anxieties about the next.'

One young friend who was popular in the male elite of the playground was a boy who would arrange a little elementary voyeurism. 'If you come home with me when my mother is having a bath, you can look through the door when she calls out for a bucket of cold water,' Terence was promised. 'This seemed a fair arrangement,' says Spike, 'so I did.'

But I remember other incidents which worried me a lot. There were these two very posh boys with very posh voices. They took me home with them one day and said 'Come and watch this,' and we climbed up onto a roof and watched through a skylight their father and mother having a terrifying row. Their father was in the Indian Army or the Indian Civil Service. The wife was in her nightgown, the man was dressed in a lounge suit and there was a bottle by the bed which was knocked over and he was trying to grab some jewellery off her wrists and fingers. I was horrified – this was like a nightmare to me. I'd never seen my mother and father fighting. They were hardly ever together so I'd never seen anything like that.

What he had witnessed remained his own, rather fearsome secret. He was essentially a lonely child and perhaps isolated to some extent by unusually highly developed powers of awareness and perception, which may sometimes have been painful and frightening. He learned early that it was prudent to subdue his rapid assumptions and feign indifference to the frequent hypocrisy and stupidity of his elders.

I remember this officer who moved into Climo Road. There was a lot of gossip at servant level about the bibbies who visited him nightly. The breakfast table would be full of *double entendres* to prevent my understanding; how dull people were not to realize that I understood everything! 'Why do the bibbies go to the Captain's house at night?' I'd ask – and they would tell me that it was to do his cooking!

Terence would draw his own conclusions on the likelihood of people requiring a cook in the middle of the night, yet some self-protective instinct warned him to remain silent. This capacity for objective and intensive study of his elders was probably the cornerstone of his precocious development as an astute and cynical observer of the absurdities of human nature. He became acutely perceptive of the adult world long before experience and maturity could insulate him from its terrors and ambiguities. So childhood innocence diminished, and adult anxieties began.

* * *

Terence spent these formative years in a world that dazzled him with its beauty and mystified him with its pain. The months passed in the curious, timeless way of childhood, but as he edged towards maturity he continued to question the social implications of an environment in which racism was endemic and human suffering a matter of virtual indifference.

From time to time Leo Milligan would be posted – to nearby Kirkee, to Belgaum in the South, finally far away to Rangoon in Burma. When the family was able to travel with him they made long journeys over a land that was too vast to hide its blatant poverty; even in the rural areas there were no ways in which the rampant, human misery could be contained or concealed. As a result Terence became profoundly aware of human and animal degradation; the knowledge came, perhaps, too early and too acutely, and it was to influence the whole of his future thinking.

I couldn't grasp the horrors of overpopulation at that stage, although at some level I realized that there were just too many people. You couldn't enclose people in institutions or hospitals or almshouses in the way the Victorians managed to do. India was too big. Seeing the suffering people was terrible, but I think I was more distraught at the needless cruelty to so many animals.

Observing, from his earliest childhood, the spectrum of animal life left Terence fascinated, shocked and appalled. In India, animals were not treated as of any importance or value. There was an overall indifference to their welfare or suffering which filled the young boy with bewilderment and painful, frustrated anger. This has spiralled over the years into a sort of mocking, hopeless despair, and though the mature Spike Milligan of today will tell you that he has no hope for the future – 'I have resigned from the human race. Look at the way we treat animals' – he has earned the respect of countless animal welfare activists by the depth of his commitment and the sporadic but valuable efforts he has made in this field.

As a young child, Terence was both horrified and distressed as he watched the Indian cookboy decapitate the live chickens for that night's dinner. The boy would drag the chicken from the coop and, amidst a flurry of squawks and feathers, behead it with a sharp blow from the axe. Then, often, would follow the ritual horror of the chicken's last, macabre dance. 'They were executed, that's what it was,' recalls Spike sombrely, 'round the back of the house, and I used to watch a chicken dance its life away, with its head off – it was unbelievable.'

Cruelty and indifference to the suffering of animals were not the prerogative of the Indian. Terence once watched in horror as British troops tried, ineffectually, to kill a monkey.

> They tried to drown it, I don't know why. They put it in a dustbin, then put the lid on. There's a small hole in the top of the dustbin with a lever, you can raise this to put small refuse in and then close it. They started to pour water in, eventually it got up to the top and they opened it and the monkey was still alive. It had got to the surface. Then they took the lid off and they beat it to death with sticks.

Most of his early memories of animals are painful ones and Terence was obsessed with what seemed to him to be mindless brutality. The army employed dog shooters to dispose of pariahs known as 'no collar' dogs. One day when he was playing outside his house in Poona he watched a dog-controller approach one of these animals and shoot it with a double-barrelled shotgun. The dog began to yelp and scream. Terence ran across and saw that it had been shot almost in two.

Its spine was still connected to its tail, and it was lying there yelping and yelping, and this was the incredible part. The man went 'tchk, tchk, tchk,' to it and it looked at him and wagged its tail at the same time as yelping – so faithful is dog to man.

Terence asked the dog-shooter to put the animal out of its agony. The man made no reply, but aimed his gun and fired a single shot into the dog's head. Terence watched in fascinated anguish as one of the animal's eyes blew out 'like a stopper on a bottle'.

On another occasion he recalls an unfortunate crow which had survived a pot shot from a bored dog-shooter. The crow was dying gradually from starvation because its mandible had been shot away. It sat listlessly on the Milligans' veranda trying to get food into its jaw. After a while, Leo was prevailed upon to shoot the bird and end its misery.

Terence was given a dog called Boxer and a pet duck named Havelock Ellis. Boxer, his first dog, was a great success until he disappeared without trace during a period when Terence was away. No reason was given for his departure; it is possible that Boxer died and the family were apprehensive about breaking the news. 'I don't remember him going out of my life,' says Spike. 'He was there when I went away from Poona, but when I returned he'd gone.'

Havelock Ellis also came to a sad end. In a search for water, the unfortunate bird positioned himself exactly beneath a bath overflow pipe where the water could drench his skin from time to time. A servant, concerned because the drain appeared to be blocked, rammed a stick down it.

My idiot family and the servants hadn't realized that a duck needs water on its skin every now and then. Just giving it a dish to drink out of wasn't enough. The outlet from our bathroom was an open drain. The poor creature saw water flowing so went and sat there, then they rammed a pole down which landed in its stomach and it was partly eviscerated.

The duck had to be killed, and Terence was given no more pets.

But such painful and anxious memories are not the predominant ones. Many of Spike's recollections hinge on the golden beauty of India, the uncluttered, open skies, the still white heat of the days and the jubilant relief of the monsoon. He remembers being allowed to take a bar of soap outside and stand naked in the rainstorms enjoying a natural shower bath. His movements, outside school hours and family commitments, were not rigorously curtailed. Children had the dangers of sunstroke and snake-bite well instilled and were allowed a good degree of freedom. Terence was often very happy in the Climo Road days. He cut steps in a high tree and sat up there for hours watching the flight of the kite-hawks.

I loved the kite-hawks, they called them shite-hawks. I used to love to watch them wheeling, and then the sound they used to make was peee-off peee-off. I loved that and it was all so timeless. It went on for ever – I never knew the time, I don't think I ever asked the time. I never knew what day it was. I never knew what month it was – and I wish that I still didn't.

Yet from the earliest days, Terence seems to have been trapped in an inexplicable isolation. He did not find friends easily, and longed for companionship.

I always seemed a bit solitary. I remember I used to think it would be a wonderful thing to have a boy visit my house and stay for a whole day, but somehow it never seemed possible to arrange.

At one time, however, he grew close to the two young sons of an Anglo-Indian family, Jumbo and Bruce Day, and spent many happy hours in their company. They ran wild together, wore paper goggles and chased each other round the cantonment pretending to be jockeys. They went to two-anna picture-shows featuring Douglas Fairbanks at the local 'West End' cinema and afterwards had breathtaking cardboard sword fights all over the gardens. They swam and ran and swapped the secrets of childhood; they became firm friends. Then came the blow. The Milligans were to leave Poona for Rangoon.

'When I knew I had to say goodbye to the Days I was emotionally desolated. I don't think my parents had any idea what it cost me to say goodbye to the first friends I'd ever had,' recalls Spike.

Half a century later, Spike looks back with a sort of wry, baffled curiosity at what he regards as his parents' limitations.

> Why couldn't they have brought to my attention the simple resource of pen, paper, and a stamp, so that I could have gone on being in touch with them? I'll tell you why. They had no feelings for relationships, no way of passing on to me the benefits that communication can mean between people. They didn't prevent me writing to the Days, they just never allowed it to seem possible. And how could I have managed it on my own? I never saw an inkwell or even a pen in my house. Writing anything was unheard of.

There is a strain of bitterness as the adult Milligan remembers this aspect of his childhood. He knows his parents were talented, intelligent and able, and he has never become resigned to what he regards as the intellectual and social deprivation of his youth. The Milligan household held no reading matter, apart from the odd comic; he states, categorically, that outside school he never even saw a book.

The upheaval of leaving Poona was considerable. The preparations for the journey, the sorting and packing seemed interminable. The time came to say goodbye to the Days. Terence accepted the parting with a sense of stunned misery, but before he left he had a final meeting with his friends. They banged holes in old coins and took one each, as a token of everlasting friendship. Terence wore his on a string around his neck for years until, eventually, it was lost.

It is interesting to speculate what might have happened to Terence Milligan if he had been sent 'home' to England from an early age, as would almost certainly have happened if he had been an officer's son. The young Kipling, at the pathetically early age of six, was banished from India along with his younger sister to a meagre household in Southsea where he lived in considerable apprehension and sadness for seven years. He was ill-cared for by a dreary foster family, and the one mitigating factor in this unhappy period was that the house was full of books. 'Ruddy' was able to immerse himself in reading, and literature, in lieu of love, warmth and kindness, became his solace. The pattern continued when he went on to school at Westward Ho! where he spent many school holidays buried in a surfeit of reading.

Young Terence Milligan, however, the child of a non-commissioned officer, was not sent to England, and spent the years between six and twelve surrounded by the relatives and friends in what would now be called an 'extended family'. He may well have fared better than the more 'privileged' children. Yet Milligan himself has never ceased to regret the curiously limited background of his early days.

We weren't even allowed to absorb any of the Indian or Burmese culture. That would, in a way, have made up for it.

They had wonderful songs and music and architecture – we were always pressed into a sort of acceptance that everything non-British was just a load of . shit. Nothing of value was supposed to come out of India. I spoke fluent Urdu, for instance, when I was thirteen. Why didn't they try and keep that alive in me, at least? I'd have had a second language then, wouldn't I? It was just never valued as being anything that could possibly be worth learning or preserving.

No criticism can fairly be levelled at his parents in this respect. They simply adhered to the customs in which they had been reared, and with a few exceptions (such as Flo's refusal to go to the hills in the hot weather) questioned nothing.

New influences of significant importance were not to be felt by Terence for many years.

3

Rangoon

In the creative individual the sensitive system
and the activity of insight remain preponderant in
an abnormal way all through his life.

Schopenhauer

In the spring of 1924, Leo's army contract was extended for
a further five years. This was coupled with his promotion to
Regimental Sergeant-Major and a move to Burma. Leo was
delighted that he was now, in army language, 'permitted to
continue in service beyond 21 years until 12 July 1929'.
Flo and Terence joined him in Rangoon early in 1925 and
lived for a time in a rambling bungalow which was divided
into two and shared with another army sergeant and his
family. The address was No 15 Godwin Road. Terence was
impressed by its spaciousness, and by the fact that their
new home was in the shadow of the Shwe Dagon Pagoda,
the 'Golden Pagoda'.

Terence was delighted when his brother, Desmond
Patrick, was born on 3 December 1925 in the military
hospital at Rangoon, but less delighted with Desmond's
lusty screaming once he had returned with Flo to Godwin
Road. On the first day he watched Desmond's ayah,
Minema, attending to his needs. With what appeared to
be a certain lack of gratitude, Desmond howled. Terence
looked on disapprovingly, then with fingers in his ears
marched into the garden to find his mother. 'Mother,' he
said. 'Couldn't we please exchange him for a quieter one?'

From the time of Desmond's birth until the end of 1929
Terence was still spending most of his time under the
matriarchal influences. For various reasons, the Milligans

were much of the time apart, and a pattern of living became established whereby Florence and the children spent a good deal of time in Poona, where she could be close to her family, and Leo remained in Rangoon. During these years Leo made numerous duty tours, went on hunting trips and both organized and appeared in army entertainments.

During the late summer of 1927, when the family were together in Rangoon, a telegram arrived from Hugh Kettleband with distressing news about Flo's mother. Apparently she had become depressed and made an attempt on her life. Flo, with the children, left for Poona immediately. Spike remembers arriving at Poona station in the early hours. Grandma Kettleband was at the station to meet them. It was the time of the hot weather, but at 2 A.M. he remembered that it was mercifully cool. The family stayed for some months, Terence attended school again and once more had to resign himself to doing without his father. Leo, perhaps with a little time on his hands, studied for a first-class certificate of education which he passed with a distinction in mathematics.

In March 1929 Leo wrote to Terence, just before his eleventh birthday:

My darling Terence,
    Your sweet letter safely to hand. I am always pleased to receive a letter from you, and to hear how you and your dear little brother Desmond are getting on. He is a big boy now and will be able to take part in the cowboy games with us when I eventually get leave. Now, son, you ask me what I am going to buy you for your birthday. Well, son, it has taken a lot of thinking out. I want to buy you something useful and at the same time something you can play with. I first thought of buying you a good hunting knife in a sheath to hang on your belt, so that when we go shooting we could dress and skin the Buck, etc., we shot. Then you would not be able to play with it, you would only be able to take it out and admire it and put

it back again. Such things as real rifles, pistols and knives are for serious business and should never be treated as toys.

Well, I have had you made up a cartridge belt with two revolver holsters hanging and a place to strap on your hunting knife when I eventually buy one for you. Here is a drawing of the belt: The belt is so made that you can put 44 bullets in it when you go out with your 44 carbine and later on when I buy you a revolver you can carry it on any side you like. In the meantime, I am going to send the money to you to buy two good toy pistols so that you can play cowboys. I can't buy any good toy pistols here so am sending you the money to please yourself with. Your birthday is on the 16th of next month so don't expect the belt until about that time. Well, dear son, I hope to get some leave soon so be a good boy. I will try and come over for your school holidays. God bless you, son. Give my love to dear Gran and Hughie, darling Mum and sweet Desmond and lots of love to you from your loving Dad.

Not long after Terence read his birthday letter, Leo arrived in Poona on leave. Before he returned to Rangoon, the arrangements were well in hand for Flo and the children to join him there. Terence was now in a state of subdued excitement at the prospect of a major change in his life.

His final school report from the Convent of Jesus and Mary at Poona was interesting. The subjects, apparently listed in the nuns' order of importance, began with 'Catechism and Sacred History'. Terence had gained 80 out of a possible 100 marks for this. Music, presumably considered the least important as it appeared at the bottom of the list, simply has a blank space. In most subjects he gained an approximate 60%, one exception being 'Composition' which netted him 90%. No doubt an eager, racing imagination tripped him at this point, for he then catapulted firmly downwards with only 14% for 'Grammar'. In his maturity Milligan, now with thirty books to his name, claims that he has not yet mastered the arts of punctuation.

This may be so, but his speech, impromptu as it so often is, is articulate, forceful, imaginative and lucid.

He did not acquire this talent at the Convent of Jesus and Mary in Poona, and why was his undoubted talent for music not developed? There were musical nuns at the convent. When he was eight or nine years old one of his teachers did suggest that he might at least be taught the rudiments of music as he was obviously musically gifted, and his mother and father asked him if he would like to learn to play the piano. But it seems that the idea was not presented with any enthusiasm or confidence, and Terence was diffident.

I'm not quite sure why. I think they made it sound like something I couldn't do. It all sounded very unexciting so I said no. They never asked me again. If they had said, 'This is something we think you could do, we think you might like it and it would be good for you and a real accomplishment,' well, I'd have had the confidence to try, wouldn't I?

At this stage he had his sights fixed on what seemed to him to be less daunting instruments – the banjo, the ukulele or the trumpet. The piano, perhaps, belonged to the grown-ups. Flo, Eileen and Leo received all the acclaim and praise. Wistful and uncertain, he had felt that it was not for him.

In January 1930 Terence was enrolled at St Paul's Roman Catholic High School, Rangoon, under the Brothers de la Salle.

Things began to improve when I went to Rangoon. To begin with, my father was promoted which meant he was at home more. The matriarchal society was ended and for the first time I went to a boys' school. It was still a religious set-up, but we were taught by fathers instead of nuns. I remember being put in one form, and after reading or talking or something they suddenly moved me up into Father Theodosiphus's form. That made one feel very important.

But Terence's educational background had been inadequate to prepare him for the high standard aspired to by the Brothers. Their ponderous approach to learning was for him more restrictive than constructive; while his high intelligence coupled with a motor ability that speeded most of the time frequently left his teachers both baffled and irritated. His mind was not attuned to learning by rote and he was not resigned to what seemed to him to be unnecessary formalities. Frequently he could answer a problem with no difficulty, but would be unable to describe the method by which he had reached the answer. Furthermore, it seemed tedious and unnecessary that he should be required to do so. Years later, on a signalling course in the army, he was jubilant that the intensive training given had little in common with the tedium of those early schooldays.

At the age of thirteen or fourteen, however, Terence was unable to question the methods of the holy fathers. For a lot of the time he made the best of an educational system that did little to encourage his slumbering talents. Occasionally, he truanted and ran almost wild with one or two chosen companions. There was plenty to interest him in the colourful markets and native compounds and the jungle-like forests that Rangoon and its outskirts had to offer. From this early age, Terence was fascinated with animal and plant life. He spent long hours watching the native snake charmers training their snakes by playing on flute-like pipes. He would crouch for hours on the river bank watching the frogs and small eels. He was not interested in fishing, and although he admired his father and liked watching his cowboy antics with guns, felt no desire to join in the frequent shoots. 'I liked the cowboy

games with guns,' remembers Spike, 'but killing harmless
animals felt wrong to me. It just seemed unnecessary.'

Rangoon meant increasing prestige for the Milligan family.
A fine large house, 'Brigade House', was allotted to them
and they had several servants – a cook boy, a house boy, a
boy who specifically looked after the laundry (the dhobi
wallah) and the ayah, Minema, whose chief job was to care
for Desmond. Minema lived in the servants' quarters,
along with her own child and her mother, Rangema. Her
child, Hari Krishna, was frequently to be found playing
with Terence. On one occasion, Terence's peremptory
request that Hari Krishna be sent to play with him met
with refusal; Minema wished her son to attend to his
homework. Terence was astonished that the ayah should
refuse his request and called on his own mother to arbi-
trate. 'I think that on this occasion she came down on the
side of the ayah,' recalls Spike (still a little puzzled over
half a century later).

The increase in Leo Milligan's military responsibilities
did nothing to turn his desires away from theatrical and
concert work. Flo was also ready to participate. During
the years of partial separation she had performed frequently with her sister Eileen and brother Hughie in
Poona while Leo had also spent whatever spare time he
had on keeping up his own high standard of performance.
There had been occasional professional jaunts when he
had taken some of the generous leave given by the army
and appeared for an odd week professionally. He was
billed as 'India's Soldier Showman'.

Rangoon meant spiralling interests for the Milligan
family. Terence was fascinated by the comings and goings
of visitors to Brigade House, and with Leo Milligan less
often away from home he seems to have benefited from
male company.

I remember how the visitors used to come, and one in particular, Sergeant Blair. He used to come out on the bus every week or so, and would sit on our verandah. Father was a bit of an authority on roads and laws and customs by now and this Blair used to come quite often. He used to arrive on the bus from the town and come walking up to our own bungalow. 'Hello, Milli,' he'd call. 'Are you there, Milli?' I remember he always wore bush shirts, and he had very thin legs. I was always excited when he came and used to sit as close as I could listening to them talking, not wanting to be sent away.

Perhaps it was then that the young Milligan felt his first longing interest in literary matters.

He used to bring a big book of papers and, I think, his writings. My father would try to answer his questions and they talked about the police and the army and India. I longed to join in, but knew I couldn't.

In due course Sergeant Blair finished the book that eventually was to bring him wide acclaim. It was called *Burmese Days* and was published under the name that he adopted for the rest of his literary career – George Orwell.

In 1931, Leo Milligan was granted long home leave. Terence, now almost 13, was overwhelmed with excitement. The idea of a family exodus to England thrilled him. He believed that England would mean one magnificent agglomeration of excitements. It was going to be *The Boys' Own Paper*, the *Hornet*, *The Magnet* and the Christmas parcels from the Army and Navy Stores all rolled into one.

The word England just meant magic to me. I'd always heard people say how in England everything was wonderful, and that you could buy chocolate and cream for a penny. I never questioned this, and to this day I don't know what it was supposed to mean. But I heard so much about this land of chocolate and cream. It sounded ecstatic.

Leo, Flo and the two boys left Rangoon in December 1930. They sailed for Calcutta and spent two months with the Kettleband and Milligan contingents in Poona and Kirkee. Then on 7 March 1931 they sailed from Bombay on the *Kaisir-i-Hind*, arriving at Tilbury twenty days later. Terence was breathless with excitement. The previous evening he had watched his talented father and mother perform in a 'grand finale concert' for an admiring crowd on the ship. In the early hours of the next day, whilst they still slept, he crept out of his cabin and up to the deck. England, the land of chocolate and cream, was in sight. The ship was making a slow progress towards the Tilbury Docks.

As the ship approached, a tug-boat came out to help. Early morning mists were rising, hooters were sounding and young Terence Milligan had a lump in his throat. Elated to be at last within moments of arriving at this strange land of promise, he threw a rose saved from the previous night's celebratory dinner into the tug – a token of joy and excitement. One of the tug-boat men slouched across the deck, crushed the flower with his heel and kicked it smartly overboard.

The lightness of Spike's tone as he recalls this incident is belied by the sudden darkening of his eyes. It seems that after almost half a century, he is still disheartened by the implicit rebuff that his youthful spirit suffered. 'I thought a sailor would have liked to put it in his hat,' he says, almost defensively. 'It was my first experience of the English working class, my own class once we returned from India. And I didn't like the look or the feel of it at all.'

This first visit to England remains blurred in Spike's mind. He remembers relatively little and it seems almost as though the disappointments he suffered conditioned him to forget everything that happened. He found South London both dirty and noisy.

One important thing I recall about India was that it was quiet. It was never noisy in the way that life was noisy in London. To begin with, there was no traffic to speak of, and no radio. Towards the end of our time in Rangoon we imported a wind-up gramophone and started playing records; some of the tunes we played were songs that I had heard my mother sing in army concerts and shows – and of course I enjoyed that sort of thing. But I was protected from the dismal caterwauling of noise that hit me like a bomb when I arrived in England. It was dreadful, dreadful. The shock was terrible. Terrible noise, and everything so cold and grey.

In the first place, Leo went to stay at the Union Jack Club whilst Florence and the children stayed with Leo's sister Kathleen in Catford. Then suitable lodgings for the year were found at the home of a Mrs Windust nearby. Both Terence and Desmond hated this. They were constantly told to 'get off the grass' in the drab little garden. The small rooms were claustrophobic and dark. The freedom and space of Rangoon seemed light years away.

Desmond was given a small car for his birthday. He promptly gave himself a rupture by an excess of enthusiastic pedalling. A badly executed operation caused further damage and several months were spent in hospital.

Terence, meanwhile, was sent to the nearby Brownhill Road School. Leo and Florence were both deeply shocked when he came home and reported that, among other things, his rough and uncouth classmates were masturbating in the lavatories. 'They were horrified,' says Spike with a reminiscent grin. 'They took me out and sent me miles away to a Roman Catholic school called St Saviour's at Lewisham and of course they were wanking worse than ever there. Godless they were – totally, totally godless.'

The South London schools were something of a burden to him. He was alone and uninitiated into the ways of the London 'board school'. Desmond was not around, requiring his protection, and he made no friends at either of the two schools. The leaden skies depressed him and his parents were too occupied with Desmond's illness and their numerous friends and relatives to pay much attention to their elder son.

There are confused memories of occasional treats at the cinema; Terence was sometimes taken to the 'pictures' on a Saturday by his father. Leo had managed to get a temporary job for the year as a 'tally' clerk. This helped with funds, and kept him occupied. The Crystal Palace was still functioning and both Terence and Desmond were taken to see it. The relatives they had never seen did their best to make them welcome, but as the days passed and their return to Rangoon drew nearer, Terence nursed a secret excitement. He was not sad that the year's leave was almost up. For his parents, perhaps the time had flown; for him it had been interminable, drab and largely unenjoyable. He relished the thought of the return to Rangoon.

Once the family returned to Burma, Terence settled down thankfully at the Brothers de la Salle. His memories of the past year faded quickly. Perhaps this was because the whole wonderful promised treat of England had somehow misfired and his illusions had not been realized.

In Rangoon, everything was familiar and real. Flo was happy to be supervising her own household at Brigade House once more, Desmond was overjoyed to find Minema and Rangema again, Leo was immediately occupied with his work, his pistols and his plans for forthcoming shooting trips and shows. The Golden Pagoda (bigger than St Paul's Cathedral) seemed to fill a sky that was bright blue and cloudless. The Milligans, as a family, were as close to happiness as they would ever be. They had no knowledge of it yet but anxiety, depression and near poverty were lying in wait for them.

Leo Milligan was one of the unlucky ones who, at the age of 43, received notice of his discharge. The decision which the Ramsay MacDonald government had made to withdraw ten per cent of the British Army in India came as a blow to the majority of those who were affected, and Leo was no exception. He discussed the situation with Florence. Neither of them could visualize a life in almost total contrast to the one they were enjoying, and Leo's half-remembered fear of the poverty that had overshadowed his Sligo childhood made him wary and anxious; he did not want to leave this country where the white man fared so well. Several colleagues made a joint request that he should remain with the Regiment, and Leo himself wrote to his Colonel. He wrote of his commitment to the army, of his dedication to the role of 'soldier showman' which he had played for so long. He reminded the Colonel of his successes as an impresario and of the contribution he and his talented wife had made to the entertainment of the troops. He reminded him further that he, Leo, had been promoted to the rank of Regimental Sergeant-Major. He wrote of the long-standing associations which his family and family-in-law had enjoyed in India. Some of the grandparents might well end up being left behind. The letter had no effect.

'He should,' says Spike bitterly, 'have written to England. To the Prime Minister or something. He should have gone to the top. You should always go to the top. Useless, wasn't it? Poor man – writing to his Colonel. What did he care, or know about anything?'

Leo was now given a final period of leave. On 24 April 1933, the family were to leave Burma for India where they were to spend the last few days with relatives in Poona and Kirkee. On 6 May they were to sail home to London from Bombay.

During the last few days that the Milligans spent in

Rangoon, Leo made a final concert appearance. It coincided with a military ball for the III Field Regiment RA which was held in the regimental drill hall. Leo wore the dress uniform of Quartermaster Sergeant; Florence wore an elaborate white organza evening gown trimmed with ruched black lace, a unique creation which she had designed and made herself. Terence was also drawn into the festivities. He was dressed as a page-boy and given the job of presenting flowers and presents to the ladies who had taken part in the concert:

> They actually dressed me up as a page in a red uniform with blue buttons and pill-box cap. I was to give away the presents at the end of the concert, I had to go in front of the stage and hand out these presents. I remember doing my first ad lib, I suppose. They were all standing in line, getting these gifts and there was one rose which must have fallen off one of the bouquets, it was a very dead rose, and I said: 'And this one is for the Sergeant Major.' I remember that, and getting a big roar of laughter. That was the end of the concert, then came the dance, a splendid affair. I remember some of the music – one song was called 'Ramona, I'll meet you by the waterfall' – there were some really romantic tunes in the 'thirties!

Leo and Flo were, in fact, soon taken over by the excitement of the coming voyage and enthusiastic preparations were made. Their furniture and goods were packed and prepared for shipment at government expense, a final army 'perk'. The family were allotted splendid outside cabins on the liner *Rajputana* which was to take them home.

As the ship sailed, Terence moved away from his family who were standing at the rail on the promenade deck waving to their friends on shore. He hid away behind some lifeboats, not wishing his family to see his distress. Many years later, when Spike was compiling a journal of his father's life, he wrote:

On 24 April 1933 sailed from Rangoon. It rained very heavily,
and as we sailed down the Irrawaddy River, the Shwe Dagon
Pagoda was lost in the mists of rain. I cried bitterly at leaving
but never let anyone see me. I was just fifteen.[1]

In the first place the family sailed to Calcutta on the SS
El Sevvico. Then they went by train to Poona, where they
stayed for several days saying goodbye to their relatives
and friends. Desmond and Terence, for a special treat,
were taken to see Boris Karloff in the film of *The Mummy*.
On 5 May they boarded the 16,000-ton *Rajputana* at
Bombay and sailed via Aden, Suez and Marseilles for
London.

My mother was truly excited. She and Father were just
marvellous in the way they seemed to take whatever life sent
along. They forgot about leaving the army and being so upset
about it. They didn't worry about the future in England in the
depression of the 'thirties. I don't think they even knew what
was in store for them. They were going home to England. It
wasn't costing them anything, and they determined to enjoy
it. My mother sent sheaves of postcards to England – and back
to India – showing pictures of the ship. She wrote on the cards
and marked them to show their excellent cabins. She was in
her element.

Flo and Leo had packed their props and music and an
ambitious ship's concert was soon in preparation. Leo did
his buck and wing dance. Florence sang. They made up
impromptu sketches with one or two other amateur artists,
and even Terence and Desmond had a small spot.

Terence designed a shadow-play behind a brightly lit
white sheet. He remembers that he played a surgeon and
Desmond – with a huge fat stomach – was a patient on an
operating table. The patient was opened up and a large
number of startling objects – brushes, dustpans, light
bulbs, hammers, etc. – were one by one lifted out of him.

Terence had to work hard to achieve his final effect. 'I remember we had a dreadful time persuading the mother to let us borrow her baby,' says Spike. 'She was convinced that we'd let it come to some harm. Well, it didn't. I lifted it out and handed it back to its mother who was waiting nearby. And I remember the great round of applause and laughter we got. I liked that. And the audience loved it.'

The voyage home on the *Rajputana* was the last time that the Milligan family were freely to enjoy the comforts and luxuries of a secure and adequate income. For Leo and Florence it was the end of the days of game safaris, camp-fires, concert parties and comfortable houses with native servants. For Terence and Desmond it was the end of an exciting life in which they lived on the edges of a different culture to their own.

> I was thrown without warning into a totally different life. We left the brilliant Indian sunlight, the white-hot blue skies, all the marvellous colours that were India, and we ended up entombed in South London. It seemed like a slum. It was a slum. And we were under this great enormous blanket of white. A terrible grey-white blanket that stretched endlessly. A damp, dead greyness that seemed to go on for ever. To begin with, I couldn't believe it. I couldn't get used to it. I think I was thrown into a state of shock from which I never properly recovered.

Leaving the East was, in fact, crucial for Milligan. It brought his childhood to a sudden end, and where once he had known only comfort, space, security and relative plenty, he was now to encounter the drab hardships that went with unemployment and the constant undercurrent of Leo's mounting despair.

Many years later, when Spike (in England) and Desmond (in Australia) were compiling family albums, Desmond sent Spike the final photographs that were taken of the Milligans in Rangoon. On the last page he wrote 'The Milligan Family, leaving Rangoon' and underneath, heavily underlined: 'THE END OF THE GOLDEN YEARS'.

4

Catford, SE6

I struggle and struggle, and try to buffet down
my cruel reflections as they rise; and when I
cannot, I am forced to try to make myself laugh
that I may not cry; for one or other I must do.

Samuel Richardson

Leo's sister Kathleen and her husband Alf Thurgar, an
insurance broker, met the four Milligans when they arrived
at Tilbury. For a short time the family stayed, as before, at
the Union Jack Club until accommodation was found for
them in Catford. The landlord was an ex-World War I
sailor; possibly this arrangement was fixed up through
connections at the Union Jack Club. The accommodation
was dismal – just two attic rooms, no bath and a cooker on
the landing. The address was No 4 Riseldine Road, London
SE23. It was a sorry contrast to Brigade House in Rangoon
and Desmond and Terence stared in dismay at their new
home.

Leo's army pension was fifty shillings per week. To
begin with, this was all they had to live on. Leo immediately began on the long, hopeless trail for work and Flo
buckled to and did the best possible for her family. Looking
back, Spike praises her courage and fortitude; she wasted
no time in self-pity but simply carried on as though cooking
on the landing and living in two small grey rooms was the
most usual thing in the world. Terence could not share her
equanimity; he was stunned and horrified at the changes
in his life. Many years later he encapsulated the moment
in a poem, which in due course was included in a collection
called *London in Verse* edited by Christopher Logue and

published in 1982. When a copy of the new anthology was sent to him he looked at his own contribution without much pleasure. 'Yes,' he said rather grimly. 'That's exactly how it was. I'll never forget that workman's tram.'

Catford 1933

The light creaks
      and escalates to rusty dawn
The iron stove ignites the freezing room.
Last night's dinner cast off
      popples in the embers.
My mother lives in a steaming sink.
Boiled haddock condenses on my plate
      Its body cries for the sea.
My father is shouldering his braces like a rifle,
      and brushes the crumbling surface of his suit.
The *Daily Herald* lays jaundiced on the table.
'Jimmy Maxton speaks in Hyde Park',
My father places his unemployment cards
      in his wallet – there's plenty of room for them.
In greaseproof paper, my mother wraps my
      banana sandwiches.
It's 5.40. Ten minutes to catch that
      last workman's tram.
Who's the last workman? Is it me? I might be famous.
My father and I walk out and are eaten by
      yellow freezing fog.
Somewhere, the Prince of Wales
      and Mrs Simpson are having morning tea in bed.
God Save the King
But God help the rest of us.[1]

Whilst the Milligans were establishing themselves in England, Terence and Desmond virtually withdrew into a boyhood idyll of military splendour. Looking back now, Spike says:

We were obsessed with our boyhood, we couldn't bear to grow up, we couldn't get on with English boys – you see, we didn't understand them. We lived in this fantasy world surrounded by Woolworth's toy soldiers, just the two of us in an attic. We called it Lamania. It had its own strange airplanes and pilots – Desmond made marvellous drawings of them. And my father encouraged us, because he also lived in a fantasy world.

Leo Milligan, once again poverty-stricken and out of work, found time to indulge his own dreams of gun-toting heroes. He used to spare what odd pence he could put together for Terence and Desmond to add to their collection of toy soldiers. He also used to make model log-cabins out of corrugated cardboard, whole cowboy towns. In the Rangoon days, when money had been plentiful, he had made photographic backcloths of these log-cabins, incorporating a duel with puffs of smoke arising from the guns of the cowboys and Indians fighting in the foreground. These pleasing effects were achieved by various eccentric and temporary inventions that involved Leo's blowing smoke through piping behind the toy models at the exact moment of exposure.

Spike looks back with tolerant affection on these capers.

He was more of a fantasist than we were. I realized that years later at Woy Woy [the Milligans' home in Australia]. He was sixty-five then, and I once took him out into the back of the bush. He'd never been there, you see. He was adventurous in his mind but not otherwise. Suddenly he started saying: 'Bang! Bang!' I was startled for a moment, then he said, 'Listen! Indians!' And I remember that there was a bush fire in the distance and he snarled, 'You see that? Indians setting fire to a fort!' I couldn't help smiling. I realized that he was much more of a boy than even I was.

After the departure from India, the days of singing and dancing receded into the past. Flo and Leo, now settled into a dreary routine of struggling for survival in South

London, would have had very little opportunity or enthusiasm for encouraging latent talents in their whey-faced, ill-clad sons. But it is curious that during the years in India they had, apparently, been unaware or uninterested in their artistic or musical development, despite the family preoccupation with concert performances. Florence and Eileen were trained singers and Leo was recognized and applauded for his expertise as a dancer, actor and performer. It is difficult to fathom why accomplished and doting parents such as these had so little interest in the dawning talents of their young.

In England attempts at further education for Terence were unsuccessful, partly because of the eccentricity of his early schooling. Leo, with a rather touching naïvety, supported his son's belief that he could become an RAF pilot and presumed that the jumbled curricula of the Poona and Burmese days needed only a little knocking into shape before his bright boy would be accepted at a Royal Air Force training school. Terence was considerably enamoured of the idea; it seems to have been the only boyish ambition he held, apart from the long preoccupation with music. Spike remembers the time well: 'I think,' he says (with a lack of his customary modesty in these matters), 'that I would have made a *stunning* fighter-pilot. I've always had amazingly rapid reactions, I make decisions quickly, I like the idea of being responsible for myself, having my own life in my own hands. I wasn't thinking in terms of organized battle and warring – but of being up there alone, romantically – I wanted to shoot down Messerschmitts.'

Leo, however, even whilst he was encouraging Terence, was being unrealistic. 'It was all pipe dreams, poor man,' says Spike. 'He really hadn't a clue about what would be required of me for that examination.'

A local teacher who charged half-a-crown for an hour's

tuition in mathematics was engaged, and Terence went along to his house every week, clutching the money and trying hard to assimilate advanced exercises in algebra and geometry on the very rocky foundations that he had acquired in Burma. The intelligent young boy was soon swimming against an impossible tide; the date of the entrance examination for the RAF training school was approaching and Terence knew in his heart that the tutoring he was receiving was wholly inadequate and that there was no way in which he would be able to by-pass his impoverished educational background. Neither Leo nor Florence had the slightest idea how to prepare their son for the forthcoming interview nor, indeed, what would be required of him. In comparison with well-prepared entrants who had been educated in England and meticulously drilled for this examination, Terence probably presented a dismal figure, and he failed abjectly.

Now that it was established that the Royal Air Force was not for him, Leo and Flo Milligan seem still to have lacked the insight or ability to recognize the latent talent in their elder son or to find for him a niche in which his developing talents might have begun to grow. Instead he embarked on a dispiriting series of dead-end jobs in which he soon began to flounder and struggle.

To begin with, Terence was enrolled at the Greenwich and Woolwich day continuation school in May 1933. This was not a success. His fellow pupils seemed rough, uncouth and totally uninterested in learning. The school did nothing to inspire him; he saw no hope of progress, and he was alienated from his contemporaries. Like Desmond, who was at a nearby Roman Catholic junior school, he was sneered at because of his 'posh' voice, although Terence seems to have suffered less than Desmond in this respect. Perhaps a capacity to mimic his new companions helped him to avoid too much notice. The situation seemed barely tolerable, and Terence was not dismayed when his parents informed him that they would be taking him away from the school at the end of the Christmas term in 1933.

Leo's inadequate funds were rapidly becoming exhausted and his attempts to earn were as lamentable as those of many other penniless ex-army rejects of the 'thirties, so it seems hardly surprising that at the age of fifteen Terence found himself work. The firm was Stones of Deptford, the first of a number of soul-destroying jobs that served to benumb any hopes or aspirations that he might have had. Many years later, Spike looks back with compassion and understanding for his father's plight at the time. He accepts today as he did then that the respectable poor had a desperate fight to keep their heads above water. The importance of the first wage packet can never be exaggerated, and it is significant that Terence preserved the first one he received. 'It was for thirteen and fivepence,' says Spike, 'and I gave my mother eleven shillings.'

Leo Milligan did not relax in his own attempts to get work. 'He bought himself this smart suit. It was pin-striped, with a smart shirt, spats – yes, even spats – and a cane. "You've got to look the part," he'd say. "You've got to look a million dollars." Poor man – the suit wore out, and he never got a decent job.'

Terence's first duties at Stones were unremarkable. He was set to work with the firm's bookkeeper, and it was his task to collect time-sheets and help the crusty old man with several tedious clerical jobs. His memory is of seemingly endless trips all over the factory, collating scraps of paper with meaningless figures, eating his sandwiches at lunch-time and going drearily and joylessly home when the hooter went. It was a long and unchallenging day which was not helped by the fact that he was obliged to arrive at work an hour early each morning. This was in order that he could take advantage of the workman's tram ticket which had to be purchased before 7 A.M. and represented a saving of one penny.

Spike can still remember the taste of his lunchtime sandwiches.

My mother used to make me the most awful food to take to work. You used to get white loaves wrapped in horrible grease-proof paper and she used to make me these banana sandwiches in white bread and wrap them in the paper off the loaves. I remember getting on this cheap workman's tram with them, and the tram was always full and I had to go upstairs and sit in the lung cancer ward.

The tram, Spike remembers, was always freezing cold. He used to stay on it until he reached New Cross, then change over to take another one which ran all the way to Woolwich Dockyard. From there he ran down the hill that led to Stones at Deptford.

During the time that Terence was employed at Stones, he was sent round the factory whilst the authorities tried to decide what niche, if any, was going to suit him:

I couldn't understand how my life had become so terrible. I was there like a sort of blindfolded donkey pulling the wheels around. I remember sitting trying to do something with boxes of matches and a man saying, 'Put them on the desk – *not* on your lap. Oh, you're no good at this. We'll have to try you with something else.'

When they found that I couldn't handle the figures they tried me with fuse boxes – I was pretty useless with them as well. But the foreman was a man called Rose. I remember I liked him, he was a water-colour artist and I used to take him the bits of pictures I'd tried to do. I wanted him to encourage me. I longed for a bit of praise.

Next Terence was moved to the Mechanics' Yard. Here he was given overalls and spanners and attempts were made to turn him into a mechanic. He was pleased with the workmanlike heavy garb and in a chameleon-like attempt to integrate himself with staff and co-workers made sure that he was always heavily smeared with grease. This, at least, impressed a young woman called Nina Hall who worked in the accounts department. She was to become Terence's first girlfriend, and he remembers how he would leave work at the end of the day hoping to run into her.

> I remember walking up Honor Oak Park and I remember I used to try and make a big thing of being in overalls. I used to leave my grease on my face and carry spanners in my pockets going home so I looked like a highly skilled mechanic of some kind – I was still acting – and I used to make sure I kept the grease on, and I thought that I looked a real Butch.

Terence was chatting with Nina as they walked up the road one evening when they ran into Phillip Stevens. Phillip was a pianist for a local group of amateur musicians, so he held a certain glamour for Terence. They stopped to talk. Phillip, who worked at a bank, was wearing a smart suit.

'I can't dress up like you,' said Terence, resplendent in his grease and spanners. 'I only earn a pound a week.'

'Well, that's all I earn. I only earn a pound a week,' said Phillip.

Nina looked at them both. 'Well,' she said. 'I bet Terry works harder for his pound than you do.'

'I remember,' says Spike, 'that I was rather chuffed.'

Eventually, Terence was moved to the factory basement. This was the machine floor, and disaster was imminent.

He was put in temporary charge of a machine which folded cardboard packets. It had a whirling metal arm which acted as a guillotine, slicing the card into appropriate sizes. Inexperienced and curious, Terence bent down to watch the operation. His thick curly hair caught in an unguarded ratchet and he was virtually scalped. Spike is morose about what happened then.

> Half the hair was ripped off my head and I was fired for inefficiency. The foreman reported it to the manager and the manager sent for me and said, 'Right now – you have your cards.' Just sent for me and gave me my cards – yet it was their negligence that had allowed it to happen. I wonder that my parents hadn't the sense to sue them for allowing me near an unguarded machine.

Leo and Florence, however, accepted this fresh adversity with stoical calm and Florence made a small cap to cover Terence's bald patches. He wore it with disdain and embarrassment until, in due course, his hair grew.

The next job that Terence battled with was as a junior assistant at Chislehurst laundry:

> What an experience it was having to wash all the shitty sheets. There was this foreman, George. I was working on the hydro; first there was a great colander or a tumbril, you pushed all the sheets in, you closed the doors. Then you turned on boiling water and threw soap powder in and it revolved. That was George's side of it. Then they would come out, all soaking wet, into a big basket on wheels and I'd wheel them to the hydro and pack them in, close the lid down, press a button and then a centrifugal force would throw all the water out; then when they'd dried, I'd pull them out and put them into another trolley and push them to where the women were, for ironing.

The workforce of ribald young Cockney girls had their own ways of passing the time. A great deal of sly laughter and obscene gesturing went on. Sixteen-year-old Terence was a target for many of their jokes. Dark-haired and blue-eyed, his bashful glances served only to encourage them and he would receive a few good-natured gropes as he went to and fro with his trolley.

Sometimes one of the girls would roll up a pillowcase, shaping it like a man's penis, and wave it encouragingly at him. 'Come on, Terry, tell us. 'Ave you got one like this?' Terence, scarlet-faced with embarrassment, would push past them and disappear as fast as possible.

One day, one of the older women spoke curiously to him, perhaps taking pity on his embarrassment. She seemed genuinely puzzled that he was working at this very menial job. 'What's an educated boy like you doing in a job like this?' she asked him. Terence had no answer for her, but her words stayed in his mind as he worked on, dully and mechanically.

> I don't know how I bore it all. They were awful days, but they seemed to be what my parents expected of me. I was glad to give my mother my wage packet every Saturday. But there was no hope in the situation. Nothing to look forward to – just the grey days stretching on and on.

Spike Milligan would be upheld by most accepted authorities as a classic example of the 'late developer'. Yet this label would not be wholly appropriate. The average 'late developer' has usually been an apparently slow or backward child, often one who has been carefully nurtured and anxiously encouraged by the people immediately responsible for his welfare. In the case of the young Terence Milligan, nothing very much had been required or expected of him by his parents or his teachers. As a consequence, it seems that he never expected much of himself. Apart from the music (which was a special private dream) and the impractical idea, soon abandoned, of becoming a fighter pilot, he seems to have had virtually no ambition. If anyone ever could be said to have expected anything of him during his youth, it must have been the

elderly lady at the Chislehurst laundry. Yet the laundry
was only one link in the chain of dismal dead-end jobs
that Terence struggled through – partly despairing, partly
apathetic. He remembers that he had been momentarily
nonplussed at the old lady's question.

Of course, I wasn't educated in the way she meant but I
suppose I was a bit more sensitive or better mannered or
something. When she said that to me, it was the first time that
I had ever considered that I could do anything different with
my life than just being a sort of boorish slob. It made me stop
and think a bit. But I didn't know how to go about anything,
except perhaps to try and get into music. What I longed to do
was to somehow get hold of a trumpet, and learn to play it
well enough to get into a jazz group.

In the evenings, and on Saturday afternoons and sometimes on Sundays after church, Terence and Desmond
would disappear into their private attic territory of
'Lamania'. Terence, at sixteen, had no difficulty in meeting
the nine-year-old Desmond as an equal and they spent
long hours designing ships, aeroplanes and landing craft
that were manned by strange, other-worldly captains.
Desmond was perhaps beginning to exhibit some of the
artistic talent that so impressed his brother; certainly the
drawings that survived show a great deal of promise. The
stories and yarns about a strange 'space age' were chiefly
made up by Terence. None was written down, but the
essence of Lamania was never dispelled. Florence knew
nothing of the curious world that obsessed her sons. Years
later, Milligan was to compare their fantasy world with the
Gondal world of the Brontës.

They were at the same thing as Des and I, I suppose. They
had this bleak time in their lives, they had their colourful
imaginations and they must have lived with their fantasies.
The world around them was harsh and unacceptable, they

surrounded themselves with a tolerable world of their own creation. Des and I were escaping as well. We wanted to escape. I know that I did.

The ease with which Terence left the unappealing world of his contemporaries to lose himself in childhood imaginings with his younger brother is interesting. Teenagers are rarely prone to desert their peer groups at such crucial stages in their adolescence. The pleasure with which Terence returned to the fantasy world of childhood can be seen as a forerunner of the days when as a tormented adult he would find so much release and delight in the lives and imaginations of young children, a rare capacity which has never deserted him.

During these interminable, unexciting days, Leo Milligan thought longingly of India. In May 1934 he wrote to the Associated Press to apply for a position as a news photographer's agent. He had been asked to produce a brief biography and a statement (in duplicate) of his ambitions. Leo wrote:

May 14, 1934

Dear Sir

As requested, I submit below the brief biography and statement of my ambitions called for.

I was educated at Blacknock College, Dublin, and after a brief period in civil life entered the Indian Army.

After serving twenty years in India, Mesopotamia and Burma, the post I held was abolished – due to retrenchment – and I was prematurely retired in May of 1933.

My premature retirement in no way reflects on my character, mine being only one of two hundred similar posts abolished at the same time.

I was at this juncture – and still am – in perfect physical condition and considered myself fit to undertake another Career.

Having through your kind intercession obtained employment in the Associated Press, and finding the work interesting, I concluded that a career in the news photo business to be in keeping with my ambitions which I append below.

Immediate Ambition

My immediate ambition is to study the news photo business from the ground up and from every other angle, and to become efficient.

To work conscientiously and industriously in the interest of the Associated Press.

To gain the confidence of my employer and to become a reliable and valuable member of the Staff and thereby gain promotion.

Ultimate Ambition

My ultimate ambition will be to approach the A.P. through my immediate employer to open an Agency in India. The possibilities for such a profitable venture I know to exist.

My knowledge of the Indian language and its peoples would make me particularly suitable for employment in such a venture.

I remain, Sir,
Yours very respectfully,

P.S. I attach extracts from my confidential reports which will indicate the esteem in which I was held during my Military Career.

Terence, already one of the family breadwinners, looked at the letter in awe. India was now only a faraway dream and to him the idea of going back was inconceivable.

Years later, Spike was to stick the letter in the family album. He wrote across it, angrily, 'He got the job. At starvation wages.'

As the years passed, letters and photographs from India arrived from time to time. Grandmother Kettleband remained at 5 Climo Road, Poona. Uncle Hughie Kettleband remained a soldier and a musician, but changed his surname from Kettleband to Bogart. It was, he told everyone, because he was a great admirer of the film star Humphrey Bogart. The beautiful Eileen married a civil servant called MacIntyre. She did not let her theatrical talents lapse. One of the photographs sent to Riseldine Road from Poona showed her, splendidly attired in top-hat and tails, leading a slightly uneven chorus of six young women in top hats and shorts. The show was a revue called *Rise Above It* and it was performed at the Ordnance Club in Kirkee.

The year was 1938, and the world was getting ready for the next war.

Leo Milligan came to terms with his greatly diminished style of living. Just as he had once left poverty behind him, he now virtually embraced it, and the 'golden years' became a forgotten dream. The cramped and uncongenial house and the despairing struggle for work limited his horizons. Florence was vehemently opposed to any suggestion of show business ambitions, and Leo lacked the confidence or the courage to oppose her. He was essentially a tender man, with an anxious, dependent love for his wife. He loved his two sons and took an affectionate pride in them.

There was, perhaps, a lot of Spike in Leo Milligan. He had a great need of peace and he had to have a certain amount of solitude. Sometimes he escaped into his dreams – as in the gun-toting days; sometimes he just went upstairs into the attic and joined the boys in the fantasy world of Lamania. In the overcrowded conditions of their small house, he chose not to fight for supremacy at the kitchen sink in the mornings but simply to get up two hours before any other member of the family. That gave him a pleasurable period of time on his own in which he would wash, shave, dress, have his breakfast and prepare for the day. Then he would make tea for the family. Spike remembers his father talking about this. 'It's a good thing to have time by yourself to get yourself in order,' he would stipulate. 'By getting up early I have time to just be myself in the mornings.'

Years later, on days when appointments and commitments would run him mercilessly into the ground, Spike has been heard to rage, 'I'd love a day, even half a day, that belonged to me only, a day when no one could tell me that I had to do this or that. A day when no one owned me, a day when I could just be myself.'

Spike has not, however, adopted Leo's practice of early rising for the sake of solitary peace and quiet. A large house with enough space for privacy has made it unnecessary. Dogged by insomnia until the small hours, he is rarely alert first thing unless a film call or early appointment demands it. On these occasions, he will arrange calls by alarm clock and telephone, as well as by human agency.

'I can't stand being late,' he says dourly. 'I try to be professional. I try not to let people down. But people let me down. That's why I don't rely on anyone to call me. That's why I have clocks as well as people. I have to be able to call myself; it's the only way to be sure.'

There are mornings, however, that find Milligan able to face the day with some element of delight. In 1972 he wrote a poem for the early morning:

> Spring came haunting my garden today
> A song of cold flowers was on the grass.
> Tho' I could not see it
> I knew the air was coloured
> And new songs were
>   in the old blackbird's throat.
> The old ground trembled at the thought
>   of what was to come!
> It was not my garden today,
>   it belonged to itself.

At the dawn smell of it
    my children fled the house
And went living in that primitive dimension
    that only they and gardens understand.[2]

As the months passed, Terence grew obsessed with his longing for a trumpet. It became the only reality in his life and an aching need for it filled his dreams at night and coloured the drabness of each morning with a haze of hope. But the grey, tedious days stretched into their allotted weeks, the pay packet was relentlessly swallowed up by his needy family, and the realization of the dream seemed to grow farther away and more improbable as time passed.

By now, Terence was working for a tobacco firm, Spiers and Ponds of Ludgate Circus, as a packer. It was an especially dispiriting job that offered no challenge to his intelligence and little apparent chance of promotion. He worked from eight in the morning until six-thirty in the evening for a salary of about fifteen shillings per week. The work entailed counting out cigarettes into packets of ten or twenty. Spurred on by a mounting sense of unfairness, inequality, longing and despair, Terence discovered that it was possible to secrete cigarettes about his person and dispose of them later in the day to colleagues whose own jobs did not bring them into such tempting proximity with the finished article. For each handful of cigarettes thus requisitioned he received a few pence, and gradually the trumpet fund was raised.

Modern criminologists lay much emphasis on the boredom of the 'conveyor-belt' job being the trigger of early delinquency, and it could well be that the mindlessness of the work was the dangerous corner for the frustrated, anguished youth. His developing intellect and his considerable intelligence had nothing with which to grapple; the need for a trumpet became the only decisive factor in his life, the only hope of release from the impenetrable gloom of the 'great blanket of white' that overwhelmed him. Music was for Terence the promised escape, music in general and the trumpet in particular.

When his crime was discovered the manager of the firm sent for him, dismissed him, called the police and had the terrified boy charged with theft. Today, Spike will discuss the circumstances which encouraged this – his first and only venture into crime – with a cold, quiet hatred of his employer which the years have done nothing to diminish:

> He was an appalling man, absolutely appalling. I'll never forget him. He sat back in his chair with his feet on the desk and his hands in his pockets, scratching his testicles through his trousers. It made a horrible scraping sound, I can hear it now, and he had a horrible scratching, rasping voice as well. I sat there in terror and even though I was shaking with fear I remember thinking quite calmly, 'Well, you hold all the cards now but I'm basically a lot better than you. You make profit all the time from poor people's addiction and pay your staff starvation wages, and all I've done is just even things out a bit.' I felt that I'd only taken what I was entitled to.

It is interesting to note that many years later, in the first *Goon Show* script that Terence, now Spike, was to write, the scene was set in a court room, and the matter under litigation was concerned with the theft of cigarettes. It showed a judge (played by Peter Sellers) investigating a defendant, Mr Jones (played by Harry Secombe). The prosecuting lawyer was Michael Bentine, and the clerk of the court was played by Spike.

There is a lead-in by the defendant, who is outlining his difficulties:

> HARRY: . . . as a last resort, I opened up a little Tobacconist's shop in Town. Unfortunately, the little Tobacconist caught me. He sent for the police and so . . . (fade out)

COURTROOM FX: Gavel on desk

SPIKE: Order in court. First case!

MICHAEL: The Prisoner, yr honour, was found to be in possession of two thousand half-smoked cigarettes.

PETER: Two thousand cigarettes? What have you got to say for yourself, Mr Jones?

HARRY: (Wheezy coughing)[3]

In casting himself as the unemotional, objective clerk of the court, was Spike at some subconscious level distancing himself from this early, traumatic experience? In the classic tradition of 'and if I laugh' was he now ridiculing the incident that had caused him such terror and humiliation? Is it significant that in the Goon court the prisoner alone appears to be isolated? There is no mention of a defence lawyer.

Spike looks back on this day without much apparent distress, but it is clear that at the time he must have suffered deeply. No doubt we should all reflect with some thankfulness on the magistrate, who seems to have been somewhat benign for his time. Terence was a working-class boy who had been caught thieving, and a spell at a Borstal would not have been considered inappropriate. Spike remembers his father's impassioned plea to the court: 'He is a good worker, my lord, and gives all his paltry wages to his mother. He wanted a trumpet so badly, and saw no way of getting one. He is an artist, sir, and wanted only to enrich his life.'

'There he was, making this great speech – I'd heard him rehearsing it the night before in front of the mirror. They were a bit floored by it because usually they get some snotty-nosed chap trying to say, "My son never dunnit. He never dunnit, I tell you." Spike remembers the day with horror. 'I just wanted to yell out, "Oh, I'm guilty, I'm guilty – just say that I'm guilty and make an end of it."'

'He will become a successful musician, and in due course repay every penny,' intoned his father, whilst Spike crouched lower and lower in the dock.

One can imagine what an impressive front soldier-showman Leo put up. With his ex-army confidence, his striped suit and his actor's flamboyance he must have bemused the court into virtually dismissing the case. Once outside, he was triumphant. He and Terence mounted a tram-car and settled themselves on the top deck.

'That,' said Leo with relish, 'will show the buggers.'

'It was rather a comedown then,' remembers Spike. 'The conductor came up for our fares and neither of us had a penny. We had to get off and walk six miles to get home.'

After this experience, Terence went to work at Strakers, a large stationer's shop in the West End of London. Once again it was a dreary, unrewarding, ill-paid job. One of his duties was to make tea at regular intervals for numerous ungrateful individuals. Being tea-boy for a few months may have had one fringe benefit for Milligan; to this day he can make a first-class pot of tea which, from choice, he will take from a good-sized mug. In the canteen one morning at the White City TV Centre, he had two paper beakers of tea on a tray. A friend running into him asked if he had someone with him. 'No,' said Milligan. 'I'm on my own. But you don't get a decent cup of tea out of one of these BBC cardboard thimbles, do you?'

Kathleen Milligan, Leo's elder sister, had been married to Alf Thurgar for two years when they bought a newly-built modern semi-detached house in Newquay Road, Catford. She was to live there until she died fifty years later at the age of 87.

Every week, usually on a Friday evening, Florence

would rally the family together and they would make the short journey to Aunt Kath's house. Newquay Road was situated a short bus-ride away in the 'better' part of Catford. No 15 must have stayed in a sort of time-warp, for it was to remain a pure and undiluted testament of the 'thirties which Milligan used to visit intermittently until his aunt's death in 1983. Back in 1933, Aunt Kath's house had the distinction of a bathroom; thus it was in a fever of cleanliness that Florence led her little band there each week. Desmond and Terry were delighted with their 'rich' aunt and her superior standards of living; they rolled up their towels cheerfully enough. 'We never discussed this sort of thing with the neighbours,' recalls Spike. 'But I imagine they must have thought that we were going swimming or something like that. And my mother was proud. She wouldn't have let on – never.' The Milligans regularly descended on No 15 and always received a kindly welcome. Bathing was not the sole entertainment; Aunt Kath was invariably good for an excellent tea. A family afternoon tea was a special occasion, and warranted the use of a small but businesslike trolley made of dark oak. It was always laid up in the same way: sandwiches on the top shelf, cakes and tarts on the second, and teapots and cups on the bottom. The trolley impressed Terry with its bountiful grandeur.

This was a whole different sort of life, you see. We were living in such a small, miserable place – it was poky and dark, it seemed to us you could have fitted our whole place into just this front room. And Aunt Kath used to make something of an occasion of it when we came. We looked forward to it no end. I remember the tea trolley, it had this rail on it, this wooden rail at the end and she always had a white linen cloth hanging over the rail.

The front room at 15 Newquay Road held an upright piano. After tea Florence would sit and play. Leo would stroll around humming and tapping his feet. He had no performances to give now, and during the hours of unemployment in 1933 he would often stroll, smartly dressed, up and down the nearby Bourne. This was nearer to his sister's house than his own, so he often slipped out during the visits for a respite from the family and for a few moments 'to be himself'. No doubt his Irish optimism and good humour kept him buoyant – but there seems to be no doubt that he was, largely, a man unfulfilled.

The house at Newquay Road had one special ornament that impressed the Milligan brothers deeply. It was an art-nouveau lamp that was fixed to the banister rail in the entrance hall. The lamp was held by a bronze boy angel, and it remained in its position for the better part of fifty years. When Aunt Kathleen died, Desmond remembered the figure and asked if it could be sent to him in Australia. Spike made a special journey to Catford where he met his cousin, Terry Thurgar, and they went on a nostalgic last visit to the house. In the entrance hall the lamp still stood. Spike fell on it lovingly and asked his cousin if he might send it to Desmond. Terry agreed and the lamp was dismantled there and then. Milligan held it on his lap during the drive back to his home in Barnet. He was anxious about its forthcoming journey to Australia; ordinary packaging would not do, he said.

A friend, shortly to visit Australia, offered to deliver it personally. 'No thanks,' said Spike. 'I want this to get there safely. Thanks all the same but I don't really trust anyone. I shall send it by Special Courier. That way I'll know that it will arrive.'

Before the cousins parted, Terry Thurgar promised to have the small oak tea trolley delivered to Spike's house. Spike was overjoyed, for afternoon tea is frequently celebrated at his home and he felt that the trolley would lend a great air of occasion. 'How marvellous to have it there!'

he said. 'We must have a small white linen cloth to hang on the rail. We can use it for afternoon tea. It will remind me of all the tea-times we had at Aunt Kath's.'

Terence had by now infiltrated a dance band – Tommy Brittell's New Ritz Revels at Brockley. They played every Saturday night at St Cyprian's Hall. He managed to croon like Bing Crosby and win a competition; he also played drums, guitar and trumpet, in which he was entirely self-taught. The next musical instrument that was to fascinate him was the double bass, but his first attempt to buy one was not successful.

Well, the advertisement in the shop window said 'Bass, going cheap. Call after 6.' I suppose the 'cheap' was the bit that made me notice. Anyway I called round at the address and the man asked me in. He looked a bit curious and said, 'Are you married?' I said no, so he asked me what I wanted the bass for. It turned out to be a bassinet, meant for a baby.

But he was not frustrated for long. One of the young musicians he knew was on the point of abandoning the double bass so he was able to acquire his instrument. Although it was cumbersome, he was proud of it and, when he took it with him to a band engagement, gladly paid an extra penny for the bass to stand at the front of the tram-car, next to the driver.

One of the short-term jobs that Terence had was at Keith Prowse of Bond Street, where he was employed as an assistant storeman. The work was uninteresting, tedious and without much hope of advancement. He scraped through the days and longed for the evenings, when he would race to London Bridge Station and congregate with several friends, all musicians or would-be musicians. One particular friend was Harold Fagg, who left his job at the Stock Exchange every day at 4.30 P.M. but hung around

until 6 P.M. or later when Terence would be free to join
him. Harold lived in Brockley and they could usually catch
the same train home. He remembers that Terence, through
the good offices of Keith Prowse, was able to supply the
group of impecunious young musicians with cut-price sheet
music and strings for instruments. The firm may well have
had another important advantage for Milligan. It was in
those days largely a music store and for the first time in his
life he found himself in an atmosphere where music was
regarded as a profession, a livelihood, and not simply an
enjoyable accomplishment or pastime. Perhaps it was via
Keith Prowse that he came to hear of a part-time evening
course in orchestral practice that was available at Goldsmith's College in Lewisham Way. He was not really of
the standard required, but he bluffed his way into the
class and it says much for both Goldsmith's insight and the
immediacy of Milligan's responses that he survived the
course.

Terence turned up at the first class carrying his double
bass. Other players were rubbing their bows with resin;
he had no bow but managed to side-step the issue by
explaining that his bow had inadvertently been left at
home. 'No matter,' said the teacher. 'You can play *pizzicato*.' Milligan knew of no way to play his instrument save
by plucking the strings. Perhaps that was what '*pizzicato*'
meant? He hoped for the best and proceeded. His contribution was acceptable, and he returned once a week for
the rest of the one-term course. The class taught him the
rudiments of harmony and counterpoint, and he learned
something of the discipline of formal music. As with the
matter of the bow, he managed to conceal the fact that he
had only a very limited knowledge of written music, and
before the term ended was no longer intimidated by a
musical score but was sight-reading with growing
proficiency.

In the future, Terence always carried a bow with his instrument and even at jazz sessions, when to use a bow would have been inappropriate, he would position it neatly, lying at a right angle across his bass. As Spike says:

> Well, Goldsmith's was the nearest I ever had to a musical education. I suppose I wanted to show off a bit. To show that I didn't only strum, and that I could play with a bow if I wanted to, and that I took music seriously.

Ronnie Scott, a friend of Milligan's for twenty years, has no doubt about Spike's musical gifts:

> Of course he could have been a musician. He is a musician. He has a true ear and a marvellous rhythm and all the talent in the world when he wants to use it. He'd have played a beautiful alto trumpet if he'd stuck at it. But you have to stick at it, and exclude almost everything else. Taking up an instrument seriously is a life sentence really.[4]

Florence Kettleband had always been a staunch Catholic. She never questioned the faith in which she was raised and it could be that the comfortable reins with which her religion allowed her to control her family were agreeable to her. Now, as Terence painfully and almost reluctantly grew to maturity, he angered and distressed his mother on several scores. He kept changing jobs, he stayed out late playing jazz music, and worst of all, he became indifferent to the basic Roman Catholic requirement of attending mass on Sundays. In time this became an issue. Flo cajoled, exhorted and finally threatened her reluctant son. Terence grew sullen and determined. Leo tried to support his wife and understand his son, probably succeeding in neither. Desmond, wide-eyed and cautious, kept his distance and did as he was told; his time for defiance had not yet arrived. Eventually a sizeable row flared. Terence stalked out of the house and took refuge at the home of Harold Fagg, whose mother philosophically allowed him house room in Brockley whilst the heat abated. He stayed for about six weeks, eventually infiltrating back home and under his own terms; he went to mass when he felt like it.

In years to come, Spike was to court his mother's displeasure by mildly mocking her religious fervency. 'My mother,' he writes in *Adolf Hitler: My Part in His Downfall*, 'had gone to church to do a bulk confession for the whole family.' In the same book, on a later page, he describes an army chaplain who lectured the battery and harangued them on the necessity of avoiding strong drink which could lead to fornication. 'If you see one of your comrades the worse for drink and sexually excited, take him home with you, and bathe the parts in cold water,' the chaplain exhorted. 'Gratifying to know that all you need to be a Christian is a bucket of cold water and an erection,' writes a sardonic Spike.

It was during these tense, pre-war days of the 'thirties that Terence at last began to stand up for himself. In 1938 he was playing in the Harlem Club Band. 'We were,' he recalls in his war memoirs, 'a bunch of spotty musicians held together by hair oil.' Spotty or not, the band was not unsuccessful and they were able to obtain a fair number of 'gigs' at South London venues, usually weekend engagements at local dance-halls. Terence discovered that when he was not working he was still able to present his mother with virtually the same financial contribution from his share of the band money. This gratified him but enraged poor Flo whose desire for her sons to have 'proper' jobs has always exceeded all other considerations.

The last job that Terence took on before his call-up was another dull and unpromising one: he became a semi-skilled fitter at Woolwich Arsenal. This entailed fitting leads to batteries, and it had the singular merit that at five pounds per week it was relatively well-paid. Leo was justifiably pained to realize that Terence was now earning as much as he himself was, but his loyalty and pride in his son overcame his qualms, for when Flo grew vociferous about Terence's continuing late nights and musical excursions Leo would try hard to pour oil. 'He's bringing home the dibs, my dear,' he would say soothingly. 'He's bringing home the dibs.'

The years of deputizing for Leo during his army absences had undoubtedly sharpened the decisive and dogmatic side of Flo's personality. She ruled the household with a rod of iron; what she said went and she never considered the possibility that she might be wrong. She was staunch, loyal and strong but she lacked understanding and had no capacity to see her sons as individuals or to recognize that they might have their own ideas and aspirations which did not, of necessity, fall in with her own. She was abysmally short of imagination. Friends were neither made nor encouraged, and the home, adequately maintained and run as it was, was never welcoming.

It is fair, perhaps, to remember under what changed circumstances the Milligan family were now living. Flo had no terms of reference for a situation where one pound must always do the work of two. To someone so inflexible, the idea of offering hospitality not linked to native servants and army pay must have seemed unrealistic.

Spike's girlfriend Lily Gibbs lived only a bus ride away from the house in Riseldine Road, yet although their association was recognized and presumably accepted by the family, it was rarely suggested that she might join the family for a meal or an evening at home.

I don't know why it was like that – she was my girlfriend, and my mother knew. She came to the house once or twice but there was only one occasion when my mother said, 'Well, have dinner with us,' or something like that. I don't know why, for she knew all about dinners and having people and all that – they'd had enough dinners and things in India. Somehow there was no real freedom at home. I had to wait until I joined the army to know any sort of freedom. My mother always wanted to have all the say. My father once told me that my mother was never so happy as when I was ill in bed and she was nursing me. 'She had total control then, you see,' he said. 'Total control.'

Lily lived with her parents, a brother and a sister at 45 Revelon Road, Brockley, SE4. Her parents were unpretentious and highly respectable. Her father, a commercial traveller, was in steady employment. Her mother stayed at home cleaning the house, shopping and cooking for the family who took sandwiches to work every morning and came home for supper every evening. Lily left school at the age of fourteen; at the time she met Terence she had been working as a shorthand typist at a wine and spirit merchant's office in Shaftesbury Avenue for two years. She commuted from Brockley Station; it was a five and a half day week and for this Lily earned a salary of ten shillings. She gave this to her mother, who returned two shillings and sixpence to her for her 'pocket money'. Lily was 5' 4", slender, pretty and congenitally shortsighted.

Every Saturday night, she and her girlfriend Joan Wood put on their best dresses and went along to the weekly dance at St Cyprian's Church Hall, Brockley. They would pay the entrance fee (sixpence) and make a bolt for the 'Ladies' where they would hang their coats, put on their dancing shoes and generally make themselves as attractive and seductive as they knew how. Not to receive any invitations to dance from the young men who frequented St Cyprian's would be a matter of absolute shame. Women had not, as yet, adopted the cheerful, post-war solution of dancing with each other; consequently no invitations meant that one was speedily branded a 'wallflower'.

It was usual for girls to go in twos and threes. They would stick together, prim but interested in the boys who would stand in a gaggle round the soft drinks bar, eyeing the girls and speculating on their chances. Girls who visited the hall together would separate only for the length of a dance, and there was an unspoken understanding that if a girl allowed herself to be 'seen home' by a special boy, she first made sure that her girlfriend was not abandoned. Very often the boy who was keen to see a favourite girl home would be required to produce an unattached friend for her less successful companion.

One Saturday evening in November 1936 Terence arrived at St Cyprian's in especially high spirits. His parents had announced their intention of taking Desmond away to visit a relative on the following weekend. This presented an opportunity too good to be missed, and a party at 50 Riseldine Road was planned. From their excellent vantage-point on the stage, the bandsmen surveyed the scene and picked out their quarry, and one of their number, Mick Wilmot, was sanctioned to step down and invite five girls to come along the following Friday night, Lily and Joan among them. Lily was in ecstasies, for though she had never joined the group of girls who hung hopefully round the bandstand eyeing the musicians, she had gazed for many weeks on the double-bass player and woven a fantasy that one day he might descend from his pedestal and invite her to dance.

'Don't be so silly. He's not inviting you specially,' said a cautious Joan. 'He's got a girlfriend. That's her sitting in the wings with a lemonade.'

'I don't care,' said Lily. 'I'm definitely going, whether she's there or not. He doesn't seem to be going regular with anyone. And just to be in the same room with him would be heaven.'

The party turned out to be everything that Lily could have hoped for. The front room at the Milligans' was warm and comfortable. It was lit only by the flickering log fire in the grate – an extravagance that would have horrified Flo. The girls sat round in a circle, the gramophone played and the boys moved round. When the music stopped, the boys halted and each sat down next to the nearest girl. A kiss was then in order before the music started up again, at which stage the boys moved on. Before long, Lily saw that Terence was drawing close. She took off her spectacles and dropped them in her lap. The young lady who had accompanied Terence to the party was at the opposite side of the room but probably within earshot. The music stopped and Terence sat down. He and Lily exchanged several kisses. When he spoke, Terence's voice was muffled.

'I don't know who I'm with, but I'm staying here.'

'No you're not,' hissed a perturbed male friend. 'Stick to the rules, Terry. Yer gotta move on.'

Terence acquiesced – perhaps he was conscious of the other young lady who was peering uncertainly through the firelight. But before he moved he whispered in Lily's ear: 'Meet me tomorrow outside the Rivoli Cinema, Crofton Park, seven o'clock.'

Lily went home delirious with excitement. Terence saw his current girlfriend to her home and left her suspicious and unmollified. Then he returned swiftly to Riseldine Road to pressgang some members of the band into helping him eradicate all signs of the party. He was not displeased with the way the evening had gone. He wondered whether Lily would turn up.

* * *

Lily arrived early the following evening. Terence was not yet there so she walked around outside the cinema watching the nearby trams for a sight of him. Eventually he arrived on foot, and walked straight past her. Lily was dressed in her best black suit and a white blouse. She was wearing a black pill-box hat with a small eye veil. She was also wearing her spectacles. After some indeterminate circling, she summoned enough courage to speak up. Terence was taken aback. The prim little bespectacled girl scarcely corresponded with his eager memories of the party game.

'Oh, hullo – there you are,' he said distantly. 'I hope you've got some money. I'm broke.'

Lily had, fortunately. She paid the two ninepences without question. She did not notice the film, but Terence sat straight up in his seat like a sentry, watching the screen intently. He appeared to be unaware that she was by his side. After the show, he turned to her abruptly.

'Well, I might as well see you home. Where do you live?'

Lily told him, and he walked with her towards her house. They did not speak, and Lily was conscious that she had in some way disappointed Terence, that he had reviewed his evening's date and found her inadequate. When they came to her road, he said a curt 'goodnight' and strode away. Puzzled and humiliated, Lily went to bed and wept for the desolation of her evening. She resolved that she would never visit the St Cyprian's Hall again.

The next day, when Joan heard Lily's tale she was dismayed and sympathetic. She agreed that Lily would be too embarrassed to go dancing at St Cyprian's in the immediate future and they made plans to visit the Laurie Grove swimming-pool dance-hall at New Cross, where, as at St Cyprian's, there was a dance every Saturday night.

For the following three Saturdays, Lily and Joan went to the Laurie Grove dances. The journey was longer, the entrance fee larger and they did not enjoy them as much; the dancers all seemed to know one another very well, and they were somewhat older and so highly professional that the Brockley girls felt themselves gauche and inferior by comparison. Undoubtedly, Lily was also longing for a sight of Terence, and when, after the third week running at New Cross, Joan spoke up and said that she now felt that the time had come for them to brave St Cyprian's again, Lily agreed without argument.

When the girls arrived at St Cyprian's on the following Saturday, they were told by the manager that they were to be admitted free. 'There's no charge for you two,' he said. 'Orders of the band, you're to go in free if and when you turned up.' Lily was shaken, but Joan took it all in her stride. 'Come on, silly,' she said. 'There's no harm in us going in free. We're not under any obligation.'

They went in and took up their usual position in the 'wallflower' area where the unaccompanied girls were gathered. The music was in full swing. Terence was on the rostrum and he saw Lily within minutes. He made no gesture of recognition. Lily accepted one or two partners, and just as she finished one of the dances, Terence deserted his double bass for a few moments and stalked over to her.

'Don't bother to let any of these people arrange to see you home,' he said austerely. 'I'll be doing that.'

Lily was stunned and speechless; Terence marched back to his place on the stage and went on playing for a further ten minutes until the band had a 'rest' period. At this point, the players left the rostrum and the dance continued to recorded music.

During their break, the musicians usually had a sandwich and a drink at the bar. They were then free, if they wished, to dance to the records. This was the moment for which many of the 'wallflowers' eagerly waited. On this occasion, Lily sat silently, not looking at Terence. He danced a few times, with several different girls. He laughed and chatted and joked and flirted, but for the whole half-hour period of the break he ignored Lily completely.

At the end of the last session, however, the instruments were packed away and Terence delegated care of the double bass to Harold Fagg. He collected Lily who was waiting demurely with Joan. The three of them walked together until Joan's road was reached, then Terence and Lily walked on alone. When they reached Lily's gate, he took her in his arms and they kissed.

'What time do you get home from work tomorrow?' asked Terence. 'I'll meet your train.'

A pattern emerged and was followed for the next eighteen months. Terence Milligan was unemployed; his energies were diverted by weight-lifting at Ladywell Athletics Track and swimming at the outdoor lidos at Brockwell Park and Bellingham Baths. He was a dedicated and tireless member of the Harlem Club Band, but unenthusiastic about seeking more formal or regular employment. Every evening he would be waiting at Brockley Station for Lily to return from work. He would walk her to her gate, and for the first year he was often invited into the Gibbs' house to share the family meal. But then, as he continued to displease his potential in-laws by failing to get work, these invitations gradually became less frequent. Terence would then go to his own home for supper, sometimes meeting Lily again later in the evening. There was no money for outings, but Sundays were often spent visiting the museums. Terence was fascinated by the Natural History Museum and the Science Museum. It was usually Lily's small funds that paid their bus fares. Once each week they managed two ninepenny cinema seats, and on

Saturday nights there was invariably a band engagement. On these nights Lily went along in the full status of Terence's girl. She was allowed to dance when invited, but her partner was never encouraged to buy her a drink or have more than one dance. Terence was possessive and jealous and would not hesitate to leap down from the band and threaten any over-eager young man. If necessary, Lily advised any would-be admirer to be wary. 'You'd better not hang about too much if you don't mind,' she would say. 'I'm actually with the band; the young man on the bass is my friend and he can get very angry.'

Terence was, by now, wholly occupied with his band engagements, and with the swimming and athletics programmes. As he earned enough from the band to give his mother a few shillings he felt it unnecessary to look too hard for work. Leo, perhaps remembering his own thwarted artistic ambitions, was secretly sympathetic, but Florence was extremely anxious. Sometimes she would rage and scold for a full half-hour. Desmond, whey-faced and worried, would scurry out of range, but Leo would stand firmly behind Flo, sometimes pulling dismal faces and making flapping motions with his fingers to suggest a duck quacking. Lily was once or twice present when these outbursts took place, but she was too apprehensive to join in and she certainly never dared to giggle at Leo's mild fun. Terence was merely mutinous and silent, and watchful for the first moment of escape.

'I don't know why she's so angry,' he said to Lily on one occasion. 'I get twelve and six from the band and I give her seven and six.'

Flo was understandably wrathful. 'Seven and six doesn't go far towards your keep,' she would yell. 'Why don't you go out and get a proper job.'

Years later Spike would say, 'She never really enjoyed

the successes I've had, you know. She can't forgive me for succeeding without working by her standards.'

But the Milligans approved of Lily. On the one occasion when she was invited to a meal she sat, silent but polite, between Flo and Leo. Terence and Desmond sat opposite. Perhaps they were awed by the unusualness of the situation. Certainly conversation did not flourish. Leo carved a small piece of meat and Flo dished out vegetables. Eventually, Leo broke the silence. He put his hand on Lily's wrist.

'What a quiet little thing you are,' he marvelled. 'You've been here two hours and no one has heard a peep out of you!'

Before Lily left, Flo took her aside. 'You are a good influence on Terry,' she said. 'You want him to get a proper job now that he's walking out with you. You want your security, I can see. And you are a nice quiet girl. We like that. Better than some of the others we've seen.'

Lily did indeed want her security, and she also pressed Terence constantly and ineffectively to get a proper job. He was not responsive, but to begin with Lily bore with him for the single reason that she was head over heels in love. Often Terence could only collect her and take her for a walk in the evenings. Her own slender pocket-money exhausted, Lily would sometimes collect a few pence for Terence's tram fare home by returning empty soda or beer bottles to the local shops. The shops generally paid a penny per bottle, and many a long walk home was Terence spared by her diligence. Eventually, Lily's mother rebelled.

'That boy's no good,' she said. 'He's been coming round here after our Lily for months now, and he's out of work and not even trying to support her. Just don't let me see him round here any more.'

By now, Lily also despaired of Terence, but she was

more in love than ever and unable to say goodbye. Her
unsatisfactory lover continued to treat her with a curious
mixture of adoration and callous disregard, yet she
remained fascinated. He was quite different from any other
boy she had known. He wrote little poems to her, he
talked about art and music and for a lot of the time he
seemed to inhabit a world that was quite outside her
comprehension. He worked hard on improving Lily.

'You can't say "I'm frozed",' he admonished her. 'There's
no such word as *frozed*. The noun is "frost" and the verb is
to "freeze" and the adjective is "frozen".'

The influence of the scholarly holy fathers of Jesus had
been cut short when Terence was uprooted from Rangoon,
and the sequence of depressing South London schools and
dismal jobs did nothing to keep his interest in academic
areas alert. Yet still he made some effort to remember the
lessons of more privileged days.

Lily listened avidly to everything he said. She tried
hard to understand him, and she gave generously of her
time and resources. It was Lily who eventually saved up
four pounds for Terence's first trumpet. She made no
demands, except for the implicit, underlying but crucial
requirement that he should conform to the standards in
which she had been raised.

Perhaps in the hope that it would prove a decisive
factor, she moved away from those standards for long
enough to lose her virginity to Terence. It was an exhausting and unrewarding experience for them both, as neither
had a very clear idea as to what exactly should happen.
The breakdown of their relationship seemed inevitable.
Terence couldn't change, and wasn't interested in changing. He felt that he was doing all right as he was. Lily met
another young man who behaved as men behaved in the
films which she watched every week. He collected her in a
car, took her to West End cinemas and then for dinner at

a Lyons Corner House. He was attentive and dutiful and he made her feel important. Lily eventually broke the news to Terence that there was 'someone else'. Terence appeared uninterested and undismayed. It was at this stage that he was called up for army service in the Second World War. From then on, he continued to write to Lily in deeply affectionate terms. As far as he was concerned, Lily was his girl and he professed his love for her. 'We will,' he wrote, 'be together after the war. Oh, yes, we will.' Lily answered with letters couched in friendly terms, but tried to impress him with the fact that they were no longer a couple. It was no use. Milligan, then as now, believed only what he chose to believe. He had shown himself to be totally indifferent to Lily's needs, and it is conceivable that her long and patient toleration of him gave him ground in which to entrench the basic disparagement of women that subtly infiltrated his adult life. Milligan, to this day, has little respect for women. Nevertheless, if you catch him on a good day he might easily show you the trumpet that still hangs on his office wall.

'That was my first trumpet,' he will say. 'A girl called Lily gave it to me. She saved up for months to buy it for me. She was my first real love.'

5

Army Days in Bexhill

Satire, being levelled at all, is never resented for
an offence by any.

Jonathan Swift

Terence Milligan's departure to join the army on 2 June
1940 was an important milestone in his life. He had
virtually never left home before and although, in the
beginning, he missed his family and his friends, he soon
became aware of a curious lifting of his spirits.

Apart from escaping from the thrall of a good servile
Catholic family, Terence now escaped from something
else: the inevitable oppressions of daily life that bedevil an
impecunious suburban city-dweller. The South London
streets where Terence lived were not the romantic areas of
Dickens' London. They were neat, grey, foggy, dull and
legion. They stretched for miles and encapsulated most of
the dispirited inhabitants with a gloomy gratitude that they
had, at least, a 'decent' place to live. Being released
into the marvellous Sussex countryside around Bexhill hit
Milligan like a bomb. He was amazed and delighted to
witness the rolling panorama of a golden English summer.
The views, the myriads of wild flowers, the farms, the
people, the industry still redolent of pre-World War II
farming communities, all these were a matter of incredulous joy to him. The space, beauty and, from time to time,
solitude of the countryside impressed him dramatically and
his exposure to all this was to affect his thinking profoundly
in years to come.

More than four decades later, he recalled the days that
still hold a kind of magic for him:

This was the English countryside – it sang at you – this was the reason Constable never wanted to paint anything else. The pleasures of those years were endless – from seeing a rare medlar tree, a Saxon dew-pond, an unspoilt bluebell wood, a working windmill, to watching Fred Vahey, a Sussex thatcher living in a gipsy caravan, make nettle soup from a Romany recipe.

He concluded with a despairing reflection on the present and a plea for the future.

Now, forty-one years later, our countryside (and I stress *our* countryside) is being eroded and mutilated. Cruel farming methods are being evolved . . . What is killing the countryside is pressure from increasing population and affluence; depression or no, people still have more money than of yore. The result is tremendous pressure on land and the fruits of the land . . . Malthus was right: if you want the countryside to survive – small families please, preferably vegetarian![1]

The boy who revelled in the joy of the Sussex countryside learned a lot as the years passed. Now a father of four, Spike will occasionally struggle for compromise.

I didn't realize these things about overpopulation in those days, very few of us did. And the children just came along and I loved them so much I just can't regret them. But there's a part of me that isn't too easy on the score. I would like to have done my bit and only had one or two, but I didn't, and that's that.

Every day he found something new to interest him. He was intrigued to think that he was part of the war effort and fascinated by the massive inadequacies of the authorities who at this stage had provided the men with a rifle each and five rounds of ammunition 'in case of invasion by sea'. The main transports at this time were heavy sanding-gravel lorries that had been commandeered from builders. Milligan marvelled at the desperate shortage of equipment and the straight-faced commanding officers who appeared to take it all for granted.

On the positive side, he was now, at the age of twenty-two, at last enjoying a sort of freedom, a release from the rigid conventions of his home and the rules made by his mother. No longer was he obliged to give lip-service to her well-intentioned but bombastic protestations. No longer would there be altercations about his unwillingness to go to mass. No longer would she wait at the top of the stairs to reproach him for coming home at one in the morning after a night playing with Ritz Revels or the Harlem Club Band.

And no longer was he to feel furtively resentful of the 'proper jobs' that he had fallen in and out of fairly regularly. For the first time in his life, in spite of all the army rules and regulations for the private soldier, Milligan felt grown-up and free.

When Milligan decided to write his autobiography, he concentrated almost entirely on his years in the army. The reason can probably be found in his preface to Volume I, *Adolf Hitler: My Part in His Downfall*, where Milligan says, 'The experience of being in the army changed my whole life.' Apart from the vividly remembered days of his childhood in India, he seems to have found relatively little interest in recording other periods of his existence, either the uncertain musical progress which followed the muted despair of his teenage years, or the gradual spiral to fame when the Goon Show flourished and took off. The five years he spent in uniform seem, in retrospect, to have brought him closer to a state of cheerful, unstructured happiness than he has experienced before or since. He has small appetite for recalling painful or unhappy memories; no doubt he softened the discipline of writing his autobiography with the self-indulgence of remembering times that were nearly always happy.

* * *

Various reasons combined to delay his call-up. Probably the main one was a matter of his temporary ill-health. The weight-lifting had resulted in a minor rupture; his trumpet-blowing had presumably not aided his recovery. He was, in fact, attending the out-patients' clinic at Lewisham General Hospital, and although call-up papers arrived at Riseldine Road in January 1940, he did not actually join his regiment until June. Like his father and grandfather before him, he was to become a gunner. He reported to D Battery of the 56th Heavy Regiment Royal Artillery, then stationed at Bexhill-on-Sea.

A former mate, Ted Lawrence, remembers his arrival.

He seemed a bit different from the lads, I think it was because he was carrying a trumpet in a little separate case. He had a suitcase, like we all had when we arrived, but he had this funny little extra trumpet case. I remember he went off in the back of an open lorry to get kitted out. Supplies had been short of everything when I first got there but it was getting a bit easier by the time he arrived. We'd been short of clothes, guns, ammunition, everything.

Training and drilling began immediately. Terence, no doubt remembering the impressive soldiers of the Raj, took the army disciplines more or less for granted. He was, up to now, accustomed to conforming and usually doing what was expected of him.

But for the first time in his life he was forced into a close proximity with strangers. He had to live, eat, work and sleep to an ordained pattern and with a group of companions he had not chosen. They were nearly all about the same age, between twenty and twenty-two. On 2 June 1940, Milligan wrote in his diary:

Joined the Regt. 56th R.A. Dumbest crowd of blokes I've seen. Nearly all N. Country blokes.

The dumb 'north-country blokes', however, turned out to be not so dumb after all, and Milligan, once he had lost something of his initial shyness and inhibition, became relaxed and interested in everything that was new to him. His companions undoubtedly found him somewhat unusual but they were all sharing the common upheaval and there was a great spirit of camaraderie. Dennis Sloggett was a conscript who had arrived just a few months before. Formerly a builder's cost clerk, he survived the war and now is a prime mover of the Battery Reunion party held yearly at Bexhill.

Well, we were all making the best of it. We were all in it together, all young lads having their first stretch away from home – not many of us had really wanted to go and none of us had much idea about what was in store for us. Spike was just another lad, but I do remember that he seemed a bit retiring, almost a bit backward or something, but he came on beautifully in a few weeks. It was as though we drew him out. The army really made a difference to him. He got a lot more sure of himself.

For the next few months, Milligan was billeted at what had formerly been a girls' boarding school, Worthingholme on the Hastings Road. It was to have an unexpected benefit for him, not apparent at the time of his arrival. The girls had been evacuated to safer parts of England and it seemed as though they had left in rather a hurry. A well-stocked library of books had been abandoned on the top floor. Milligan had never really seen a collection of books before and he was enthralled.

I went to one of the officers – I remember his name was Mostyn – and said I'd like to collate all the books, list them and so on, and let the chaps all borrow them. I said that we were very short of reading matter in the Battery. He just said

'Oh yes, Milligan, good idea, Milligan,' but he wasn't bothered, so in the end I just took the books over for myself.

Perhaps with a foretaste of the future, Milligan, the convivial man who is yet strangely solitary, choosing for preference always to sleep alone, removed himself from the barrack room and took his mattress upstairs where he slept with the books and began reading for the first time in his life.

There was Dickens, I read a lot of Dickens – I loved *Bleak House* – and George Eliot. *Silas Marner* I read, and *Mill on the Floss*. It was a new world to me. I just somehow got started reading. It was marvellous.

The war was very close. The sound of gunfire could be heard, faint but persistent, across the Channel. Within a few days of Milligan's arrival, the evacuation of Dunkirk was under way, and the young recruits and conscripts sat around, awed and uncertain, waiting for something to happen.

The day of the actual Dunkirk evacuation the Channel was like a piece of polished steel. I'd never seen a sea so calm. One would say it was miraculous. I presume that something like this had happened to create the 'Angel of Mons' legend. That afternoon Bombardier Andrews and I went down for a swim. It would appear we were the only two people on the south coast having one. With the distant booms, the still sea, and just two figures on the landscape, it all seemed very strange. We swam in silence. Occasionally, a squadron of Spitfires or Hurricanes headed out towards France. I remember so clearly, Bombardier Andrews standing up in the water, putting his hands on his hips, and gazing towards where the BEF was fighting for its life. It was the first time I'd seen genuine concern on a British soldier's face; 'I can't see how they're going to get 'em out,' he said. We sat in the warm water for a while. We felt so helpless. Next day the news of the 'small armada' came through on the afternoon news. As the immensity of the defeat became apparent, somehow the evacuation turned it into a strange victory.[2]

Right from the start of his army days, Milligan managed, one way or another, to promote his musical talents. He did not allow his trumpet to go unnoticed, and well before he succeeded in getting the Battery band together, established himself as unofficial Battery bugler. He was roped in to sound the reveille in the early mornings. Never eager to leap out of bed, but pleased to have his musical ability respected, he contrived a manner of sounding the reveille before rising each morning. He managed to position his mattress just below a low window which opened well above most of the adjacent (and more official) sleeping quarters. At the required time, he would raise himself on one elbow, blow a clear and strident reveille on his trumpet, pause, blow it a second time, and then relax under the blankets until he just had to get up.

Reg Griffin, another friend from the Battery, recalls:

You used to see the trumpet, just on its own, poking out of that upstairs window. The Sergeant used to wake him with a bell, or something like that, then Spike used to blow the trumpet himself to get us all moving. But he didn't move himself until the last possible moment.[3]

During the first weeks at Bexhill, Milligan made tentative steps towards fulfilling his vague but determined musical ambitions. He spent a lot of his free time lying on his bunk playing the trumpet. One of the boys told him that he should meet the Battery pianist Harry Edgington who was also a talented composer, song-writer and arranger. The meeting was propitious and highly productive. They began playing together and as jazz enthusiasts inspired each other as much as they delighted their listeners. Milligan warmed to the approbation of his audience and his confidence soared.

> Harry and I were giving the lads a tune one evening and there was this gunner Doug Kidgell sitting there, he was banging away on his mess-tin with a knife and fork, keeping time with us. He was great. I said 'Right, you're our drummer.' And he was, from then on. That's how it happened. That's how we got the Battery band together.'

The band was not yet complete, however. Bombardier Alf Fildes was discovered to be an accomplished guitarist. There was no escape for him. They now had four musicians with an average age of twenty years. They had been thrown together by the advent of a war which none of them had welcomed or necessarily understood. But music was their forte and they all knew about that. Battery D recognized its good fortune, a drum kit was commandeered, and life in the barracks became considerably less drab.

In September 1941, a smudged, two-page newsletter was produced 'on behalf of the Semi-Pro Musicians in the Forces'. One item reads:

> TERRY MILLIGAN, THE WILD MAN OF THE HARLEM CLUB BAND who played bass, guitar and, latterly trumpet, with that aggregation is now in the Army and is probably driving his section NCO potty. Just the same, we'd like a word from him.

Apparently no word arrived. Subsequent newsletters seem not to have referred to him again.

At about this stage in his life, Terence Milligan got to know Anthony Goldsmith. Goldsmith, a second-lieutenant in the Battery, was eight years Milligan's senior and by all accounts a young man of exceptional promise. It seems too that he had a rare capacity for transcending the barriers of class, education and the strange convention called, for want of a better word, protocol.

Anthony Goldsmith was a scholar at Harrow, and an exhibitioner at Balliol College, Oxford. There he read Greats, edited *Cherwell* and subsequently wrote what the critics agreed was a masterly translation of Flaubert's *L'Education Sentimentale*. At the outbreak of the Second World War, he joined the 56th Heavy Regiment RA. It is to his everlasting credit that he was able to become something of a guide, friend and mentor to Milligan. Goldsmith was the scion of a good Jewish family where learning was taken for granted and every room in the house was full of books. Milligan was a conscripted private soldier whose formal education had finished at fifteen and whose parents had been wholly gratified when he became a semi-skilled fitter at Woolwich Arsenal. The two men had nothing in common save their sensitivity, their humour, and their as yet unrealized potential. They were hopelessly dissimilar by birth, rank, background, education and culture.

> I started talking to Anthony about serious things. He knew a lot about books and writers and literature and music. He would find time to talk to me about these things. We'd talk about music. I'd talk about jazz, and he'd talk about classics. He'd say 'You must listen to this, Milligan, try this, see what you think of it.' It was exciting for me – and I knew I could learn things from the officers that the lads knew nothing about. Most of them had no interests except boozing and bawdy jokes and sex. I loved the lads, I really loved them but I knew there was no mental food for me there. Sometimes I'd hear things being said between the officers that I knew were important, they talked about things that mattered. So this way, gradually, I began to get the gleanings of an education.

This first summer of the war was memorable in other ways for Spike.

There didn't seem to be a war on at all, it was a wonderful 'shirts off' summer. Around us swept the countryside of Sussex. There were the August cornfields that gave off a golden halitus, each trembling ear straining up to the sun. The Land Girls looked brown and inviting and promised an even better harvest. On moonlight nights haystacks bore lovers through their primitive course, by day there was shade a-plenty, oaks, horse chestnuts, willows, all hung out hot wooden arms decked with the green flags of summer.[4]

Milligan had lived within easy reach of the countryside for five years, but has no memory of ever spending any time there.

My parents became unadventurous once they had left India. They just didn't stray far away from home. They somehow lacked some sort of vital imagination or something. They just had no ideas of introducing us to a world outside our own narrow little home. They once took Desmond and me and we went on a trip, a day trip I suppose, to the seaside. It was a failure – all grey and raining. Nobody enjoyed it. We never went again.

In Lewisham, Leo was still working for the Press Association. He had also enrolled as an air-raid warden and fire-watcher. On 7 September 1940, a daylight raid of great intensity took place. Leo and Desmond were sitting in the Astoria Cinema at Rochdale Road, Lewisham, watching *Stagecoach*. As was customary, a warning flashed on the screen for patrons wishing to leave the cinema. A particularly heavy raid was accurately forecast and a good number of the audience left. Leo was too enraptured with the early Western spectacle to contemplate leaving and they sat on till the end of the programme. The firing of the pistols on the screen blended well with the more immediate thunder of ack-ack guns and the whine of incendiaries. The little cinema reverberated, a shower of plaster fell from the ceiling and clouds of dust almost obscured the screen.

When the film ended, Leo and Desmond emerged cautiously. In the distance, the whole of the East India Docks seemed to be on fire. Leo came back to earth with a jolt. 'Good heavens, son,' he said. 'Who would believe we sat clean through an air-raid of that size?'

After several weeks' training with howitzers, guns and explosives, Spike and one of his good friends, Bob (Dipper) Dye, went on a signalling course. Dipper, three years Spike's senior, has a protective, affectionate attitude towards him, and his memories of shared wartime experiences are recalled with clarity and a certain stolidity:

> We were close together most of the time – once we were sent off on a signalling course together. Spike took to it, but I hated it – I really hated it. Couldn't take to it, I couldn't. He understood it all and he wanted to go on doing it. I think he thought it was something new.

Spike's memory confirms this:

> It was great for me. It meant using my head a bit – even just learning Morse code was an excitement. It was a great feeling to know something so painlessly, to get knowledge so easily. Maths, physics, all the boredom gone, no having to show how you reached answers that you just knew – that's the sort of thing that had got in my way at school.

Dipper, however, was taken off the course and returned to driving heavy artillery. He was thankful to escape from the signalling, but sad to be parted from Spike.

> Dear old Dipper – I love Dipper – I love that man. No, Dipper couldn't take it. The officers made him feel a lemon. He couldn't handle it, he didn't want to know. He didn't need to learn; I did and I wanted to. Not out of ambition – just wanting to be interested. It made the days pass. And Dipper

was happy. We got the Scammels about that time, he started driving a Scammel. He loved that. It suited him fine.

Years later, at one of the Battery reunion parties, Spike managed to negotiate with army authorities and produce a Scammel lorry. It stood resplendent on a cold April morning outside the De La Warre Pavilion on the sea-front at Bexhill. The middle-aged men gleefully scampered around it, pointing out its attributes to their shivering and somewhat mystified wives.

'Grown men making such fools of themselves – just look at them,' said a disapproving Mrs Alf Fildes.

'Oh, well, they had a lot of good times together, didn't they?' said Connie Kidgell, wife of Doug.

Mrs Dipper Dye, with the superior status of a Battery wife whose husband had actually driven the Scammel, agreed with Connie. 'Yes,' she said. 'It's nice to see them enjoying themselves.'

Milligan, swarming all over the Scammel, was enjoying himself more than anyone.

His loyalty to his old friends is legendary. There is no savour of duty in his long association with the Battery reunions; he actually wants to go down to Bexhill and spend time with his old mates when the reunion weekend arrives. He is indifferent to any publicity which arises from his visit, and keeps a fairly low profile at the actual dinner, perhaps falling in with a bit of impromptu cross-talk with some of the stars whom he might have cajoled into appearing, but never choosing to perform himself. He has no sympathy for one or two reluctant wives who turn up rather sourly. 'What's she here for? Why doesn't she piss off if she doesn't enjoy it?' he will say, angry blue eyes snapping. If his calendar permits, he will arrive several hours in advance, book into the Granville Hotel and, after a preliminary grumble about the proximity of his room to a lift or extractor vent or some such noisy adversary, race over to the De La Warre Pavilion, park his Mini neatly at an angle outside the stage door, usually on the double yellow line, and then happily spend the next few hours sorting out the technical arrangements for the bandstand, adjusting spotlights and so forth. He will test the piano critically and fume if it is not perfectly in tune. If there is a spare moment he will divert from the task in hand and show any interested person exactly where his band, the 'Boys of Battery D', used to play. 'The bandstand was just there,' he will say with pride. 'Sometimes the dancers would stand around and applaud our music. Honestly, in 1941 and '42 we were the Beatles of Bexhill.'

Part of the army training consisted of going 'under canvas'. This was hailed by most of the young lads as something of a treat, a new experience. Apparently it went to Spike's head. In Dipper Dye's words:

> In those days under canvas, we saw such amazing sights. Spike would be wearing a sort of loin-cloth like Tarzan or something, he'd just start racing around in the woods carrying a huge club, waving it and howling. We all took it somehow for granted, just accepted it. Didn't seem unusual at all – it was just him being him.

Several weeks after Dunkirk Milligan was dispatched to duty at the lookout post on Galley Hill, one of several local defence points on the outskirts of Bexhill. He was not displeased to be away from the centre of the Battery for a while. A group of four fishermen's cottages on Galley Hill had been commandeered for army use and he was delighted with his new billet. The lookout post was a small brick tower with a machine-gun supposedly at the ready positioned in front of it. These were the eerie days which immediately followed the fall of France, and the two-men watches would sit idly discussing the possibility of invasion and the various plans for this contingency.

As we had no ammunition to speak of, it didn't look as though there would be much that we could do if they did invade. But we always kept the watches, always two of us together; the idea behind that was that one would keep the other awake I suppose. And we would sometimes see the French coast burning in the night. It was a sort of torrid glow. It was unbelievable. God knows what we'd have done if we'd been invaded. We'd have copped it. Alanbrooke was supposed to be in charge of the area; his idea was to let them land and then attack them.

Whilst on duty at Galley Hill, Milligan had a brief meeting with General Sir Alan Brooke, afterwards Lord Alanbrooke.

I was at Bexhill, at the observation post on Galley Hill, and he arrived one mid-morning with a small retinue. I remember he wore leggings and had on a brown camel-haired jacket which was just down to his knees. I'd never been in close contact with the high brass with red tabs on, they came in like a swarm – they always seem to be as if there's no room in the world, they came close together in a great lump these men – with the important one a sort of Queen Bee in the centre. I just looked at him and he said 'Who are you?' I said 'Gunner Milligan, Sir.' He said 'What do you do?' I said 'I do my best, Sir.' He looked hard at me and said 'Well, the way things are it might not be good enough.' I was amused at his quickness, at the way he topped me. I'd no reply.

At what stage did Terence become Spike? Few friends from his army days and later know his baptismal name. When asked about this, he shows a faint ironic amusement. The story goes that he had been talking to Harry Edgington about his musical ambitions. 'I'd like to play the trumpet as well as Spike Hughes does,' said the young, enthusiastic

Terence. 'Oh, I see. We're going to have Spike Milligan next, are we?'

So Terence became Spike, and Spike, along with the band, flourished. The music was a great military bonus and band members were excused guard duties and various chores so that they could practise and perform at social functions. Spike's musical development was rapid and joyful, his inherent creativity growing, and the band's presence was also welcomed by the civilian population. The long Indian summer turned into a bleak wartime winter of barbed wire, blackouts and food rationing, and the dances given under military auspices were popular and well attended. For Spike, it was a matter of some import-ance that the band, for which he felt personally respon-sible, was receiving praise and acclaim.

> We became the darlings of Bexhill. They loved us. We were all young and we loved the music and we liked playing for them. We played requests, and of course we all flirted with the girls and the officers' wives and made eyes at them. Some of the officers used to bring their wives over to the bandstand and liked to introduce them. Of course I was on trumpet and that had a bit of glamour and the wives would like talking to me. 'OEouoe, come and meet Milligan,' their husbands would say, so I'd try and chat them up a bit if they seemed a bit attracted.

Up to now, Milligan had no political affiliations. But now there was the mind-opening freedom of escape from his mother's benign dictatorship. And he could sit around, listen and talk with the men, eavesdrop on the officers and form his own conclusions. Not surprisingly, a socialist conscience began to infiltrate the murky depths of con-fusion left behind by his days in the Raj. The music to 'The Red Flag' intrigued and stimulated him. He decided that it would be a salutary tune to play for the 'last waltz'

instead of the tacky 'I'll See You Again'. The band practised
it willingly enough, and it slipped effortlessly into the
repertoire at the next military dance. Spike, on trumpet,
surveyed the scene with approval. The officers and their
ladies swirled around the bandstand, deep in each other's
arms. Some of the men grinned furtively. They recognized
the tune and saw the joke. The officers, from OCTU and
Sandhurst, didn't. One sergeant, however, knew what was
going on. Older than the average rookies, he had probably
been to militant meetings and Labour Party rallies in the
hungry 'thirties. However, he knew his duty, and insti-
gated a speedy audience with the band. He was full of
wrath.

'Listen, you lot – if you want to go on playing as the
Battery Band you can cut that lot out for a start.'

Milligan was spokesman; his blue eyes opened wide.
'Why, Sarge? What's the matter? What have we done
wrong?'

The sergeant glared and thundered. 'You know well
enough. I'm just warning you. We'll have no more of that
nonsense. *And* in the presence of officers! You know what
I'm talking about.'

The Boys of Battery D were not seriously put out. They
had had their bit of fun. 'The Red Flag', however, was
dropped from the repertoire.

Before long, the band acquired a compère called Arthur
Edser who introduced the numbers. Bookings were many
and various, the main venue being the De La Warre
Pavilion on the sea-front. The band also played at the
requisitioned premises named 'Forces Corner' situated on
the corner of Sea Road and Cantaloupe Road in Bexhill.
There, the canteen was run by the Women's Voluntary
Service. Spike tells us that it was open daily for 'Teas,
buns, billiards and deserters'.

A playbill announcing the band is still in existence, and

is proudly displayed on the Battery notice board when the reunions take place. There is a rough sketch of a howitzer anti-aircraft gun and over it details of a dance.

NON-STOP R.A. DANCE
GRANVILLE HOTEL
4th DEC 1942
SPIKE & THE BOYS
FORCES 1/6. CIVILIANS 2/6.
DANCING 8-11.45 p.m. DOORS OPEN 7.30.
Refreshments Free.

Spike inevitably was the leader. Doug Kidgell remembers how effortlessly he seemed to assume this responsibility.

> He was the mainspoke, obviously. He was the front man. Actually, he was the only musician amongst us. I can't read music – Alf could read his chords but Harry doesn't read music either so Spike was the only musician amongst us. It was more or less automatic that he sort of took charge, but we were a get-together group, there was no set pattern. When the call came 'Everybody on the stand' Spike was always standing up there with his trumpet, ready.

Dances were also given at nearby Cuckfield, the Regimental Headquarters of the Battery. A photograph of the band shows them perched on a small platform in Cuckfield village hall. They all wear battledress and have smartly slicked-back hairstyles with the exception of Milligan, on the trumpet, who wears a tin hat. Harry is seated at the piano, Doug at his drums, Alf has his guitar and Arthur Edser is standing behind the mike with his finger raised admonishingly as though at the punch line of a joke. They are all smiling; the blurred lines of the photograph do not detract from the youthful ebullience and happiness of the moment.

On one occasion, the band was summoned to the home

of an ex-officer to play for his daughter's twenty-first
birthday party. Spike covers the incident in *Adolf Hitler:
My Part in His Downfall*:

> A Wednesday night, late in summer 1940, the band was doing
> a gig at a private house in Pevensey Drive. A well heeled ex-
> army major was throwing a house party on the occasion of his
> daughter's coming-of-age. It had the cobwebs of a dying
> empire: men wore slightly dated evening dress, and there was
> one joker from the Blues with Cavalry spurs; the ladies were
> in gowns of chiffon that seemed straight from the wardrobe of
> *Private Lives*. It was pretty horsey, but not outrageously so,
> though I'm glad to say the moment we played a 6/8 they all
> did 'cocking of the legs' and shouted 'Och Ayes'. As a parting
> gift our host gave us each a fiver. We stood stunned. 'I'm
> sorry,' said Kidgell, 'we haven't any change, sir.' He waved us
> off. Outside, in the dark, we loaded our gear onto the fifteen
> hundredweight truck. Looking up I saw the night was alive
> with stars. In the Eastern sky I could make out Saturn,
> Pegasus, Castor and Pollux. I could hear the distant sound of
> sea washing the pebbled beaches of Pevensey. The Romans
> must have heard it once. We drove back in silence until Alf
> Fildes spoke. 'Five pounds? He'll ask for it back when he
> sobers up!'[5]

The band gradually increased its repertoire. Milligan jokes
that at their first session they played the 'Honeysuckle
Rose' twenty-six times. They played 'swing' music, and the
poignancy of imminent parting and wartime separations
must have influenced the musicians so that they played
most of the sentimental and nostalgic melodies of the day.
Favourites were 'These Foolish Things', 'The Song is
Ended' and 'You Stepped out of a Dream'. Perhaps in a
token revolt against the sweetness of it all, Harry Edgington composed the spirited 'Boys of Battery D':

> We're the boys from Battery D
> Four Boys from Battery D
> We make a rhythmic noise

We give you dancing joys
And sing the latest melody.

Now we make the darndest sounds
As we send you Truckin' on down
And if it's sweet or hot
We give it all we've got
And boy! we got enough to go around.

We'll set your feet tapping with a quick step
We've a waltz that'll make you sigh
And then the tempo we've got
For a slow fox-trot
Would make a wallflower wanna try.

Come on along you he and she
It's the dancers' jamboree
Come on and take a chance
Come on and have a dance
To the band of Battery D.

Forty years later, Spike gave Doug Kidgell a copy of the
first volume of his war memoirs. He inscribed it:

> To The Best Drummer Ever
> Always Your Pal
> Spike

After the signature, he added:

> The Best Musical Years of my Life

These early days in Bexhill were crucially important to
Milligan's development. The gauche boy began to give
way to the grown man. The talents which had earned
disfavour now began to clarify. He realized that he had a
gift for making people laugh. The fact that they laughed
when he joked became gratifying and important to him.
He found himself the innovator, the man with the ideas.

He was the one who could get the band on and off the stage to the sound of appreciative laughter. It might spring from a straight task such as a large drum needing to be carried up a narrow stair. Somehow, Milligan would manage to turn a difficult job into a joke, and inspire other people to see it with his clown's vision. Almost without realizing it, he was producing virtually unrehearsed half-minute comedy 'spots', spontaneously igniting his colleagues into explosions of ad lib hilarity.

When words were inappropriate or would have gone unheard, Milligan would surmount any situation by using the instinctive clowning skills which are the font of his diverse comic abilities.

He became practised in the art of the 'send-up'. Doug Kidgell had a good tenor voice and as a change from playing the drums at the garrison dances would often come forward to sing. One song went:

> Deep in my heart there is rapture
> And I hope one day to recapture –

He was inevitably well received, but the dancing couples who drifted romantically past in each other's arms were grist to Spike's mill. Under his crisp direction the boys in the band continued backing Doug, but with a new and strident lyric:

> Deep in my guts I've got rupture,
> Except for that, dear, I'd have upped yer.

There were other jokes, all spontaneous and ridiculous. Spike's mind whirled continually with kaleidoscopic fantasies and he was never slow to exploit them.

'Gunner Milligan will now play the *Invisible Trumpeter*,' the MC announced one evening. There was a moment of hush and then Milligan's trumpet rose from behind a sofa.

The trumpeter remained on his back, invisible, but a neat tune issued from the cushions. 'It was all very unrehearsed stuff,' comments Spike, looking back. 'We just got an amazing amount of fun out of the band, and each other. And it made the army a lot of fun. And we all felt a bit important, being part of the band. And we were always in demand.'

As the laughter escalated, so did his confidence. His letters home began to ring with the sort of optimism that had been lacking in the Milligan family ever since the exodus from India. 'I am definitely going to find a future in show business,' he wrote to his mother. Predictably, her replies circumvented this perhaps unwelcome news and she confined her letters to the usual motherly concern for his health and safety, coupled with voluminous instructions as to his religious welfare. 'Pray to St Anthony and St Francis every day, my son, always say your catechism and wear all your holy medals.'

'If I had,' says Spike reflectively, 'by the time we went overseas I'd have had to crawl into battle on my knees.'

After some weeks, part of the Battery moved to Hailsham, still in East Sussex, and the change of scene led to one interesting development for Spike. Harry Edgington and he would sit at the duty point filling in time by sketching cartoon-type drawings and making up jokes. One-liners began to develop into embryo sketches. As the men sat at their post giggling a tall young captain more attuned to the theatre he had left behind than the war he was trying to face found himself irresistibly drawn, intrigued with the spontaneous fun. A wartime officer, he did not find it difficult to lay aside protocol. One evening, when the laughter and muttering were particularly enticing, he asked the men what was amusing them. 'We're just making up a few jokes, sir,' said Milligan politely. 'It makes the time pass.' The young captain was intrigued, and stayed long enough to listen to the next few ideas. He left with reluctance, presumably to return to an officers' mess which he found less stimulating than the company of two private soldiers making each other laugh at an observation post.

After that, he used to come to the post regularly and he and Milligan would discuss ideas for sketches in a show that they were hoping to produce at Hailsham.

> We told him that we would be rehearsing something and I'd suddenly see him sitting out there in the front – laughing away. He was interested in us and wanted to see what we were doing and how we were getting on. We didn't ask him to come – but we were quite pleased when he turned up.

Captain John Counsell had left a promising career in the theatre when he joined up. After the war, he went back and made a success of running the Windsor Repertory Company, which for many years was recognized as a hotbed of talent. Counsell had an acute eye for spotting new performers and giving them a chance. He undoubtedly gave Milligan a degree of encouragement and Milligan never forgot it. After the Goon Shows brought his name to the public eye, Counsell got in touch and told Spike that his young daughters were great fans. Spike sent them a copy of *Silly Verse for Kids*. It was inscribed:

> To my old Captain's daughters
> With love from Spike Milligan

Milligan's links with his family remained fairly close although the letters were infrequent until he went overseas and he seems to have spent relatively few leaves at home. Almost certainly he failed to take advantage of many weekend passes because his time was fully occupied with the band, but he was deeply attached to his young brother and as his own horizons widened began to plan for Desmond's future. He wrote to Leo and Flo and emphasized the need for Desmond to apply himself to his studies whilst still at school and, more importantly, to plan for further education in art, an area in which he showed great promise. Desmond would append drawings of ships, aeroplanes and guns to brief boyish notes and Milligan would show them to his close colleagues with pride. Eventually, when the Battery went overseas and he saw unfamiliar sights and architectural wonders, he tried to pass something of this awakened enthusiasm over to his young brother by sending him postcard views and descriptions. In due course, Desmond did indeed go to art school and even today his elder brother takes a considerable pride in his achievement:

> I made sure that my parents knew the importance of a proper training for him. I said that he had to go to art school and train to be an artist. I remember all the soul-destroying jobs I'd had as a boy and I decided that Desmond must have it better. I knew he had the talent, and I kept on at them so that they saw to it that he got the training. So that's how he got into art school. And now he's a professional artist and that's how he earns his living.

Things were now looking up in Leo Milligan's life. He rejoined the Forces and was given an administrative job in an Army Supply depot at Reigate. He was now a commissioned officer, and the family moved to live in army housing nearby. The location was to prove fortuitous for Desmond; in due course he was enrolled in the Reigate College of Art, the first step in his successful career as an artist.

Spike made a new girlfriend about this time – Beryl Southby, who sang occasionally for the BBC. It chanced that her family lived near Norwood and on occasions Spike would pay a flying visit with Beryl to both families. She was an intelligent, pretty and talented girl and her musical expertise was part of her attraction. It was she who encouraged Spike to go up to a BBC recording studio at Maida Vale in the summer of 1942 to enter an instrumentalists' competition. Milligan, on trumpet, won hands down and his prize was the opportunity to make a record with the band. The pianist was George Shearing, who at the end of the session complimented Spike on his playing. 'I hope that we play together again one day,' he said. Spike went back to Bexhill-on-Sea, his head well up in the clouds.

Meanwhile one of the wartime officers was talking to Spike about music. He suggested that Spike, already dedicated to modern music and jazz, might well enjoy classical composers. He lent him records and obviously enjoyed a musical rapport with the eager, intelligent young gunner.

The enthusiasm with which his talents were greeted was in complete contrast to his earlier experiences of music. The excitement of the ten-shillings-a-night gigs had been perpetually overshadowed by the gloom of Flo's anxiety for his 'future'. Now his army admirers gave him the sort of warm approval that was essential for the nurturing, let alone maturing, of his talents. Even when Milligan had become famous, the affection and approval of a few friends always gave him more pleasure than the delighted roars of audiences; Bexhill and Hailsham were largely instrumental in bringing confidence and aplomb where formerly he had felt only uncertainty and a kind of isolation. Perhaps it was the dawning recognition of his own potential as a performer which allowed him to turn imperceptibly towards the beginning of his career as a writer, as an innovator of a new kind of Goon comedy for which, in time, he was to become famous.

6

D Battery to Africa

O Providence I will not praise
Your blundering and cruel ways

Frances Cornford

The Battery embarked for North Africa on 8 January 1943.
They sailed from Liverpool on the SS *Otranto*. The ship
sailed round the north coast of Ireland, through the Bay of
Biscay and the straits of Gibraltar. On 18 January they
landed. Milligan noted their arrival in his diary: 'Arrived
Algiers at Dawn'. Thirty years later, he recalled his
impressions of his first adult landfall:

> Harry and I got up early to enjoy the sight of Africa at first
> light. We saw it bathed in a translucent, pre-dawn purple
> aura. Seagulls had joined us again. A squadron of American
> Lockheed Lightnings circled above. The coast was like a wine-
> coloured sliver, all the while coming closer. The visibility grew
> as the sun mounted the sky; there is no light as full of hope as
> the dawn; amber, resin, copper lake, brass green.[1]

Spike Milligan has written five books of autobiography.
They cover the years he spent as a soldier and they suggest
that those years were not only very happy for him, they
were also curiously fulfilling. They were a period of
immense growth, and although Milligan showed a diffidence and limitation that was partly consequent to the
abrupt cessation of his schooldays and the atrophying years
in South London, he was fast developing acute powers of
perception and awareness and was growing crucially aware
of every new facet of his existence. An open mind and
wide vision encompassed every fresh sight instantly and

almost painfully. But his capacity for expressing the new images crowding his mind lagged far behind his powers of observation. He was stunned by everything he saw, but as yet virtually unable to transmit any of it either to his mates or to his family and friends back home.

> My letters home seem pretty functional, just Hello Mum, Hello Dad, I'm all right please send socks and cigarettes – all very ordinary sort of stuff – but I remember how incredible it all seemed to me and how I wanted to pass it on, share it with someone. The lads were great, but I couldn't get them interested in Doric columns when they were hopping about waiting to be let loose on Arab tarts.

When the Battery arrived in Algiers, the men had spent a crowded ten days on board a troopship. Army discipline had of necessity to be relaxed. Rough seas had weakened many who were not good sailors. Crossing the Bay of Biscay the latrines were flooded with vomit, and three-quarters of the men suffered from diarrhoea. The sick men clung to their hammocks and the fit ones handled the necessary battery fatigues. Storms raged until the ship passed into the relatively peaceful Mediterranean.

Before the Battery embarked at Dover, severe threats had been issued by Commanding Officers anxious to deter men from attempting to export any 'large' personal items. However, once the worst agonies of the voyage were over, a dance was mooted, and the Battery D boys produced their camouflaged instruments in front of the gratified 'blind eye' of authority. A bevy of service ladies, mostly nursing sisters, emerged. Milligan never forgot them, either. Thirty years later, he included them in his autobiography. 'And where were *they* when the decks were strewn with seasick sailors?' he enquired.

After ten days, the SS *Otranto* docked and by some devious manipulations Spike was able to disembark at his leisure, taking with him Alf Fildes, Doug Kidgell and their collective musical instruments. Whereas the main body of men left the ship burdened with full kit at the march, the musicians stood back, a self-appointed 'Band Party'. They were almost the last to leave and marched off the ship at their ease, Doug shouldering his drum kit, Alf his guitar and Spike (quietly bubbling with delight to have once again thwarted authority) his trumpet. 'It was,' recalls Doug regretfully, 'a shame about Harry. He had to go on ahead with the lads. We couldn't reckon that he had to carry his piano.'

Their first night in Africa was spent in a stadium close to the docks already partly occupied by soldiers who had been sent down from the front line for 'rest'. Some of them were jaded with battle fatigue, grey-faced and silent. Spike was somewhat awed. He whispered to Doug: 'These are real soldiers. Fighting men. We're still rookies, really, aren't we?'

Thus D Battery arrived in Algiers. Nearly two weeks with virtually no exercise, a good deal of sickness and a final night of drink and near-debauchery (albeit with the prim nursing sisters) left them in poor shape for what was to come. First, a restless night on the concrete floors of the stadium, a parade in full kit and then a daylong march. There were no transports, except for equipment, and many of the men were very soon failing and falling behind. Milligan writes:

> The march of the Regiment from the ship to Cap Matifou had been a mild disaster. It started in good march style, but gradually, softened by two weeks at sea, and in full F.S.M.O., two-thirds of the men gradually fell behind and finally everyone was going it alone at his own pace.[2]

In his book, *Adolf Hitler: My Part in His Downfall*, Milligan records unemotively the death of Driver Reed, who died whilst trying to jump a lift. When he speaks of this, however, he shows a stubborn anger undiminished by the years:

> There was this poor wretch, absolutely done in – blisters, weighed down, struggling under his kit. Weeping, I tell you – he'd had enough. Not a coward or anything – just a lad that couldn't make it. Bloody Army Bureaucracy. Do you think they'd say 'Right, up the transport.' No – rule of thumb. 'All men have got to march – strengthen them up – make men of them.' Well, it did for him, didn't it? That was the end of him.

Reed had fallen between a lorry and a trailer when, his strength having given out, he tried to snatch a forbidden lift. He was killed instantly. Another tragedy befell one of the older men – Gunner Leigh survived the march well enough but awaiting his arrival at the camp was news of his family. His wife and three children had died in a Liverpool air-raid. 'He went mad, never spoke again,' Spike recalls sombrely. 'He's in an institution in Yorkshire to this day, I think. I remember asking myself who is writing this scenario? Who is in charge? Somebody must be – but they are not doing very well with it, are they?'

The day after Driver Reed's death, several of his companions who had been strong and lively enough to jump the trucks successfully were ordered on a further march. The route covered several miles. The men marched silently, slogging along, sullenly resigned. They were not going anywhere in particular. It was a matter of military discipline.

Spirits rose once the Battery was established at Cap Matifou. The majority of the men had never been abroad and they had to get accustomed to extremes of temperature and repetitive, unpalatable meals. Army food in wartime Bexhill had not been particularly exciting, but here it was deplorable. Milligan describes it as *crap*. 'Hard biscuits,

soya links, bully-beef, jam, tea, every day for *all* meals.'
Physical training went on non-stop, long route marches
were plotted for every day. Singing en route was encouraged; this kept everyone cheerful.

They marched through war-scarred country and found
the people friendly. In the ruins of their villages, they
would welcome the British soldiers and give them whatever small presents they had to hand. Fruit and cigarettes
were pressed upon them, and on one occasion they were
offered a large number of fresh eggs. There was no obvious
way of transporting the delicate cargo, but the officer in
charge was unwilling to forgo the promised improvement
to the diet and he gave the order that the marching men
should carry an egg in each hand. This was done, and
omelettes were added to the supper rations that night. 'Of
course,' recalls Spike, 'that march holding the eggs called
forth a lot of laughs. The lads were flapping their arms like
wings and calling out cluck, cluck and all that sort of thing.
There was plenty of that.'

The excursions through the neighbouring villages
brought many unfamiliar sights. Milligan was enchanted at
the profusion of frangipani and bougainvillaea and fascinated by the sense of timelessness. 'Nothing seems to have
changed in a hundred years,' he wrote in a letter home.

After they had been confined to the camp for two weeks,
the men were given an evening 'pass' and transport into
Algiers. Some of them made for the brothels, some for the
booze. 'I was a good Catholic boy,' writes Milligan smugly.
'I didn't frequent brothels.' Flo and Leo were not, however, greatly reassured when they received Spike's first
letter home:

My Dear Mum, Dad and Des,
Safe and sound. The crossing was uneventful except for some

very rough weather which put nearly everyone down with sea-sickness except myself and a spare few. Conditions on the trip were terrible, packed in akin to cattle, food very meagre, no real system of organisation. When anyone wanted e.g. a wash – dinner – purchase of sweets it all boiled down to a queue ¼ mile long and a period of waiting no less than ½ an hour. We are allowed to state we are in North Africa. We had an unfortunate accident here on the first day. A young soldier was crushed under a lorry. We had to march to a transit-cum-prisoner of war camp, with full equipment. More than 20% of the men dropped out with utter exhaustion which in my opinion is proof of the poor physical condition of the men. I had the luck of the Irish as I was on baggage party and rode up on a lorry. Meals to begin with were Bully, Biscuits, spam, cheese and tea, but as things are getting more on an organised basis we are receiving veg, tinned fruit, tinned stew but no bread. The tobacco ration is 7 cigs per day. Wages 150 francs per week (about 10/-). Dates 15f, tangerines 5f per kilo, wine 2f per glass (about 4d) are plentiful and as you see very cheap. If you could, I would appreciate a parcel of writing paper, a cake, capsules, hair-oil, soap and razor blades. No more news as my paper supply is finished.

Loving son, Terry.

Whilst in the aftermath of Alamein battles were being fought five hundred miles to the east, around Tunis, the 19th Battery was allowed to break itself in gently. The musicians were summoned to Fort de l'eau to take part in a military concert. Harry, Alf, Doug and Spike were collected by an imposing staff car and delivered at a large opera house. Nothing like this had ever happened at Bexhill and they were in alternating states of delight and awe as they tuned their instruments with as much confidence and panache as they could muster. There was much discussion about the repertoire. Doug was all for starting with an easy favourite. 'Let's get them in the mood,' he said. 'Let's start with "Honeysuckle Rose" and then go on to "The Boys of Battery D".'

In spite of numerous difficulties, like the curtain rising whilst the men were still humping the piano, their act was a great success. For Milligan, it was an important evening. The theatre in which they appeared was a far cry from Cuckfield village hall and the various Bexhill and Hailsham venues. It was a large and imposing French-colonial style opera house with massive tiers of seating. The fauteuils, dress circle and upper circle seemed to stretch endlessly, and even cloaked and dimmed by the wartime austerity of black-out and air-raid precautions, it was a thrilling and stimulating occasion.

> It was my first real appearance on the stage, after that one as a boy, as a clown, in the Nativity at the Convent of Jesus and Mary in Poona. I think the concert was planned because there was such a lot of troops coming in, going wild, getting drunk – no entertainment. So we were all in it. It was a big French Provincial theatre at Fort de l'eau. I realized I couldn't stand still so I did an impression of Louis Armstrong playing in a band – I remember running across the front of the footlights playing the trumpet, and jumping down into the pit, and playing, and getting up onto the stage – I couldn't believe the ovation. Doug Kidgell said to me afterwards 'Spike, you're a showman.' We did once try to get a concert party together at Hailsham, but we got orders to move before it came to anything. But that night at Fort de l'eau, well, the ego got the first taste of honey.

By early February, the Battery was once again under orders to move. The morale, on the whole, was high. The men were young and excited about what was to come. 'Well,' Spike recalls, 'it was a fact that about ninety-nine per cent of the lads had never been abroad, and this was a bonus in their lives even though it took a war to give it to them.'

By now, Milligan was well established as something of a clown. He had a manner of light-heartedly reducing wearisome routine to fun. His sense of the ridiculous, dormant throughout the grey years in South London, began to bubble in earnest. He had learned that he could make people laugh. He must have presented quite a problem to officers concerned with protocol, military etiquette and discipline. Although the mature Milligan insists that he had 'a working-class attitude to the officers' there were times when he certainly seemed to lack the customary inhibitions that exist between service ranks. The officers, like the men, were grist to his mill if he saw a joke looming. On the road to Setif the banter went on non-stop.

'Right, Milligan,' says Lt Budden. 'World War Two at twenty-five m.p.h.' He looked back at the long line of vehicles. 'My God, what a target for the Luftwaffe.'

'Don't worry, sir. I have a verbal anti-aircraft curse that brings down planes.'

'Keep talking, Milligan. I think I can get you out on Mental Grounds.'

'That's how I got in, sir.'

'Didn't we all.'

There was a throttle on the steering column. I set it to a steady 20 m.p.h.

'I said twenty-five,' said Budden.

'Trying to economize, sir. The slower we go, chances are by the time we get there it might be all over.'[3]

The long trek to the fighting continued. A night was passed at Tizi Ouzou, about eighty miles east of Algiers. The column came to rest in an orange grove at the side of the road. Milligan curled up in his sleeping-bag and stared at the stars in the night sky. What had war to do with all this beauty?

Being in charge of the musical instruments undoubtedly gave the band boys a military advantage. They rode whilst others marched, and Milligan was quick to devise ways of making the miles roll by. One day, as they sat on the back of the lorry, he pointed to the almost empty desert road. The talk, as often, was of women. 'Let's imagine,' he said, 'the next one we pass is going to be Harry's future wife.' After a while, a bent old lady, shrouded in the traditional black robes, came into view. They all hailed her with shouts of glee. She gave them a happy, toothless grin and continued on her way. When the mirth subsided, Spike continued. 'Right. That's Harry fixed up. Now, next one is Alf's.' Alf was luckier. A beautiful young woman holding a pitcher on her head and leading a young child came into view. She must have been startled by the whoops of joy and 'You lucky sod' which filled the air. Doug Kidgell chuckles at the memory.

> He never wanted to waste a moment. And he didn't like to see any of us wasting one either. We'd just be sitting in the lorry waiting for time to pass and he would chivvy us up with a new idea. 'Come on now,' he'd say. 'Who can tell the daftest joke?' He'd get us all playing along as well. And it made the time pass by and the journey shorter.

Spike recalls pleasurable moments of the long trek in *'Rommel?' 'Gunner Who?'*

> We bivouacked just outside Setif. We'd had a good day buying Arab supplies, eggs, potatoes and chickens, so a great meal was in the offing. We backed two wireless trucks together, threw a blanket over the join, inside we rigged an inspection light, and picked up the BBC on the set. The food came steaming in the chilly night air as I uncorked the Vin Rosé. I can still see the scene, the young faces, poised eagerly over the food, all silent save the odd 'Cor, lovely' and the clank of forks on mess tins. We listened to the news.
>   'I think it will all be over by Christmas,' said Gunner White.

4

After the relative inactivity of Camp Matifou, the next few days sped by. The Battery bivouacked at Souk Arras and Le Kef. Eventually, on the outskirts of Tunis, gun positions were dug in; the city, held by Rommel, was virtually under siege. The young soldiers were a little daunted; they had just passed through the smoking ruins of Arab villages. Spike's first job in action was to help lay a communication line to the operation post, and he and several other signallers provoked the attention of enemy guns. The shellfire seemed louder and closer than he had ever experienced. Line-laying began at dusk, was abandoned for a few hours, and recommenced at dawn. If there was a period of sleep in between, it was virtually unnoticed. Milligan ached with fatigue, fear and cold. Their officers were close by; at one stage in the long night he cracked a few jokes with Lieutenant Tony Goldsmith. Like Spike Goldsmith had a bubbling sense of fun and could find a source of humour in the most unpromising material. And as had happened frequently before, the barrier between man and officer, for a few moments, ceased to exist.

Fighting continued during the next few weeks. Ground was won, then lost, then won again. Important landmarks were nicknamed 'Grandstand Hill', 'Dead Cow Farm'. The noise of the guns was shattering and, for some, demoralizing. Spike, as a signaller, was constantly crawling over exposed ground trying to establish and re-establish communications. He began to feel depersonalized, perhaps bemused or withdrawn from an unfathomable world of ear-splitting noise. He looked anxiously at the faces of his friends – Jack Shapiro, fellow signaller, laying lines and subsequently unlaying them with gusto; Doug Kidgell, driver, going back and forth cheerfully enough between the waggon lines; Major Chater Jack who, after one hasty retreat, smiled at the men equably and said 'I'm sorry we

had to móve, gentlemen.' Were they all less frightened
than he was? Milligan wondered. He would bite his lip
hard to stop his teeth chattering. Sometimes, when he was
not standing to, he lay fully clothed on his bunk-space, or
in the back of Kidgell's transport. His balaclava would be
pulled down over his face, his head buried in his arms and
his knees drawn up under his chin.

March found Milligan promoted to Lance Bombardier,
and billeted in an abandoned farmhouse in Munchar.
There were a few days of partial escape, a mile or so away
from the thunder of gunfire. Spike explored the house,
fascinated at the signs of its former occupation. The roof
had caved in during the bombing, and fire had caused
considerable damage. Beds were made up on floors and at
one stage he drew a sketch-plan of the room he shared
with several other soldiers.

Being in a house for a short time was therapeutic. He
attended to his signalling and wireless equipment, brewed
up tea, chatted with Lieutenant Budden, the officer in
charge, and the men, did the required chores and waited
for orders. They were actually a support-base for the
Observation Post (OP) which, at this moment, housed
among others Lieutenant Goldsmith and Bombardier
Deans. Wireless contact was maintained at all times, the
farmhouse contingent ready to jump to with fresh supplies
of food, ammunition, medical supplies and relief.

During his foray in the house, Milligan had found a
piano. It was rather precariously positioned in an upstairs
room, the floor of which had caved in, and, wisely as it
transpired, he had not approached it. Then Harry Edgington arrived on a line-laying expedition. 'There's a piano
upstairs, Harry,' said Spike slyly. The musicians hugged
each other, and Harry ascended the rickety stairs at the
double. Spike followed with his trumpet; Harry was already

seated at the piano. The floor looked so dangerous that
Spike stood in the doorway to play and soon the strains of
'Honeysuckle Rose' were heard. They played several of
their old favourites until the driver of Harry's truck grew
belligerent. Loud bleeps filled the air; reluctantly the
pianist had to leave. Spike descended and waved his friend
off. As he went back into the house, the piano fell through
the floor and landed in the room beneath in a thousand
pieces. It narrowly missed one of the gunners, who was
sitting on the floor cleaning his boots.

During the days of fighting, it was not uncommon for
the men to write down their last wishes. Spike scribbled
his in a notebook which survived. It reads:

> If anything happens to me
>
> 1st My trumpet goes to my brother
>
> 2   My girl's letters burnt
>
> 3   My savings (about £50, £25 in my
>   money credit and £30 at home) I give
>   to my mother
>
> 4   My girl's photograph I would like to
>   be painted in oils by Patrick Carpenter
>   (contact Daily Worker for his address)
>
> 5   My epitaph –
> > I died for the England
> > I dreamed of
> > Not for the England I know.

On 18 March 1943, Terence wrote one of his frequent
letters home, on sheets of small, squared paper. 'Excuse
the paper,' he scribbled across one corner. 'It was
scrounged from the Battery Office.' The letter was
addressed to 'Dear Mam, Dad and Des'.

The day of St Patrick was a fine, sunny cool day. I spent most
of the time driving around on a very bumpy road sitting on a

load of junk, looking for a salvage dump. The countryside about us is very rugged, en route we passed the ruins of what looked like an old Arab Moorish castle. Through centuries of decay it has now become almost a rubble but here and there are signs of a once magnificent castle. We also passed some in a good state of preservation, the stone work was not bad, even the faithful reproduction of Grecian Doric fluting was evident in the columns. The temple itself seemed to be the centre of what was, at some past era, a thriving town. Traces of villas, baths, were prominent, but as they had only local, African rock to work with it hadn't the lavish appearance of the marble buildings of the city of Rome. Arabs are living a pitiful, hand-to-mouth existence, yet happy people they are just the same. Farming is the main industry on the land round about, they manage (the Arabs) to plough land in the most inaccessible places at say a gradient of 1 in 3. They could, if properly trained, make a good show on a collective farm.

He continues with a few comments about postal allowances, then continues with a terse little statement about the fighting.

Our O.C. told us that we (the 19th Btry) have a very good name in this section as we have done much good work during the short time we have been in action (3 to 4 weeks).

Shortly after, he wrote a further letter to his family. It was on the same squared 'scrounged' paper. He wrote carefully, in ink, underlining certain passages.

It's still early morning, 8.30 to be precise, very misty indeed. I'm sitting in my wireless tent waiting for various information, quite interesting. You will have noticed that I have now been endowed with a tape [stripe]. This was for good work at O.P. whilst under fire from enemy mortars, it's a nasty feeling as these mortars don't whistle like a bomb or shell, the first thing one knows is the explosion. *I have been under more fire than anyone else in the battery!!!* That's the truth!!! Along with me was my pal Jock, a real Scot with plenty of guts. We were in the O.P. every day from Dawn till Dusk for seven days during which time we did not (could not) wash, shave, or have hot meals. It was quite exciting watching Stukas dive bombing (that is, when he's not after you) but I found my nerves getting bad. I would drop flat at the sound of a motor backfiring – I watched a ding dong between our boys and Jerry, it was a hell of a do.

Milligan dated the letter, incorrectly, 21 May 1943. The sequence of military events and, indeed, the paper he used suggests that it was probably written only a few days after the earlier letter of 18 March. It was a trivial error, but perhaps a warning light for the state of shock and confusion that was eventually to overwhelm him and bring about his removal from active service.

On 16 April 1943, Spike was twenty-five years old. He celebrated his birthday in action behind the OP which was now situated a few miles from the village of Toukabeur. The noise of the gunfire was constant; most of the 56th Heavy RA were now involved in the last serious fighting before Tunis fell to the Allies. On 24 April, during one of the savage battles which raged over Long Stop Hill, Lieutenant Goldsmith was killed. His death had come simply as he plotted gun positions from a shallow trench or foxhole. A mortar bomb hit him squarely on the chest, killing him instantly. The bombardier with him was blown to relative safety and survived. The men of the battery were shaken. Goldsmith's popularity had been immense and his loss was mourned deeply. Milligan was stricken; the pain and sense of loss that submerged him on that day have stayed with him, in some degree, ever since.

Fighting on Long Stop at a crescendo all day. OP under murderous fire – support group at bottom of hill also under heavy shellfire. Gunner Collins hit in hand. At about 11.10 I heard the dreadful news, Lieutenant Goldsmith had been

killed. Alf Fildes noted in his diary 'Learn with regret we have
lost our best officer.'

I went back to my cave and wept. I remember calling his
name. After a few minutes I straightened up, but the memory
of that day remains vivid.[5]

Anthony Goldsmith had an appreciation of 'black' humour
well in advance of his time. Like Spike, he could find
something hilariously funny in what was simply intended
as a formal statement. Writing to his wife only six days
before his death in action, he described a letter he had
found from a German woman medical student to her
boyfriend at the front. She said that she was getting on
very well indeed: 'Yesterday I was actually asked to be
present at an amputation. You can imagine how pleased
and happy I was!'

Being able to share a joke like this had been an unexpected bonus for them both. Goldsmith's spirit was as alien to
the fighting as Spike's. Writing wistfully to his wife about
the reception of an article he had published in *Horizon*, he
said, 'It is consoling to think that one can maintain a
vicarious literary existence in London, while being physically in Tunisia.'

He was not like an officer, not in the sense 'I have to be
superior to you.' I could talk to him closely. We were as real
friends, there were no barriers between us. He was another
me, the one that went to University. I was the wild spirit that
he'd like to have been, had he *not* gone to University. His was
a controlled intellect, mine was one which ran free, like a horse
without a saddle. I read his book, *L'Education Sentimentale*. Of
course, I'd never read Flaubert before. I thought he was a
stunning writer, it seemed somehow like the first coming of
journalistic writing. With someone like Tony Goldsmith, your
whole appreciation of things just rocketed. He enthused people
so easily. He was that sort of man.

When that excellent translation of *L'Education Sentimentale* went out of print some years ago, Spike spent

fruitless hours on the telephone trying to persuade the publishers to reprint. He tried to enthuse an uninterested female executive in his proposition. 'If you are considering reprinting the book, I'd like to write a short foreword on Anthony Goldsmith,' he said. 'I wouldn't want paying for it.' The lady was startled by the phone call out of the blue. 'I'm sorry,' she choked with some surprise. 'I can't quite believe who I'm talking to.'

After he had put the telephone down, Spike was bitter. 'Oh Christ, I suppose she expected me to start telling jokes. Why the hell can't people just behave normally sometimes? I wanted to do something for Tony Goldsmith, that was all.'

He has never ceased to honour Goldsmith's memory and has been at pains to collect every possible memento or piece of work that could be associated with him. He sent for photographs of his grave, and copies of his citations. Spasmodically, he sought out his family and friends. When he began to compile his war memoirs, he got in touch with one of Goldsmith's relatives, who seemed bewildered.

'Why this sudden interest in Tony Goldsmith?' she asked me. I said, 'It's not a *sudden* interest. It's a constant interest. There's nothing sudden about it. He befriended me at a time in my life when it was valuable to me. I know that he was a man of immense promise. If he had been alive today I know we would have been close friends. It's not a sudden interest. It's been an interest all my life, and I've never ceased to regret his loss.'

Perhaps unjustly, Spike shows some bitterness now. 'I daresay they feel embarrassed that an outsider crops up and wants to see his memory honoured. They can't take it that he's of more importance to an outsider than he is to his own relations. That's the English for you.'

Many years after Tony Goldsmith died, Milligan wrote a

poem. It stayed in first draft and was not included in any of his collections. It was eventually published on the next page to a poem by Tony in 1982 in *Oasis*, a collection of war poems and diaries from Africa and Italy.

> That April day
> Seems far away
> The day they decided to kill
> Lt Tony Goldsmith R.A.
> On the slopes of Long Stop Hill.
>
> At Toukebir
> The Dawn lights stir
> Who's blood today will spill?
> Today it's Tony Goldsmith's
> Seeping out on Long Stop Hill.
>
> One can't complain
> Nor ease the pain
> Or find someone to fill
> The place of Tony Goldsmith
> Lying dead on Long Stop Hill.
>
> In Germany
> There still could be
> A Joachiem, Fritz or Will
> Who did for Tony Goldsmith
> That day – on Long Stop Hill.

Someone suggested that perhaps Spike should have worked on his poem a little. Milligan listened carefully, but answered firmly:

> I couldn't. It wouldn't be possible. It wouldn't seem honest. It's just how it came to me, so if it's not good as a poem, I can't help that. I wrote it the way it's got to be.

Milligan was not alone in his appreciation of Goldsmith. Part of an obituary, written by his Oxford contemporary Terence Rattigan, read:

The loss in action of Anthony Goldsmith at the age of 31 will be most bitterly felt, not only by his many personal friends but by all those who, through his writing, recognized his great gifts and were hopeful of the promise they gave.

The writer Derek Hudson, in his autobiography *Reading Between the Lines*, makes numerous and affectionate references to Goldsmith. Thirty years after the war, Spike came to hear of the book and lost no time in getting in touch with the author. They spent several hours together talking incessantly of Tony. Derek Hudson and Tony Goldsmith had been friends at Harrow and Oxford and just before the war they collaborated on a play. 'You were so lucky to have him for a friend for all those years,' Milligan said. 'I only knew him for such a little time.'

Lieutenant Goldsmith was buried on 27 April on Long Stop Hill. Milligan, ordered to hospital with an infected leg, was not present.

The first days of May found the 56th Regiment RA Heavy Artillery massing with units of General Alexander's First Army. They were preparing for what was to be the final battle. On 12 May 1943 the war in Tunisia was over.

The danger was now abated. The weather was beautiful. The men took part in the victory parade through Tunis, got drunk, wrote ecstatic postcards home. Milligan was a part of all this but the euphoria was cut with a strange feeling of not belonging, of being an outsider. For many nights he was to roll feverishly in his bed, a prey to nightmare and hallucination. He relived the scenes of carnage and death; one tragedy in particular obsessed him. Two weeks before the fall of Tunis, when the Battery had been sporadically engaged in 'silencing' the enemy guns, the Command Post suffered what at first sight appeared to be a direct hit. In fact, it was the premature explosion of a

shell from one of the 19th Battery's own guns that had
devastated its neighbouring gun positioned only a few feet
away. This almost unbelievable loss to the Battery of its
own men had been bitter and traumatic. Forty years later,
at Battery reunions, this occasion is sometimes spoken of.
The pain, dissipated over the years, is never forgotten.

The early summer of 1943 found them still in North
Africa. The Battery established a new camp near Hammam
Lif, outside Tunis. Short leaves were being granted and it
was arranged that Milligan, Fildes, Kidgell and Edgington
could go off together. There was much excited discussion
about where they should go. Spike recalls that he wanted
to visit Carthage.

> 'What's Carthage?' said Doug Kidgell.
> 'A great archaeological site.'
> 'Oh?' said Kidgell. 'Why we goin', you got friends there?'
> 'It's to improve my education.'
> 'Can't we go to the pictures,' said Kidgell. 'There's Bing
> Crosby in *The Road to Bali* in Tunis.'
> That evening, excited as schoolboys, we drove off along the
> Tunis-Bizerta road. It was as though the war didn't exist.
> Eventually we pulled up on a sandy beach for the night.

Thirty years later, Milligan remembered the impact that
this moment had for him:

> There was no moon, but the sky was a pincushion of stars.
> Great swathes of astral light blinked at us across space. We
> made a fire, glowing scarlet in cobalt black darkness, showers
> of popping sparks jettisoning into the night air. Tins of steak
> and kidney pud were in boiling water, with small bubbles
> rising to the surface.[6]

After the brief leave, the men returned to base and the
Battery moved on to camp at Ain Abessa, an uninspiring
chunk of desert on the road to Setif. The weather was
blisteringly hot and a jaded boredom rapidly replaced the

post-Tunisian relief and euphoria. It was a matter of delight
when the band were approached by a French concert
party who wanted support for their rather depleted show.
The performances, which were to be given on the back of
a 30-ton lorry, were in preparation and were much
enhanced by the addition of the Battery D band. The men
knew their limitations – they couldn't sing in French or
join in the sketches – but they could supply a solid belt of
hot jazz and this they did with their customary enthusiasm.
To the bored and frustrated garrisons massed around the
area, the entertainment was an unexpected bonus. The
band numbers were received to rapturous applause, howls
and whistles. The impromptu nature of the set-up and the
difficulties of collaborating with the French performers
were a challenge which the Battery D band met with
honours.

Meanwhile, a few miles away, a piece of British Army
theatrical history was in the making. The RA 140 Field
Artillery was under the command of one Brigadier Rogers.
A regular army man, he was determined to keep his troops
entertained, and he had already been instrumental in
getting several HM Forces amateur variety shows presented both in England and overseas. Now it was his
ambition to rally together a top-ranking pool of talent
drawn from all available forces in North Africa.

Bombardier Kenneth Carter from the same regiment
was a peacetime professional actor and dancer who had
been working with the impresario George Black just prior
to the war. Two of his fellow officers, brothers Graham
and John Leaman, were talented amateur actors wholly
addicted to the theatre. The time was ripe, and 2 AGRA
(Army Group Royal Artillery) concert party was formed
from the nucleus within this entirely military enclave. It
was decided that auditions must be held to select the most

promising soldiers and an order was consequently sent to five regiments stationed between Tunis and Algiers:

19th JUNE 1943: Part Two orders: 'It has been decided to form a concert party. Anyone who has the ability to entertain will parade tomorrow at 10.00 hrs. Map Reference 345 675.'

The selection panel consisted of Ken Carter and Graham Leaman; Leaman at this time was twenty years old, Carter a year or so his senior. Their youth and inexperience did not affect their self-confidence, or, for that matter, their judgement. They had watched the Battery Band performing with the French concert group before the actual auditions were under way. Ken turned to Graham in delight. 'We must have them in the show,' he said. 'Absolutely no doubt at all.'

Almost forty years later, Jack Leaman still takes part in the annual Battery reunion. Graham, who had a successful career as an actor before he became a victim of multiple sclerosis, is absent, but not forgotten. Recently, Spike, along with Doug Kidgell and Dennis Sloggett, collected him from his home in Kensington and took him out for lunch. 'We had a marvellous time rapping about the old days,' said Milligan afterwards. 'He's a good man and he didn't deserve such a cruel blow. He was a very popular officer with us all and he had a lot of talent.'

Rehearsals began immediately after the soldier-artists had been selected. The band, delighted to be part of all this, sat on the sidelines and went through their repertoire whilst the various acts were put through the hoop. Regimental duties received the absolute minimum of attention now, and boredom, for all those involved in the show, was light years away.

The company, named 'The Jolly Rogers' in honour of the brigadier who had drawn them from the ranks of fighting soldiers, gave their first performance on 4 July 1943. The show was called *Stand Easy* and was an immediate and riotous success. They had been unusually lucky in finding and commandeering a splendid little theatre in Setif. Like the theatre in Fort de l'eau, it was built in the tradition of a French opera house, and the professional facilities afforded for scenery, backcloths and lighting were all fully exploited. The plush seating in the little auditorium was filled to overflowing with appreciative troops who roared and stamped their approval.

Milligan revelled in the music once again and began to feel some relief from the bouts of tension which racked him intermittently. The days on Long Stop Hill began to fade.

> After the shelling, all the noise and the destruction it was marvellous just to involve ourselves in the music again. We'd played together for a long time, so we were fairly professional by now. We had at least two good spots in the programme and we more or less produced ourselves. And some humour started creeping in, the men went mad for it. I made Doug into a sort of dwarf and added a trombone case to the top of my head so that I looked like a giant. We used to cross the stage in the middle of some poor blighter's act and the Tommys out there went mad. It was pure lunacy, no rhyme or reason in it, it was *meant* to be just pointless. Just like the war!

There were, of course, difficulties. The army authorities were reluctant to allow their performers any concessions for duties, kit inspections and so forth. This meant a tight schedule for most of the people as parades and fatigues went on as usual. Occasional lapses and clashes had to be sorted out by the officers, Carter and Leaman, and occasionally all their diplomacy was called for.

After the little theatre in Setif had been solidly packed out for a month, it was decided to take the company out on a coastal tour. The performers were delighted at this proposed extension of the show, and the members of the band in particular were jubilant at the thought of fresh audiences.

Milligan was in his element. An almost incredulous, naïve confidence in his ability to entertain was beginning to take shape. His talent for innovation and his flair for mimicking and 'sending up' establishment figures and values were developing fast. The critical abilities which had been so curiously stultified during the pre-army years were now becoming acute. Milligan himself believes that 'being shot up' actually triggered his release from a sort of psychological straitjacket that he had struggled with since adolescence:

> It was as though everything that had been bottled up inside me suddenly started spilling over. It was a continuation of what happened at Bexhill when I found I had the power to move an audience. But it was all high-tension stuff, hysteria really, and ideas coming to me so fast and so many I could hardly contain them, or process them on the way out.

Sadly, the Army authorities refused to sanction a full tour. They were not prepared to risk the inevitable departure from discipline that the drift away from unit-based military exercises would entail. They did, however, grit their teeth for three or four weeks while *Stand Easy* played at Djelli, Bougie and Philippeville. The company revelled in the pleasures of touring and also, it must be said, and none more than Milligan, in the escape from all the tedious military duties and formalities. Carter and Leaman, travelling with their protégés (Captain Leaman in fact acted as compère), were euphoric at the success of the show and, knowing that a return to base was imminent, prepared a blue-print for a follow-up. It was perhaps with a view to assuaging the tantrums of authority that they decided on the title for the sequel; when *Stand Easy* was laid to honourable rest in the archives of army entertainment, *Stand Up* was to take its place. Not surprisingly, Spike Milligan and the Battery D Band were scheduled for star billing.

Stand Up, however, was never to materialize. About the time that the first rehearsals were due to begin, the 19th Division, D Battery were suddenly reminded that they were at war. At only a few hours' notice, they were en route for Salerno.

7

Italy

Shell fire is often not nearly so lethal as machine-gunning, but it batters the mind to a pulp of insanity, from which every return is slower and less certain.

John Brophy,
from the preface to
Soldiers' Songs and Slang

On 22 September 1943, the Battery sailed on HMS *Boxer* for Salerno in southern Italy. Preparations for war had taken over once again and the exciting, rewarding happiness of the concert parties faded abruptly. Milligan felt both anger and despair at the prospect of the thundering guns, the carnage and the wastage of human life that he was to be a part of once more. He had no philosophy to help him and he tried to combat a certain shame because he felt it must be almost cowardly to find war so reprehensible and painful. Some of the lads were almost eager to get going. They had been bored silly by heat, flies and inactivity in the camps. Spike, enthralled in *Stand Easy*, had been more fortunate.

During the journey from Setif through North Africa to the point of embarkation at Bizerta, the men witnessed many scenes of destruction and the sorry aftermath of the desert war. Spike marvelled at the sight of very young and very old peasants stoically ploughing round bomb craters, trying to re-start their lives.

It was not the fear that I was going to die that upset me so much, although I believed I wouldn't return again from the fighting, it was the horrific needless suffering I saw all around me. What had all these people done to deserve their lives shaking up and destroying? They seemed simple, good people to me, kicked around by unbelievably crazy or greedy men at the top.

The feeling of not belonging, of being isolated from what was happening had begun during the first period under gunfire. Now, subtly against his will because he hoped to feel 'one of the boys' with some of his kindred spirits in the Battery, these feelings of being, in psychiatric jargon, 'depersonalized' were reinforced.

On the voyage, Doug Kidgell and Spike slept side by side on top of Doug's Scammel. In the early hours of the second day Doug awoke alone. Dawn was breaking; he got up and wandered round to the ship's prow. He found Spike watching the sunrise sipping a mug of cocoa provided by the sailors on watch. A second mug was soon found for Doug. 'It was the best cup of cocoa I've ever had in my whole life,' he recalls. 'That's all I remember about the voyage. Just sitting there in the early hours of the morning, Spike and me wondering about our future, wondering if we had any future, and drinking this lovely hot chocolate. Best I ever had in my life.'

A few hours later, the men disembarked at Red Beach, Salerno. Among the stores and equipment that were carried ashore was Lance Bombardier Milligan's carefully concealed trumpet. 'I wanted my trumpet with me at all times,' recalls Spike. 'I thought it would be useful in case I was ever buried alive.'

After the usual hitches and setbacks, Milligan was detailed to leave for Mango. His transport on this occasion was a Bren-gun carrier driven by one Bombardier Sherwood. Spike was unenthusiastic about the journey, which he felt might very well end in his death, but he was overwhelmed by a powerful excitement when the convoy approached Paestum and he was able to see the Temples of Neptune and Ceres. The Doric columns glinted in the morning sunlight. His spirits rose and he begged the driver to go slowly. Years later, he recalled the moment:

> I had appealed to Sherwood to drive slowly past the temples.
> 'Wot temples?'
> 'You'll never get another chance to see them close at hand,'
> I said.
> 'You're right,' he says. '*You'll* never get another chance to see them again,' and he drove on.[1]

The next few days passed in the journey towards Naples. The guns went into action in the regions between Monte Mango and Monte Stella; no OP had been established so Milligan, as a signaller, on this occasion at least avoided imminent danger. Sheltering in a trench to escape from the reprisal attacks of German fighter planes on their gun positions, Spike bent his head low and wrote a letter home.

> Dear Mum, Dad and Des
> We've been moved, I'm not allowed to say where, we had spaghetti for lunch. The lunacy continues and has every chance of becoming a way of life unless we stop it soon . . .

The following day, among the chaos of orders to move or orders to fire, cancelled and reinstated orders, Milligan fell ill. Vomiting and dizzy, he reported sick. His temperature was 103, sandfly fever was diagnosed and he was sent to a forward dressing station to await transport to hospital. His departure was delayed by an influx of badly wounded and dying men who had been fighting on Monte Stella:

> Three jeeps arrive with stretcher cases. Among them is a German, his face almost off. Poor bastard. There was a trickle of wounded all afternoon, some walking, some on stretchers,

some dead, the priest went among them carrying out the last rites. Was this the way Christ wanted them to go? The most depressing picture of the War was for me the blanket-covered bodies on stretchers, their boots protruding from the end.[2]

Christmas Day 1943 was spent on a farm close to Naples. As was the custom in the RA the men dined first and were waited on by the officers. The food was as near to a traditional Christmas dinner as could be managed and the discrepancies, such as tinned turkey, were rendered less noticeable by large amounts of good Italian wine. After the food, nostalgic thoughts turned to homes and families. Milligan, Kidgell, Edgington and Fildes, among others, had no time to remember past Christmases; they were fully occupied with the present one and at 6 P.M. that day a concert given by the 19th Battery took place.

The programme was ambitious and ran for hours. It was introduced by Spike on trumpet. One riotous item was 'The Royal Horse Hillbillies' (otherwise Gunners Milligan, Edgington, Fildes, Kidgell and White). Later, Milligan led the audience in community singing and Doug Kidgell had his own spot: Songs you all know and hate. The hand of Milligan seems evident in the writing of the programme as well as in 'The Command Post Follies' which came near the end of the programme. The evening was an unqualified success; Milligan's adrenalin was still flowing in the early hours. He sat on the now deserted stage with Edgington, recapitulating. By now, he had no doubts about the future. 'If there is any future for me, I want it to be in show business,' he said to Harry. 'It'll compensate, in a way, for all the misery of war, won't it? Something so good as laughter coming out of something so evil as war.'

A short leave in Amalfi at a rest camp brought an interval of mixed delight and frustration. What amenities were available in an Italian resort in winter were largely unavailable to the soldiers because of lack of cash. The rest camp provided the usual stodgy army food, and the nightlife, as Spike comments in his war diaries, consisted of going to bed early. Yet, it was a memorable time for him:

> It was sunset. Standing on an abutment of the Villa Cimbrone, we were looking out on to a sea that lay like polished jade. Away to our left, about to be swallowed in an autumn mist, was the sweep of the Salerno coast running away into the distance like an unfinished song. I stood long, next to Harry Edgington. There was no noise, no trains, motor cars, motor bikes, barking dogs. It was a moment that was being indelibly etched in my mind for life. I felt part of past history.[3]

The first days of January 1944 took Milligan to Lauro, a small town that was to suffer some heavy casualties during the advances towards Cassino. He was still involved in line-laying and establishing new Observation Posts. The noise of the Infantry was close and constant. Shelling was continuous and enemy bombers were still flying overhead. On 22 January Milligan was on his way to an operation point under orders to deliver fresh 50lb batteries and a new transmitter set. He was at this time suffering from bleeding piles and had been ordered bed-rest for 48 hours but the situation was such that he had reluctantly volunteered for action. Following, as it did, a mammoth period of 72 hours on duty, he was both exhausted and in considerable pain. The route that he and a fellow soldier followed was mountainous and exposed. The enemy were shelling the area heavily with mortars and Milligan was wounded in the left leg. Light-headed with shock, fatigue and the severe pain from both the wound and the piles, he passed out. The soldier with him, Dipper Dye, picked him up and carried him to the nearest first-aid post. Milligan was now shaking, weeping and incoherent. An ineffectual major, snarling and sarcastic, admonished him for not reaching the OP. 'You could find your way back, but you couldn't find your way to the OP,' he said.

The words, and the implication, were to live in Spike's memory. At the back of his mind the fear that he might, at some level, have acted in a cowardly way tormented him. Milligan is fundamentally a courageous man – the lifelong battle he has fought with his manic-depressive illness would seem to confirm this – but he has never quite assuaged the self-doubt that began that day.

He explores the whole situation in his novel *Puckoon*:

The Milligan had suffered from his legs terribly. During the War in Italy. While his mind was full of great heroisms under shell fire, his legs were carrying the idea, at speed, in the opposite direction. The Battery Major had not understood.

'Gunner Milligan? You have been acting like a coward.'

'No sir, not true, I'm a hero wid coward's legs, I'm a hero from the waist up.'

'Silence! Why did you leave your post?'

'It had woodworm in it, sir, the roof of the trench was falling in.'

'Silence! You acted like a coward!'

'I wasn't acting, sir!'

'I could have you shot!'

'Shot? Why didn't they shoot me in peacetime? I was still the same coward.'

'Men like you are a waste of time in war. Understand?'

'Oh? Well den! Men like you are a waste of time in peace.'

'Silence when you speak to an officer,' shouted the Sgt Major at Milligan's neck.

All his arguments were of no avail in the face of military authority. He was court martialled, surrounded by clanking top brass who were not cowards and therefore biased.

'I may be a coward, I'm not denying dat, sir,' Milligan told the prosecution. 'But you can't really blame me for being a coward. If I am, then you might as well hold me responsible for the shape of me nose, the colour of me hair and the size of me feet.'

'Gunner Milligan,' Captain Martin stroked a cavalry moustache on an infantry face. 'Gunner Milligan,' he said. 'Your personal evaluations of cowardice do not concern the court. To refresh your memory I will read the precise military definition of the word.'

He took a book of King's Regulations, opened a marked page and read 'Cowardice'. Here he paused and gave Milligan a look.

He continued: 'Defection in the face of the enemy. Running away.'

'I was not running away, sir, I was retreating.'

'The whole of your Regiment were advancing, and you decided to retreat?'

'Isn't dat what you calls personal initiative?'

'Your action might have caused your comrades to panic and retreat.'

'Oh, I see! One man retreating is called running away, but a whole Regiment running away is called a retreat? I demand to be tried by cowards!'

A light, commissioned-ranks-only laugh passed around the court. But this was no laughing matter. These lunatics could have him shot.

'Have you anything further to add?' asked Captain Martin.

'Yes,' said Milligan. 'Plenty. For one ting, I had no desire to partake in dis war, I was dragged in. I warned the Medical Officer, I told him I was a coward, and he marked me A.1. for Active Service. I gave everyone fair warning! I told me Battery Major before it started, I even wrote to Field Marshal Montgomery. Yes, I warned everybody, and now you're all acting surprised?'

Even as Milligan spoke his mind, three non-cowardly judges made a mental note of Guilty.[4]

After some hours in a dressing station, Milligan was sent to Afrigola, a reception centre for the walking wounded and battle-scarred near Naples. The pressures on the medical authorities were great. Once checked in the new inmates were left to their own devices and virtually abandoned. For Spike, it was the end of an era and, although it ended so painfully, the years in Battery D remained in his memory as a time of uncomplicated and almost total happiness.

* * *

The days passed. Milligan was unhappy, frightened, shaken, cold and ill. He gazed for long hours at the mud-soaked countryside. The camp was ill-equipped to cope with its residents, and since the authorities had only recently begun to recognize the existence of the battle-scarred 'PNs', the 'Psycho-neurotics' were given virtually no treatment other than sedation. Ideas about therapy were mixed: some of the establishment made no secret of their belief that the patients needed to 'pull themselves together' and get back to some sort of active service. There were long hours of unmitigated boredom broken only by dismal and tasteless meals. The men wept on each other's shoulders and helped themselves by a process of listening and talking. The stories were muddled and confused, apologetic and guilty, tormented and angry. Milligan remembers his own bewilderment clearly.

> I just felt thankful to be away from the shelling, from the appalling noise. But I worried all the time about being a coward, yet I knew I wasn't really because I knew I hadn't behaved as a coward at the time. And then every day men were turning up at the camp in worse states with terrible stories, sometimes crying and screaming out and some of these men had already received bravery citations and awards. That made you realize that the same sort of thing had happened to you. That you weren't one of nature's cowards, just that you couldn't take any more. In some way you opted out, but you hadn't been a coward. You'd come to the end of your stamina, of your courage.

Forty years later, when Spike has a particularly difficult day on his hands, he is still liable to opt out. He will swallow a large dose of sedatives, seeking a brief oblivion. Sometimes he chooses what seems to be an incredibly selfish time for this action. One Christmas, when he had not been able to offset the numerous frustrations and anxieties that can be a regular part of the preparations, he blanked out from Christmas Eve until Boxing Day. His daughters sat dismally downstairs sipping at a bottle of sherry with their former nanny trying to make the best of it. When he reappeared, his face was set in a rigid mask of pain. He seemed to find it difficult to speak. He was not contrite, but he was deeply sad.

'I feel so miserable,' he said. 'It's been a lost Christmas in my life. And I was looking forward to it. I really was looking forward to it so much. I wanted it to be wonderful for my family.'

After he had spent several months in rehabilitation camps in Afrigola and Banio, Spike was recommended for a transfer to Portici, an officers' rest camp south of Naples. He missed his chums in D Battery and had pleaded to be sent back to his regiment but was told that this was not on. He was unfit for further active service. By now he had been downgraded to a fitness classification of B.1; the shelling had left him physically debilitated as well as mentally torn; he was weak, suffering from bleeding piles and stammering badly.

'Then give me a job of some sort away from the fighting,' he had asked. 'I can't sit around here for ever. I can't spend the rest of the war doing nothing.' He was now a mass of conflicting thoughts and feelings. The posting to Portici consolidated his final parting from D Battery and from the freedom and security of his first adult happiness, yet by that token he was also released permanently from the shattering pain and anxiety of the gunfire. He wrote to his mother, guardedly and almost without emotion: 'It was a bit hard leaving the regiment after so long, but I can't stand gunfire any more. I'm OK where I am, lovely and peaceful.'

However the decision to post him to Portici was a good one. The surroundings were tranquil and beautiful. The

Officers' Club was a miniature Palladian villa. It had marble steps, fountains, a Venetian balustrade and a portico which housed marble busts of Homer, Apollo and Athena. The terraced gardens were hung with jasmine and bougainvillaea; there were fig, pomegranate and olive trees in profusion.

Milligan was not displeased with his new job. He became wine waiter in the officers' dining room. The work was interesting and relatively undemanding; it was something with which he could cope. It was here that he first learned about wine and began to understand about vineyards and vintages, and to this day he will demonstrate the correct way to hold and serve a particular bottle. It is not uncommon for the present-day Milligan to gaze disparagingly at an apparently accomplished wine waiter and remark cryptically that he is useless because his thumb is in the wrong position.

There was a neglected piano in a corner of the Officers' Mess and one afternoon, as Milligan sat strumming away in a melancholy fashion, one of the officers walked by and paused to listen. The outcome was that the wine waiter was occasionally pressed into service as pianist:

> Sometimes the officers would have lady visitors, and they would bring them over and introduce them and ask me if I could play some certain tune. That used to make me feel good. It was a bit of a lift to feel that you were really giving these people something that they couldn't manage on their own. I began to heal up a bit, and remember the marvellous days of the band at Bexhill, and I could almost begin to see a future for myself again, in music, with my old friends like Doug Kidgell and Harry Edgington. It gave me a real lift to think that even on my own I could be an entertainer.

Milligan also found that there was plenty of opportunity at Portici to demonstrate his talent for organization. He was adept and adroit, sensitive to the needs of the officers. He would move speedily around, emptying ashtrays, polishing glasses, taking orders and responding immediately to requests. He was skilful and courteous. Major Tony Clark soon noticed him and asked him if he would like to become his personal driver:

> I was a fool to accept promotion from him. He came up to me one day and asked if I'd like to work for him. I don't know why I accepted. I wasn't forced to. But it was something my mother had filled me up with, recognizing my betters and being grateful. I must have been mad. Portici was a beautiful place. Marble halls, gardens, fountains, everything. It was away from the fighting. I was perfectly happy there, but it was the last bastion of being humble and working-class and saying to the officers, 'Yes, Sir, thank you, Sir.' And that's what happened. I agreed. So he made me up to a Bombardier again and took me off as his driver, and that's how I arrived at that dreadful place O2E [the Second Echelon]. When he turned out a pouf, putting his hand up my shorts, grabbing my balls, I hit him and he said, 'Very sorry, Terence, it won't happen again.' I could have had him cashiered but I didn't. I just thought well, first they take my stripe and say I'm a coward, then they give it back to me because of some pouf major, what sort of man am I? I was shaking and stammering and half the time still feeling like crying.

So it was with difficulty that Terence settled down at O2E, at Maddaloni south of Naples. He was discomfited by the knowledge that his major was a homosexual and deeply concerned that his colleagues should not presume that he was also 'queer'. He tried to get a fresh posting but it was difficult as Major Clark was in charge of the department that handled transfers.

Officially Milligan was a clerk-driver, but he soon found that the duties were negotiable. He began playing his trumpet again and before long was absorbed into the large O2E dance orchestra. Inevitably, this reminded him of D

Battery and he continued to be obsessed with feelings of guilt that he was out of the fighting and safe whereas his former comrades were still risking their lives. He wrote several letters, ill-spelt and almost illegible, to his Battery Commandant pleading for the chance to return. His span of concentration was probably short; most of the letters came to a despairing end after a few lines. One such scrap has survived:

> Dear Sir, I beg of you to let me get back to the Regiment. I can't stand it here. I will do what you say but please help.

He felt morally as well as physically downgraded. However, as was to prove so often in the future, the music was therapeutic; he could once again lose himself in the excitement of a large band. Playing for army concerts and dances brought back memories of the irrepressible happiness of the Bexhill days. He continued with the drawing and painting which had occupied a lot of his time in the hospital and rehabilitation camps, and won a prize for art which drew him to the attention of Robb, the well-known *Daily Express* cartoonist.

Lieutenant Robb had been sent to the Second Echelon to recuperate after an operation. He was an officer in the Seaforth Highlanders and was made responsible for the design of the bar in the Officers' Mess at Maddaloni. At this time O2E seemed to be full of homesick Londoners, to judge by Robb's murals in the Mess. The bar was called 'The Tudor Rose', and the paintings covered several nostalgic views of London including Hyde Park, Piccadilly Circus, Covent Garden, London Bridge, Battersea Power Station and Saint Paul's Cathedral. One street scene depicted a London bus. Whilst the work was in progress Milligan was an interested observer. He approached Robb and said, 'I shan't ever be in this bar, sir, as it's only for the officers, but will you make that a No. 159 bus for me?' It was the early morning workman's bus between Camberwell and Lewisham that I used to catch to go to work on!' Robb acquiesced. 'He was an interesting lad,' he says now, looking back. 'I remember I was rather touched. There was a lot of emotion in him.'

Before long, Milligan had been drawn into the work and spent many hours painting the mural. This gave him a lot of pleasure and he wrote cheerfully to his family:

> I am well away in this job and liking it very much. I am doing well at music . . . and now I am making a name as an artist . . . A Major . . . (security) who was the official artist for the *Daily Sketch* before the War, was very interested in my sketch book . . . and said he would like me to work for him after the War . . . He gave his address in Maida Vale . . . I thought that was the last of it but next day the O.C. of this unit comes up to me and details me to do the interior wall murals for the new Officers' Mess . . . So last night saw me on a raised platform . . . producing some 7' high drawings . . . consisting of coy Victorian maids being given the 'eye' by be-whiskered soldiers in Hyde Park setting. If it is possible I would like to get a photograph. If so, I will send them on to you. In the meantime I'm being paid for the band jobs I do . . . 200 lire (10/-) so I'm saving that. I will be sending home another 20 quid soon for you to bank for me.

The letter was carefully typed in block capitals on an army air-letter form. Milligan was now 26 years of age. There seems to be a need to placate his mother – a need to convince her that art and music would be a 'proper job'.

Lieutenant Robb was a friend of John Henry Wood, O2E's Brigadier – a fierce old soldier who had spent years in India. There was massive boredom in barracks at Maddaloni – nicknamed 'mad and lonely' by the 2,000 soldiers incarcerated there in 1944 – and ENSA shows tended to by-pass O2E and go straight from Naples 'up country' to where the fighting was. Nevertheless Robb recalls that he oversaw the laying down of a splendid outdoor dance floor. They managed to provide music and drink.

> But never an ATS girl did we see – here was this marvellous dance floor, a band, a bar – a night-club in fact and no girls to dance with. The men were dancing with each other – big husky guards dancing with the batmen and so on. I went to the Brig. and told him 'We can't have this, can we, sir.' I *had* to tell him! The Brigadier ran true to form. 'I don't see why not,' he thundered. 'Indian men dance together, and they are the best fighters in the world.'

Greater attempts, the Brigadier decided, must be made to mitigate the boredom and frustration of his men. A derelict farmhouse which stood a distance from the main building was commandeered, and Robb got to work on a design for converting this into an 'other ranks' club – the men's equivalent of the officers' Tudor Rose Bar. Robb planned a huge mural to camouflage the decrepit walls. The design was of a great lobster which went right up one wall and across the ceiling. Robb approached Milligan and discussed the mural he envisaged; the outcome was that Spike executed the paintings from the small designs on squared paper which were given to him by Robb.

Thus, Spike spent his days peacefully painting, his evenings playing with the O2E band which was always in demand. His stammer, never to leave him entirely, began to fade. The solitary hours he spent painting, and his involvement with the music, began to work restoratively for him.

The next important development in Milligan's life came about by pure chance. 'I didn't know it at the time,' says Spike, 'but the finger of fate was beginning to point.'

In common with other war casualties who had been

posted to O2E Spike came under fairly stringent medical supervision, and before long one of the army doctors advised him to hang up his trumpet. He was told that he must stop playing because of a chest condition. In retrospect Spike firmly believes that this was not necessary, but at the time he accepted it.

> I don't know why I listened to him. Doctors! They don't know much, do they? I think I'd just had a chest pain, and when he told me that I ought to stop playing the trumpet I thought it was my mother's warnings all coming true. She was always telling me that I ought to stop playing the trumpet, that it was bad for me, that I'd die like my grandfather from aneurism of the heart – it was echoes of her warnings, I suppose. And it was all rubbish. I'm still here, and still playing the trumpet!

Yet in 1944 Spike accepted the dismal premisses of his mother and the mistaken diagnosis of the doctor. The outcome was positive. Milligan had now arrived at an important stage in his development. Deprived of his music, he began to turn his eager, fertile mind in other directions.

Milligan, scriptwriter, comedian, satirist and clown, was on the point of making his entrance.

The Combined Services Entertainments had just presented a production of Leon Gordon's *White Cargo*. This worthy, wordy play with its stilted dialogue, contrived attitudes and overtones of melodrama sent Spike into infectious paroxysms of giggles. The play is set on a tropical island between the wars. The theme is the white man's grave. The male characters are all in various conditions of ambition, frustration, pessimism and finally alcoholism. The one female character is a sultry desert island temptress who first captivates and then appals the drink-sodden Englishmen, rejects of the Establishment, muffled in their own red tape.

Milligan was already developing his formidable hatred of bureaucracy. The idea of a parody came to him and within days a full-scale, satirical comedy revue was presented with Spike directing and playing in several sketches. The show was called *Black Baggage*. Each character that had appeared in the original production was parodied and such plot as there was became non-existent as new and bizarre dialogue appeared. Much of this was at an impromptu and ad-lib level, and it is especially interesting because it illustrates the start of one of his most important contentions in comedy writing.

How do you know which character can say which thing and when? You can't put words into people's mouths until you've tried them out. You write a line for a character, but when he speaks it can sound totally wrong for that individual. You can't be sure of what is right for him to say until he says it.

This was the principle on which his first comedy writing was based, and no doubt the surviving 'Goon' producers of several years later will nod their heads in anguished memory. Spike has never seriously deflected from this stance – it has been both his making and his undoing. His capacity for finding the right treatment of the comedy situation rarely fails, but the mercurial speed at which his mind races can pose almost insuperable problems for fellow actors.

White Cargo, originally produced in 1923 at the Greenwich Village Theater in New York, had a cast of nine men and one woman. This may have influenced its eventual choice by ENSA who, rightly or wrongly, seemed hesitant about sending more women than absolutely necessary into the fighting areas. Milligan's *Black Baggage* company found no difficulty in casting the female role – Tondelayo. The part went to a member of the Welsh Guards, in drag. He

came from the Records Office. Before the war he had
played the cello.

> Of course, I was a bit dumb about homosexuality. I never
> could understand why the chap was all dressed up in his make-
> up and hula-hula skirts hours and hours before the curtain
> went up. Just didn't recognize it – sometimes he went to bed
> wearing his make-up and still had it on in the morning. I
> suppose he was having a marvellous time for a change, poor
> fellow. The army was very down on his side of things.

After *White Cargo*, the troops were entertained by a
performance of *Men in Shadows* produced by Sergeant
Lionel Hamilton, a former English actor attached to the
forces' welfare department of O2E. It was the first play
written by the young Mary Hayley Bell. She was married
to actor John Mills, who played the lead in the first London
production. The play, a story of the underground resistance
movement to enemy occupation, had encountered difficulty with the censorship and security departments in
London, apparently because of the authenticity with which
its theme of sabotage was treated. The author had lived
within close range of the situations around which the play
was written, and her privileged knowledge was of concern
to the Home Office's security department. However, the
authorities were eventually pacified and the play opened
with great success at the Vaudeville Theatre in September
1942. Mary Hayley Bell wanted to call her play *To Stall
the Grey Rat* but was persuaded to retitle it *Men in
Shadows*. After Lionel Hamilton's successful production
on the stage of the O2E theatre, Spike Milligan persuaded
the stage manager to let him 'borrow' the sets for the
following weeks. Rehearsals for Spike's brainchild *Men in
Gitis* began immediately – it was a further essay into the
sort of satirical, surreal comedy that was to soar into
the highly original, escalating mirth of the Goons. Each

character was faithfully produced and parodied; whereas the opening scene of *Men in Shadows* shows an old partisan in the background outside a remote farm patiently chopping away at a pile of logs, to muffle the sounds of the men in hiding, *Men in Gitis* opened to Signaller Tompkins, wild and woolly in a frizzy scarlet wig, downstage front, chopping violently with such roars of manic glee that wood chippings showered the first few rows of the stalls. As usual, Spike's performance delighted the audience and infuriated the Brigadier, who was wont to sit in sullen rages whilst the mercurial bombardier was on stage.

The *Valjean Times*, the official journal of the officers of the Second Echelon, gave *Men in Gitis* a cautious, somewhat bewildered review on 2 March 1945:

Music Hall

The high spot was undoubtedly *Men in Gitis*, a satirical sequel to *Men in Shadows*. This type of show is either liked or hated, and quite a few did not care for it at all, but the majority of people present gave the distinguished performers a really good ovation. Spike Milligan was at his craziest, and the show was a cross between 'Itma' and 'Hellzapoppin'.

To be 'either liked or hated' was the sort of uncertain accolade which Milligan's work seemed destined to attract. Five years later, BBC critics were to take the same guarded stance, hedging their bets in a precisely similar way about a show that was to change the face of comedy. It was called *These Crazy People*, shortly to be renamed the *Goon Show*.

After the riotous success of *Black Baggage* and *Men in Gitis* Spike was approached by one of the officers who had theatrical ambitions. He was dubious about the officer: 'Milligan, Ai laike what you are doing most awfully.' Spike mimics him distastefully forty years later, but he was, by this time, anxious to try his luck in straight theatre and he accepted a lead part in a forthcoming one-act play *The Thread of Scarlet*. He wanted the chance to prove himself capable of serious acting, and he might have succeeded had he not broken down before the planned production date. It is not clear whether this was because of his lack of experience, or ineptitude, or whether it was because the producer strained his capacity beyond its limit; Spike believes that the rehearsals had gone well, and that he had made good progress. 'It was my head,' he says dismally. 'I was just crazy at the time. I just broke down.'

We need to remember that by now Milligan had been virtually invalided out of the war. Ruth Conti, one of the very few women in O2E, believes that it was largely a matter of army mismanagement that a considerable number of unhappy active service rejects were still in Italy. As personal assistant to the Brigadier, her opinion is worth noting. The shelling had taken a grievous toll on Milligan's stability, yet when we consider these curiously productive months after the bombardments it could be that he is right when he asserts that his war experiences were closely linked with his artistic and creative development.

'All the ideas and the words and the scenes seemed to start tumbling out of me. It was as though all my imagination had been dormant until then,' he says.

Certainly the capacity for a sort of visionary, satirical comedy-writing erupted and flowed almost incessantly from the moment when the music had to stop.

It was not long, however, before Spike began surreptitiously to practise his trumpet again. He dismissed the MO's advice and his mother's gloomy forebodings from his mind; he was an active member of the entertainments group, constantly visualizing new ideas and putting them into practice with frenetic energy. Meanwhile, Lionel Hamilton was fighting a running battle to keep him at

O2E. The Brigadier had by now formed a violent antipathy towards him, unable to reconcile himself either to Spike's sort of humour or to his re-established trumpet-playing. 'It's too loud,' he would bellow. 'I'll have the idiot posted.' The Brigadier was perhaps deserving of a little sympathy, for it appears that Spike frequently played his trumpet while lying on his bunk bed, and the sounds apparently percolated not only to the Brigadier's office but also to his sleeping quarters. Lionel spent a good deal of time soothing the Brigadier, albeit firmly. 'I can't get any shows together if you get rid of the most talented performers,' he insisted. 'OK, he may blow the trumpet rather loud occasionally, but he's a real leader with the entertainments lot and we can't do without him.'

Spike looks back with a grin that holds just a flicker of guilt. 'He was right, of course. I did play it too loud. I was an exhibitionist, wasn't I?'

Len Harvey, a former Warrant Officer in O2E, recorded something of the situation when, thirty years later, as a Pensioner at Chelsea's famous Royal Hospital, he compiled his war memoirs. It is interesting that although Spike and Len had not met, Len recalls the tale of the trumpeting bombardier with humour:

During one of my occasional visits to Maddaloni, I heard one of my friends, Captain Brian Clarke of the Hampshire Regiment, talking at length about a certain medically down-graded Field Gunner named Milligan, who answered to the name of 'Spike' and was a veteran of the North African and Italian Campaigns. It seemed that this character not only played a devastating trumpet, thus being of great value to the O2E Band then newly formed, but also had something of a reputation of a comedian, and was therefore quite an asset to O2E!

Gunner Milligan's official employment was that of a clerk, but whether this was a convenient cover for his other qualities I do not know. Neither did I ever meet him on my visits, nor hear the O2E Band, both circumstances being to my obvious disadvantage, but I do remember his murals!

Len remembers these days with a dignified, wry smile. 'I believe he constantly annoyed the Brigadier, quite apart from his trumpet playing. I'm not sure how – but he made the old man absolutely determined to get rid of him.' Years later, when both Spike and Len were in the throes of preparing their war memoirs, they corresponded and exchanged photographs. Eventually, a meeting was planned and Len Harvey was heard to comment: 'I think it ought to be an occasion where I could reasonably wear the scarlet!'*

They did, in fact, meet. In-Pensioner L. A. Harvey was invited to tea at Milligan's impressive Victorian home in Hertfordshire.

'What do I call you?' asked Len as they shook hands. 'Spike or Mr Milligan, sir!' Milligan welcomed the old man with his customary warmth. 'Just call me Gunner,' he said, with a grin. They reminisced for a couple of hours about the days in O2E, and Spike accepted a manuscript copy of Len's book *Chairborne Warrior*, as yet unpublished. 'I shall read it in bed tonight,' he said, and he probably did.

Len went back to the Royal Hospital in a warm glow. 'What a wonderfully kind man he is,' he said. 'I didn't exactly expect him to be jumping about and doing tricks or anything like that, but I never thought he'd be so concerned and thoughtful, or so relaxed. We could have talked until midnight and still had a lot to say. He is kindness itself.'

In the end, however, the Brigadier had his way and Spike was summarily dispatched from the interesting and productive corner that he had established for himself. He

* The full-dress uniform of the Chelsea Royal Hospital, worn on ceremonial occasions.

admits that he was upset at being removed from a niche in which he was beginning to feel a success:

> It seemed a bit hard to be sent away just because he didn't like my trumpet-playing, but when they told me that I was going to be posted to the Central Pool of Artists I thought, well, that can't be bad. An artist is what I think I am so maybe it's where I belong. Anyway, it sounded more like where I wanted to be than in a war so I decided it would be all right.

Lionel Hamilton has other views about the posting. He remembers the speed with which Spike would satirize or 'send up' some bureaucratic misadventure. He would hold up some of the long-treasured army procedures to absolute ridicule and the audience would roll in the aisle, with the single exception of the Brigadier. 'Not funny. Not at all funny,' he would hiss. 'Get off. Why don't you *get off?*' Comments which of necessity went unheard whilst the audience rocked and shouted with mirth. In later years Milligan was to inject his war memoirs with much of this anti-establishment ridicule. Lines like 'Silence when you speak to an Officer' were not only uproariously funny when they appeared in 'top brass' sketches – they were, in essence, so innocuous that the unfortunate targets of this 'insubordination' had no redress. They had to bear it all with as much stiff upper-lip as they could muster. It was not possible, even for the enraged Brigadier, to put the whole audience on a charge, but he could send Gunner Milligan to the Central Pool of Artists in Naples and he did.

It seems sometimes that Spike, innocently and without intent, has a disastrous way of upsetting people. Ruth Conti, sometimes called upon to act as a buffer between Milligan and the Brigadier during the O2E days, says, 'For such a sensitive man he was at times curiously insensitive about the feelings of other people. He lacked a sort of "nous". He had an extraordinary capacity for putting his foot in things. It was as though he wasn't able to appreciate the effect that he sometimes had on people.'

Harry Secombe, with all the warmth of his sanguine, uncritical and generous heart, has an affectionate, long-standing awareness of Spike's facility for crashing headlong into disaster. 'He can't always help it. He's a great man – always espousing causes, putting himself out – he'll drive himself to the end and beyond. But from time to time he gets into a twist about things and yes, he can put his feet in. Both feet. Takes his socks off first, and all!'

8

Central Pool of Artists

> Of course you bear the cross that all Milligans
> carry, I'm still carrying mine, we come from stock
> that have been and are emotionally unstable, we
> can't bear to be frustrated, it hurts us like hell
> inside.
>
> Letter from Leo Milligan to Spike,
> 28 September 1958

Milligan's arrival at the Central Pool of Artists must have
seemed something of an anticlimax. He was, of course,
still suffering intermittently from shellshock. He slept
badly, sitting up and chain-smoking for half the night,
dreaming and jumping and having short, frenetic night-
mares for the other half. Belonging to the Central Pool
was in itself no guarantee of working as a performer and he
felt cheated and angry. At O2E he had achieved some
success; here, no one knew him or cared about him.
Several other soldiers were in the same plight, and they
made a habit of going over to the CPA offices on the
outskirts of Naples where they occupied a room on the
third floor, and where an unfortunate NCO tried to prevent
their besieging the harassed director whose job it was to
get the shows on the road. The director was a young
musician who had worked as both composer and conductor
before the war. His name was Raymond Agoult.

Raymond Agoult is a man of interesting origins. He
was born, by chance, in Budapest, where his father was
conducting an orchestra and his mother was singing in
opera. His parents came from Alsace-Lorraine and young
Raymond travelled extensively with them in pursuit of

their careers. How he came to rest in the Pioneer Corps in the Second World War is something of a mystery. He certainly had no military ambition, which was just as well as he never left the rank of private. He was, however, earmarked for his musical prowess and his talent for organizing and arranging concert parties. July 1945 found him, one afternoon, hiding in his office in Naples from the wild young men on the third floor. They were, by all accounts, an unsavoury lot: unruly, unshaven, wearing their khaki-drill uniforms anyhow and bypassing any lingering army disciplines or parades. Suddenly his door flew open and Milligan burst in. He was, as Agoult recalls, 'a thin fellow, unkempt, unshaven, looking a proper mess. He didn't say who or what – just came in and threw himself on my table practically and yelled "Give me a job, will you? Please, just give me a job."'

Agoult remembers that Milligan looked 'wild and almost insane', and that he quickly identified him as one of the fellows from the third floor. 'I said to him: "Well, what can you do?" And he answered me: "Do? I can do any damn thing. I play the trumpet, I play the guitar, I can play any instrument. I sing, I dance, I make jokes, anything, but for God's sake give me a job."'

Agoult was exasperated. 'Could you,' he said 'jump out of the window?' Milligan took him at his word and leapt for the sill. The office was on the second floor and Agoult grabbed him, just in time, by the ankle. 'For God's sake,' he said, 'I was joking.' He then entreated him to come back in and sit down.

'I don't want to sit down,' yelled an infuriated Spike. 'I want a job.'

Agoult, in spite of himself, was impressed. He took his number and details of service. He promised to 'let him know' and, in contrast to what this usually means in theatrical circles, he actually did. A week or two later he put Spike in a show called *Over the Page*. Spike never, as Agoult recalls, '. . . applied himself to a script, but he was magnificent as an "ad hoc". He could really make them laugh. I gave him a lot of freedom in this show, and that suited him. At that stage in his career, and in the state he was in, freedom to develop was what he needed.'

Over the Page was a variety show, largely musical with singing, dancing, sketches and funny stories. A Combined Services Entertainment, it toured Italy in December 1945. The leading comic was a gifted young Welshman of great talent. He was also a man of warmth and generosity, and he was to become a lifelong friend to Spike Milligan; his name was Harry Secombe. His early promise was not missed by the critic who wrote for the army paper *Union Jack*: 'Rubber-panned, burlesquing Harry Secombe proved that he has a big and bright future ahead of him in British music-hall sketches when he gave us his ATS officer, his voice-pill seller, his nervous man at a village concert and his Western drummer in quick succession.'

Like Spike, Harry had been pigeonholed as 'battle weary' after he had served a long stint in North Africa, and it was a source of some relief to him when he was posted from his regiment, the 14th Welsh Hussars, to the Central Pool of Artists.

But Harry looks back on the time with equanimity:

It wasn't so bad with me as it was with Spike. I was battle weary all right, but I wasn't as shattered by it all as he was. Some of the time he was in a really bad state – crying, shaking, stammering and he couldn't sleep properly. I was just a bit liable to jump a few feet in the air if a car exhaust went off near me, that's all!

Before rehearsals for *Over the Page* began, Spike and Harry had managed to get themselves one or two 'gigs' in the Officers' Club at Naples. These were largely unrehearsed musical turns. Spike would play his trumpet or the piano and Harry would sing. Sometimes, a crossfire of spontaneous comedy would erupt and the musical clowns would prolong their spot, revelling in the applause.

Two other musicians were also in residence at the Central Pool barracks, Bill Hall and Johnny Mulgrew. Bill Hall was a tall, lanky Irishman who played a magnificent jazz violin. Johnny Mulgrew was a double-bass player who had played pre-war in the popular big band, Ambrose's Orchestra. Like Milligan and Secombe, Mulgrew had been downgraded after battle. Bill, Johnny and Spike – on the trumpet – were all in the orchestra for *Over the Page* under the direction of Raymond Agoult.

Milligan had long been an admirer of Stephane Grappelli, and the moment he heard Bill playing he was seized with excitement and inspiration. He made an immediate foray into the stores and emerged with a mixture of triumph and nonchalance holding a guitar. The music of the duo was stunning, and before an hour had passed they were joined by Johnny Mulgrew on the double-bass. From then on, they played together every free moment. Harry Secombe listened to the trio in delight and solemnly gave judgement. 'I think you three should stay together,' he said. 'And keep in the comedy bit.'

The 'comedy bit' was born of the curious appearance of the trio. Tall, lanky 6' 4" Bill always seemed to have too many arms and legs. He was a great imbiber, and frequently in his cups. Johnny was short and determined, not much bigger than his double-bass. Hyperactive Milligan was the ideas man, swarming all over, dressing up, reducing the other two (and in due course the audience) to hysterics. The standard of jazz music was superb, and it was as the Bill Hall Trio that the three stole the show in *Over the Page*.

The local paper in Naples gave them a gratifying review after their appearance at the Bellini Theatre.

Hit of the show in Naples so far has been Bill Hall's Trio, consisting of Bill himself on the violin, Spike Milligan (guitar) and Jock Mulgrew (bass). On Monday night they were called back for two encores, and exhibited an amazing ability for playing first-rate hot music in comedy style.

There were a few setbacks. On one occasion, largely through Bill Hall's tendency to riotous celebration, they all three landed under detention in the army guard-house. Raymond Agoult looks back with wry affection overlaying the remembered exasperation.

They were a bit of a nuisance. After all, they were still in the army, and every time they misbehaved they got in the guard-house. I had to go to the Colonel who had locked them up and say, 'Now look here, I want them out. You must release them' – and so forth. One fine day I remember I got hold of Bill Hall and I said, 'Now look! You know your own worth. You are a brilliant artist on the violin, but if you carry on like this you'll be forcibly demobbed, and you'll find yourself in the gutter.' And he said to me, 'I should worry – that's where I came from.' That was Bill Hall. The others weren't so bad – but of course they led each other on.

The *Union Jack* reviewed the Trio with enthusiasm:

The hit of the night was Bill Hall's trio. Bill's eccentric hot fiddling will take him far, and his partners on Bass and Guitar make up the best act of the night.

One of the places that the Trio visited was Trieste. It was an important date for Milligan, for it was there that he met Maria Antoinette Pontani. Toni Pontani was destined to play a special role in his life, and it is probably true to say that the generous and undemanding love that she lavished upon him brought him the greatest happiness in women that he was ever to know. Their love affair was short but entirely joyful: nearly forty years later they both spoke of each other with an almost mystical awe.

Toni had been a ballet dancer in an Italian opera company. She was young, talented, beautiful and intelligent. Her family came from Rome, where her father was a musician and a successful artist. Both of these accomplishments he passed on to his second daughter. Toni had been well-educated and spoke several languages, including English. Like most carefully brought-up Italian girls she was almost totally inexperienced with men. Perhaps she was lucky in her first love. Milligan, overwhelmed, treated her with a tenderness and admiration that was almost reverential.

The next production sent out by CSE was called *Barbary Coast*. Toni joined it as a ballet dancer during early 1946. The war was over, but the successful show was to tour Italy and Austria playing wherever the armed forces were still gathered. When she saw Spike for the first time Toni was sitting on the top deck of a stationary charabanc in Trieste. The charabanc, which transported the ballet girls, was parked in the market-place, and Toni was watching the local traders offer whatever they had happened to lay their hands on to the unsuspecting servicemen passing through. Milligan was inspecting a wristwatch. It was not a particularly good one and the price was high. An Italian 'spiv' was eloquently describing its valuable attributes. Spike looked as though he was weakening. Impulsively, Toni called out, 'Don't buy it. It's too expensive.'

> He looked up to see who was saying this and we looked straight at each other. He had this beautiful tanned skin and blue, blue eyes, lovely curly hair. We looked at each other and it was *coup de foudre* – for us both, I know. For him, and as well for me.[1]

About this time, Spike wrote an enthusiastic letter to Leo and Flo. He was elated with his success, with his good salary and with the comfortable perks of the officer status afforded to serving soldiers on the tour.

At the moment I am staying at the Albergo Universito in Rome and having a wonderful time – I am broadcasting this afternoon at 3.30 and again tomorrow at 6.30. I will send you the newspaper cuttings later. Look after them, they are all I have. How would you like an Italian girl as a daughter-in-law – ? Well, it seems as if you are [sic], because I am more than fond of her and she's mad about me – I will let you know as soon as I have seen her family. They are fairly well to do and very strict – I am never allowed out with her alone, always a chaperone – the redeeming feature is my being R. Catholic.

March 1 1946 was an important day for Milligan. The Bill Hall Trio was invited to appear as part of the Central Mediterranean Arts Festival finale in Rome as a 'non-competing' act. The judges were to award prizes in several areas to army finalists, unit dance bands, singers, double acts and the like. To enhance the standard of the show, the organizers added several well-known artists, the best known of whom was Gracie Fields who had spent a great deal of time entertaining the troops in the Middle East. On this occasion, Gracie – at No 13 – closed the bill. The Bill Hall Trio, nervous but exhilarated, were to precede her. In the event, the Trio had a resounding success, and encore after encore was demanded by a hilariously enthusiastic audience. Gracie, great favourite as she was, had to wait patiently whilst Bill, Johnny and Spike took their calls.

The judges were Lieutenant-Colonel Phillip Slessor – the chief broadcasting officer of the Central Mediterranean Forces, and the famous impresario A.C. Astor. There were, of course, no prizes for the Trio, but the hilarity and

enjoyment which their act evoked was not wasted on one
of the judges. A.C. Astor scribbled a note on the back of a
programme. Printed on cheap, wartime paper, folded and
refolded many times, it survived what were probably many
months in the Trio's back pockets. The note reads:

> Will book your act as seen tonight
> if you want to play variety.
>
> Let me know
> 1.) When likely to be available.
> 2.) Where to *find* you.
>
> My card is attached.
>
> A. C. Astor.

Barbary Coast toured Italy and Austria during the long
and wonderful summer of 1946 that was to remain so long
in the memories of both Toni and Spike. The tour was
well organized by the Combined Services Entertainment.
Officer status meant good hotels, linen sheets, meals on
tap and the princely salary of £10 per week. Travel
arrangements were taken care of, and the tour was exactly
what a young, over-sensitive, highly-strung artist needed.
He was protected, to some extent, from the wear and tear
of a life in show business. There was no responsibility save
being ready on time to perform, and performing for Spike
was almost always a pure delight.

Toni Pontani took Spike well in hand. She took him to
hear *La Bohème* at the open-air theatre in the Baths of
Caracalla, Rome. She took him to Roman ruins, to art
galleries and museums, to flower gardens and grottoes.
She sat with him for hours at pavement cafés, holding
hands and talking about their future. She also marched
him firmly into an Italian couture shoemaker and saw that
he invested in a pair of light, handmade Italian shoes.
Spike was amazed at his new comfort.

I'd no idea that there was anything wrong with my feet. They were like blocks of concrete. I just accepted that all army issue shoes were normal and I had these great John Bull boots weighing half a ton. When Toni kept pointing me towards shoe-shops I'd no idea what she was up to. The penny suddenly dropped. I bought the shoes and she made it seem like my idea. I'd never known such comfort. I walked out and felt airborne, my feet so light I wanted to take off and fly.

Before the *Barbary Coast* tour finished, Spike and Toni went on holiday together to Capri. They stayed for two weeks at the Albergo Grotto Azura. Years later, Milligan stuck the snapshots that he and Toni had taken of each other in his album. One was of them both; they are lying on their stomachs smiling at the lens. Spike's hand is blurred and he is obviously delighted to have moved the shutter by poking at the camera with a long stick.

'It was a time of no tourists,' he wrote under the photographs. 'It was paradise.'

On 20 August 1946 Spike was medically examined by the Military. On the bleak army form W 3149 his medical history was brief.

Before war service: MALARIA. INDIA.

During present war service:
SANDFLY FEVER.   SALERNO. NOV 1943.
BRONCHITIS.   AFRIGOLA (ITALY). 1944.
WOUNDED.   JAN 23 1944.

He was given first-class sight, hearing, teeth; no physical defects or scars, no varicose veins, hernia, VD or gastro-intestinal disturbances. His age was now 28 years and 4 months, he was five foot ten and three-quarter inches, weight 155 lbs, skin clear and physique good.

To question No 9 – 'Any obvious evidence of psychoneurosis, mental disease or allied conditions?' – the MO wrote simply 'NIL'.

Spike was then granted local release pending discharge. His final discharge certificate was given on 9 October. He had been in the armed forces for six years and two hundred and twenty-eight days. He was awarded several medals – Africa Star with First Army, 1939/1945 star, Italy Star and the Defence Medal. Next to 'Military Conduct' the Records Officer wrote 'Very Good', and on the reverse side of the document, as though after further thought, he added, 'Testimonial: A steady and reliable man who has carried out his duties satisfactorily.' The discharge certificate has a curt sub-heading 'If this certificate is lost, no duplicate can be obtained.' T.A. Milligan 954024 must have heeded the warning. The certificate is still in his possession today.

Finally the day came when Bill Hall and Spike Milligan accepted the inevitable. The party was over; it was time to go home. A decision had to be made about where to be demobbed. Home, or in Europe? The tour of *Barbary Coast* had just played Klagenfurt in Austria. The nearest European centre for demob was Villach, so Bill and Spike made for there.

The formalities of demobilization were few, and soon completed. Each soldier was given demob pay, ration-book vouchers, clothing coupons, medical certificates and a new suit. Bill and Spike looked aghast at the choice available and, after a burst of quickly suppressed laughter, proceeded to enjoy themselves. Spike, to the mounting and incredulous horror of the quartermaster, chose a chalk-striped suit several sizes too big for him. The sleeves extended well beyond his arms, and the trousers had to be rolled up at the ankle.

'Well, I've got to allow for growth, haven't I?' he told the gaping staff.

Bill Hall diligently persisted until he had found a jacket which would not button across his chest and trousers that reached only an inch or two below his knees.

'I suppose we were feeling a bit high,' said Spike. 'We just felt like fooling about a bit.'

Being demobbed touched Spike with exhilaration and apprehension. His adrenalin was flowing but deep down his basic insecurity stirred. Notwithstanding the pain and misery of war, the army had been a protective shield, he had gone through late adolescence and early manhood in the staunch camaraderie of friends who were destined to remain close to him for the rest of his life. He had known appreciation and a degree of adulation. With a certain incredulity he realized that he was attractive to women, well-liked by his mates and able to command a good degree of attention from people in general. The gauche, uncertain youth receded as the apparently confident young man, albeit carrying the seeds of a deep anxiety, emerged.

9

Post War: Pre-Goon

Life is not a spectacle or a feast, it is a predicament.

George Santayana

Back in England, Leo had managed to resume his former job at the Associated Press in Fleet Street. During the war years, he had been recalled to the colours and given officer status. He was appointed to an administrative job in a supply depot and he, Flo and Desmond moved for the time being to Reigate in Surrey. This meant a considerable improvement in his circumstances, and his extra income meant that he was able to enrol Desmond at the Reigate School of Art where he began his training. However, by seeking early release from his army post, he relinquished his army officer's pension; presumably his anxiety about possible unemployment after the war had triggered this move. It looked as though the family could now be trickling home. Flo was anxious to have rooms for her sons, and through the good offices of Alf Thurgar's mother they managed to rent a small terraced house – No 3 Leathwell Road, Deptford.

After the demobilization formalities, Spike and Bill Hall set off for London. To begin with, they were both in high spirits and looking forward to seeing their families. They travelled by train through Switzerland and France, and embarked for Dover in the cold grey light of a November morning. For some reason, a snapshot of Spike was taken on board the ferry, probably by Bill Hall. It shows him looking rather sombre and dubious. He made no attempt to smile at the camera, and many years later he wrote on the back of the photograph '*1946. On the voyage home. I was very unhappy.*'

> Well, I was saying goodbye to a life that had given me a lot of freedom, a lot of companionship. I'd had everything. I'd survived death and lived again, I'd seen Pompeii, I'd had success as a musician and a performer, I'd found something that I was really good at. I saw a future for myself in the entertainment world. I'd fallen in love and known a wonderful love affair. I should have died then. Really, 1946 would have been the year for me to die . . . By the time that photograph was taken, I must have been foreseeing something of the nightmare that was in front of me.

At Victoria, Bill and Spike parted. Bill went off to find what remained of his family, and Spike caught a train down the line to Deptford. It was mid-afternoon, there was a fog and it was beginning to rain when he arrived at Leathwell Road. He braced himself for the shrieks of delighted welcome and rang the bell. No one answered. He rang again, knocked, and peered in the gloomy window. The house seemed empty. A neighbour, sour and inquisitive, looked over the fence. After first querying his credentials, she informed him that his parents were away for the weekend with his brother. She asked him suspiciously why he had not informed Leo and Flo that he was arriving, and was contemptuous of his somewhat lame reply that he had wished to surprise them. She did, however, hold a key to the house, and after Spike had convinced her that he was indeed part of the family grudgingly agreed to let him in.

Once he was inside, Milligan's mercurial spirits sank rapidly to zero. The disappointment of finding his family away was acute, and after the brighter Mediterranean skies the overcast grey clouds of South London seemed oppressive and foreboding. He sat in the chilly house, stared at the drab surroundings, and wondered what he had come home to, what the future held. His memory of this homecoming is still dismal.

> It was freezing cold and I couldn't make the gas work, or something was wrong – it was foggy, raw, and with them all away it was just unbearably depressing. I remember feeling very dejected and without much hope for the future.

Milligan found it virtually impossible to settle down at Leathwell Road. His mother was unimpressed with his potential career as an entertainer and never failed to repeat her desire that he should get a 'proper' job. She was dubious about the Bill Hall Trio, as well she might be, for the gifted Hall did nothing to reassure her. He lacked the conventional glamour that she associated with a successful artist and she could not accept his messy appearance; in particular she was appalled at his long, shoulder-length hair. In the 'sixties, Bill would have caused no surprise, but back in 1947 long hair on men was seen only in the history books.

Nevertheless, in the early days of 1947, the Bill Hall Trio managed to get sporadic engagements at various London night-clubs or 'bottle parties'. These included the Windermere Club, the Blue Angel and the Coconut Grove, where Edmundo Ros was reaching a height of South American popularity. Sometimes it was possible to 'double' and play two clubs. This meant a lot of rushing about carrying the instruments. The winter of 1946–7 was viciously cold; London was not to see such another until 1963, which almost equalled it for harshness. Both winters were to be memorable for Milligan and both brought him pain and anxiety.

The new year came in with a solid carpet of snow in London which caked all streets save the very centres. The

cold was bitter and exhausting; getting to work in the
morning and home again in the evening became a cumulative strain on all but the most hearty. People passed each
other in the street with bent heads and a bare, nodded
acknowledgement – it seemed that every scrap of energy
had to be husbanded. Socializing dropped to the minimum.
Theatres, cinemas and places of entertainment were having
the worst season on record.

It was at such a time that the Bill Hall Trio strove to
take advantage of A. C. Astor's former promise. 'Get
yourselves a booking within reach of London and I'll get
Val Parnell along to see you,' he promised. In the event,
the booking the Trio got was at the Hackney Empire.
A few shivering 'paper' customers were sitting almost
resentfully in the stalls. The snow fell gently outside; grey
vistas of frozen roads stretched as far as the eye could see.
It is hardly surprising that the riotously funny Bill Hall
Trio received nothing but a titter of lukewarm sniggers
from the few miserable recipients of complimentary tickets
who had made it to the theatre. It is not on record what
the impresario Val Parnell thought of their performance.
Suffice to say that no offer of work was forthcoming.

On 25 January 1947, the Bill Hall Trio made its first
television appearance as part of a variety programme. One
week later, on 2 February, they appeared again in *Paging
You*. The programme included a rendering of 'The Flight
of the Bumble Bee' by Rimsky-Korsakov, arranged by the
Bill Hall Trio. The piece must have been something of a
favourite with them because they used it again on 28
August 1948, when they appeared as a supporting act on
the popular television programme *Rooftop Rendezvous*.
Thirty-five years later, with Bill Hall dead and Johnny
Mulgrew gravely ill, Milligan played it briefly, on a comb,
when he opened in his one-man show at the Gaiety Theatre
in Dublin. It brought the house down, which probably

surprised Spike, who almost certainly included it more
from a feeling of nostalgic affection for his old friends than
a belief that it might stop the show.

The next few months were not easy. Milligan stayed
with the Bill Hall Trio and played various provincial dates.
Neither Bill, Johnny nor Spike were good administrators.
They tried various agents, and accepted what work they
were offered at whatever salary was going. For Spike,
commuting to Leathwell Road became difficult on several
counts. Firstly, the bottle party and night-club cabaret
dates were ruled out because of the obvious transport
difficulties. Secondly, and more importantly, Flo was
becoming increasingly restive about her talented son's
failure to find regular work, and she was also upset about
his status as a lapsed Catholic. She knew that he did not
attend mass or go to church regularly. To a certain extent
she had lost control. Fortunately, Desmond was proving
rather more satisfactory. He had work as a designer, he
still went to church, and during the summer of 1947 he
fell in love with a good Catholic girl.

Doing 'the rounds' of agents, Spike ran into old army
acquaintances. Reg O'List was now with Jennie, a beautiful
long-legged girl from the Windmill. He was delighted to
meet Harry Secombe and Norman Vaughan, both ex-CSE
and trying to make it as comedians. Between them they
established a little colony in Notting Hill Gate: at No 13,
Linden Gardens. This was a house of bed-sitting rooms,
mostly let to theatricals. A lot of coming and going went
on there, and occasional doubling up, for none of the
occupants could afford to pay rent when they went on
tour. The rooms were serviced, and the residents had to
bear with the ministrations of Blanche, a stout, cryptic
woman who 'did' for them all with varying degrees of
affection. She was never seen without a cigarette drooping

from her lip; when the ash grew long she would occasionally flick it neatly into her apron pocket. She frequently expounded on her dislike of Harry. 'She must have been the only person in the world who didn't like Harry Secombe,' says Norman Vaughan, still a little mystified. 'I think it was because he was so untidy. "That Secombe," she used to say. "I can't stand him." Everyone in the world loved Harry, even then. Everyone except her, that is!'

Living at Linden Gardens brought a certain freedom to Spike. According to Norman and Harry, he was surrounded by pretty girls. Milligan denies it. 'Name one!' he will say stoutly. 'I was still thinking of Toni, or trying to get something going again with Lily Dunford.' Certainly it is on record that Spike had a room to himself – unusual for this very hard-up group as the double rooms worked out much cheaper. A guitar hung on the wall, an uncommon sight in those days. 'I remember being very impressed with that,' says Norman:

> It seemed very sophisticated – well, trendy. Only no one said 'trendy' at that time. Those were the days when we were all looking for work – and we didn't get much. Harry Secombe was the luckiest – the phone would ring and we'd all charge downstairs and it always seemed to be for Harry. He was starting to get in, getting quite popular in [the radio programme] *Variety Bandbox*, and we all waited for him to cash his cheque. None of us had bank accounts, so he would have to get someone with an account to cash it. I remember it was usually Jimmy Edwards. We all managed with the Post Office. These little cheques would come in from the BBC for five guineas, that sort of thing. The rooms cost about two pounds ten shillings a week – that was a lot at a time when £4 was a man's weekly wage.

In 1947, the Bill Hall Trio appeared at the Princes Theatre in Blackpool from 5 May for one week. Then they played Glasgow Pavilion, Colchester, Liverpool and Bolton. Spike tried to organize his life and made a brief diary listing the letters he wrote and the way his salary was spent.

During the week at Blackpool he wrote to both Toni and Lily, and he listed some of his outgoings. 'Cigs 3/4, Dance 3/6, Drinks 1/6, Food 2/-, Sweets 6d.' The following week, in Glasgow, he appears to have written more letters and spent less money. He wrote to Reg O'List, his mother, Toni and Margot. Margot was the landlady at 13 Linden Gardens; no doubt he was writing to confirm his return to London for a 'break' in the engagements. The only outgoings he listed were connected with work: 'Orchestrations 4/-.'

Whilst his own show was playing at Liverpool, Spike had been able to fit in a visit to the opera. He wrote to Toni:

> Darling,
>   I have just come back from the opera – *La Bohème* – beautiful! Beautiful! But not as beautiful as when I saw it at the San Carlo with Gigli and Pina Esea. It had the effect of taking me back to Italy for a few lovely hours. What do you do all day my darling? Tell me all. I want to hear about my too-beautiful dream.

Although it seems that by now both Toni and Spike had abandoned any real hope of a future together, the relationship was still important to them both; letters were written and received avidly.

It was during the Notting Hill Gate days that Spike first began to linger in the second-hand bookshops. The thirst for reading which had begun in the abandoned school library at Bexhill was steadily developing. He was drawn to the poetry shelves and would occasionally find a spare shilling or two which would pay for a cheap odd volume.

At least one of these has survived the wear and tear of his life. At first glance it might seem a strange choice for a penniless young man trying to make it in show business – it is a translation of a book of Virgil.

The Virgil was the first book Spike ever bought. Over the years he has spent a fair amount of time in old bookshops and at the stalls in the old Farringdon Road. He has bought books for their content, their antiquity or their curiosity – never for their potential intrinsic value about which he knows little and cares less. As his family grew up, he established a small library in a ground-floor room at Monkenhurst. He has labelled the shelves carefully: 'History', 'Politics', 'Encyclopaedias', 'Fiction'. He has not included his own books on these shelves. A few of these he keeps for reference purposes in his bed-room; the rest are neatly shelved in a cellar which also houses files, odd bits and pieces which he can't bear to throw away, and tools.

In July 1947 his grandmother, still resident in Poona, visited England, and in August Desmond was married in London. Spike, wearing a suit and with a very short, neat haircut, was best man.

In between the tour dates, Milligan was a frequent visitor at Allen's Club, close to the famous Windmill Theatre in Soho. This was a regular haunt for show people. Keeping an ear close to the ground at Allen's Club meant that you heard what might be likely to happen next in the business. It was here that gossip circulated and rumours grew. One interesting rumour went round that Harry Secombe was now in London with a lovely, dark-eyed Italian girl who had a cream-like complexion and beautiful black hair. Envious old army friends (perhaps Spike was one of them) surrounded Harry one day demanding to know how he had managed to bring his wartime lady to London when most of them had settled for tearful partings.

Harry was amused. 'Don't be so daft,' he said. 'She's no Italian. That's Myra, from Wales. She's been my girl since we were kids.' It seems that Harry, as Norman Vaughan had said, was certainly 'doing best'. Nearly forty years later, his luck still holds. Lady Secombe (Harry was knighted in 1981) is the same dark-eyed girl from the Welsh valley.

Harry was the most generous of friends. No sooner had he gained a precarious foothold for himself at a club or other venue, than he would do all in his power to bring in his friends. He loved Spike with a protective warmth and a profound understanding of his talents and needs that grew from his own compassionate and intuitive intelligence. He was tuned in to Milligan's mercurial wavelength, and the bond of shared war experiences had helped to establish a lasting friendship that was to prove wonderfully creative.

The role of Harry Secombe, the least presumptuous of the four men who were ultimately to know lasting fame as the creators of the *Goon Show*, was immensely valuable. His rock-like stability, his warmth, his firmly entrenched sense of values would spread through the company of four with a centrifugal force that held the gifted eccentrics together in a whirlpool of creative joy.

Both Spike and Norman Vaughan failed their auditions when they applied, at Harry's instigation, for the 'resident comedian' spot at the Windmill. It was in any case a thankless job for the artist, who had to try and amuse the audience of excitable men who barely tolerated these short intervals between the nude tableaux. Many years later, Spike and Norman recalled the old days over afternoon tea at Monkenhurst.

'I never got a chance to even show what I could do,' said Spike morosely. 'I just walked on stage and said "Oh, please excuse me for appearing fully dressed," and the blighter at the back yelled out "Thank you. Next please."'

Norman was indignant on Spike's behalf. 'Shows how short-sighted they were,' he said. 'It wasn't a bad beginning. They could have listened for a few minutes. Bastards, weren't they?'

Things began to look up a little in the early autumn of 1947. Through the medium of Foster's Agency, Will Collins, an impresario, booked the Bill Hall Trio to appear as part of a freak show called *Would You Believe It*. They were to travel to Zürich, and their act was to be sandwiched between performing pigs who stood on tables and a man with xylophone skills. They were to appear for a month as part of the ZUKA Exposition, a massive sort of carnival show under a big canvas roof. Spike remembers that he and Johnny Mulgrew stayed overnight with his family at Leathwell Road before leaving for Switzerland. He was excited at the thought of more travel and they were both in high spirits when they started out although it was a damp, grey morning with leaden clouds and a promise of rain. Flo, making the best of it, gave them a huge breakfast and then stood out in the middle of the road energetically waving goodbye until their taxi disappeared.

They journeyed to Zürich by boat and train where accommodation had been secured for them with a Herr and Frau Hitiyi. Milligan's stay with them was made memorable by a Swiss girl called Laura Gagalty who fell in love with him: 'It wasn't an affair or anything like that,' he recalls, 'but she seemed to get very attached to me.' He was not quite certain how to handle the situation and in any case was still in a state of confusion over both Lily and Toni. Laura, however, must have made some impact on his life. A few years later, he chose that name for his first-born daughter.

Whilst appearing in *Would You Believe It*, Bill, Johnny and Spike were seen by an Italian agent, Ivaldi. Ivaldi was loud in his admiration of their act and promised great things, including impressive salaries. The suggestion was that the Bill Hall Trio should tour Italy with a popular band, Angelini and his Orchestra. The Trio came back to England briefly, negotiated their contracts between their agent in London and Ivaldi in Milan and set off for Italy. Milligan was delighted at the promised extensive tour. As often before, he and Johnny Mulgrew travelled together and Bill Hall arranged to meet them in Rome. This was almost a disaster as Bill turned up only minutes before the show opened at the Teatro Del Arte. Johnny and Spike had spent an anxious few hours awaiting his arrival. Their part in the show went on with barely a run-through, yet it was, as nearly always, a riotous success.

While the show was in Rome, Spike saw something of Toni, although this was no longer the joyous idyll of the *Barbary Coast* days:

> We were at the Teatro Del Arte in Rome. I remember I saw Toni again. But something seemed to have happened. We went out and everything, but we were somehow distanced now. I think I was very irresponsible, like I was with Lily. I wouldn't name a date or a day or anything. I just wanted it to go on as it was. I never thought about marriage seriously. I know I wrote to my mother and said, 'How would you like an Italian daughter-in-law?' but that was a bit of bravado when I was in the army and I had my head in the clouds going out with a ballerina, going out with an upper-middle-class girl. But now, she thought my life was just going to be wandering around with the Bill Hall Trio. Toni wanted stability by now. She'd given up the profession, and we were being a roaring success. The Continent were much more into clowns and we were playing jazz which was new to the Continent, very exciting, so we were winners everywhere we went. I was sad about Toni and me, but I don't remember feeling that there was anything I could do. I don't remember being invited to her home again. I think I just didn't come up to her standards.

Toni Pontani recalls her own sadness at this meeting: 'He was such a special and brilliant person. I would say to him,

"Why do you stay with these Bill Halls and people? They will be no good to you in your future." But he wouldn't be serious, not really. He would say, "He plays magnificent jazz violin", and "Johnny is my friend", and I could see no future for him, with them, or for us together.'

Toni was right. There really was to be no future for Milligan with the Bill Hall Trio, and even before this last tour commenced, he was beginning to be aware of it:

> I knew really that we'd not get anywhere. You can't just go on trailing the same act round the same places, not really moving. Bill was a great artist, but he was a piss artist as well. It was obvious that there was no future. But they were marvellous people. Both of them. And I loved Johnny. We had some really tough times together. On that last tour we ended up in Trieste or somewhere. We had digs but absolutely no money – we hadn't been paid. We had a box of crystallized fruit which I'd bought as a present for my mother. We were so hungry we sat up in bed one morning eating it for breakfast. Johnny had a bottle of red wine and we drank that and the landlady came in and couldn't work out why we were both pissed in the early morning when we'd been in bed all night. We couldn't stop giggling. I remember I hid the bottle under the bed.

Milligan still remembers the box of crystallized fruit that Flo was never to receive. It was an antique-looking gold box, with an old master reproduction on it. He thinks it was a Raphael. There is no doubt that it would have delighted his mother.

The tour continued in some sort of fashion. They played Rome, Milan, Pistoia, Verona, Arezzo, Savona, Trieste, Bergamo and Genoa. Very frequently the organizers ran out of money and couldn't pay the artists. On one occasion, before the journey to Trieste, they were not able to pay even the travel expenses. Spike sold his gold watch (a relic of his last journey through Italy) and bought the train tickets for himself, Bill and Johnny. Bill went off to celebrate this smart move with a drink or two. Unfortunately he overdid things, and as a consequence failed to arrive at the station on time. Spike and Johnny waited on the platform with failing hope and growing exasperation as the train steamed out. The only alternative now was to travel by road. They took a coach that travelled through the night. After a while Milligan ceased to regret the missed train as the journey by road was so impressive.

> I remember waking up early in the morning and going past a magnificent view, it must have been Lake Como. It was stunning. It was winter, I remember, and there was snow on the mountains, and this beautiful lake was next to my window, the whole length of the road we were driving along. It was such a marvellous scene, silent and beautiful as the dawn came up. I've never forgotten it.

During the tour, on one of the occasions when there was a break and no money, Spike and Johnny found themselves staying in a small Italian town near the Yugoslav border. Penniless and hungry, they looked enviously at a small eating-house with steamed-up windows which was full of young men waving their arms, shouting enthusiastically and tucking into large helpings of spaghetti. It was the local Communist headquarters. Milligan discovered that if you joined the Communist Party you could get a free meal. Hungry as they were, it seemed a fair exchange. They both joined, and dined well that evening.

On another occasion, they found that a local taverna was willing to feed them handsomely in return for music. The taverna was a typical small Italian restaurant where artists congregated. It was no hardship to the hungry musicians, who loved to play and needed to eat. They enjoyed the food, the quantities of red wine and the friendly, appreciative Italians eating there. In the years to come, Milligan's favourite choice of restaurant would be Italian, and his most favoured main course, however imposing or luxurious the venue, a plate of spaghetti with Neapolitan sauce.

Eventually, the tour faltered to an impecunious finale. Spike and Johnny were quite penniless; their only course seemed to be a visit to the British consul to ask for repatriation. They presented themselves at the British Embassy in Rome with their tale of woe. They were interviewed by a serious-faced Indian who regarded them with considerable suspicion. 'I think,' says Milligan, smiling sheepishly, 'that Bill Hall had already been round there on the tap.' The official rather reluctantly parted with a small sum of money. He was unimpressed at Spike's attempts to be funny. 'I would walk,' he offered, 'but I'd lose the way.' 'Do not be making these silly jokes on a serious occasion,' he was told. 'You must remember that this sum of money is only a loan and you are under an obligation to pay it back.' They accepted the stricture with equanimity. 'He suggested,' says Spike, 'that the whole British economy would collapse if we defaulted.'

Their spirits were not broken by this humiliation, for on the way back they dropped off at a beautiful villa at Cannero on Lake Maggiore belonging to a rich Swiss family, the Roccas. The daughter of the family, Jean Roccas, had invited them both to call in on their way back to England. They stayed for several days, enjoying the good food, wine and company.

> I remember we were quite penniless – we had no shame. I think we just took it for granted. They had to feed us and wine us and dine us, and thank God they did or we'd have starved to death.

There is a photograph in existence of Milligan lying flat on the ground with his eyes, arms and legs crossed. Against a background of a gracious marble piazza it looks funny enough. Perhaps the fact that he might have been unaware of the two large holes revealed in the soles of his shoes makes it seem funnier still.

10

Goons Arising

Observation is sharpened by suffering.

Balzac

A new and important influence now came into Spike's life.
Jimmy Grafton was a young man who had survived the
war, was demobbed, as a major, in 1946 and found himself
with a burgeoning talent for scriptwriting, a young family
to support and very little else. He opted for a livelihood
that would allow him security for his family and time to
develop his own interests, and the Grafton Arms at No 2
Strutton Ground, Victoria, became a convivial meeting-
place. It was a popular public house and its enterprising
licensee had a good deal of success with his scriptwriting
ambitions. The pub was the haunt of a good number of
show business people – some of them well-established.
Jimmy Grafton's break as a scriptwriter came when one of
the comedians he wrote for, Derek Roy, was installed as
resident comedian in *Variety Bandbox*, a popular radio
feature that gave opportunities to a number of young
artists. Grafton, therefore, was getting well-acquainted
with the BBC. Sensitive and intelligent, he had a perceptive eye for talent, a great sense of humour and a youthful
enthusiasm for innovation. He met first Michael Bentine,
then Harry Secombe. Next he met Peter Sellers and finally
he was introduced to Spike.

When Michael Bentine first met Grafton he had already
made his début in the West End of London – he was a
newcomer, along with the twelve-year-old Julie Andrews,
in the show *Starlight Roof* which put him well onto the

show business map. A brilliant short comedy spot at the famous Nuffield Centre, a sort of superior post-war Naafi where members of the forces could drop in for food, music, dancing and entertainment, brought him immediate recognition and the chance to move on to, first, the London Hippodrome and then the London Palladium, a Mecca for all would-be comedians. Bentine, who had served in RAF Intelligence during the war, was already well in with the BBC, having appeared in *Variety Bandbox* and a show called *Third Division*, which was a follow-up to a clever radio series called *Listen My Children* starring actor Robert Beatty, with Benny Lee, Benny Hill, Carole Carr and including the as yet unknown Peter Sellers.

Peter Sellers, a man of rare and special talents, was the only Goon to come from a professional show business background. His mother, Peg, the archetypal Jewish mother, was a formidable character who loved, cherished and dominated her young son. She predicted, rightly, that he would reach international stardom and the whole of her life was dedicated to that aim. For the first seven years of his life he had no settled home but endured an unenjoyable childhood being dragged around variety theatres where his parents were performing. They separated when he was six years old and from then on he lived solely with his mother. As with Milligan, Peter's formal education came to a stop when he was about fourteen years old. Some time was then filled in by working in a theatre doing front of house and backstage chores and, like many teenage boys, he took up drumming. Peg, of course, provided a drum kit. Eventually, he was called up into the RAF. Bored with groundstaff routine (Sellers had bad eyesight) he volunteered for entertainment duties. He was speedily selected and posted to India with the *Ralph Reader Gang Show*. His mother, distraught at losing her boy, made many attempts to frustrate this arrangement, but fortunately she was unsuccessful.

Sellers did not enjoy his relatively low status and whilst touring enlivened numerous occasions by borrowing appropriate costumes from the wardrobe for various masquerades. Here, buying a drink in the mess and playing the part of an officer, he began his career as a mimic. His talent for impersonation and mimicry was quite outstanding. Jimmy Grafton was as impressed with Peter Sellers as he was with Bentine and Secombe. Finally, he was introduced to Spike Milligan and the quartet was complete.

Much water was to go under the bridges, however, before the *Goon Show* got under way. Grafton took Spike under his wing in all senses of the word. Fascinated by his articulate humour and capacity for repartee, he encouraged him to write comedy scripts, in the first place for Derek Roy. They worked together well, but were limited for time by the constraints of the Grafton Arms. Jimmy was rarely free until midnight. Linden Gardens seems to have faded out of the picture now, and Milligan, doubtless feeling something of a non-achiever, was still not eager to commute to Leathwell Road, even if transport had been feasible. Jimmy and his wife found room for him in the attic at Grafton's, where he slept beneath a pile of old coats and blankets under (reputedly) a large painting of Franz Kafka.

Often, after midnight, Jimmy would join Spike and they would crouch on the floor together, writing, laughing, hysterical with mirth. And the jokes would flow freely as though from some bottomless pit. Milligan's creative imagination and unstoppable flights of fancy into a land of increasingly surreal humour were not coupled, at this time, with the more mundane talents of spelling and punctuation. A shorthand that could keep pace with his

speed had not yet been invented. His debt to Jimmy
Grafton, who recognized this exploding talent and helped
to proliferate and harness it, is considerable.

Before long, Michael Bentine, Harry Secombe, Spike
Milligan and Peter Sellers were inextricably involved.
Understanding and appreciation flared between them like
forest fire. They met on a dimension denied to most of us
and revelled in the joy they found. All ex-servicemen,
they were united in their hatred of bureaucracy and time-
wasting officialdom. High rank impressed them not at all
and the pretensions and idiosyncrasies of quite ordinary
people reduced them to helpless laughter. It was an
extraordinary, explosive combination of clever, intuitive
minds and it was Milligan who seized his long-neglected
pencil and began, in his ill-spelt and unpunctuated writing,
to commit chunks of it to paper.

Jimmy, of course, was delighted and did everything to
encourage and support the four who came daily to the
Grafton Arms. Sometimes they were in funds, more often
they were penniless. He helped them with food and drink
and encouragement. The Goons, as they now began to call
themselves, were in any case good for business. When
they were on form (which was nearly always) they could
reduce the other customers to hysterics. The crowds round
the bar listened in delight to the exchanges of wit and
ribaldry. It was new, riotous, anarchic and unbelievably
funny. The most dour of *Goon Show* critics (and there
have been some) could not deny that in this inauspicious
corner of London, in 1948, a uniquely important stage in
the history of comedy was being reached.

The next months were full of action, with hopes regularly
raised and dashed. The Goons as such were not yet ready
to emerge, but the foundations of their future success
were being built. Their affinity and delight in one another
intensified, and Jimmy Grafton looked after them, made

introductions that sometimes led to jobs, and acted as an unofficial extra agent. Grafton was still writing for Derek Roy, who was to feature in two popular radio shows – as well as *Listen My Children* there was *Hip Hip Hoo Roy*. Milligan had a hand in the scriptwriting, and Harry Secombe appeared in both shows, along with the actor Robert Beatty who remembers some of the hilarious rehearsals: 'We were in fits of laughter nearly all the time. I remember the poor producer, Pat Dixon, trying to control Harry. Harry giggled non-stop and Milligan used to be there, not exactly in the shows but egging us all on. He used to appear in the studio and then vanish, only to return and corpse us again.'

A follow-up series to *Listen My Children* came up. Scripted by Frank Muir and Denis Norden, again produced by Pat Dixon, the show was aimed at an 'educated minority' audience and went out on the Third Programme. Once again Harry Secombe appeared, as well as two young comics who were rapidly gaining notice – Peter Sellers and Michael Bentine.

Pat Dixon and another BBC producer, Roy Spear, were now taking a keen interest in all four Goons. Milligan was scribbling untidy comedy scripts with growing confidence; these were being hilariously received and occasional after-hours parties went on in the upstairs room at Grafton's when Peter, Harry, Mike and Spike himself would read. Frequently they were joined by other Grafton customers, who would be invited to participate. These included Jimmy Edwards, Tommy Cooper, Dick Emery, Alfred Marks, Graham Stark and many others who were ready to make their mark in comedy.

But Milligan was getting fewer radio opportunities than the others, not because he was less talented but because he lacked the confidence to compete for the work.

When Alfred Marks offered me a job as his dresser for a few weeks I was thankful. It earned a bit of money and kept me independent and I still had time to practise the writing. He also gave me a job to sit out in the stalls as a sort of stooge and answer him back. One day I was late taking my seat out front and he was calling out the lines to me and getting no feedback. He was very good about it. Didn't sack me or anything like that even though it must have ruined his act that day.

For Milligan now began the first agonies of what one of his younger doctors was to dismiss as 'the cyclothymic personality'. Bluntly, this means simply a situation in which the highs and lows of normal behaviour, cheerfulness and depression if you like, are regularly vying for supremacy in the individual concerned. It seems arguable that the states of elation and despair through which he has to battle, almost daily, sometimes hourly, whilst working, performing, socializing and generally going about the normal business of his day can be thus so simply disposed of. However, we do know that from about this time there were periods of despondency which alternated with the hours of ebullient and creative mirth. One such period was recorded by Milligan in a yellowed scrap-book of loose, lined pages. He wrote in pencil:

Feb. 1948

Here am I in my 31st year of life – nowhere. I who have served every task set me with zeal – I who have loved all things good, I who have never harmed nor brought pain to the smallest of God's creatures – nowhere. I live in an attic covered with 3 coats lent me by a friend – is it not hard to contain one's hatred for life – is it wrong to laugh at proverbs, try try try again. Yes it is easy because they mean naught. Mozart loved, again and again, but his was a miserable life, a pauper's grave – and in death *attained immortality* to a world that gave him no pleasure – he gave just *that* in return – but for poor Ludwig he can never know – he lives with never having known

joy in full measure. Now I sleep and if I never awake – who
cares – ! Not I.

Spike Milligan
1st Feb. 1948
12.30

About twenty years later Spike has written on the original:

Written in the Attic of No 2 Strutton Ground – when I was
writing odd jokes for Jimmy Grafton.

During early 1948, Spike was offered work as a musician/
comedian in a Combined Services Entertainment show
starring Ann Lennor called *Swinging Along*. This was to
tour Allied Occupied Germany and Austria. He accepted
it, grateful to have a solo engagement now that he had
split from the Bill Hall Trio. Rehearsals took place in
temporary CSE rehearsal rooms in Eaton Place, SW1. On
the first day, Milligan noted with approval a beautiful
young red-head, Dorita Stevens. He approached her when
a break was called at midday and said, 'I'd very much like
to take you to lunch, but as I'm skint I can't.' When the
company met some days later at Liverpool Street Station
Milligan searched the reserved compartments until he
found Dorita sitting alone:

I went and sat next to her and we talked and talked. All day.
All the way in the train, in the boat, all the way to Hamburg.
She was a marvellous person to talk to, not educated in the
official sense but bright. We got on like a house on fire. I don't
remember us making love until later in the tour. Of course we
were growing closer all the time but she was engaged to a
sergeant or someone. She left him for me during the tour. We
became lovers in Trieste, I think, and it filled me with guilt
because it had been one of the places I'd been to with Toni. I
felt badly about it. She was not élite as Toni was, but sort of
working-class and very bright with an enquiring mind. She
lived in South London and when the tour ended she invited

me to meet her parents. She warned me her father was an alcoholic and not to trust him, and when it was time to go I had to admit I'd lent him the only five bob I had and I had to borrow my bus fare back to London from Dorita.

Dorita came along to Grafton's and saw something of Spike once the tour was over. As Jimmy remembers her, 'She was a smart young girl, quite ambitious, very attached to Spike, but I think she tried to impose too many conditions on him. He didn't want that. He couldn't be regulated or tied down, he was much too much of a free spirit.'

Dorita was around on and off during the days that followed the *Swinging Along* tour. She disappeared occasionally for work or family commitments but it seems she was very loyal to Spike. Loyalty has figured predominantly in Milligan's life. Over the years, total loyalty has been both given and received by him in enormous quantities. Sometimes, almost to excess.

The Nuffield Centre was flourishing in London at this time. It opened at the old Café de Paris in Piccadilly in 1943, and Mary Cook – who was mostly in charge there – remembers what a splendid little stage it had. In 1944 enemy action destroyed the building, but not the concept, for a fresh Centre was established within weeks at Adelaide Street, WC2. Constantly changing entertainment was provided by way of cabaret and musical acts. These were given freely by the aspiring artists for whom it provided a valuable 'shop window' where they had the chance of being seen working by agents and impresarios.

Mary Cook was a kind, friendly woman, extremely sympathetic to the impoverished young artists returning from the war and desperately needing a start. The artists gave their services free, but most of them gratefully received the liberal amounts of tea and substantial, delicious sandwiches which she provided.

Established artists already appearing in the West End were generous in giving their time to the Nuffield Centre also, and consequently some excellent late-night shows were produced.

Harry Secombe, who had fared better than either Norman Vaughan or Spike at the Windmill, also had success at the Nuffield Centre, and Clifford Thornton, the bandleader, remembers him coming 'round the corner' after his Windmill spots to perform at the Nuffield, replenish himself with the sustaining tea and sandwiches and then nip back to the Windmill for his next appearance. 'Harry Secombe was always a big success at the Nuffield,' he recalls. 'But the Windmill were never privileged to hear his fine tenor voice.'

Spike Milligan made an appearance at the Nuffield Centre on 10 December 1948. It was his first solo opportunity there, though he had appeared earlier as one of the Bill Hall Trio. At his solo appearance he clowned, ad libbed, told jokes, fooled with his guitar and generally reduced the audience (mostly servicemen) to hysterics. The laughter and applause he received bolstered his surprisingly frail confidence, and he began to feel that perhaps he too could perform.

And now and then, in quiet hours at the Grafton Arms, Milligan would find great pleasure in the company of Jimmy Grafton's young children. He told them stories which kept them enchanted. He left notes for them, and made tiny parcels of sweets which purported to come from the good Hobbely Gobbely men, or cross notes from the wicked Alfie of the Boneyard if they misbehaved. These hours dedicated to the children brought Spike a good deal of relaxation and pleasure. With them, he was in his element, rarely too tired or occupied to give them his attention.

Yet if the hours he spent in the Grafton's attic brought him the solitary peace he often craved, by the same token he knew loneliness and depression. There were also troughs of sadness into which he sank and floundered helplessly. Sometimes in the early morning he would wake before anyone was stirring. He would dress and leave the house quietly, making for St James's Park at a fast step. It was often cold and sometimes still dark, but he would stand on the wooden bridge and talk to the sparrows and small birds that were about. Sometimes, when he had remembered to fill his pockets full of crusts the night before, he would feed them. To some extent, the birds seemed to mitigate the loneliness that obsessed him:

> I felt very alone for a lot of the time. I never felt that I made friends easily, it was a sort of isolation – perhaps a self-inflicted isolation some of the time. I'd feel, Oh well, the birds are my friends, anyway.

These moods contrast oddly with the euphoric sessions he was having almost daily with Bentine, Secombe and Sellers.

On 31 December 1948 there was a special New Year's Eve concert at the Nuffield Centre. Harry Secombe was performing, and with him were Trevor Howard and Helen Cherry. Milligan was not present.

Desmond had become eligible for a grant as his education at the Reigate School of Art had been interrupted by call-up. He was accepted at Goldsmith's College for a three-year Diploma of Art course. Now that he was married, he was subject to considerable financial strain and somewhat missed out on the supposedly carefree student years. Flo and Leo were also finding life in this post-war Britain hard and drear. They had never ceased to remember the Indian and Burmese days of hot sun and cloudless blue skies and began to dream of emigrating to Australia, where opportunities and the promise of a sunnier climate seemed very enticing. More importantly, Desmond and his wife showed interest in joining them. Perhaps by now Spike had been given up as lost. Flo was still despairing about that 'proper job', and although she took what interest she could in the ups and downs of his theatrical career it all seemed too insecure and uncertain for her approval. She had lost control, and Spike's failure to meet her social and religious standards was a constant irritant. She was quite resigned to saying goodbye to her unrewarding son.

On 3 June 1949 Spike gave another performance at the Nuffield Centre. On the same bill were Frankie Howerd and a girl called Lynette Rae who had been on the Ann Lennor tour. It is possible that Spike used his influence to get her 'on' at the Nuffield. Spike's performance was noted, and on 16 June *The Raven* (an RAF paper) printed an inconspicuous paragraph:

> *The Raven* doesn't go in for racing tips, but here's a tip straight from the horse's mouth. Keep your eyes open for the name of Spike Milligan. Spike – real name is Terry – is the British answer to Danny Kaye – and how!
>
> I watched his act recently and he brought the audience to the verge of hysterics with his burlesquing.
>
> Spike believes music-hall humour needs a tonic and this former BBC scriptwriter has joined forces with three other rising comedians and formed the Goon's Club. Object – to get decent (and clean) comedians on the air again.
>
> So scan your *Radio Times* for the name of a comic who promises to be the biggest thing since Charlie Chaplin.

Milligan looked at his first write-up uncertainly. No special offers of work had flowed in from his Nuffield exposure, whereas Michael Bentine had been lucky enough to do his five-minute 'broken chair' act at the exact moment the theatrical agents Dennis Selinger and Monty Lyon walked in. His brilliance was recognized and within weeks Michael was appearing at the Palladium.

In the late autumn of 1949, Spike appeared in the *Hip Hip Hoo Roy* radio series. There were thirteen instalments between October and the end of December. Jimmy Grafton, writing about the show in his memoir of these early years, is modest in the extreme:

> Since I was writing for Derek Roy who wanted to progress from *Variety Bandbox* to a series, we conceived a programme rather cornily entitled *Hip Hip Hoo Roy*. The series did not exactly break any windows, but we had great fun writing it and many a long night was punctuated by shrieks of laughter at jokes that amused us if not the listeners.

The early part of 1950 found Spike touring American army and air force centres in East Anglia, appearing as a solo comic with the Frank Weir Orchestra. His own recent army experience was invaluable to him now. He knew what made the men laugh. He spent every free moment concocting jokes, often scribbling down a few lines on the backs of cigarette packets when he ran out of paper. The musician Denny Piercy often sat next to him on the coach as they toured the Norfolk air bases from their hotel in Downham Market. He remembers that Spike was continually writing odd bits of script for his own show, or to send back to Jimmy Grafton in the hope that they would be included in a forthcoming radio programme. Spike was also thinking endlessly of his companions, Harry, Peter and Michael, missing the sessions that went on at Grafton's and wanting to be back.

When the tour wound up, Milligan moved his few possessions from Jimmy Grafton's attic to the flat belonging to Peter Sellers' mother in Golders Green. Hardly an improvement, but change seemed now to be agreeable to

his restless, anxious and excitable nature. The scriptwriting
continued, and the ideas of the Goon Club were in a state
of constant flux. The extraordinary, intuitive and immediate
recognition between the four of them churned under an
almost chemical compulsion whenever they were together.
Milligan, his mind racing far in advance of his writing
capacity, was the most volatile, and perhaps the most
fragile. Jimmy Grafton, in between his duty sessions in the
Grafton Arms, worked tirelessly. He produced an early
tape-recorder and recorded impromptu sessions in the
attic which were sometimes played back to an invited, off-
the-cuff audience after the pub closed. The sessions
'upstairs at Grafton's' became the place to be after closing
time.

Plans were now forging ahead for a trial recording of the
Goons. Pat Dixon and Roy Spear were the ones with their
feet firmly planted in the BBC, and they worked tirelessly
along with Jimmy Grafton to bring the idea of this very
different sort of comedy show to fruition. Another BBC
producer, Jacques Brown, arranged an audition recording
for Spike under the title Tatters Castle. This seemed to
come adrift, and Milligan recalls another attempt that was
also doomed to early extinction – Sellers Castle, featuring
Peter Sellers.

During these frustrating months, Leo and Flo made
the decision and sailed for Australia. Spike said goodbye
cheerfully enough but the feeling of being deserted lurked
in the corner of his mind. Dorita was still around but the
relationship was faltering and work often divided them.
Desmond and his wife lived in South London and were
occupied with arranging their own departure to Australia.
The closeness that both men wanted to find was never to
materialize. Seven years is a long time-gap between two
brothers, and by now their lives had divided sharply.
Spike, for all his nomadic life, had a basic yearning for a

home and was drawn to situations like the Grafton family
and then Mrs Sellers' house. With the Sellers he was
probably able to bask in Peg's approval as someone close
to her son and to stand outside the atmosphere of almost
vitriolic love-hate which existed between Peter and Peg.

Jimmy Grafton was deeply disappointed when Jacques
Brown, rather than Pat Dixon or Roy Spear, was chosen
by the BBC for the early presentation of a pilot *Goon
Show*. They differed largely on the matter of a studio
audience. Jimmy (rightly) felt that an audience was essential to appreciate this sort of humour. The listeners at
home could join with the studio audience, who spent half
their time rocking helplessly with laughter. Jacques felt
otherwise, and presented the pilot to the BBC planners in
a capsule of sterile silence. It is hardly surprising that this
strange and extreme humour with its unheard-of sound
effects fell on mystified ears. Jimmy was deeply angered
by the inevitable failure of a show that had been his
protégé.

The next months were frustrating in the extreme for
Spike, who now conceived a despairing hatred for the
bureaucracy of the BBC which he would never lose. Peter,
Harry and Michael were all achieving success in their
separate shows. Milligan had odd weeks in variety, but
they were not in any way fulfilling, and in financial terms
barely kept body and soul together. A lucky break came
for him when bandleader Joe Loss heard him acting out
bits of his scripts. Spike was engaged for a few weeks as
part of Joe Loss's 1951 *Band Show*.

Joe introduced him at his début in Nottingham with
characteristic generosity. He informed the audience that
the British were relying too much on American talent and
that it was a pleasure to greet a new comedian from 'within
our own shores'. The local paper gave Milligan some
guarded praise:

Spike earned the build-up that Loss gave him. He has a new line in humour which can be described as grotesque knockabout, mingled with the witty rather than the funny story. He was warmly applauded, and when, with experience, he can link more smoothly the peak points in his act, he will be capable of keeping an audience laughing continually.

In the light of what we now know about Milligan's achievements, in the light of our knowledge that he is a man in advance of his time, it would seem that this reviewer may have missed an important point. No doubt Spike did need experience, but perhaps the audience, listening to a radically new sort of humour, needed it even more.

By the combined efforts of Jimmy Grafton, Pat Dixon, Roy Spear and a new producer, Dennis Main Wilson, a new pilot show emerged in February 1951. Then, on 28 May 1951, the first *Goon Show* (then billed as *Those Crazy People, The Goons*) went on the air. The show was to bring fame to all four Goons, three of whom were already well-advanced in their careers; the fourth, Spike Milligan, was to reach heights of superb and unquestioned brilliance as the writer of the scripts.

11

Goons Ascendant

The regular *explosions* in the *Goon Show* grew
out of Milligan's own unpleasant experiences in
the war. By creating a world where explosions
hurt no one, he made his own memories of the
reality more bearable.

Roger Wilmut,
The Goon Show Companion

The *Goon Show*, as it eventually emerged, cut no corners
towards its important place in the history of British
humour. It did not follow a sterile patch in British radio
comedy. Richard Murdoch and Arthur Askey's *Bandwaggon* and Tommy Handley's *ITMA* were hard acts to follow,
and there was also an upsurge of safe, conventional comedy
acts vying for present notice. Denis Norden and Frank
Muir were leading with a highly successful programme
Take It From Here which starred Jimmy Edwards. Jimmy
was a good friend to the embryo Goons and frequently
turned up at the late-night sessions. Another brilliant and
unusual man came into the picture about now – Tony
Hancock, who was to become a close friend of Milligan's.

In addition the BBC hierarchy was unenthusiastic to the
point of churlishness about their gifted fledglings and never
allowed them to feel appreciated or secure. For a good
part of the time they were barely tolerated, and it was
probably this that fuelled the insecurity that has been so
much a part of Milligan's artistic functioning. His youthful
sensitivity had been deeply jarred by the abrupt change
from the relatively affluent 'golden days' in India, when
privilege and plenty gave way almost overnight to deprivation and penny-pinching in South London. Certainly it

seems to have been a very insecure Milligan who, during the early *Goon Show* days, conceived a massive and persistent resentment of the BBC which has never abated.

Yet the BBC, on their side, were perhaps deserving of some degree of sympathy. Perhaps the Goons made *them* feel insecure. Certainly they may have felt that even their jobs would be at risk if the Goons had their way. In the early days they were not a popular programme with producers, and it is no rumour that the threat of being given the Goons to produce made several quite able people go 'sick' or take overdue leave. It cannot be entirely coincidence that at least three producers fell by the wayside before Dennis Main Wilson produced the first successful series.

Two men who were both to become important in Milligan's life were now on the scene: Eric Sykes, busy carving out his own successful career as a scriptwriter but generous with time, skill and encouragement, and Larry Stephens, an ex-Commando captain who was script-writer for Tony Hancock. Both gave Spike a good deal of support and help with his writing. Larry was also a talented pianist, which delighted Milligan whose longing for music as a part of his life has never abated. When they were together they would work on the scripts until they dropped – Milligan, quite literally, under the piano. He would sleep there, undisturbed by Larry, until the morning.

It has been suggested that Milligan's scripts for the *Goon Shows* have been influenced by touches of Kafka, Ionescu and Dylan Thomas. Milligan finds this irritating.

How can I have been influenced by them? I never read Kafka, or Ionescu, or Thomas. I believe people make these protestations just to show their own learning, just to remind people that they have read all these important writers. I didn't need to go to books for influences. I got my influences listening to the Members of Parliament making fools of themselves in the House of Commons – listening to the bus conductor grumbling about the crowds and arguing with the man who tried to bring a dog kennel or a double-bass on the bus. My influences were all around me, in real life. I didn't have to go to books to look for them.

After the first six weeks, *Crazy People* had moved up gradually from a not very prestigious 6.45 P.M. on a Monday to peak time on a Thursday. The *Radio Times* item read:

7.45 CRAZY PEOPLE

RADIO'S OWN CRAZY GANG

THE GOONS

HARRY SECOMBE, PETER SELLERS, MICHAEL BENTINE,

SPIKE MILLIGAN

WITH

THE RAY ELLINGTON QUARTET

THE STARGAZERS, MAX BELDRAY

THE DANCE ORCHESTRA

CONDUCTED BY STANLEY BLACK

SCRIPT BY SPIKE MILLIGAN

ADDITIONAL MATERIAL BY LARRY STEPHENS

AND JIMMY GRAFTON

PRODUCED BY DENNIS MAIN WILSON

BBC RECORDING

(Peter Sellers is appearing in Variety at the London Palladium; Michael Bentine at the Winter Gardens Theatre, Morecambe; Harry Secombe in *Happy-Go-Lucky* at the Opera House, Blackpool.)

In 1951 *London Entertains* was released, a short film directed by E. J. Fancey in which all the Goons except Michael Bentine took part. The screenplay (about girls from a Swiss finishing school running an escort agency in London) was written by Jimmy Grafton. It ran for 50 minutes, and attracted little notice. Copies exist (on video) of *Let's Go Crazy*, another short film released about this time. Only Spike and Peter Sellers appeared in it. Pressed to remember the occasion, Spike says succinctly, 'I think that it was a load of shit.'

The Goons were not without a little publicity. The *News Chronicle* gave them an interesting advance notice: 'GOONS TAKE THE AIR – A STRANGE PHENOM-ENON IN RADIO'. The article ended:

> Optimistically (because it has really no idea what is going to happen on May 28th), the BBC officially describes GOONISM as 'A rather extravagant form of humour.' On May 29th they will probably consider this definition a remarkable understatement.

After only twelve broadcasts the Goons also received the accolade of being discussed by *The Critics* on the BBC's prestigious Third Programme.

Spike was first introduced to June Marlowe by Peter Sellers in the winter of 1949. Peter was enthusiastically courting Anne Howe, a young actress of great beauty and charm. June was her friend, and as Peter and Anne were planning an evening out at the Edgwarebury Country Club Spike was persuaded to come along and make up a foursome. Milligan, at this stage in his life, was no longer inexperienced with girls but he was still shy and uncertain of himself and more so with the confident and sophisticated young women he was meeting in show business circles. Perhaps he was at some level trying to mitigate his shyness when he told Peter that he would come on condition that he was allowed to masquerade as a foreigner who spoke little English. Make-believe was normal for Sellers, so he raised no objections and Spike dressed carefully for the occasion in a velvet jacket that he had purloined from the wardrobe of the Combined Services Entertainments depot.

> I had no money at all. Peter had the money, but I said I would go on condition that I could pretend I didn't understand a word they were saying. We agreed my name was Jules, and that I was an Italian. I had very curly black hair then. We had to go pick her up at Sherwood Road in Hendon. June Marlowe greeted me at the door in a bathtowel. She was like a sexbomb, statuesque, jet-black haired, dark-eyed. I'd never been to an expensive house, it was very upper middle class, I suppose, an elaborate house, grand in a modern way. Her father was a well-off Italian who made money by manufacturing expensive clothes for the gentry.

At the Edgwarebury Club, June and Spike danced together and sat out between dances, chatting. He maintained his act of baffled foreigner and his pidgin English drew laughter from the people around. He was being mildly scorned as some sort of idiot when June sprang to his defence. 'No, don't be so cruel about him,' she said. 'He's a very charming person. He's a very nice boy – he just doesn't understand our language, that's all.' This was too much for Spike, who capsized with laughter and owned up to the masquerade. June was not pleased, but she must have forgiven him, for before the evening ended they arranged a future meeting. Dorita, away on tour whilst all this was happening, now dropped finally out of the picture.

Spike's conscience about her was never quite dormant. In 1984 he received a note from Dorita when he was appearing in his one-man show in Sydney, Australia.

> I thought that I must ring her up, so I did and I said 'I owe you the greatest apology in the world' and she burst into tears. I'd always felt awful about the way I dropped her for June. Anyway, we went out for dinner and she was still a lovely person, hadn't changed at all.

But the impact of June must have been considerable in 1950.

I met June again and again. I suppose I was sexually attracted to her. I was still pretty immature as a person at thirty. I'd never known anything except my mother's home, and then the army took over from her and arranged everything for me. I'd never known any responsibility at all, toured around in the war a bit but never had any real responsibility.

June's family, like the Milligans, were on the point of emigrating to Australia. June's passage was already booked; perhaps this gave a poignancy to the situation that existed between Spike and June:

Well, I thought that would be it and I'd never see her again. I suppose I thought that I'd write to her in Australia. We went to a little restaurant near Leicester Square, and she said to me, 'Look, why don't we get engaged before I go.' So I was so stunned I said, 'Oh! All right.' I never asked her to marry me. I just wanted to please everybody, so I said, 'All right, then.' So we got engaged, then she said, 'Look, why don't we get married before I go away.' So I said, 'Well, all right, but you're going away?' And she said, 'Well, my father insists that I go to Australia with him first and then I can come back.' So we got married at Caxton Hall in Victoria – we had a couple of days' honeymoon in a hotel on the Bayswater Road and then she was away and gone.

Spike and June married on 26 January 1952 – their wedding day was four days after the transmission of the first programme in the second *Goon Show* series. Enmeshed in this, Spike was working at such intense pressure that he hardly noticed June's departure, which is not to say that he had not enjoyed the brief and ecstatic Bayswater Road honeymoon. June, in a blissful daze, acquiesced willingly enough to her parents' demands, and sailed with them to

Australia. Before long, her seasickness gave way to morning sickness. The Milligans' first child was on the way.

In England, the people mourned the death of George VI, and the young Princess Elizabeth became Queen. Spike barely noticed these events, barely thought of his new and absent wife, barely ate and slept spasmodically in a variety of places, under Larry Stephens' piano or in Peter Sellers' mother's kitchen whenever fatigue completely overcame him. Day and night, he thought of nothing except the next week's *Goon Show*. The need for more and funnier scripts obsessed him. Larry Stephens, talented and experienced, was by now enrolled as official assistant scriptwriter and there is no doubt that his disciplined approach was of value to Milligan, who acknowledged no rules and accepted no conventions in comedy. His mind whirled in a continuum of new and still more far-fetched ideas. The battles with the BBC became fiercer and wilder. Harry, Michael and Peter had learned to trust him, and dissent, once the script was flung together, was rare. Similarly, Spike knew that once he had triggered the gun, his mates could be relied upon never to let him down. Spontaneous and absurd improvisations embellished the scripts. The moment the four of them got together the magic began. The rare and superlative chemistry never seemed to fail.

When Spike received the news from Australia that June was pregnant he became in rapid succession startled, excited and dismayed. The idea of a child thrilled him, but he felt a certain apprehension. He had no settled home, no money and even arranging some finance towards June's return journey put him into debt. He discussed the matter with Peter Sellers, who was helpful. Peter had a relative who was connected with Mendoza, the house agents. Some small flats were to become available at Shepherds Hill in Highgate; he and Anne were taking one so what could

be more delightful than for Spike and June to set up
housekeeping nearby? This seemed to be a solution; Spike
accepted it with relief. That flat would not be ready for
several weeks; as a stop-gap he was able to rent a furnished
flat on Hornton Street, behind Kensington High Street.
June arrived back from Australia; there was a happy
reunion and for a while all went well. She rested and
began preparations for the baby. Spike kept constant trysts
with his *Goon Show* confederates, and the scripts emerged
each week, feverishly and just on time. It was a period
of domestic happiness which partially insulated Milligan
against the stress he was under at the BBC. The second
series of *Goon Show*s came to an end in July 1952 and
the BBC authorities afforded the Goons no grounds for
complacency about their future. They still met with constant threats and rebukes, and the innovative ideas that
bubbled endlessly from them were regarded with a suspicion, disdain and general lack of co-operation which
drove Milligan – as the scriptwriter – to the end and
beyond.

The first and second series of *Goon Show*s ran from 28
May 1951 until 15 July 1952. There is no doubt that they
were both hilarious and unique. They were also never far
from annihilation by the shocked and unmollified administrators at the BBC.

A new producer, Peter Eton, played a vitally important
role now. Peter Eton was a highly professional man, and
something of a stickler for discipline. These admirable
traits, however, were cut with the rare gift of being able to
step ahead of his age; with the awareness of a visionary he
would meet Milligan's apparently outrageous ideas with
delighted recognition, even when that recognition was
coupled with necessary rejection. His considerable respect
for the Goons' ideas and his immediate joy in them was
beautifully laced with a firm certainty that at the end of

the day he knew best. He forged a splendid relationship with Peter and Harry but he was particularly close to Spike who, to him, seemed the most talented, the most vulnerable and often the most in need. Milligan found a great deal of strength in Peter Eton, a well-read, well-informed man who understood the disproportionate yet ineradicable frustration that Spike's lack of formal education caused him. Perhaps he was the first person since Tony Goldsmith who had actually recognized a mind that was seemingly starved for knowledge and was capable of soaking it up like a giant sponge.

Peter and Harry had no such hang-ups. Peter possibly suffered inherent feelings of inadequacy, but he had a capacity for isolating himself from unacceptable details, and he could, almost at will, become a university professor or a Guards officer. Harry, secure from childhood in warmth, love and an admiring family, applied himself decisively to the present, and even in these early days had his feet firmly planted on the road to success. He was the least trouble to Peter Eton, who found him the most delightful of all the Goons to work with, and Spike probably the most demanding, even though the most rewarding.

Michael Bentine, the only one of the Goons who already had something of a name in show business, left after the second series. Rumours flew that there had been a big quarrel. Everyone – including Michael – gave different reasons. No ill-will seems to have been generated, however. A few years ago when Milligan received a letter on 'The Goon Show Preservation Society' writing paper, he wrote to them to say that Michael's name should be on it, along with Peter's, Harry's and his own. 'Well, they shouldn't have put us all on it and left him off,' said Spike. 'He was one of the Goons, wasn't he, in the beginning? And he was marvellous as Dr Osric Pureheart; he was so funny we used to cry.'

The film *Down Among the Z Men* was released in 1952. This film had the single distinction of showing all the Goons. Even allowing for the low budget and relatively early days this jape about stolen atomic secrets is a poor film, with only Peter Sellers showing anything of the mammoth amount of talent that the director, Maclean Rogers, had on his hands. Milligan's performance was dismal.

Asked about it years later Spike was vague.

Well, I never thought I had any talent to perform. I thought the others were the performers, and I was the writer, just chipping in now and again. They only wanted me as a fool and I was a fool already, so there was nothing for me to do, was there? I just took it for granted, and said things how they told me to say them.

Now well advanced in her pregnancy, June was anxious to go with Spike on shopping expeditions to equip their future home at Highgate. Money was a constant problem. At this stage Milligan was receiving a salary of £25 per week as a scriptwriter and this had to cover the rent of the furnished flat as well as their current living expenses and what necessities they could afford towards their future home. They went together to buy a three-piece suite for their sitting-room and Milligan has a confused memory of rushing around buying sheets and kitchen items and, above all, of worrying deeply about money.

On the morning of 1 November 1952, June went into labour. Spike was terrified. He rang his friend and colleague Graham Stark, who raced round in his small two-seater car to collect them. On the way to Southwood Hospital, N6, they were stopped by the police for speeding. Spike, white-faced and stuttering badly, explained. The police were sympathetic and let them go. They drove with more caution until they arrived at the hospital. The

three extricated themselves from the car with difficulty and
it was with some relief that Spike and Graham prepared to
hand June over to medical care. Their relief was short-
lived. The Matron emerged from her office, firmly rebuked
June and her baby for arriving two weeks ahead of schedule
and, after a short telephone call, informed them that they
must now make all haste to the Royal Northern Hospital in
Holloway Road.

Stunned by this further complication the anxious trio
packed themselves once more into the car. They drove a
short distance without any clear idea of the route they
should take. June's labour was steadily advancing and
beads of perspiration were rolling down her face. Spike
was so frightened he was quite unable to cope. Then
Graham spotted one of the new Hendon-trained police
officers sitting astride his massive motor-bike glumly sur-
veying the busy road junction by Highgate Station. He
parked the car and ran across to get directions. Graham
recalls:

From then on it was all stations say go. This chap had been
sitting there on his bike with nothing to do for weeks, waiting
for something to happen. Now it had – we'd turned up. 'Follow
me,' he said, and roared off down Archway Road, blaring his
horn. He was in his element – for months he'd been waiting.
Now he was finally cast – he had a role.

The little car jolted into action once again as Graham
put his foot down. According to its owner it never went so
fast before or after that day. In the attempt to keep up
with their powerful leader, they bounced at speed all over
the road. In the early hours of 2 November 1952, June was
safely delivered of a baby daughter. Thirty years later,
Spike is still distraught at the recollection. 'They held her
up for me to see, through a pane of glass,' he remembers.

'I think she had a broken nose or something, but she was lovely.'

Nine days after Laura was born, the first *Goon Show* of the third series was broadcast. The Milligans had moved into their new home just a few weeks before Laura's birth, and immediately after seeing his baby daughter Spike went back to the empty flat where he began painting the small room scheduled for Laura's use. He covered the walls with strange and curious creatures. He remembers a huge, cartoon-type of fly, and a weird, crab-like crawling animal.

> They were most unsuitable for a baby, I suppose. I don't know what got into me, I daresay I was a bit mad. I wanted to make a special welcome for her. I don't know what June felt about all this. She must have thought me a bit mad.

The day before June and Laura arrived home Spike began work on the next script. After all the months of writing in Jimmy Grafton's attic or Peter Sellers' mother's flat, or even a convenient shake-down under Larry Stephens' piano, it had seemed highly desirable to work in his own flat and up till now working at home with June had been reasonably successful. But both June and Spike were totally unprepared for the advent of an infant into their lives. Spike remembered the birth of his brother Desmond in Rangoon. An experienced mother and capable ayah had managed the event with efficient calm, and life had progressed for the seven-year-old Terence with hardly a ripple on the surface. Baby Laura's advent was by comparison catastrophic. A few hours after she had arrived home, June went down with a serious bout of post-natal fever. She was running a high temperature, ill and incoherent. 'Please take care of the baby,' she said, handing a wailing Laura to Spike. 'I think I'm ill. I must lie down.'

The nightmare now began in earnest. June was indeed
ill, with puerperal fever. A doctor ordered a full-time
nurse to care for the mother and baby. Spike was sleeping
on the sofa and trying to care for the baby during the
times that the nurse required her time off. He had difficulty
in mixing the feeds, and a couple in the flat above tried to
help. It would seem that they were more kind than
competent, for Laura was given the wrong strength of milk
mixture and she in turn became ill. The nurse, a New
Zealand girl of little sophistication and no experience of
scriptwriters, decided that her distraught and wild-eyed
employer was surely an alcoholic, and this information was
gratuitously given to all comers.

Milligan reeled under the cumulative pressures of
responsibility for the *Goon Show* scripts and (to him) the
more arduous responsibilities of marriage and fatherhood:

> I'd never known this sort of responsibility in my life. It'd
> always been my mother, or the army or something. And of
> course there were no grandparents to call for help from –
> June's parents and mine, all gone away to Australia. I didn't
> know what to do or where to turn and the worries of the *Goon
> Show* were escalating, and I was needing pounds a week for a
> nurse – it was an impossible nightmare.

Living almost next door to Peter Sellers was not an
invariable advantage. There were occasions when Spike
had, with difficulty, fallen asleep in the intervals between
frenzied scriptwriting and attending to the domestic needs
of Laura, June and the nurse when Peter would arrive in
the Milligans' flat, at any hour of the day or night (usually
the night), to consult Spike on ideas for the *Goon Show* or
to play a new gramophone record. Not to accept his
arrival with some apparent pleasure would have been
inconceivable to Spike, so further inroads were made on
his already minuscule periods of sleep.

At the BBC, Milligan was having constant rows over the failure of their technical departments to produce the complex sound effects he demanded, and over their censorship in areas that he considered to be integral to the show.

Harry Secombe recalls this time with a warm sympathy:

> It was enough to make anyone go off the rails. It was worse for Spike than for us. He was the writer, and they put up enormous blanks in his way. Everything Spike said would be funny, half the things he put up, they would say 'Oh no, you can't do that.' We took it more in our stride but it drove Spike up the wall.

Milligan is seldom happy to talk about the *Goon Show* days: it would seem that the hours of their great success are for him permanently overshadowed by the memories of the frustration and struggles that constantly ensued.

> We were trying to break out into satire. We were ripe for it. Peter could do any voice of any politician in the land – the Queen included. That made us lethal. They were all frightened of their little fucking jobs. We were ready to break out – we could have beaten the Fringe by ten years. The BBC did frustrate me very badly.

The constant, unending frustration in work and the bewildering anxieties of marriage and fatherhood were now capped by what was perhaps the most grotesque pressure of all – the recurring need to produce a very funny thirty-minute script every seven days. Milligan was fast reaching a crisis.

Spike received a stream of letters from the BBC. One arrived after a particularly bad night when June was in great pain caused by a breast abscess and Laura had been crying almost without pause. Milligan, light-headed from lack of sleep, was working frenetically on the current script. The letter read:

Dear Mr Milligan,

It has been reported to me by Mr Peter Eton that despite his constant requests for early delivery, your scripts for the above production continue to arrive late – in some cases not until the morning of the pre-recording.

Perhaps the letters were the last straw. Milligan pressed his hands to his head. His head felt full of agonizing pain and he had the frightening sensation that his brain was going to burst wide open. He believed he was going mad. Weird hallucinations raced round his mind. With a frightening clarity, he knew that his sanity was deserting him. He felt in desperate need of help, but had no idea how to seek it. Perhaps the way he chose, consciously or subconsciously, was as good as any. It certainly worked. He grabbed a potato knife from the confusion in the kitchen and ran into Peter Sellers' flat:

I was so mad I thought that if I killed Peter it would all come right. I think I just wanted them to lock me up. I was totally demented. Poor Peter hadn't done anything.

For the next three months, Milligan was out of the *Goon Shows*. He was taken to a nearby hospital in Muswell Hill, where he was for some time put in a straitjacket and kept in an isolation ward. He was treated mainly with sedating drugs and given some therapy. Psychiatrists counselled absolute rest and quiet, but within days he was sitting up in bed, struggling with the scripts. His hair was matted and tousled, his skin pallid and his eyes staring. His mood veered between anger and anxious despair. The memory to him now is of wretchedness and misery:

It was just a terrible nightmare of doctors who couldn't help me and nurses who kept taking away my pencils and saying 'You must rest', and all the time I kept knowing for certain that I must go on writing. I felt frantic because I knew I had a wife and baby to support.

Meanwhile Leo and Florence were establishing themselves in Australia without much knowledge of what was happening to Spike. Florence sent a photograph of herself, looking very firm and capable, her hair tied up in a scarf like the munition workers of the 'forties. She was working in a factory assembling electrical components.

June, recovered from her illness, took baby Laura in a pram to visit her sick father. Sometimes Spike stared miserably at her, afraid to touch her. Sometimes he would take her on his lap and talk to her. His moods towards June also were variable. Sometimes he was pleased to see her, sometimes he would refuse to have her near him. It was a very difficult and unhappy time for them both.

Yet one way and another, the *Goon Show* prospered through its third series. When Spike first collapsed, Jimmy Grafton took over, and in the absence of both Milligan and Larry Stephens (Larry was also unwell) he wrote the fifth show completely alone. On other shows in the series Eric Sykes also helped. There was barely time to get in new actors. Peter Sellers' legendary capacity for mimicry was never needed more: he was able to take over all Spike's parts. With typical and unobtrusive generosity, Harry Secombe took care of some of Spike's housekeeping bills. In subsequent weeks Dick Emery and Graham Stark joined the cast from time to time, and by the middle of March 1953 Spike was able to go back into the show.

He was apparently restored to health, but there was an added dimension of rigidly controlled pain which he struggled to mask. His sense of isolation had been heightened, not lessened, by his experiences.

Seventeen years later, the film director John Goldschmidt made a documentary film in which Milligan relived the traumatic time of his admission to hospital. He said, 'I was in the hands of the human race, which as you know can be the very worst thing to be in the hands of.'

It was Peter Eton who had the brilliant insight now to give Milligan Rabelais to read. Milligan revelled in the Rabelaisian language and the exuberant imagination of the sixteenth-century French writer. They fired his own imagination and ideas of fantastic comedy.

During its third series the *Goon Show* continued to grow in popularity, and Spike, even in the midst of his breakdown, seemed to learn a great deal from Larry Stephens, who was thoroughly experienced in working for radio. The last few shows of this series were linked to real events – *The Ascent of Mount Everest*, for example, almost coincided with the real event in the summer of 1953.

This linking of many of the *Goon Shows* to their time in history in no way detracts from the contemporary pleasure people still take in listening to the original recordings. The humour has some nostalgic value, but its very freshness seems to have worn so well that we can still laugh. What was so new to the radio audiences of the 'fifties now seems almost timeless, classic.

The death of Queen Mary in March 1953 resulted in holding over the twentieth *Goon Show* for a week. It was now almost the end of the series; all the Goons – and Peter Eton – breathed sighs of relief.

Spike returned to the family flat at Shepherds Hill. He was still working frenetically but seemed frustrated and on edge for much of the time. June eyed him warily, and with some dismay. His breakdown had shaken her equilibrium very deeply. She felt that in some way she had become alienated from him and this was a source of distress. She had no experience of mental illness, no yardstick by which to measure her strange and talented husband. The disappearance of both sets of grandparents undoubtedly had a bearing on the growing feelings of isolation and despondency she felt. Even their mutual delight in Laura was to some extent clouded by the anxiety that the new responsibility brought them both.

June would see young couples proudly pushing a pram and doing the weekend shopping together, and feel thwarted that her husband, brittle and unapproachable, was hunched over a manuscript, his eyes staring and his hair tousled. Spike would feel overburdened with the responsibility for the scripts, even though he had valuable help from both Larry Stephens and Eric Sykes. An inability to delegate responsibility successfully is an integral part of his functioning now: almost certainly it was one of his failings in the past.

In July 1953 Peter Sellers was playing a summer season in Bournemouth. Spike, June and Laura, now eight months old, booked into an hotel for a short visit. Now that the third series had successfully ended, Spike was already occupying himself with the fourth. Whenever the Goons were together, they chipped in eagerly with their ideas and reactions to what Spike had in mind. Roger Wilmut, who produced an impressive book called *The Goon Show Companion*, writes of this time: 'The Goons had now reached the plateau which *ITMA* occupied for most of its run – though by their own route and in their own style. Ahead of them were some of the greatest comedy performances ever broadcast.'

12

Associated London Scripts

Pull the blinds
  on your emotions
Switch off your face.
Put your love into neutral
This way to the human race

Spike Milligan,
Small Dreams of a Scorpion

Being able to go to an office every day was a fringe benefit
which Milligan gained from the establishment of a company
he founded called Associated London Scripts. The nearest
thing that this impressive-sounding body could be likened
to is perhaps a writers' co-operative. Ever since the early
days at Grafton's the established scriptwriters in their
group had been asked to write material for performers
who needed it, while would-be scriptwriters were looking
for artists who wanted material. It seemed a good idea to
get a group of scriptwriters together, who could both write
for their own needs and help to find outlets for other
writers. Spike and Eric Sykes were joined in this enterprise
by Alan Simpson and Ray Galton, who were already well-
established writing for Tony Hancock. Eric Sykes wrote
for Jimmy Edwards and Frankie Howerd. Milligan, of
course, was writing full tilt at the *Goon Show.* Associated
London Scripts was not established primarily to make
money, and it ran on a fairly modest budget for some
time. Its first office was at 130 Shepherd's Bush Road,
over a greengrocer's shop.

Spike first went to 130 Shepherd's Bush Road to visit
Eric Sykes.

Eric was working with an agent called Scruffy Dale. I went up
to this office, there were two floors of empty offices, Eric
Sykes sitting in one of them wearing an overcoat that really
looked like a djellaba, you know, those things that go right
down to the ground. It looked like a shroud, he was so thin. I
said to him – I had a mind to business – pity that all these
offices are empty. Why don't we form what is desperately
needed in this country, a writers' commune?

The idea worked well. The writers were all grateful to
have a place where they could work and discuss ideas,
pace one another mentally and generally keep in contact.
Scruffy Dale, probably by virtue of owning the offices,
became a director of the company. This didn't work out,
and before long he was given a large farewell gift for his
rather meagre part in establishing the business. The office,
of course, was usually in an unbelievable mess, four
men working frantically in their shirtsleeves, telephones
ringing, loud calls for tea going on all the time. There was
a lot of fooling about as artists dropped in to discuss scripts,
and often, when business was apparently at its height,
everyone in sight feverishly occupied and the telephone
ringing non-stop, someone (usually Milligan) would suggest
lunch, and within moments the office would empty as
company directors, assistants, friends and hangers-on
would make a beeline for Bertorelli's. On a good day,
lunch could take all afternoon; then would come the
procession back to work. There was often some burning of
the midnight oil to make up for the long lunch hours, and
it was not unheard-of for Spike to wrap himself up in a
couple of old coats and sleep in the office to save himself
the long tube ride back to Highgate.

As the confusion mounted, Milligan, Simpson, Sykes
and Galton made an important decision. What Associated
London Scripts lacked was a typist or secretary to whom
they could give orders. Giving orders to each other was

getting four hypermanic writers nowhere. At periods of
high activity the calls for tea were constant and frequently
unheard. Also, not all of them were capable of making a
decent cup. Spike, with his early training as tea-boy at
Strakers, reinforced by the army years when 'brewing
up' (even, sometimes, under shellfire) was constant and
therapeutic, undoubtedly made the best tea. But as he
was invariably struggling with *Goon Show* deadlines he
was usually too fraught to take on the task himself. The
idea of a girl who would act as handmaiden, tea-maker,
telephonist and typist was born. For a few more weeks
they went on assuring each other that this was what was
needed. Not surprisingly, none of them was sufficiently
organized to make the obvious move of contacting an
agency or advertising. Alan Simpson was the one who
consolidated the idea with a firm suggestion that he would
bring along a young girl he knew who had excellent
secretarial skills and lots of intelligence. 'She's exactly what
we need,' he said. He was, in fact, absolutely right, and
the engagement of Beryl Vertue was an important event in
all their lives, especially, perhaps, in the life of the young
woman herself.

Beryl Vertue was twenty-one, married, and newly
recovered from an attack of tuberculosis of the lung.
She was a bright young woman, quiet, intelligent and
unambitious. Looking back at herself, she says now, 'I
really was Miss Suburbia 1954.' Her doctor had ordered
an easy job without much travelling. The journey from her
home at Eltham to Victoria took half an hour by train, and
Beryl found an easy post in an insurance office only a
stone's throw from the station. This seemed to be what the
doctor meant and Beryl was quite happy. Then Alan
Simpson persuaded her, rather against her will, to make
the tedious trolley-bus journey from Victoria to Shepherd's
Bush for an interview. It seemed a bad idea to Beryl, who

liked getting home on time with a minimum of travelling and effort. 'I really don't want to change,' she told Alan. 'Honestly, I'm happy where I am.' 'OK,' said Alan. 'But please do just come and talk to them. I've told them about you and at least they'll see that you exist.' He assured Beryl that there would be no need for her seriously to consider the job, so more to oblige Alan than anything else she went.

Beryl's first sight of Spike was startling. He was tow-haired and dark-eyed, without jacket or tie, and was sitting hunched in a crumpled shirt and braces. She was unused to such informality with a prospective employer. Eric Sykes was sorting wildly through his papers and Alan, her friend, was sitting on the floor surrounded by a litter of scripts. It all looked extremely unusual to Beryl after the formality of the Legal and General office with its actuarial executives and well-groomed clerks. Beryl sat down gingerly, holding her handbag nervously and straightening her skirt. She was the model of a prim secretary. Milligan immediately took charge of the interview and fired questions at her. None of them seemed relevant. What made her laugh? Where did she live? Had she any sisters or brothers? Most importantly, did she make good tea? Beryl sat it through with a growing sense of unreality. No one questioned her references or asked about her speeds (which were excellent) or even whether she could spell or add up. She looked at the dishevelled four in wonderment. Milligan suddenly jumped to his feet. 'Well, I think you'll be perfect for us.' He beamed all round. 'Don't you agree, fellas? How much do you want for salary?' Beryl saw a loophole. She had, apparently, committed herself to a job she did not want and to take on work which she could not visualize. She added several pounds to her existing salary and asked for ten pounds a week. It was an unusually large salary for her qualifications at that time. Milligan wasn't dismayed. 'That's OK,' he said. 'That's two pounds ten shillings each for us. We can manage that, can't we?'

The interview ended in cheerful confusion and Beryl caught the trolley-bus for the long ride back to Victoria. She was baffled and bemused by the outcome. How had she managed to get an indeterminate job with these very strange people? Amazed and a little apprehensive, she caught the train at Victoria and went home to discuss these extraordinary events with her young husband.

Any possibility that Beryl was to end up as 'Miss Suburbia 1954' ended that day. For the next twelve years, she was to be almost totally committed to Spike Milligan and his associates. Even the birth of two little daughters during that time hardly made a ripple on the surface of her new life. 'They gave me six weeks off when Debbie was born,' she recalls, 'but I only got three for the next one. I expect they thought I'd got the hang of it by that time.'

The Goons were all too active to be cautious or conservative, and they were ever ready for experiment. Before the next series of shows commenced, they tried, unsuccessfully, to link themselves with the Peter Brough programme *Educating Archie*. Archie was the ventriloquist's doll. He brought great success to his owner but he did not happily mix with the Goons, although he had encountered Harry Secombe at an earlier date. Eric Sykes was scriptwriter to Archie and it was during the attempt to get Archie in Goonland going that Milligan and Sykes formed a friendship which has endured through many difficulties, rarely of their own making. After this initial working together they collaborated frequently, and Sykes came in to stand by with help on the *Goon Shows* when Larry Stephens was not available.

The next experiment the Goons tried was piloted almost entirely by Spike and very nearly resulted in the show's being axed once and for all. *The Starlings* was broadcast on 31 August 1954. It was within the *Goon Show* format, with the musical interludes, but was presented as a straight radio play. London, apparently, is suffering from a plague of starlings in Trafalgar Square and the methods used to disperse them are riotous and pure anarchic Goon. Bureaucracy is ridiculed and the BBC heartlessly mocked. Peter Sellers excelled, as usual, in a number of roles, one of them Dinglebee, the announcer who addresses the crowds gathered in the square. The Tannoy, of course, faults perfectly as a preliminary.

DINGLEBEE: Here in the Great Square of Trafalgar which, as we all know, takes its name from the great Underground Railway that runs directly beneath its flagstones – here all is in readiness for the great Explodable Bird Mixture inauguration –

Dinglebee's hushed tones, of course, are curiously like the famous Richard Dimbleby's, and when Harry introduces Lady Boil de Spudswell she is a near-to-perfect replica of the Queen.

HARRY: Ahem, my Lords, Ladies and Gintlepong. Pray silence for the Duchess Boil de Spudswell, Dim of the Empire and at present appearing in Television's "That's Your Lot", "Where's Your Bonce", "What's Up Now", "Who's Your Dad", "Look What's Come" – and other edifying panel games. She appears here this evening by arrangement with the makers of "Footo", the wonder boot exploder.

DINGLEBEE (Hushed): With that great, dignified sound – she steps up to the great microphone.

LADY B (On Tannoy): Ladies and Gentlemen – it is – (Tannoys go dead, except for odd noises).

ENGINEER (Tannoy): PHOO phoooo phoooo hello hello testing one two three four. Yus, that's alrite, gel.

LADY B (Tannoy): Ladies and Gentlemen, it is my privilege and provelege to name this experiment "Operation Explodable Bird Mixture" and may all who stand on it perish –

We move then to "FURIOUS SCENE in the House of Commons".

> OMNES: YOU SWINE – HOW DARE YOU – WE'VE LOST MILLIONS – THE MARKET'S FALLING – IDIOT – IMBECILE – DOLT –
>
> W.C: Lads, lads – Quiet now. Let's have a fair hearing. Now Mr Bladdock, Minister of Bird Pest Control?
>
> BLADDOCK: Mr Prime Minister – Hon. Mems. I fear that the explodable bird-lime was a mite too powerful – but fear not, St Martin's will be rebuilt.
>
> TIM: But the starlings will only roost on it again.
>
> BLADDOCK: If they do, we'll blow it up again. Naturally we would rebuild again – but if the starlings still persist in roosting there – we'll have no compunction but to blow it up yet again. We'll see who gets tired first.

The play ends with an announcement by the long-suffering Andrew Timothy (Tim):

> That was the starlings that was. A comment by Spike Milligan, author of the *Goon Show*, on the recent efforts to rid Trafalgar Square of starlings. All parts were played by Peter Sellers, Harry Secombe and Spike Milligan. Other Pests were played by the Starlings themselves. Technical Production by Harry Green and Barry Wilson. I am the Announcer. Andrew Timothy is the name. I am asked to say that any resemblance to a *Goon Show* is due to the laxity of the producer, Peter Eton. Good Night.

Andrew had begun with the Goons as their straitlaced announcer. The Goons were lucky; a sense of the ridiculous lurked beneath Andrew's staid exterior, and he allowed himself to be bullied and chivvied into every comic diversion possible. He was loved by all of them, and in due course became godfather to Harry's son.

The BBC took tremendous exception to this particular programme and the Goons might well have reached the end of their rope had it not been for the intervention of

John Snagge, a senior announcer who commanded a good deal of respect and who, not surprisingly, was also a committed Goon fan. The anger of certain BBC officials can be assessed by their urgent demand that the show should be summarily axed. It was now at the end of the fourth series, the fifth set up and ready to start. The Goons had now reached a height of popularity which they were to retain to the end.

On 19 September 1954 June gave birth to a little boy. Conditions at home were not tranquil, but the domestic situation was improved by the fact that Spike now had an office to work in. The boy was called Sean, and at the age of six weeks he was baptized along with his sister, two-year-old Laura, whose own christening had somehow been overlooked. The service was at the Church of Our Lady of Dolours in Hendon. The christening photographs show an attractive young couple, ensconced in their comfortable home with two delightful children. Their future was not to be as promising as it might have looked.. There was a lot of unhappiness in store for this family, as unavoidable as it was undeserved.

The next series of *Goon Shows* (the fifth) ran from September 1954 to March 1955. They were again produced by Peter Eton, and now they had the advantage of magnetic tape which meant much easier editing: unacceptable 'ad libs' could be removed without difficulty. Eric Sykes and Larry Stephens continued to collaborate with Milligan intermittently over the next two or three years, but by now Spike had become a polished and able scriptwriter in his own right. His capacity for work was quite extraordinary. Eric Sykes has said that during these *Goon Show* years Milligan, single-handed, did the work of several people every week. He did not achieve this without a good deal of mental suffering, and the massive burden he carried must bear some relation to the unhappiness that lay ahead for Spike, June and their children.

Another severe depression sent Spike into a private nursing home for a few weeks. June wrote to her parents-in-law in Australia:

> I *hate* this beastly flat. Spike's been ill since we got here. He has nowhere to be alone – still, I'm here all the time, at least he is away for weeks and all day. I go out one evening a week, otherwise I'd go barmy. The children have been in quarantine for measles, luckily Spike was in the nursing home so it doesn't matter, but *has* he had them? I couldn't stand it if he gets them as well as the children.

June was, at least, delighted with her children. She sent photographs of 2½-year-old Laura and Sean aged 7½ months to Leo and Flo and concluded her letter with the news that Sean had now got two big teeth and two more coming, that Laura was wonderful and that Spike had put on weight.

Interest was now turning constantly to television. If the Goons were seriously worried about the influence this might have on their by now famous radio series, none of them showed it. On 21 September 1955 the *Daily Sketch* carried a short article by its television critic, John Balfour.

> Half of civilised Britain tuned in to TV or the Light programme last night – to celebrate Wilfred Pickles' 25 years of marriage. It was an extraordinary tribute to the nation's common man number one.
>
> But me and 2,999,999 other listeners were over on the Home Service with the Goons. After a wintry absence of six months the highly esteemed *Goon Show* returned to the air. And it would have taken more even than mixed pickles to keep the followers of the uncommonest band of comics in Britain away from 303 metres last night.
>
> The *Goon Show* is pure radio. It is surrealist fantasy –

involving the brilliant use of sound effects and the combined talents of Spike Milligan, Eric Sykes, Peter Sellers and Harry Secombe.

It gained a million listeners last year and remains something of a radio enigma. Thousands of listeners profess not to understand it. But a vast army of others – including a worthy spattering of highbrows – claim it is the most original and rewarding radio series since *ITMA* said its farewell.

I asked Spike Milligan if with the new TV coming up the Goons might try their hands at visual comedy.

'Not a chance,' he said. 'This will always be radio.'

Wasn't he scared of TV competition?

'No. Anyway, our listeners are fanatics. They stick with us. Because movies came in, oil-painting didn't go out, did it?'

Milligan played occasional variety dates. In June and July he had joined with Harry Secombe and Max Geldray, who played the harmonica in the *Goon Shows*, on a Moss Empires tour. But in general Milligan got fewer chances to appear than the other Goons. He was to be the one who stayed back home with his head down in the Shepherd's Bush Road. 'It was all fun for Peter and me,' says Harry generously. 'Spike had the worst of it. He had to stay back and get on with the work half the time. He had all the responsibility.'

During the musicians' strike at the end of 1955, Spike, not always impressed with the quality of popular music even when it was available, announced that he could easily write a top Christmas song. He composed 'I'm Walking Backwards for Christmas' one night going home on the Underground. He sang it during a *Goon Show* and was plagued by listeners who wrote in and begged him to pass on words and music. Several companies competed to record the number, which in due course rose to the top of the charts.

In February 1956, a late-night series for Independent Television, *The Idiot Weekly Price 2d*, commenced a six-week run. The programme was promoted as a 'sort of visual *Goon Show*. Peter Sellers, Valentine Dyall, Patti Lewis, Graham Stark, June Whitfield and Max Geldray were among the artists in the first show. Milligan and Sykes were responsible for the script. Guest critic to the *Evening Standard* Wolf Mankowitz was enthusiastic:

> At last here is humour which is intelligent, pointed, skilful, professionally conducted, specifically television and very, very funny.

Richard Lester, who was to be successfully associated with Milligan in film, was the producer.

The BBC had not encouraged this sort of show, and the defection of the Goons to ITV did not seriously embarrass them as the series, in spite of a good press, ran for only six weeks. However, from this format grew a series that was to make television history – *A Show Called Fred.*

A Show Called Fred was also produced by Richard Lester for Associated Rediffusion. The first series ran to only five programmes but their memory has never sunk into oblivion. *A Show Called Fred* heralded the arrival of surrealist TV comedy. The natural progression of this show, which had its origins in the *Goon Show* and *Idiot Weekly*, went on via *Son of Fred* and the *Q* series until it culminated in *Monty Python*.

Both *Son of Fred* (booked for sixteen shows, axed after eight) and the *Q* series (which began in the late 1960s) were massively undervalued by the majority, yet impressively applauded by the comedy cognoscenti. Comedian John Cleese of the *Python* team, speaking to the writer David Nathan about Milligan's *Q* series, made a comment which could be fairly back-dated to include the *Fred* shows:

> Shows prepare the way for other shows, and sometimes shows that make genuine breakthroughs are missed. Spike Milligan's *Q5* was missed. Milligan is the Great God to all of us. The

ABOVE LEFT: Florence Kettleband outside the Roman Catholic church in Kirkee, India, where she played the organ and met her future husband, Leo Milligan. This photograph was taken on her engagement day in 1913.

ABOVE RIGHT: In the early days of their marriage, Florence and Leo Milligan performed in army shows in India. Here they prepare for a 'trick' cowboy routine.

BELOW: Leo and Florence relax outside their army bungalow in Kirkee in 1922.

LEFT: Florence Milligan (left) stands next to her sister Eileen Kettleband before joining the men in a shoot near Poona, 1923.

BELOW: Nearing the end of the golden days in Rangoon, Burma: Terence and his small brother Desmond wearing new suits, which were probably bought for their first visit to England in 1931.

OPPOSITE: Scenes from the childhood of Terence Milligan in Kirkee, India, 1922. Terence was four years old.

ABOVE: Playtime in Rangoon, 1932: Terence on the left, brother Desmond second from the right. The little boy at the end of the line was the son of Desmond's ayah.

BELOW: Terence and Desmond in topees watch the snake-charmers in action on the Milligans' tennis-court in Burma.

LEFT: Spike's mother Florence standing at the door of their Lewisham, South London, home in 1950, with her mother Margaret Kettleband, on a visit from Poona.

BELOW: Spike acts as best man at his brother Desmond's wedding to Kathleen Roberts in Lewisham, 1947. At this stage Spike was struggling for a foothold in the entertainment world.

Spike on the day of his Caxton Hall marriage to June Marlowe, 26 January 1952. The second series of *Goon Shows* had just begun.

ABOVE: Spike visits his children on the occasion of Silé's second birthday. They were living in Richmond with their mother, but after the divorce custody was given to Spike.

RIGHT: Spike admires his father's gun collection on a visit to his parents in Woy Woy, Australia, in 1959.

LEFT: Bobby Limb, the well-known Australian radio and TV personality, appeared with Spike in *Idiot Weekly* for the Australian Broadcasting Commission in 1958.

BELOW: Rehearsing with Peter Sellers for *Son of Fred,* one of ITV's most popular shows.

RIGHT: Spike's second wife Paddy with Laura, Silé and Sean in 1964.

BELOW: Paddy Milligan in the early 1970s. After her marriage to Spike she did very little professional work but her beautiful singing voice delighted her family and friends almost up to the time of her tragically early death in 1978.

LEFT: Spike Milligan and Joan Greenwood as they appeared in *Son of Oblomov* at the Comedy Theatre, London, 1964-5.

BELOW: An historic evening at the Mermaid Theatre, London, on 21 June 1966. Left to right: Tomás Graves, Daniel Black, Spike, Paddy and Robert Graves, with Isla Cameron out of shot. The evening was given to raise funds for Bernard Miles's famous theatre.

ABOVE: Spike Milligan in Richard Lester's film version of *The Bed-Sitting Room*, 1969.

RIGHT: In the summer of 1964, the young Prince Charles – a great fan of the Goons – paid a private visit to Peter Sellers's home in Elstead, Surrey. The photograph was taken by Britt Ekland, at that time married to Sellers.

ABOVE: Milligan at work on the Elfin Oak in Kensington Gardens. A magnificent piece of wood sculpture by the late Ivor Innes, it would have rotted away completely had not Milligan taken charge and mounted a skilled rescue operation. He describes the bureaucratic and technical problems in a letter to Robert Graves. LEFT: Some of the 'fairy letters' which Spike wrote for his children and hid in the garden during the early days at 127 Holden Road, North Finchley. The letters are less than 10cm high.

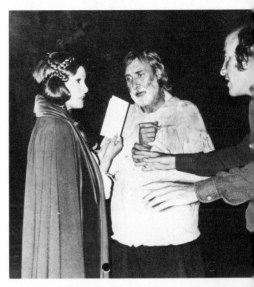

RIGHT: The director Richard Lester explains a point to Raquel Welch and Spike Milligan on the set of *The Three Musketeers*, 1973. Spike played the part of an old innkeeper married to a lovely young wife.

BELOW: Spike and Raquel Welch during a break in the filming, on location in Madrid.

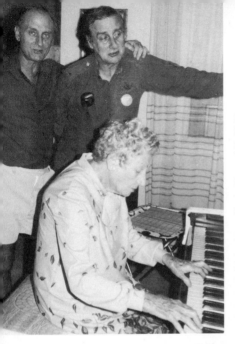

LEFT: Desmond and Spike with their mother (aged 89) at Woy Woy in March 1983. Spike was touring Australia with his one-man show.

BELOW: Spike shares a joke with his old mate Harry Secombe at Silé's wedding in April 1984. Silé, the second of Spike's daughters, was the first to marry.

OPPOSITE ABOVE: A recording session with Secombe and Sellers, shortly before Sellers's death.

OPPOSITE BELOW: At a book-signing session in Leeds during his one-man show tour in 1982.

Spike and his third wife Shelagh with Jane and Silé at the latter's wedding, April 1984.

Goon Show influenced us enormously. When we first saw *Q5* we were very depressed because we thought it was what we wanted to do and Milligan was doing it brilliantly. But nobody really noticed *Q5*.

Colleagues Terry Jones, Michael Palin and Terry Gilliam all concur.

'Watching *Q5*', says Terry Jones, 'we almost felt as if our guns had been Spiked! We had been writing quickies or sketches for some three years and they always had a beginning, a middle and a tag line. Suddenly, watching Spike Milligan, we realized that they didn't have to be like that.'

The critic Bernard Levin, writing for the *Guardian* at this time, paid the team a compliment that delighted Milligan. He claimed that they had done for television what Gluck had performed for opera. 'That is,' he said, 'they have added a new dimension.'

In the early spring of 1956 the Milligans moved to a new house, No 127 Holden Road in North Finchley. It was semi-detached but spacious, with a large garden that ran down to the Dollis Brook. The garden proved to be a great bonus for all the family.

June had coped with the major effort entailed in the move, and there is no doubt that she was doing her best to make home conditions more pleasing for Spike. Yet she was growing understandably discontented with her lot: she saw very little of her husband and his critical, abrasive moods were not conducive to any sort of marital happiness. Besides, they had grown apart. She confided in Anne Sellers, still a close and trusted friend, and Anne, who perhaps had a greater vision to understand the situation, consoled her with stories of Peter's impossibly difficult temperament. Anne had a certain built-in wisdom that seemed to insulate her against almost insuperable difficult-ies. Poor June had not. Milligan is quick to take the blame (a rare phenomenon).

> It was the pressure of the work. I was going mad half the time. She couldn't understand how it was destroying me. I loved the kids and I wanted to be a good father, I couldn't handle the whole responsibilities of being a husband and father, and there was never enough money. The poor girl wasn't really extravagant, but she bought a lot of clothes. I once counted thirty-seven pairs of shoes. How can anyone need thirty-seven pairs of shoes?

The new house was a great success, but Milligan had a difficult time ahead. Tensions mounted both at home and at work. His sleeping pattern, never very stable, became more agitated. The insomnia that was to plague his later years was beginning to be a serious problem. Some aficion-ados of the *Goon Show* believe that Milligan was now reaching a peak of brilliance that was never to be surpassed. For Spike, the only certain thing was that he must go on writing new and funnier scripts. His appearance, not a matter of concern to him at this stage in his life, grew increasingly untidy and neglected. When June suggested a haircut he snapped at her in rage. At the BBC he knew frustration at every turn – his sound effect needs were no longer ridiculed, but his success had not brought his scornful, brilliant persona any real respect. He fought constantly to have the programme go out on a different wavelength. It was normally transmitted on the Home Service, then repeated within the week on the Light. He was convinced that it should go out on the Light Pro-gramme in the first place and could never understand why this was not allowed. Nearly forty years later Milligan met René Peltier, former Light Programme chief, and the conversation turned to the Goons. 'Well, actually, we didn't like the programme much,' said Peltier. 'In fact, my wife couldn't stand it. We always had to turn it off.' Milligan was very quiet for a number of hours, but that evening he exploded. 'So that explains it!' he said. 'I always knew that there must be some reason but it makes me wild to know that it was as personal as that – and that I was in the hands of a little tin-pot bureaucrat!'

Milligan's resentment of bureaucracy has sometimes been unnecessarily destructive to his peace of mind, but it also spurred him towards overcoming the difficulties that beset the Goons, even at the peak of their achievements. In 1957, during one of the regular exchanges with the BBC's sound effects team, Spike asked for a record of wolves howling. The BBC were unable to help. In desperation, with the date for recording imminent, Harry, Spike and Peter did the howling themselves. It is said that they performed with impressive credibility.

Philip Oakes captured a fleeting but accurate picture of Milligan about this time.

> Blue-eyed, bearded and wearing the look of an Austrian Archduke expecting assassination, he ticks off his frustrations as another man would count his assets. His spiritual home is a condemned garret.
>
>   In fact, he lives in a large Edwardian house in Finchley, where, propped up in bed at 4 P.M., he talked eagerly to me of the chemistry of Goon humour.
>
> 'Essentially,' says Milligan, 'it is critical comedy. It is against bureaucracy, and on the side of human beings. Its starting point is one man shouting gibberish in the face of authority, and proving by fabricated insanity that nothing could be as mad as what passes for ordinary living.'[1]

One evening when Spike was at Shepherd's Bush Station waiting for his train to North London, he read a poster which advertised philosophy classes. The idea interested him, and he decided to pursue it. He found that for a very small sum he could sign on for a course of lectures which encompassed Western philosophy.

> I was fascinated. You could go any evening during the week, Monday to Friday about 7 or 8 o'clock. It went on for a couple of hours and they discussed all the philosophers. I was so impressed with Bertrand Russell, and Jung. One or two of the lecturers were friendly and interesting, sometimes a few of us went for a drink and a talk afterwards. I liked it very much but I had the feeling it was all subsidized by a political group. There was something a bit odd about it.

A few years later, Spike met Bertrand Russell. He was deeply impressed by the immense enthusiasms of the now ageing philosopher. They discussed many of their mutual interests – humanism, educational reforms, non-violence and something that was now beginning to attract Milligan – vegetarianism. He did, in fact, become a vegetarian a few years later.

During this year, Spike appeared in *The Case of the Mukkinese Battlehorn*, a 30-minute film made by Richard Lester. He enjoyed making this movie, which also featured Peter Sellers and Dick Emery, with a story by Larry Stephens. This was a very funny film and was considered a success, but Milligan's best short film was still to come.

Associated London Scripts now moved their office from Shepherd's Bush Road to Cumberland House in High Street Kensington. The company was flourishing. Beryl Vertue had become a director, and her young sister was helping out with the workload.

That summer a large canvas swimming-pool had arrived at 127 Holden Road. There were shrieks of joy as Laura (now at nursery school) and Sean, a slim, nimble child who had inherited his father's good proportions, learned to swim.

On 2 December, June gave birth to the Milligans' third

child, another little girl. She was called Silé, a Gaelic rendering of Shelagh.

At about this time Peter Eton was threatening to defect to London Weekend Television. June was pressing for more attention to be paid to herself and the children. Bills came in thick and fast; and whilst he sometimes longed for the stress of writing the *Goon Shows* to be somehow lifted from him, Spike fought a constant fear that the show would come to an end and he might, one day, be out of work. He saw a doctor from time to time, who would suggest unlikely solutions, like a complete break or a change of job. Sometimes he swallowed whatever medicines the doctor suggested; on other occasions he would hurl them into a dustbin. Harry and Peter were at a loss to help him. Somebody suggested a referral to a Dr Joe Robson who practised hypnotherapy. The suggestion was timely and fortuitous.

Spike and Joe first met in the autumn of 1955. Mrs Robson drew her husband's attention to the name on the appointment pad. Dr Robson was overworked and unimpressed.

'I'd never heard of him,' he recalls. 'Charlotte said to me, "But Joe, he's a leading English comedian. He writes the *Goon Shows*. He's famous."'

This meant nothing to Joe, who privately found the *Goon Shows* noisy, disruptive and unfunny. 'It wasn't my sort of humour,' he says mildly. 'I think it was above my head. I just quietly left it for the others to enjoy.'

However, no doubt to placate his wife rather than impress his new patient, Joe Robson changed into his most formal professional wear: a black jacket and striped trousers. Milligan arrived at five o'clock. He looked distraught, dishevelled, unshaven and wretched. The overall impression was of a vagrant who had been sleeping rough. He disregarded Joe's courteous greeting.

'I've got to tell you that I don't trust any doctors. And I don't trust you.' His voice was harsh and angry.

Joe regarded him without emotion. He was an intuitive man, experienced, unegotistical and very able.

'I see,' he said quietly. 'Then I can't help you. There would be no point in your staying.'

'But I need help. Someone must help me. I can't sleep. I have to write a script every week to make a lot of idiot people laugh. Every single week. How can they fucking laugh when I'm in such fucking pain? I'm desperate. I can't make people laugh when I feel I'm going mad with strain. I must have help.'

Joe looked at him dispassionately. He was not perturbed by Milligan's attitude.

'I can only help you if you want me to,' he said. 'If I am to treat you, it will be a question of fifty-fifty. It will be half and half – half your effort, half mine. It would be a matter of collaboration and mutual trust. If you are not able to trust me, then I cannot help you.'

Milligan was in despair. He said, with some difficulty: 'Please try and help me if you can. I will do my best. I can try.'

Joe Robson had a method of helping a patient, in the first instance, to reach a degree of tranquillity. He would persuade him to lie down and then try to imagine a peaceful scene that the two of them could think about and discuss. Quite often it would be a remembered country scene with flowers or bees or haystacks. Or it might be a waterfall or lake. Spike began to tell him about India. He talked of the remembered heat, of the light, of the vast spaces, of the silence. As was the doctor's intention, he shortly drifted into a light doze. Joe Robson stared at his turbulent new patient and waited. Milligan woke up, agitated and startled. He confided in Joe that he had felt himself to be in a large double bed on the very top of the Himalayan mountains.

'The bed was rocking,' he said. 'First it rocked on the mountain peak, then it would slide a few yards down one side, then somehow it would be on the top again, still rocking, and then sliding down the other side. I was always on the point of falling out.'

Years later, Joe Robson looks back on this first encounter.

'That was the point, I think, when I began to realize that here was a very exceptional man. A rather extraordinary man, really eccentric and very, very, very gifted. He had too many things going on in his head at once. It was hard for him. But here was genius. And I don't use that word lightly. I'd seen a good number of patients by that time. Some very bright ones – but I never remember one with such a fertile and extraordinary imagination. In my experience, his was quite unique.'

Five days later, Milligan returned for a further appointment. His appearance had not changed and his anguish was undiminished, but at least his manner was less hostile.

'I have to apologize for my behaviour last time we met,' he said, 'I know I was unpardonably rude to you, and you were very forgiving. I'm sorry.'

Joe Robson may well have a selective memory when he recalls his long and predominantly happy relationship with Spike. He can speak no ill of him.

'There is only one thing about him that makes me sad and cross,' he will say. 'He's not at all anti-Semitic, but he will make these terrible racist and anti-Semitic jokes. And then I do get cross. After all, I am a Jew. And he demeans himself, in a way, doesn't he?'

* * *

Milligan now embarked on a course of treatment. It was not run on conventional lines and Joe Robson was generous with his time and patience. Very often Spike would come bounding in at nine or ten o'clock in the evening, after an agonizing day trying to get the script together. He felt under no compulsion to confine himself to the consulting room, and would be quite likely to wander round the Robsons' flat looking at books and pictures and not infrequently ending up in the kitchen. He was usually hungry, and he developed a great fondness for the bowls of chopped liver which Charlotte Robson was often preparing. Hunger assuaged, he would return to the consulting room.

'I'm so grateful to you, Joe,' he would say. 'I don't know how I could manage without you.'

Spike was closely involved with the Robsons throughout the critical last years of the *Goon Show*. The relationship developed from professional to social. Often Spike would invite Joe and Charlotte to the Sunday night recording and would try to organize a dinner afterwards which would include Peter and Harry, their wives, and other participants from the show – at this time often Max Geldray and Graham Stark. Spirits ran high after the show. Harry and Peter would usually have worked a variety date during the previous week; this meant a hectic dash after the curtain came down on a Saturday night and a few hours' sleep before presenting themselves at the recording studio (invariably the Camden Palace) on Sunday morning. If their last engagement had been in Llandudno the drive would take all night and they would have to manage without the few hours' sleep. They would have a riotous reunion with Spike who would be in varying states of anxiety and hilarity and would fall on their scripts with nervous energy and tension running high. By the time the recording hour approached the whole scene would be carried along on a high of nervous tension. Fifteen minutes

before recording began, the audience would filter in.
Milligan would scan their faces, his mercurial spirits lifting
when he caught a sight of Joe. Peter, Spike and Harry
would cluster around the microphone; the introductory
music would play and the *Goon Show* would commence.

There is no doubt that Dr Robson was extremely supportive to Milligan during this time. 'Please come to the
recording, Joe,' he would say. 'I feel a lot better when I
see you. I don't know if I can get through if you are not
there.'

In 1968, Milligan published his fifth book, *A Book of
Milliganimals*. The dedication reads:

> To Dr and Mrs J. Robson
> Who helped me through a sticky* time.

In true Milligan style, he adds:

> *I used to be a fly.

When Spike seemed somewhat restored to health, Tony
Hancock came up with what looked like a good suggestion.
He and Spike could join forces and hire a cabin cruiser to
sail up the Thames. It would be an 'away from it all'
holiday for both of them. Spike liked the idea of no
telephone or commitments, and they met at Hampton
Court to pick up their boat. Tony had done most of the
shopping and the galley was stacked with innumerable tins
of baked beans and some alcohol.

The journey began well enough, and they passed
through the first locks without difficulty. Milligan was
grateful for the peaceful serenity of the river. Being on a
'low', he appreciated the relative quiet and solitude. 'It's
great,' he said. 'No one can get at us or interrupt us, can
they?' Hancock, however, was in a more gregarious mood
and frequently feeling the need of company other than

Spike's. He constantly wanted to tie up outside riverside pubs which showed some sign of jollity. Milligan would acquiesce unwillingly. He would sit apart at the pub and glare angrily at Hancock, who would soon become the centre of a friendly and noisy party. Inevitably, their different moods hastened the unsuccessful culmination of their sailing partnership and before long Hancock, peeved with Spike, jumped ship. Milligan was partly angry and partly relieved. He made the next lock on his own, but absolute solitude soon began to pall even on him, and the next day, when he reached Abingdon, he went ashore to telephone. He rang Graham Stark and told him that Tony had deserted him in midstream.

'Will you come and join me? I've fallen out with Tony. He wanted to stop every ten minutes or so for a drink and I got fed up, so he's gone off and left me. I'll not manage this boat on my own, and you're good at this sort of thing.'

Graham was always ready for a lark, and in any case the idea of the non-sailing Milligan, alone on the middle reaches of the Thames, was a little disquieting. The protective instincts of those close to Spike are seldom far below the surface.

June agreed to accompany Graham in his car, deposit him with Spike and then drive the car back to North London. Stark remembers the occasion well. 'I must have been very keen to join Spike,' he says. 'I was never eager to let other people drive my car in those days.'

Once Stark and Milligan were together on the boat, the sailing holiday really took off. Stark remembers the occasion with clarity and pleasure:

I think I had one of the best holidays of my life – and that probably went for Spike, too. We were in absolute accord, got on marvellously. We wanted the same things, we shared the same pleasures. Spike then was getting involved with archaeology. I remember he always wanted to stop if he saw any ruins or anything that looked old and interesting. He always chose the place where we would tie up. We would go to the odd riverside pub for a glass of wine. The weather was beautiful. I think I fitted in with his mood then, more than Hancock had been able to.

The journey upriver continued slowly. At Windsor they decided to go ashore for baths. Booking into the public wash-house they were given towels and soap and a cubicle apiece. Several already occupied cubicles separated them, but they found this no handicap. 'Are you OK, Spike?' Graham called. 'No, I think I'm drowning,' yelled Spike, pitching his voice above the roar of the plumbing and the splashes and gurgles of the intermediate bathers who must have been bemused at the mini-Goon show to which they were unexpectedly treated. Back on the boat, they negotiated the next lock with confidence. The old lady in charge handed them a cat in a basket with instructions to deliver it to Mrs Elvers at the next lock, who would be expecting it. 'And tell her that Friday night is OK and I'll bring the rabbits,' she yelled after them for good measure. Milligan was delighted with this small commission and carried it out faithfully. At the next lock, it was Graham's turn. The lock-keeper here was a somewhat seedy individual who bore, nevertheless, the signs of a *passé*, somewhat decadent naval glamour. He chewed on a Woodbine and gazed at them speculatively. He must have decided they would be trustworthy for he gave a message to be passed to the 'red-haired girl' at the next lock. 'Tell her I'll see her tomorrow night, same place, same time,' he said with a huge wink. 'But if you see her husband around, forget it.'

The tryst appealed to the romantic in Spike, and even more so when the lock was reached and he saw an attractive young woman handling the heavy equipment whilst a large unkempt man slouched within earshot. Graham assessed the situation as being sensitive and, resigned to not passing on the message, was at the boat's controls intended to sail straight through the lock. Spike, emerging from the ship's galley, stopped him. 'Look,' he said to the young woman. 'We've got overstocked with these beans. We'll never finish them before our trip ends. Would you like some?' 'That's very kind of you,' she said. 'Thank you.' Spike looked hard at her as he gave her one of the large tins. 'Mind you open it the right way up,' he said as they passed on through the lock. Graham was mystified. 'What was that all about?' he said. 'There's only one way to open a tin of beans, isn't there?' 'Don't be so dumb,' said Milligan, delighted with himself. 'I put the message on the tin, didn't I?'

The establishment of Associated London Scripts gave Milligan an incentive to develop his own writing. The fundamentally solitary craft was often therapeutic for him. In a letter to Leo and Flo he outlined his feelings:

> I am still very busy writing and, well I like it. I've packed up all stage work, it's too much rushing about so unless I'm desperate for the money – it's goodbye to the variety stage. However, the stage in another sphere beckons – Sam Wanamaker, an American Producer, wants me to write an intimate revue. I might start work on it this summer. As to the *Goon Show*, it is going out to America weekly on the NBC. I had a press cutting from the Christian Science Monitor (Boston) – which gave it a very good write. I don't think the Australians will take to it.* In England it is now a firm favourite. In last week's *News Chronicle* Gallup Poll voted it No. 1 comedy show – it has been a lot of hard work but it has been worth it. It means (God willing) that I can be sure of work for at least another five years.

---

* Spike was wrong in this surmise.

In April 1956 the BBC mounted an exhibition of manuscript doodlings made by the Goons. Some minor news
value was stirred up and one or two papers reproduced
some of the Goon cartoon figures. The exhibition was not
taken seriously, least of all by Milligan, who established
himself on the pavement with his drawings around him
and a hat to receive donations.

News arrived regularly from Australia. Flo and Leo had
finally settled on where they wanted to live. It was then
still a country district, called Woy Woy, about an hour's
train journey from Sydney. The sea almost lapped the
garden of their bungalow. Leo was still whirling his guns
and writing articles for *The Gunner*. Florence was overwhelmed when she read of her 'famous son' in the English
papers. Desmond, working as a designer on one of the
Sydney daily papers, had divorced and was contemplating
remarriage with what Flo felt to be rather indecent haste.
By now, the Milligans were not doing too badly. They
went for a holiday trip on the Hawkesbury River. Photographs were taken and sent back to England. Leo and Flo
looked bronzed and well, and ten years younger than
Spike remembered them. Years later, Spike stuck the
photographs carefully into one of his large red morocco
albums.

Spike still wages war with the BBC. For the Christmas
of 1957 he made an adaptation for TV of a book that had
deeply impressed him – Paul Gallico's *Snow Goose*. Harry
Edgington, still his close friend from the army days,
wrote most of the music. Spike himself wrote one song.
Enthusiasm soared – *The Snow Goose* was a simple and
beautiful story, and lent itself well to a TV adaptation.
BBC TV, however, saw fit to turn it down. It was just
another action for which Milligan never forgave them.

The *Goon Show* was by now achieving almost worldwide
fame. Seven million listeners in England were being joined

by audiences in Australia, New Zealand, Rhodesia and the United States.

In December 1957, a *Goon Show* recording session received its first royal visit – from the Duchess of Kent, her daughter Princess Alexandra, Princess Olga of Yugoslavia (the Duchess's sister) and her daughter, Princess Elizabeth. The recording on this occasion was at the BBC's Paris Cinema studio on Regent Street. The show that week was 'The Great British Revolution', and the royal visitors enjoyed a backstage party after the session. When Milligan left the premises, he greeted the still waiting crowds by flinging both arms in the air and shouting 'Well! I've been knighted!'

As soon as Spike had a garden for his children, he began to spend hours of his time conducting a correspondence between them and the 'fairies'. Laura, Sean and Silé were all a party to the fantasy which was a matter of shared delight. Over the years Spike wrote innumerable 'fairy letters' for his children. The children wrote to the fairies and received answers, the letters being 'posted' behind flowerpots or under stones. They were enclosed in minute envelopes, painstakingly designed. Always fascinated by calligraphy, Milligan derived great pleasure from perfecting a minuscule handwriting adapted to the tiny pages. He has undoubtedly spent many of his most rewarding hours with children. He can re-enter the child's world, by his writing, by his unstinted clowning and by his capacity for losing himself utterly in a child's mind. This rare ability probably springs from a genuine childish curiosity, a curiosity and interest which has somehow never grown up.

In recent years, Milligan has been made President of the Australian Puffin Club, a book club for young children. Asked why he had been elected, a spokesman said, 'Well, it is so marvellous to see him with the children. You can see that they feel such a closeness to him, he can step out of his world straight into theirs. Not many people can do that.'

13

Australia

Turrets catch the King's grief
　　　White handed he paces the air
　　with mindless fingers.

> Spike Milligan,
> *Open Heart University*

The desire to visit his family in Australia had been uppermost in Spike Milligan's mind for some years. He had been held back by pressure of work, by financial anxieties, by the births of his children and by his own ill-health. Now, however, the moment seemed right, and in April 1958 Spike, June and the three children sailed for Australia on the SS *Arcadia*. The eighth series of *Goon Shows* had just finished, the ninth was not due to start until November. Spike had been in touch with the Australian Broadcasting Commission for some months and a successful contract to produce the *Idiot Weekly* on television had finally been negotiated. This made the visit to Australia economically viable. He had fought another round or two at the BBC over increased fees for the next Goon series before he left England and some advance publicity based on his hatred of the BBC preceded him to Australia. Unflattering references made by him appeared in the Australian newspapers:

> Of the BBC, Milligan said 'I can't destroy the BBC though I'd like to. Likewise, they cannot destroy my spirit. I'm a rebel. A revolutionary. They want a quiet, timorous fellow they can swallow up.'

He went on to describe the BBC as 'these torpor-ridden people'.

'They're a private club that barely tolerates the artist. They're a cancer between the surgeon and the patient,' he said. 'The only kind of writer they like are dead writers. Look at them – Shaw, dead, Giraudoux, dead, O'Neill, dead. They do *The Women of Troy* by a dead author who was a success 2,000 years ago and everybody says congratulations. Where's the challenge in that?'

The voyage to Australia was unhappy for both Spike and June. The enforced proximity was not helpful to either; Spike yelled and June screamed. Laura withdrew into her own little girl's world, but Sean was frightened by the rows that escalated all around him. Spike was in agony:

It was a nightmare. Everything was on top of me, I couldn't face the future. We had these dreadful rows – and June played up because I suppose I was giving her a hard time, and she'd go off round the ship drinking in bars at night, and I'd have to go and search for her and ask her to come back to the cabin and look after the children. And Sean, he was so little, when he heard this dreadful shouting between us he would put his fingers in his ears and call out 'Oh, please stop this dreadful noise, please stop.' It made it all worse. I was demented, crazy. Off my head. I didn't know what to do, I loved them so much.

When the *Arcadia* arrived in Sydney, a crowd of first-year medical students swarmed on board in an attempt to 'kidnap' Milligan, intending to release him for a 'charity' ransom. Whatever they had planned didn't quite work out, but it certainly added a lot of delay, noise and confusion to the Milligans' arrival. At one stage, Spike locked himself in his cabin. Bobby Limb, a well-known Australian actor who was to appear with Spike in the new series, was also kidnapped when he threatened to intervene. Eventually, after a press conference and a photography session on deck, the Milligans were allowed to disembark. A photograph that appeared in the Sydney papers the following day shows a smiling June holding a five-month-old Silé, and Spike pretending to strangle four-year-old Sean, who wears a sailor suit and looks pensive. The five-year-old Laura stands a little apart, demure and aloof. The newspaper article labelled Spike as 'the famous English funny man'.

The *Goon Shows* were already popular in Australia and were, in fact, running concurrently with *Idiot Weekly*, an ABC TV Light Entertainment which was shown during the Australian winter, from June until August. Critics seemed bewildered by it, and most of the reviews were cagey. During the visit, Milligan gave an interesting interview to John Query for the *TV News*, a weekly magazine published by the ABC. He spoke emphatically about the great and as yet unrecognized potential of television, 'Not as a medium for year-old films but as something new and exciting' and blasted the existing approach: 'Have you ever seen a television show about which you could have said "This can be done only on television"?' But he reacted favourably when Query asked him for his views on children's television programmes.

> I do think they're admirable, the ones that I've seen. This is the one saving grace of TV. I think that the conscience of the adult has been stirred to giving the child very, very fine programmes, many of them educational. Not in all cases, mind you. There are those that want to sell kiddies Y-front shoes and they will put horror and death in great gulps in front of the young child. They have no conscience at all. But I am talking of BBC television. It's admirable. All these wonderful little programmes of Hank and his little machine. *The Flower-Pot Men*, you see. I watch them all!

The time in Australia was fraught and unhappy. June was living with the children in an outer suburb of Sydney. Spike spent most of the time in an hotel close to the studios. He would try to be with June and the children, his parents, and his in-laws from time to time, but it was an unsatisfactory arrangement and no one was happy. June felt burdened by the responsibility of three young children in an unfamiliar country. On one or two occasions she visited the studios with Sean and Laura to watch a recording of the show, but she knew no one on the set and missed the convivial friendship of her friend Anne Sellers with whom, in London, she had often shared this sort of visit. By the time the recording was finished the children would often be fretful and tired, and a taxi would collect them and whisk them back to the isolation of the suburbs.

Leo and Flo were delighted with their grandchildren and gave them a genuinely loving welcome, but the difficulties inherent in the marriage between Spike and June were of great concern to them. Predictably, Flo made it quite plain that she felt June was at fault. As June was known to say in later years, 'No one was good enough for her darling boy!' June's own parents were surprisingly unhelpful. They made it no secret that they felt it was June's duty to make the best she could of this difficult situation. Spike, whenever they saw him, seemed to be a delightful father, deeply attached to the children, who obviously adored him. 'My father,' said June, looking back, 'was one of the old Italian school. Girls got married and put up with what came, but he was upset when he saw how things were between us.'

As the weeks went by, Leo and Flo were at a loss to handle the situation, which worsened every day. Spike was more fortunate than June on two counts – firstly, he had work to do, which has always assuaged his pain at some level; secondly, he was very much in the bosom of his family and his insecurity was offset, as ever, by Flo's protective love. He was less fortunate than June inasmuch as he was ill – he was struggling with what was almost certainly a severe anxiety state and he was either hyper-manic or depressed in bewildering succession. For June, this must have seemed the final let-down. Perhaps she had vested unrealistic hopes in the voyage; she had felt a certain optimistic idea that once they were in Australia under the benign and loving administration of his parents Spike would cast off some of the heavy armour with which he shielded himself, become her lover once again and, naïvely perhaps, she hoped that he would get rid of his 'nerves'. None of this happened. Leo rubbed his head anxiously; Flo never considered it possible that her boy could be in the wrong. He was simply 'misunderstood' and 'ill, the result of the war'. As always, he was over-indulged, and this was detrimental to him at a point in his life when he might have bolstered his fundamental courage with a thread of self-discipline.

In London, Peter and Harry were well away in their own careers. Harry was developing his splendid voice; Peter was pressing towards a future in films. Beryl Vertue had given birth to a daughter, Debbie, in July. Work was still in progress at Associated London Scripts, and once home again Spike settled down to write the ninth series of the *Goon Show*.

Money remained a problem. BBC pay was notoriously low and Spike was almost always hard-up. One day, he was driving with June through London. As they went along, they were discussing their joint bank account. 'At least,' said Spike hopefully, 'we've got £500 in that, haven't we?' June had to confess that she had laid out this entire sum as a single-premium payment for a famous school of ballroom dancing. Its representative had encouraged her to do this on the grounds that the payment would cover her for dancing lessons for the rest of her life. Spike was so horrified and enraged by this piece of news that he jumped out of the car there and then, leaving June to make her own way home as best as she could. It was fortunate that she could drive.

The year 1958 saw the beginning of the Aldermaston marches, the early days of the Campaign for Nuclear Disarmament. Milligan became involved, and made a friend who was to remain close, Michael Foot. Foot, a lover of Jonathan Swift, was intrigued with Spike.

> Milligan is like Charlie Chaplin or Jonathan Swift, whom he much resembles. I think he's a comic genius. I always have thought that and everything that I have ever seen about him has confirmed it, not only in his public appearances but in his private performances, if you can put it that way. He would come into a room in our house, he'd come in with his first wife, I remember, they'd come and have a meal with us and almost from the very first moment when he arrived in the room he'd be commenting on everything, not a matter of repeating jokes or anything like that, but a reaction to the world he sees around him. He'd be commenting on a different world that he inhabited and that's what I mean when I say he's a genius. Of course he's isolated, but that doesn't prevent him from making a connection from time to time, he's well able to communicate.

Spike and June visited the Foot household occasionally, sometimes taking the children. Michael Foot remembers Spike's closeness to them.

> It was absorbing to see him – he was devoted to them and a very good father, he cared about them and was always helping their minds along, expanding them and interested in all their imaginations. His early writing for children, I believe, sprang from his own deep interest in his own family.

Milligan was now writing and performing again for the penultimate *Goon Show* series. He was also involved in constant activities outside the immediate show. Prince

Philip had chosen the Goons to be in his team for a forthcoming tiddlywinks match against the Cambridge University Union; this was receiving an enormous amount of publicity. Difficulties were arising at Associated London Scripts which needed his full attention. A further royal visit to a *Goon Show* recording was planned and, as always, Milligan took upon himself the burden of extra work which he found difficult to delegate. His own capacity for rapid thought and action is so immense that his patience quota with less well-endowed people is often negligible. Almost masochistically, he tries to do everything himself. If he doesn't, he will go to enormous trouble to demonstrate the relative lack of achievement of those who try. He is often an unrewarding and frustrating person to help, which causes inevitable pain all round.

This stress and strain in the early part of 1959, coupled with distress about the state of his marriage, brought him once again to the edge of a severe breakdown. His distrust of doctors makes him an impossible patient most of the time; on this occasion he refused to go into hospital but was treated at home, mainly with drugs. June was quite unable to cope with him as he either ranted and raged or lay despairing and unresponsive on his bed, refusing food or drink.

The cyclic nature of the condition eventually reaches a stage when Milligan can, with an enormous effort, take control and move towards the routine of his life once more. At this stage, he can be helped (or hindered) as he reaches tentatively towards 'normal' life.

By a pure fluke now Spike Milligan made a record for Parlophone. It was entirely straight – 'Will I Find My Love Today' and on the flip side 'Wish I Knew'. Mystified critics gave the record a reasonably good write-up and it sold well. Spike had been at the recording studios waiting for Peter Sellers when he decided to cut the disc for fun.

George Martin, the record producer, was impressed and decided to bring the record out. Many years before, in the pre-army band days in South London, young Terence Milligan had had ambitions to croon like Bing Crosby. He won a local competition, but that must have fulfilled his desires, for he afterwards forgot about singing for twenty years. Now it seems the same thing happened once again. 'Will I Find My Love Today' is still the only straight vocal record that Spike has made.

The much publicized tiddlywinks event at Cambridge came off successfully on 1 March 1959. All monies raised were for the National Playing Fields Association. The match was filmed and was also broadcast on the Saturday night on the Light Programme. The Goon team included Peter, Spike and Harry, along with announcer Wallace Greenslade, Max Geldray and Graham Stark, and script-writers Alan Simpson and Ray Galton. Harry Secombe added to the attraction by leaving Cambridge by helicopter for Coventry, where he was appearing in pantomime. The helicopter was loaned by a famous Cambridge pest control firm. This in itself was good for a few jokes, grist to the mill of the three who were at their most joyful when they were together.

Since their first Australian visit had been such a strain on June, it was not surprising that, when a further offer of work for the Australian Broadcasting Commission came through for the early summer of 1959, Milligan accepted it gratefully and the decision to leave June and the children at home was mutually agreed. The breakdown of the marriage was looming, but neither June nor Spike had any clear idea of what was to happen. Spike lived from day to day. He got together his material for Australia and hugged the children and shouted at June. June pleaded and wept and shouted back. They were both deeply unhappy.

Spike left for Sydney on SS *Dominion Monarch* at the end of April. His passage was booked under the name of Alan Mills. He was in despair about his marriage and spent a lot of time locked in his cabin avoiding contact with other passengers. When he felt able, he turned his mind towards a new endeavour. It was almost masochistic, but it helped to bring him out of the frenzy of distress into something approaching tranquillity.

In February 1957 he had received a letter from the publisher Dennis Dobson. They had been successful with various humorists – Hoffnung in England and Robert Benchley from the USA. The letter was short and to the point.

Dear Mr Milligan,
    Have you ever thought of writing a book? I believe you could bring some of your humour to print, etc. Do get in touch,

Yours sincerely,
D. Dobson.

The letter had arrived when Spike was ill, so it had not been answered immediately, but in time he telephoned the Dobsons and they met to discuss the project. Dennis Dobson was a sensitive and able man with a tremendous feeling for talent. They got on well, and Spike showed him the only things that he had written to date – the *Goon Show* scripts. At that stage (perhaps mistakenly) the publishers could not visualize the scripts in saleable book form. They were incredibly complicated at first glance, with pages of instructions for the outlandish sound effects that were so much part of the success. However, Dobson was not willing to discard his ambition, and he kept in touch with Spike over the next two years. Spike frequently entertained Sean and Laura with rhymes that he made up on the spur of the moment; some of these were scribbled down and shown to the publishers. The idea of a book of children's poems was born.

Spike took his manuscript with him to Australia. He had work waiting there, which always solaced him, and he was able to go to earth under his mother's triumphantly protective wing, but he was struggling all the time with an almost unbearable feeling of loss. He was accepting, at this stage, the fact that he was likely to be separated from his children. In a few months he would be returning to England to sort out the threads of the disaster area that was his marriage. He felt guilty and wretched about June, but the predominant pain was for Laura, Sean and Silé. He remembered the happiness he had shared with them, and how they had laughed with delight when he entertained them with the funny rhymes and stories that were now going into the book:

> I had to do something for my children to prove to them that I loved them, that I didn't want to leave them. It was really a desperate attempt. My marriage was dying. I thought 'What can I do to make them understand how much I loved them? If I died now, what is there to say how much I loved them?' I thought I would write this book of poems for them. They sent me the proofs to Australia to be corrected. That's how *Silly Verse for Kids* began.

Spike spent four months in Australia, mainly in Sydney where he worked on the new series of *Idiot Weekly* for the ABC. The audience ratings were favourable, and there was much talk of future opportunities. On a different front, he was moving towards an area which was to become increasingly important to him as the years passed. He was becoming actively interested in conservation. From Sydney he made a television appeal for funds to save the old cottage that had been the home of the Australian poet

Henry Kendall. Milligan was consumed with determination to preserve this important bit of Australian history and an enormous amount of energy and interest was generated by his spirited and moving appeal.

Shortly before Spike was due to leave for home, he received a letter from June telling him that their marriage was over and she had left home, taking the children with her. The journey back to England was a tormenting one for Spike.

> Up to then I'd been living for the children. It was the only point of fixation for my love. When I was at this distance in Australia, mentally very ill, certainly not normal, I thought I was going to lose them. I sailed home on the *Willem Ruys*. I was getting these telegrams from a secretary I had then, I can't remember his name, and they were telling me that they'd left the home, they'd moved away, 'your wife is suing you for divorce', just bland, stark, bloodless telegrams. I wrote to June and said 'Please let's try again' but she'd had enough and I think she'd met this bloke by then.

It was during this voyage that Milligan made an attempt on his life.

> I just couldn't take it, we were cut off at sea, I couldn't get to a telephone, we were crossing the Pacific, the next port of call would be Panama. I couldn't stand the tension so I did take a massive dose of sleeping pills. I think it was a token suicide but I had forgotten that I'd invited the ship's doctor to come for a drink in my cabin. All I remember was a stomach-pump and he was saying 'How many did you take?'

When Spike returned from Australia the home was empty. June had filed for a divorce and had taken the children to live at a house in Richmond, 14 Maze Road. She told Spike that she had met a man who wanted to marry her. Spike was alternately demented with pain and incensed with rage. He became determined to get the custody of

the children himself. He based this on his assessment of
her new friend.

> June had taken up with this man who was a Covent Garden
> porter. I just had to fight the divorce and get custody of my
> kids. The children started saying things like 'Look at that
> fuckin' dog' when I took them out. And I know he was a
> violent man, violent and abusive. He abused *her*. She had
> great bruises on her arms where he had been violent. She
> used to wear long gloves to cover them up. I couldn't think of
> my children in that set-up.

The feeling that he had been primarily responsible for
the break-up of his marriage never left Milligan. The
capacity for self-deception, for exaggerating or diminishing
hard facts is an integral part of his make-up. Sometimes it
seems like an almost wilful going into overdrive, a surging
forward and stampeding of what may seem to him to be
the trivia of accumulated facts. But where the break-up of
this marriage was concerned, Milligan's powers of self-
deception have been absent. He saw and felt the acute
distress of his children, and he relived his own distress
and agony constantly in the years that followed.

> I can always remember a strange little smirk on Laura's face,
> the way her mouth worked when she knew her mother wasn't
> coming back. This sad little smirk, I can still see it today on
> her face. She never lost it. It never went away. And I have to
> blame myself for the break-up of the marriage. I was shattered
> in every way. The whole business of being responsible for a
> family somehow crushed me – I felt inadequate. I think I *was*
> inadequate. It wasn't June's fault. Poor girl, she couldn't cope
> with me and you couldn't blame her.

When he returned from that second trip to Australia,
Milligan was unable to face the solitude of 127 Holden
Road. The children's voices seemed everywhere, and every
corner of the garden reminded him of hours that had been
wonderfully happy.

14
Single Parent

In the middle of my life I found myself in a dark
wood.

Dante

Milligan was by now famous and there was a certain news
value in the break-up of his marriage. This distressed him,
and he avoided interviews and usually refused to speak to
the press. He lived mostly in his office at 2 Cumberland
House, but even the office had ceased to be a wholly
comfortable refuge as Associated London Scripts had now
become such big business that there were constant board
meetings there. A new formality was approaching which
was alien to Spike's ideology. Dissent and trouble were
brewing.

He saw a lot of his children, and took Sean and Laura on
outings to the London Planetarium and Bertram Mills
Circus. Broadcasting in the BBC programme *Tonight*, just
after the sad return from Australia, he was full of apparent
jocularity. 'I'll say goodnight to Sean, Laura and Silé now;
it'll save me a phone call.'

Despair and depression still overwhelmed him in great
waves. Visualizing his life without the children tormented
him; at times he locked himself in his office without
company, food or drink or any sort of medical help.
Friends tried to do what they could. Michael Foot sent his
stepdaughter Judy round in the hope that she could help.

She was a ministering angel. I think she might have saved my
life, I was so bad at that time. I got very fond of her and we
did get engaged, but I think we both knew it couldn't really

work. I was very sensitive about the children at that time and I think she really thought she couldn't cope with me, but she was a wonderful friend and she helped me a lot.

Silly Verse for Kids came out in time for Christmas 1959 and was immediately reprinted. Its success was an enormous boost to Spike's flagging spirits. The first long-play *Goon Show* record was also released.

Eric Sykes, always a generous and understanding friend, made the first Christmas of the broken marriage as happy as humanly possible – Spike and the children were invited to the Sykes' family home in Surrey. There were Christmas trees, presents, parties, balloons and all the festivities for a happy Christmas.

During December 1959 and January 1960 the last few *Goon Shows* were broadcast. Milligan was grateful for his mammoth success, and utterly thankful that it was over. The tenth and last series ended on 28 January 1960.

Spike was silently jubilant about the good reception for *Silly Verse for Kids*, but the strong feeling of inadequacy remained. He was able to accept the success of this particular book because it had been aimed at young children, the age group to whom he could most easily relate. Their world was still his world and he felt safe. Writing for grown-ups would be different. The familiar self-deprecation appears on the first pages of his first book, *A Dustbin of Milligan*. The title alone suggested that he held himself up to ridicule and did not presume to be taken seriously.

Two very amusing introductory pieces, supposedly written by his parents, are geared to show a lumpish, foolish, backward boy, in fact an unlettered, amiable ass:

My son has asked me to write this, he is a good boy, and very kind to his mother. It was never more than flesh wounds he gave me. He bought me a washing machine for his birthday,

but every time I got in, the paddles nearly beat me to death,
oh how we laughed. He is a good boy and kind to his mother.
We make big bonfires for him, but he never goes in. He
climbed a tree for his summer holiday. He likes climbing
trees. We gave him one for Christmas. He fell off. Oh how we
laughed. He is a good boy and kind to his mother. Oh how we
laughed.

His Mother
X
Her Mark

His 'father's' contribution is even funnier.

My Son has asked me to write the 'blurb' for this, his second
book. What can I say? When he was a lad, he showed a natural
inclination to write so I sent him to Eton. By the time he was
twenty-one he had mastered the alphabet. He filled his note
books with his own stories. One day he came to me, 'Father,'
(he knew that much) 'Father,' he said, 'I have this feeling of
literary genius, do you think that one day I will take my place
alongside men like Shakespeare and Chaucer?' Straight away I
told him I couldn't wait for him to join them. He took to
travelling everywhere by pram – said it made him look
younger. In 1940 he was invited to join World War Two (with
an option on World War Three). Partly out of his mind, he
accepted. So, with one stroke of a pen, he put three years on
the war, eight years on Churchill, and 2d. on the rates. He
was fired on by both sides. Montgomery asked to see him and
threw a brick at his head. When the war ended he was found
wandering in a Y.W.C.A. near Yarmouth, but still clutching
his option for World War Three. At the Court Case he was
granted custody of his body and a maintenance claim against
him for a small lad called Tom Lengths. All this is getting us
nowhere and that's exactly where I came in.

Signed
(In script) Dad Milligan

Orange Grove Road,
Woy Woy
Orstrilia

A *Dustbin of Milligan* established a pattern of humorous self-denigration and that suggestion of a basic lack of confidence which survives, in various guises, throughout almost all of his career as a writer. Yet even in this very early book he shows enough presumption mildly to mock his readers.

Author's Note: I know this story lacks that vital something, but what the hell.

S.M.

He is anxious to establish that he does not overtly seek their approval. In the same short story (which was originally written for *Varsity*, the Cambridge University magazine, in 1955) he demonstrates a certain aloof disdain and a curious mixture of egoism and self-effacement.

'Why did you thrust that note under your nose?' asked the detective. 'It's not under my nose, it's under yours, it's the way this story's written that makes it confusing.' (How dare he! That's the last time he's in a story of mine – Signed, Spike Milligan.)

References to his own name are not infrequent in Milligan's work. In particular, he brings himself into his novel *Puckoon* under the guise of 'The Milligan'.

A *Dustbin of Milligan* is a better compilation than some of his later books, which have the appearance of being thrown together too hurriedly. Milligan's uneven temperament, the rise and fall of the cyclothymic personality, is always his enemy. Apart from the fact that he has, sometimes, energy enough for ten (and this in itself is capable of causing him frustrating and despairing pain), the battles with ill-health have been detrimental to his development in every area of his creative life.

The book is a collection of poems, stories, letters (all to

Harry Secombe), fairy-tales and a section headed 'Politics and Other Nonsense'. In the last-named section, Milligan concentrates his serious anxieties in a flippant manner, yet the reality of what he sees is vivid. The first item is impressive – 'Come On In, The Fall-out is Lovely' or 'They're walking backwards to Aldermaston'. In the story section Milligan has included a little gem called 'The Violin'. He tried hard and unsuccessfully to be allowed to read this for the BBC.

One of the fairy-tales is a wistful little fable called 'The Gingerbread Boy'. Both macabre and tender, it tells of a baker's home-made son with a peppermint heart, who owing to adult carelessness is occasionally allowed to melt. The Milligan children loved this story.

The hardback version of *A Dustbin of Milligan* was reprinted many times and most of the text is still available in a 1984 omnibus edition. Milligan had a hand in designing its original dust-jacket. It shows the author squashed in a dustbin, his eyes peering between the bin and the lid. One spindly right-hand index finger points to the word 'DUSTBIN' on the cover, and the left-hand one to 'MILLI-GAN'. The full title reads *A Dustbin of Milligan or Concentrated Rubbish*.

Spike Milligan was awarded the custody of his three children in March 1960, prior to the divorce. He is still a little mystified as to how this came about, for no criticism was ever levelled at June, who was undoubtedly a loving and capable mother. He discarded his first intention, which had been to sell 127 Holden Road, and moved back there to live with his little brood. Flo wrote anxious letters from Australia. Leo and she had received a request from June's parents for news and photographs of the grandchildren. They had also suggested a visit. Leo wrote a kind but firm refusal to Mr Marlowe; Flo outlined her opinion in a letter to Spike.

> I left the whole decision to Dad. He was *most* adamant about the reply. I wish them no harm, but I must say in view of R.M.'s attitude re his daughter's extravagance coupled with the letter he wrote to us after you left, which we sent to you, his daughter had a halo and his son-in-law horns of the devil, and did not study our feelings in the least. Under the circumstances, as much as my religion teaches me to be charitable, we would be disloyal to our own son and it would be painful to both of us to meet.

Flo concluded her letter with other matters. She had just received news from Poona that her sister Eileen had suffered a heart attack whilst playing tennis in the greatest heat ever recorded there – 107 degrees Fahrenheit – and 'COMPLETE REST for SOME MONTHS' had been ordered. There's sturdy blood in Spike.

During the spring of 1960, there was a reshuffle at Associated London Scripts. The offices at Shepherd's Bush Road had moved first to 2 Cumberland House, W8, and then to Orme Court in Bayswater. Milligan now felt that as a main contributor to the company's funds he should be given a personal typist and helper to take some of the strain. This was discussed at a board meeting and was not agreed; he was upset and talked of resigning.

> What I didn't know was that the company was on the point of selling out, being taken over. They had had an offer from a Yorkshire television company which they took, but as I'd resigned I didn't get the golden handshake that they all got. I felt very badly treated as, if I'd known what was happening, I could have stayed in long enough to get a share. After all I started the company. Eric Sykes was the only one who behaved honourably to me. Eric was decent. He was fair to me. He said, 'What you're doing to Spike isn't right and I don't want

any part of it.' So we joined together and I cut him into 9, Orme Court, the new offices which we then took over, and that in the end made a really good result for him which he deserved.

The new offices were impressive. The houses had been built during prosperous times for the well-off middle class who wished to reside close to Hyde Park and Kensington Gardens. Spike took for his own use a small upstairs room which faced south-west and had a balcony. He had it fitted up with floor-to-ceiling bookshelves and installed a desk and a basket-chair. Encouraged now by the success of *Silly Verse for Kids* he was writing and rewriting *Puckoon*. His lack of experience and his obsession about his lack of formal education sapped his confidence, but his inbuilt sense of timing must have helped him, because the book that eventually emerged – it took four years – was perhaps the best thing he has written to date.

Life, meanwhile, at 127 Holden Road was not easy. Spike spent a lot of time with the children and the domestic arrangements rarely satisfied him. He wrote fairly often to his mother to keep her well acquainted with her grandchildren and his own intentions.

One of the main reasons for my coming to Australia next year would be to enable me the peace I require to finish my novel, and as it is going on for two years since I started it I feel I should like to finish it in Australia where I first commenced to write it. The children are absolutely magnificent, very fit. I now have three servants, a housekeeper, a maid and a Roman Catholic Maltese nannie, the last one being the best. I will be sending some first communion photographs of Laura to you. It takes six months to get photographs printed in London, whereas in a local village you can get them in 48 hours.

Milligan was doing some filming during this time. He appeared in a number of undistinguished productions;

none of them as good as *The Case of the Mukkinese Battlehorn*. There was one, however, in which Peter Sellers and Dick Lester were also involved. It probably had the lowest budget ever for a professionally made film – Spike claimed that it was £50. It ran for eleven minutes and received several awards: *The Running, Jumping and Standing Still Film* is a classic.

Peter Sellers, now married to the Swedish filmstar Britt Ekland, bought a magnificent manor house at Elstead in Surrey. The former Goons met there on several occasions; one well-kept secret was the visit of the young Prince Charles, who was a great Goon fan. Britt took a splendid photograph of the Goons with the 16-year-old prince. Milligan guarded it closely and it was not released for almost twenty years, and then only for a special *Goon Show* celebration, and with the approval of HRH. In April, Laura and Sean, resplendent in party clothes and Cromwellian buckled shoes, were driven to Michael Sellers' birthday party.

During the summer, Spike took Laura and Sean on holiday to Winchelsea. One of the places they visited was Hastings Castle. They lived in a rented cottage and were looked after by a kindly Australian woman called Elizabeth Wiltshire. Spike wrote in his diary 'She was like a mother to them.'

Another unimportant film was going to become important, at least to Milligan. Whilst appearing in *Invasion Quartette*, an unsatisfactory World War II story played for farce, he met Patricia Ridgeway, who had a small part in the film. Paddy (Spike's name for her) came from Yorkshire. She trained for the theatre at a North Country drama school, then came to London to study opera. She was twenty-five and of striking good looks. When Spike met her, she was singing in the London production of *The Sound of Music*. After a few false starts, a dinner date was established. When they faced each other across the table, Spike took her hand and said, 'Miss Ridgeway, you may not believe me – but a year from now we shall be married.'

During 1961, Spike went to stay with Peter Eton and his wife. 'Squirrel' Eton had been a vision mixer in a Manchester TV studio. When she met Peter, she abandoned this career without regret to marry him, and they lived in various beautiful cottages around the South Coast. During times of depression Spike had often visited them. Squirrel was a kind and understanding woman who knew by instinct when to speak and when to stay silent. Like Peter, she had a good understanding of Spike.

On one occasion, when Spike was in the lowest depths, Squirrel looked after him for a few days. He stayed alone, in a small cottage adjacent to theirs. She observed him discreetly and made him a few nourishing soups without allowing him to feel hounded. One evening, Peter decided that Spike was now sufficiently restored to go out to dinner. He knew a good, quiet restaurant on the other side of Rye. Spike agreed cautiously. He was very silent on the drive but his spirits rose during the meal.

On the way home the full moon shone with astonishing brilliance. Spike was enthralled as they drove along the narrow Sussex lanes. He turned off the car lights. 'It's amazing,' he said. 'It's like bright daylight. We can save the battery, we don't need lights!' Going through Rye, the mists came swirling around and at several stages they stopped whilst Spike investigated some of the old smugglers' passages and lanes.

'I remember he was just like a child,' says Squirrel. 'Tremendously enthusiastic, bubbling over with interest and excitement. You couldn't have stopped him, and Peter and I just went along. Of course, he got us fascinated as well.'

It was to Squirrel and Peter that Spike turned now. He visited them with Paddy and the children, afterwards questioning them closely for their observations on Paddy's suitability as future wife and stepmother to his children.

Paddy did not agree immediately to Spike's proposal, but asked for a month in which to make up her mind. This month was a strain for Milligan, who was unaccustomed to waiting, and it was with great delight that he eventually received her answer.

Milligan has had a long and treasured friendship with the Mermaid Theatre. Bernard Miles gave him his first straight acting role there – that of Ben Gunn in *Treasure Island*, a lively adaptation of Robert Louis Stevenson's classic adventure story. When Milligan and Miles first met, Miles's perceptive and acute antennae were well alerted; he understood and appreciated Milligan with a keen insight that had nothing to do with tolerance or patronage. He gave him the part of Ben Gunn because he could see Milligan's potential and was prepared to accept the challenge. And Milligan, formidably unpredictable as he was, toed the line. He was interested in his part and gave a creditable performance. Bernard Miles was delighted:

> Milligan is a man of quite extraordinary talents. He is a man on his own, a visionary who is out there alone, denied the usual human contacts simply because he is so different he can't always communicate with his own species. He is a man marooned, half the time he might as well be on a desert island. I dare say that's why Ben Gunn was his part. He is a man marooned, really. You could say he is Ben Gunn.

On 24 December, Spike took Laura, Sean and Silé to a children's carol service. He kept the programme, and wrote on it 'It was bitter cold, but fun.' It was the last Christmas for a long time that he would spend as a single parent.

Throughout the winter of 1961–2, *Treasure Island* played two houses every day. There was a long pause between the end of the matinée and the beginning of the evening show, but no time is ever wasted when Milligan is on form. He began talking to Bernard Miles about the idea he was exploring with John Antrobus of a dramatized post-nuclear world.

Antrobus had been approached by a newly-formed Canterbury repertory company called Tomorrow's Audience, one of whose members was Richard Ingrams, the future editor of *Private Eye*. They were pressing for the play to be ready for their second production, which was scheduled for 12 February 1962. The time was short, but Milligan and Antrobus related to each other with spontaneous ease. Joyfully they swapped ideas and capped each other's lines. Antrobus, already a successful and disciplined playwright, was exactly the collaborator Spike needed. Spike was eager to introduce him to Bernard Miles, so he invited him to come to the Mermaid and now there were three of them, all in the throes of creative mirth. It is probably fair to say that *The Bedsitting Room* was born of Spike's incarceration between houses of *Treasure Island* at the Mermaid Theatre, Puddle Dock. And Bernard Miles will rightly claim that he was the midwife.

Ben Gunn's dressing-room became the writing-room. Antrobus arrived faithfully every day and work was perpetually in progress. Ben Gunn, though never actually 'off', must have kept the Mermaid stage management crew (let alone the cast) in a state of perpetual hazard. He was eternally rushing from the stage, fleet of foot and fiery of eye. 'Quick – put this down – it's an idea – right – OK –

back soon,' and he would leap back to the stage in time for his next cue.

Bernard Miles, another one ahead of his time, had a visionary's courage and decided to stage *The Bedsitting Room* at the Mermaid. 'It was fantastic,' he recalls. 'As the play got nearer and nearer production the scriptwriting became faster and faster. There were so many additions, alterations, take-outs, put-ins, extras – at the final analysis we had four secretaries, all with typewriters, all typing away at full speed and all of them well-trained, efficient girls begging to know "Where do I put this in – what number is the page?" Of course they could never tell the girls because they never knew themselves. The script was in a constant state of flux. "Call it 14A," Spike would say helpfully. "But we've already got pages 14, 14A and 14B," the girl would murmur. "Well, call it supplement to pages 14A/14C," Antrobus would declare. "Just you type it," Spike would yell. "We'll find somewhere to put it," and he would snatch up his Ben Gunn hat and tear down to the stage for his next entrance.'

Carol Crowther, a young arts student (now author of *Clowns and Clowning*), was temporarily seconded to the Mermaid on an arts studentship at this time. It was, for her, a baptism of fire. 'There was always this anxiety: would he get on the stage in time? He always did, I dare say we all grew neurotic about him, but I remember people going down and sort of chatting him up and getting him into the right mood for going on. I was very interested in clowning, and I used to watch him with something approaching awe. He had every attribute of the great clowns. And he could act.'

Milligan has been heard to say, 'I wish I were ten people. There is so much I want to do.' During the performance of *Treasure Island* and the writing of *The*

Bedsitting Room it must have sometimes seemed as though he were.

At the Marlowe Theatre in Canterbury, *The Bedsitting Room* received good local notices, but it made little impact on London's theatrical scene. It was not to achieve full recognition for over a year, when Bernard Miles kept his promise and put it on at the Mermaid.

15
Puckoon and Oblomov

The midnight agony of things undone

L. A. G. Strong

Terence Alan Milligan married Patricia Margaret Ridgeway on 28 April 1962 at the Church of Our Lady of Good Counsel in Rawdon, Yorkshire. A reception was held at the Old Swan Hotel in Harrogate. Spike's memories have sad overtones.

> I was taken over by a very highly organized father-in-law, and he organized it superbly. It was to be a proper wedding. I'd always fought shy of anything very grand – I'd got married very quickly to June at Caxton Registry Office. I was taken over, really. Paddy was very strong. I don't think Paddy ever had much confidence in me at any level, she thought I was a nice guy and all that, and she loved me, but when it came to any business matters she seemed to shy away. I was still very mental in those days – still very prone to dives, emotional dives, and deep down I suppose I wanted a mother for the children who was decent and didn't drink and didn't smoke and who wasn't a tart. This was a nice country lass, in the profession, musical, honest, kind, and I did fall in love with her; yes, I did.

Peter Sellers was out of England, but Harry Secombe was present at the wedding. It was a fashionable occasion, and Spike was rather mortified that he was expected to wear the full Moss Bros outfit.

> George Martin, of Beatles fame, was my best man. It was a very upmarket wedding, marquee in the garden, all that sort of thing. It was a tiny church, and I remember I didn't like the Moss Bros suit I had to wear, black striped trousers, terribly

heavy and old-fashioned. Made me feel like a bandleader or something. But the thing that concerned me most about the wedding was that Laura, the bridesmaid, burst out crying. Burst into tears. All these things – secret cracks in children. She'd lost her mother, now her Daddy was being pulled further away. This sadness dominated the whole proceedings for me really, in fact I remember it to this day. The one thing I can't stand is the despoliation of a child's character by adults' indifference, or inability, or immaturity. Really, I don't think anybody's mature enough to get married until they are about fifty; unfortunately the child-bearing age has then gone past so God was a very bad judge of psychology and conception, he didn't get the two together at all. By the time you're clever enough to get married you are both sexually impotent, which might be very good for the human race, believe it or not.

After they had been married for about six weeks Spike and Paddy sailed for Australia on the *Arcadia*. The children were left as boarders at the convent school which Laura attended in Finchley. Spike had been invited to work on a further production of *Idiot Weekly* for the ABC. Once again it featured Michael Eisdell; also in the cast were Ric Hutton, John Ewant and Al Thomas. Paddy was included in the show as the 'featured vocalist'.

Leo and Flo were now well established at Woy Woy, about fifty miles from Sydney. Spike had arranged to have an extension built onto their house, a 'log cabin' which Leo used as a place to store and display his large gun collection. The Milligans seemed happy in their retirement.

During this visit, Milligan appeared in *The Spike Milligan Show*. In one scene, he says, 'It's a great wide wonderful world' against a film background showing atom bombs exploding, buildings crumbling, politicians snarling, wars, fighting and general violence. The *TV Times* covered the show under the headline 'TOP PROFESSIONAL IDIOT SPIKE MILLIGAN ON VIEW AGAIN'.

During the long absence of their father and new step-mother, the Milligan children were well looked after at the convent and they received a good number of large, illustrated letters from both Spike and Paddy. They arrived back in time for Christmas, which was spent at 127 Holden Road. Spike was now in the throes of rehearsals for *The Bedsitting Room*, scheduled to open at the Mermaid in January 1963.

The children settled down. The separation from their adored father had gone badly with Laura, whose extreme sensitivity had taken a hard knock when Spike disappeared for what seemed a very long time. It is a curious aspect of his almost overwhelming love for his children that he had found it difficult to be honest with them about how long he intended to be away. Perhaps he had an ostrich-like need to avoid the possibility of seeing them distressed. Indeed, if this had happened, it is doubtful that he could have gone, contracts or no contracts, parents or no parents.

Laura never quite fell in under Paddy's yoke. Paddy had very determined ways of trying to bring up her little stepdaughters. Her plans to pin up their hair in curls and nets before they went to bed each night were accepted by Silé but secretly despised by Laura who thought it unnecessary and uncomfortable. Yet Laura longed for her stepmother's approval and love; perhaps she tried too hard. Sean, docile and handsome, was eager to please and had no difficulty. Silé, a beautiful fairy golden child – the apple of her father's eye – was everybody's angel. Spike looked pensively at Laura from time to time. His own over-perceptive antennae could not be ignored. He accepted the situation and his guilt soared. Laura was an unhappy little girl.

Silly Verse for Kids and *A Dustbin of Milligan* were still reprinting. *Puckoon* was now in its final draft and being vaguely 'looked after' by one of Milligan's friends from Associated London Scripts. In one of those inexplicable confusions that sometimes occur, whilst Spike was in Australia *Puckoon* was given to another publisher, Anthony Blond. This was rather hard on the Dobsons, who had been instrumental in giving Spike the confidence he needed to start writing books in the first place. Spike, sensitive to injustice, always felt upset about this.

> I don't know what happened exactly. It's the story of my life how things get messed up when I don't do everything myself. I left it to this chap and he gave it to another publisher. I think it was the old boy network. I felt bad about the Dobsons. It was unfair. I owed it to Dennis Dobson that he had started me off on this trail. To me it was inconceivable that I would be a writer. I remember finishing off the last of the children's poems sitting in the front room of my mother's house at Woy Woy. I was sitting in the window-seat, wonderfully quiet, looking out over Brisbane waters in the early mornings. There's no peace like that any more – not even in Woy Woy. Then I sent the last few off to the publisher and I think they came back in proof form. Printed. I just couldn't comprehend that this was my work actually in print. To me it was a mind-blowing achievement that someone like myself could get a book published. So of course I was always upset that they didn't get *Puckoon*, which turned out a big success, and which they richly deserved.

The Bedsitting Room opened at the Mermaid Theatre on 31 January 1963. Several rapturous weeks later it transferred to the Duke of York's. The programme (good value at one shilling) included interesting photographs of Milligan, Antrobus, Graham Stark, John Bluthall and Valentine Dyall, who were all in the cast. The musical director was Alan Clare. Although there is no doubt that Milligan was surprised and gratified when the show transferred from the Mermaid to the West End, his pleasure in appearing gradually diminished over the year

until, eventually, the strain of coping with eight performances a week on top of a busy film schedule, complications
over the publishing of *Puckoon* and his commitment to the
French play *Ubu Roi* began to reduce him. He wrote an
article on 'Relaxation without a Hypnotist' which appeared
in a daily paper. In this he said that he achieved rare
moments of relaxation when he went on stage. 'I actually
feel better when I've done a performance,' he admits.
However, his nervous tension increased. Paddy, married
less than a year to Spike, was concerned and distressed.
Her experience of mental illness was negligible and she
was undoubtedly out of her depth. When Spike's understudy had appeared several times, vaguely differing causes
were given to the press. The stage manager said, rather
wanly, 'I think he is just overtired.' His agent veered
between a slipped disc and 'mental exhaustion'. Paddy,
doing her best, blamed 'a severe migraine'. Once again
Milligan's joy had turned to ashes. He wanted nothing so
much as to be released from the strain of facing a different
audience every night.

It is certain, nevertheless, that *The Bedsitting Room* was
a solid brick in the frail wall of Milligan's self-esteem. After
the first night at the Duke of York's, he sent a copy of the
programme to Florence and Leo. He penned a short letter
on the back cover.

My Dear Mum and Dad,
  Well, at last I have my name up in lights in the West End.
Mind you that's nothing as far as security goes, Sir Laurence
Olivier still has to appear there to make a living. It does mean
that I have made a success in a new field, once more putting
to flight those critics and doubters who thought I was just a
gag-writer. My novel is now coming out in September, which
is a better time for sales than April (as originally scheduled). I
hope you and the Edgingtons had a nice meal. Don't forget I
want to pay the bill. Well, I'll write a longer letter tomorrow.

                                        Your loving son, Terence

1963 had started rather sadly for Flo and Leo. Desmond's second wife, Nadia, had just given birth to a still-born daughter. Flo wrote comfortingly to Paddy and Spike: 'The poor little soul weighed only 2½lbs. It is as well that God took her back to Heaven.'

Leo and Florence read press reports on the success of *The Bedsitting Room*. Leo wrote:

My dear Spike & Paddy
  We have received all the good news about the success of your *Bedsitting Room*. It has had a good press out here, and Mum and I are full of excitement regarding it. We hope that some film rights will follow. It's Spike's breakthrough onto the gravy train. I knew it had to come some time and we hope it's going to have a long run.

But by the time this letter arrived in England, Milligan was already fighting the onset of further bouts of depression. Most nights he would manage to get through the performance, leaving quickly by an unlikely exit and rushing home. Some nights he would sleep in his office; either way he would usually need silence and his own company. It was an uncertain introduction to married life for Paddy, and all the more bewildering for her because of the erratic course of the illness. The manic-depressive syndrome was still barely understood by the vast majority of people; sometimes the very rapidity of the mood swings, the constant leap from despair to elation – and back again – would suggest an element of wilfulness on the part of the patient which could bring useless feelings of guilt to both patient and his family, the patient feeling that the sometimes transient nature of the depression should by its very irrationality be controllable. In this way, suffering and anguish for both the patients and their relatives can be doubly hard. It was so for Spike and Paddy.

* * *

In the August of 1963, Milligan agreed to open one of the first 'Adventure' playgrounds. This particular playground had been achieved partly by a voluntary committee acting with the CND, who used their 'construction service' facilities to get it under way. In his role as celebrity and CND supporter, Spike was an ideal choice. He went along willingly enough, but no doubt received something of a setback when he found that he was expected to take his place on a flower-filled platform between the Member of Parliament for St Pancras and the civic dignitaries of Finsbury and Holborn. At first glimpse of the flashing chains of office he side-tracked into the extensive display of children's art which was on the walls of the large wet-weather wooden hut. Many of the paintings and drawings had been decorated with CND signs. Milligan returned to the platform, called for silence and immediately discharged his responsibility.

'Look, why should I be the one to open it? It's your playground, isn't it? So we'll all open it together!'

The children found this more promising than speeches and roared a cheerful assent.

'Right,' said Spike. 'I call one, two, three and we all shout "OPEN" together – ready?'

Thus, the playground was opened, and Spike then grabbed handfuls of the flowers decorating the platform and threw them into the crowds of lively children. 'And take these home for your mothers,' he yelled. When the excitement abated somewhat, he strode among the children distributing chocolates and sweets. As a friendly parting gesture, he gave Mars Bars to the startled dignitaries.

'Let's hope,' he said sombrely, just before he left, 'that these children grow up before there is another war.'

Milligan was still not free of financial worry; three children, a wife and a large household to keep afloat proved a constant and unremitting strain. The Goons had not made him rich but at least the income had been more or less regular; now it seemed that Peter and Harry were forging ahead into new and remunerative careers whilst he remained behind. Michael Foot remembers him about this time.

> I don't think he in any way begrudged the others their great successes, but I think he felt it a bit hard that he had been so much in at the launch and that they sailed on without him, as it were. Of course they all had brilliance; Peter Sellers was a wonderful performer, a mimic, but not a genius in the same sense as Spike, and he was always ready to acknowledge it and I'm sure that Harry Secombe does. Harry Secombe, in fact, was always very good to Spike. I saw them all occasionally at parties and picked up this sort of thing.[1]

Puckoon came out in October 1963, published by Anthony Blond. It received mixed reviews, some dismissive, some laudatory. The *Evening Standard* was severe:

> At last, folks, the book that Spike Milligan took years and 14 secretaries to write. Unfortunately, a sad disappointment for Goon fans, the zany humour concerning many goings-on in an Irish town doesn't translate easily to the page. And (this may give an idea of the level) too many old jokes spoil a broth of a novel.

The *Daily Mail* was kinder:

> *Puckoon*, Spike Milligan's first novel, has a surrealist sanity, is extraordinarily well written and pops with the erratic brilliance of a careless match in a box of fireworks –

The Times Literary Supplement concluded its review with a few lines that are interesting because the writer has made a clear thumbnail sketch of a Milligan that is recognizable today but must have been harder to point to in 1963.

. . . he dances happily from one verbal extravaganza to another, throwing in everything which comes into his head (sometimes rather disconcertingly, a perfectly serious diatribe about abortion or a note of real tragedy mixed up with the nonsense) and making cheerful jokes about Negroes, Jews, Roman Catholics, homosexuals and other convenient occasions of liberal sympathy just as if they were people like you and me instead of painful special cases to be handled with care. The book is funny, unpredictable, and sometimes salutarily disturbing; one could hardly ask for more from a novelist who knew all the rules.

In *Puckoon*, set in rural Ireland, the reader is instantly exposed to a highly articulate Milligan whose immediate impact is not a cue for laughter.

Joyous voiced children fought for turns at the iron pump, their giggling white bodies splashing in the cool water from its maternal maw; bone-dreaming dogs steamed on the pavements and pussy cats lay, bellies upwards, drinking the gold effulgent warmth through their fur; leather-faced fishcatchers puzzled at the coarse Atlantic now flat and stunned by its own salt hot inertia. Shimmering black and still, it lay at the mercy of stone-throwing boys; the bowmen of the sands took respite from the endless cavalry charges of the sea. Nearby, Castle Hill groaned under the weight of its timeless ruins, while the distant mountains came and went in the mid-morning haze.

Puckoon is really a very funny book indeed, but it is interesting that Milligan apparently felt no need to capsize his readers with mirth on the first page. His acutely perceptive opening paragraphs would be more likely to arouse nostalgic childhood memories than laughter, and *Puckoon*, his first full-length book, was rewarding to Spike both commercially (it became a best-seller and is now in its 22nd paperback edition) and artistically. It was published three years after Spike said in a press interview that he would like to write a serious book if society would accept it but that 'it would have to be satirical'.

How did Milligan come to write with such an authentic confidence about the Irish? His father had left Ireland in his youth, his mother had never actually lived there, family recollections and memories must have become distant and diffused.

> It must have been my father. He had a marvellous memory and my grandfather had told him all the old tales, some of them almost mythical by now, and they must have been exaggerated. And my father was a fine actor and a wonderful raconteur. He talked so much about Ireland to me whenever we were together. We used to cry with laughter when he told us the story of the cat that pissed on the matches.

Over the years, he has nurtured a curious, tentative affection for his unknown Irish antecedents. He has delved deeply into the past and his persistent and meticulous researches have revealed some interesting stories, some of which have been noted by him in the large photograph albums. Some of the stories that Leo told Spike must have impressed him. One in particular referred to an ancestor of Flo's, a fierce old lady named Mary Burnside, née Ryan, who remembered being evicted, along with her family, from their cottage in Sligo by English landlords. She would tell the story of the eviction, and recall how the landlords' agents set fire to the cottage, and how she stood with her parents watching her home burn down. She nursed a hatred of the English for ever, and for the rest of her life, whenever she heard the word 'England' mentioned, she spat on the ground.

Many years later, Spike earned his mother's displeasure because of his dilemma when he was invited to the wedding of the Prince of Wales and Lady Diana Spencer. The Anti-Blood Sports associations, who had always received Spike's support, asked him to boycott the wedding on the grounds of the Prince's involvement with blood sports. This was a difficult decision for Spike, for whilst he respected and liked Prince Charles, he deeply disapproves of any sport which involves the suffering of animals. There was a certain amount of family conflict.

'Of course you must go, son. It's an honour to be invited to the wedding of the future King of England,' Florence rebuked him firmly.

'Don't talk to me about England,' retorted Spike. 'What do you owe to England? Don't you remember your own great-grandmother telling you about the English burning her house down? Why all this chat about England all of a sudden? We're an Irish family, aren't we?'

Nevertheless, Spike did go to the wedding.

As befits a true Irishman, Milligan can occasionally call on a talent for the 'blarney'. Vocally, he is articulate and persuasive. He is capable of making a well-ordered and disciplined speech, yet at the slightest opportunity he will leap off-course with a series of spiralling asides which can either endorse a point with clarity and panache or alternatively demolish an argument with cutting disdain and (occasionally) inadequate grounds. Because of this, his keen intellect is constantly a prey to his heightened emotional reactions. His awareness is sharp and profound, and because it reacts so forcibly upon his extreme sensitivity it disallows him the comfort of compromise.

Several interesting things were happening in 1963 for Milligan. He had been asked by impresario-producer Oscar Lowenstein to adapt and direct *Ubu Roi*, a play by the French writer Alfred Jarry. It had been a controversial macabre play which, with its sequel *Ubu Enchaîné*, had shaken French audiences at the turn of the century, with the wild indecent farce satirizing the petty dictators of everyday life. André Gide called *Ubu Roi* 'the most extraordinary thing seen in the theatre for a long time' and confessed that he, Picasso, Cocteau and Apollinaire all owed it a debt.

Spike was fascinated with *Ubu Roi* and anxious to take up the story. The ill-fated *Telegoons* were on the point of being launched on BBC TV. Milligan had little pleasure and no pride in their production, but he did accept the unusually high fees which Sellers, Secombe and he were offered to vocalize these 'Goon' puppets. He was more confident about the revival on ITV of some of the *Fred* series. *The Best of Fred* was once again hailed by some critics as ahead of its time and thrown out by others who 'didn't find it funny'.

As well as *Puckoon*, Spike also brought out *The Little Pot Boiler* in the autumn of 1963.

Leo wrote from Australia:

> Mum and I were much impressed with its context especially the stupid little sketches, odes and verse. But most of all Mum is impressed with the Dust Jacket photo of you. She thinks it's a grand photo of her son, real handsome 'should have been a serious actor' she says, in spite of the puckish pose.
>
> Mum also thinks the costume, the period coat and neckwear suits you, and you should *always* dress that way.
>
> Congratulations, four books on the market. You said some years ago that you were a writer, not so much of a goon, you have certainly proved it. In no small way.
>
> Mum sends her love to you all. Cheerio and God bless.
>
> > Affectionately
> > Dad

During this year much correspondence was exchanged on the possibility of Flo and Leo visiting England. They had been in Australia for eleven years and the idea was very appealing. Spike, of course, was funding the holiday and to begin with several dates in 1963 were discussed. It was not an ideal year from Spike's point of view as he was fully occupied with *The Bedsitting Room* as well as his other areas of work; but perhaps the shadow of the boy who had not got a 'proper job' wanted to be seen working? Once, when he was asked why he didn't do more theatre work, Milligan was firm:

> I don't know. I'd like to. I like the theatre. It's my working-class origins – the feeling of going to work every day at the same time and getting a weekly pay packet. Very secure. I like working in a theatre.

Towards the end of 1963, Milligan's condition deteriorated sharply. He came out of *The Bedsitting Room* just before Christmas and was replaced by an understudy, the play closing in the early weeks of 1964. Milligan's name had been a great draw, and the traditionally difficult post-Christmas period did not survive without him. Plans for *Ubu Roi* did not come to fruition. Spike was now in a state of collapse. He went into a nursing home where he was kept heavily sedated. After two weeks he returned to his home, still under a deep blanket of depression. He lay on his bed, taut and still, staring at the wall. Paddy was in despair. The children went around the house on tiptoe. No fairy letters had arrived for them for a long time. The psychiatrist suggested electro-convulsion therapy.

About this time the musician Alan Clare went round to 127 Holden Road. He found Spike threshing about in his bed, haggard and disorientated.

'I feel so ill,' he told Alan, 'and I'm hearing the most beautiful music – all the time going round in my head.'

Alan was distressed. He had no inkling as to how he could help his friend, but music had always been his own strength, and he knew it to be Milligan's solace. He spoke anxiously, guardedly.

'Well then – can you get any of it down? Are you writing it down?'

Milligan groaned and writhed in his bed. 'No, I can't, I can't. It's too fine, you see, Alan. It's too fine.'

Alan, baffled, sat at the foot of the bed. Two men arrived in white coats. One was carrying electrodes and the paraphernalia for electric shock treatment in an old Oxo tin. Spike had obviously been expecting them.

'Oh, here they come. I'm sorry, Alan. You'll have to go now. It's this rotten business now. They've come to electrocute me.'

The men disappeared into the bathroom for the moment and Spike glared bitterly after them.

'Look at this gear. An old Oxo tin. What a bizarre way to look after anyone. What a way to carry medical supplies, I ask you – and do you know, Alan, they actually use my electricity, what do you think of that? For two pins I'll have a slot meter put in here, then they'd have to put a shilling in.'

Alan Clare never forgot the incident.

It was marvellous, really. There he was looking as ill and sick as anyone could, really in the deepest depths, you couldn't help him or say anything, it was all a terrible disaster, what with the play having done so well and everything but it was amazing he could still somehow manage to make a joke of it, in the midst of all that.

In Australia, Florence and Leo read of Spike's breakdown in the press. Flo wrote immediately:

We knew you were ill from the newspaper reports. It's very difficult to keep these things away from the news world when one is in the public eye. Of course I didn't need the newspapers to tell me for I wrote long ago to say I knew you were ill. There is a telepathy between you and I the same as existed between my darling mother and I.

The news of Spike's illness and the uneasy context of such letters as he managed to write to his father troubled

Leo profoundly. It would seem that Leo had for many years avoided any real confrontation with his son on the matter of his mental and spiritual suffering, but something now precipitated his release from a self-imposed burden of silence. The letter he wrote brought Spike a fresh vision of his father, but not a surprising one.

My dear Terence,
   Thanks for your letter of Feb 17th.
   Yes! I'm certain the children loved the snowfall and the pleasure of making a snowman. It's one of those simple joys provided by nature that children love, and remember, when they have grown to adulthood.
   However, I was disturbed to read in your letter that you are still in a sort of mental twilight state, and that you find it difficult to obtain human understanding.
   How often have you remarked to your Mother, 'Dad doesn't understand,' but of all the people in your life – who should?
   I can honestly and sincerely say that as I battled through life I suffered mentally the same as you. I was, and still am, just as sensitive, and felt every kick that came my way. I too, had a creative mind, but was frustrated all the time. Only my sons appreciated it in the form of bedtime stories, they were my best audience.
   I left home at the age of 14, and had very little contact with my Father and Mother after that. So I had no one to turn to for comfort and advice.
   My school days were a torment, my army days were worse, I served in a brainwashed army, 'You are not paid to think,' came from NCOs and officers, 'you are paid to obey.' I just had to grin and bear it.
   Civilian life brought no relief from torment. I suffered the most intolerable indignities at the A.P. I worked a twelve hour week day, and a 16 hour Sunday, with disreputable men and women whom I loathed. I was the 'bleeding chicken in the run', as you described it.
   Often during my active life responsibility weighed so heavily upon me, that I felt my reason would cave in, but I must have had some Irish O' Maolagain toughness in my moral fibre that carried me through.

Your mother never knew about my suffering, neither did my children, I told no one, I suffered in silence, outwardly I was a happy and contented family man – I was a born actor.

There was no relief for my suffering, no drugs, or psychiatrists, to which I could turn for comfort. It was 'Cold Turkey' for me all the way.

Can you wonder then, that all my life from early childhood, I envied the character 'Robinson Crusoe', alone and away from the torment of a hard and cruel world. Even the savages did not attack him, he attacked them, to save a fellow white man from being devoured. It was prompted by love of his fellow man.

I write in this strain to assure you that you are not alone, we are two of a kind, you and I, so I DO understand, and better than anyone else.

This search for 'human understanding', does it really exist, the kind you seek, I mean, or is it a 'Will O' the Wisp'. I could never find it.

I mention this because the man who gave 'Madame Butterfly', that beautiful operetta, to the world had a fixation in his mind that no one fully appreciated the lovely music he had written for it.

Millions could have told him he was wrong, but he died with this fixation on his mind that no amount of assurance from his fellow creatures could erase.

In this cruel world, one is either a 'somebody', or a 'nobody'. You are one of the former, a somebody, you are a figure in the public eye with fans by the thousand. They appreciate you because you have given them an artistic personality, humour, and laughs, the medicine for all ills, and they love you for it.

Mum and I have been bombarded literally with kind enquiries and best wishes for your speedy recovery, and from people so many thousands of miles away from where you sit reading this letter. It's a true reflection of human understanding there are thousands of good and appreciative people who are with you in spirit.

So, my Son, carry on and go forward, you have the sympathy, understanding and love of your Mum & Dad, your Brother, your Wife and children, Aunts Kathleen and Eileen, Uncle Bertram, and other near and not so near relatives, and many close friends.

You also have your Mother's prayers, still being said, and

the thousands of Rosaries she has recited for you since before you were born, and the numerous Holy Masses offered up, and still being offered for your bodily and spiritual welfare, to strengthen you physically and spiritually to enable you to bear up and carry on.

Our combined love to you our Son, God and his Blessed Mother keep you safe and well. We will be seeing you very soon.

Affectionately, Dad

Spike grieved over the letter; he found it unbearably sad to think that his father, now in his seventies, had borne himself with such reserve. He was moved by the massive unselfishness in Leo which had made him so steadfast to the conventional image of a happy family man – a role that he was temporarily abandoning now solely to assure his son that he was not alone in his misery. It made Spike's own failure to gain any real comfort from either June in the past or Paddy now much more acceptable. The year 1963 had started badly with a viciously cold, frozen winter; the frost was so severe that skating was in full swing on the Serpentine for many days. The year for Spike ended miserably with his almost total breakdown.

Plans went ahead now for Leo and Flo to leave Australia at the beginning of May 1964 and spend the summer in England with Spike, Paddy and the 'darling grandchildren'. Laura was now eleven, Sean nine and Silé five. Spike reserved a fine cabin for them on the SS *Himalaya*. It had two large portholes and its own bathroom. As an afterthought, he sent them a cheque for 'spending money' on the voyage. Leo wrote a note of grateful thanks:

This gift has assured our dignity for the voyage, and we have no need to worry over finance any more for a time. Our grateful thanks to you son for this kindness which we will never forget.

It was a great pity that the show folded, from a financial point of view, I mean. I did think it would run for another year.

However, you have other irons in the fire, and it has proved to the many that it was Spike Milligan that the public wanted to see in *The Bedsitting Room*. Furthermore, these theatrical managers will now know your worth, if they wanted proof of your drawing ability, they have had it in full measure. You should now be in a position to dictate terms, should they require your services in future.

Mum is at church this morning. It is Ash Wednesday. She is a great believer in prayer. I'm afraid after a long life in which I have seen and endured much, suffered so much and gained so little I have lost faith, but not completely. There is still a spark left, it might be kindled again before I pass on, but at the moment I'm not sure.

His parents' visit was a success. Desmond and Nadia saw them off at Sydney and Desmond pronounced their cabin magnificent. 'It's more like a hotel suite than a ship's cabin,' he said. During the long voyage the *Himalaya* called at Bombay and Flo was reunited with her sister Eileen who had driven 600 miles to spend a few hours with her. The sisters had not met for fifteen years.

Once in England, the children were happy to get to know their grandparents again. Leo and Flo visited their friends and relatives and Paddy's relatives in Yorkshire. They had a celebration party for their 50th wedding anniversary before returning to Australia in the autumn.

Spike had reserved return first-class tickets for his parents on the *Canberra* for the journey home but during the voyage across, Flo had discovered that if they wanted to change and return on the one-class *Himalaya* they could have the same delightful cabin again, and that Spike would be refunded £200. Leo contacted Spike with details of this. 'You can be sure that your mother is delighted about the £200,' he commented crisply.

* * *

Milligan's fans and the theatrical world in general found it hard to believe that he was to appear in a straight play – *Oblomov*. He refused to be serious when questioned about his motives. In the story, Oblomov decides to spend his life in bed. Spike decided to identify with his character, and told disbelieving reporters that he thought it would be a nice comfortable rest for him.

This was, of course, prevarication. Spike was actually intrigued with Oblomov and had read a translation of Ivan Goncharov's novel. Goncharov was the son of a wealthy merchant family and a graduate of Moscow University. *Oblomov*, his second novel, was published in 1855 and considered to be important in Russian literature. The story draws a powerful contrast between the aristocratic and the capitalist classes. Oblomov is a well-meaning but fairly useless young nobleman. He cannot 'pull himself together', and is constantly bedevilled by the traditions of his class conflicting with what he sees of ordinary life. He loses the woman he loves to a more practical and robust friend, and gradually sinks into what appears to be sloth. He stays in bed and is cared for by his old landlady, but the descriptions of his condition make it sound curiously like a deep depression.

The play was to open at the Lyric Theatre in Hammersmith on 6 October 1964. The producer was Frank Dunlop. During the rehearsal period, the cast were concerned about their own parts and no one paid particular attention to Spike, who seemed to be having a lot of difficulty in learning his words. The optimistic feeling was that he would be 'all right on the night'. He wasn't, and neither was anybody else. Joan Greenwood played Olga, a part which she recalls as being fairly thankless in any case, and she remembers the horror with which her husband, the late André Morell, greeted the first night. He thought that it was appalling.

'It's too awful, my dear,' he told her. 'We must get you out of this.'

Nobody seemed at all comfortable in their roles and the audience began to hoot with laughter when Milligan's slipper inadvertently went spinning across the stage into the stalls. That was the end of Spike's playing straight. The audience demanded a clown, he became a clown. When he forgot his words, or disapproved of them, he simply made up what he felt to be more appropriate ones. That night there were no riotous first night celebrations and most of the cast seemed to go home stunned.

The following night Milligan began to ad lib in earnest. The text of the show began to change drastically. The cast were bedevilled and shaken but they went along with him and shared some rapturous applause. Incredibly, the show began to resolve itself. The context changed completely. It was turned both upside down and inside out. Cues and lines became irrelevant as Milligan verbally rewrote the play each night. By the end of the week, *Oblomov* had changed beyond recognition. André Morell came again on the Saturday night.

'He was staggered,' recalls Joan Greenwood. 'He came round to my dressing-room and said, "My dear, the man is a genius. He must be a genius – it's the only word for him. He's impossible – but he's a genius!"'

The press, on the whole, was either uncomplimentary or patronizingly tolerant. But the *Sunday Telegraph* carried a review by David Nathan, who was of the same mind as André Morell. 'Milligan', he wrote, 'is a clown of genius.'

Joan Greenwood carried on bravely. She was the only person in the cast who could not be 'corpsed' by Milligan, and he admits that he tried very hard. She looked beautiful, and played the part of Oblomov's unfortunate lady with total integrity. 'She never left the script,' says Milligan with a guilty smile of something between irritation and admiration. 'I just couldn't make her crack up. All the rest of us did. She never lost her dignity for a moment.'

Joan must have been a model of generosity and tolerance.

Oh, Spike – I love him dearly, but he can be terrifying to work with. One day he'll be standing next to you in the wings, desperately sad about an ecological crisis or baby seals being clubbed to death or something he cares most fiercely about, and he'll look all drawn and pale and say, 'How can we go on with all this idiot laughter, tell me that?' But he'll go on and do his piece perfectly and get all the laughs in the world. Then on another day he'll be jumping about full of nonsense, on and off the stage even – he'll do the most unbelievable things like jumping into the audience and taking a chocolate from someone, then back up, and continue the scene with his mouth full, and even stuff a chocolate in *your* mouth so that you can't speak or swallow or anything. He can be paralysing.[2]

After *Oblomov* had run for a record-breaking five weeks at the Lyric Theatre, Hammersmith, it was retitled *Son of Oblomov* and moved to the Comedy Theatre in the West End. Frank Dunlop was once again the producer. Milligan had been hurt by the bad press, though after the first night at the Lyric it was difficult to see what else he could have expected. However he got his own back by inserting scathingly polite invitations in the papers. One in the *Evening Standard* read:

To Milton Shulman, Esq.
Drama Critic

Son of Oblomov
Comedy Theatre

Dear Milton Shulman,
   I am happy to tell you that we have been evicted from Hammersmith after breaking all box-office records there.
   Joan Greenwood and I look forward to seeing you and all

our other friends next Wednesday, 2nd Dec, and onwards at
the Comedy Theatre.

Yours,

R.S.V.P.   Spike Milligan

Milligan's experiences and achievements in television are
difficult to categorize. To begin with, he did not find it
satisfying and was vociferous about the medium on his
visit to Australia in 1963. Probably, as has so often been
his pattern, he was unable to accept what happened to *A
Show Called Fred*, which had such an excellent reception
by many critics and was then axed almost simultaneously
with winning an award. This sort of frustration was miserably destructive, and right through his career, with both
Independent Television and BBC Radio and TV, we sense
what seems to be almost a bureaucratic clobbering of a
gifted and forward-looking artist whose survival is always
uncertain.

One BBC 2 programme that does seem to have brought
him a good deal of pleasure and reward was a poetry and
jazz series which began at the end of 1964. *Muses with
Milligan* was to be a Sunday evening half-hour programme
with music by five jazz musicians, led by Alan Clare, and
guest jazz soloists, intermingled with poets reading mostly
their own work. Spike was to link the items with a few
jokes and funny limericks. As always, the clown's hat had
to go on, but his love of poetry and music made this a
programme that gave him a great deal of satisfaction.

The first show went out on Christmas Day 1964 and
included Cleo Laine, the jazz singer, who sang 'When
Icicles Hang by the Wall', and poets Kingsley Amis and
Charles Causley, who read their own works. Joan Greenwood, in spite of her current agonies in *Oblomov*, cour-
ageously joined the programme and read poems by Edward
Lear and others. It was the first of an immensely successful

series that was repeated within the year because of its great popularity. Huw Wheldon, head of Documentary and Musical programmes for BBC TV, wrote:

> This is only just a little note and I have only got one thing to say in it, and that is that I am enjoying your BBC 2 programmes no end. As you know, when I originally saw Peter Rawley, it seemed to me that this would be a fine thing to do. All I want to say is that the results are better even than I dreamed of. I hope you are pleased yourself. Anyway, there you are. It seems to me that they are bang on.

Spike talked a lot about the programme, and made the best of his own part although his role was sometimes alien to his own inclination.

> I was always expected to turn up and be funny. The literati were allowed to reflect on what they had just heard but Milligan had to jump to it and be hilarious. It wasn't ever meant to be a heavy programme, but sometimes it was hard, very hard, to appear between artists who were immensely moving and be funny.

Maurice Wiggin wrote about this facet of the programme in the *Sunday Times*. Spike dictated a letter:

> I did like your little write-up in the *Sunday Times* (this should be an honour for you, I have never written to a critic before). Anyhow I thought I would explain that the BBC insist on me reading bits of comic verse in between the literati. I love poetry and find no greater strip-down of the mind than when reading someone like Alun Owen or Yeats, but alas as I say the dictates of those that pay us have made it part of the programme to be Milligan reading nonsense in between. While I am writing to you I might as well say that you are that rare bird, the critic who has a genuine critical contribution to make and not just a critical comment made to destroy. I thought you ought to know. Did you know that there are no dry cleaners in Tibet?
>
> Regards as ever,

Perhaps the single and most important pleasure that Spike took in the programme was his meeting with Robert Graves. On 17 November 1964, the producer, John Furness, wrote to Spike: 'I have been doing some sums this afternoon, and it looks as though we are still a bit short of material, and I intend, therefore, to ask Dannie and Laurie to have an extra poem up their sleeves for both programmes.' He was referring to Dannie Abse and Laurie Lee – both poets much admired by Milligan. Across the bottom of the typed page Furness added in ink: 'P.S. Marvellous line-up for the 2 programmes on Dec 6th. Adrian Mitchell, Robert Graves, Annie Ross who will sing a jazz setting of a poem by Graves – a first performance in this country.'

Spike prepared himself to meet Robert Graves. He was, unusually for him, more than a little awed.

16
Poets Clowning

> Those blind from birth ignore the false perspective
> Of those who see. Their inward-gazing eyes
> Broaden or narrow no right-angle;
> Nor does a far-off mansion fade for them
> To match-box size.
>
> Robert Graves

Spike Milligan first met Robert Graves on the stage at what is now the Riverside Studios. It was to be a memorable meeting for them both.

> I couldn't believe it. There he was, this great man, this smiling giant, this wonderful apparition sitting there – it was as if we'd known each other always. I was so overwhelmed with him, I thought is this the great scholarly poet I've read about? Here he vas with a stetson on his head and a great medallion thing round his neck, somehow untrammelled by the pressures of the world.

In spite of the fact that *Muses with Milligan* was, in a sense, built around Spike, he was not entirely at his ease. Robert Graves, in the way that he had, soon counteracted that. He had a glorious disregard for the intricacies of television; he accepted no rules and took no advice from anyone. Like Spike, he defied conformity and within the space of minutes they were confirmed allies.

That evening, at the end of this first meeting, Spike and Robert dined together. Their friendship was forged, solid and enduring.

Immediately after returning to his home in Deya on the west coast of the island of Majorca, Robert wrote to Spike – a splendid letter in his untidy, scholarly hand. Spike replied in high spirits and huge writing using his favourite thick nib and black ink. Thus began an intriguing correspondence between two gifted eccentrics who met in the no-man's-land of Graves's 'fifth dimension'. It is hard to say exactly what drew them together, why they were so perfectly attuned. It wasn't just the rare identical sense of humour, nor the sense of camaraderie that was very much a feature of this unusual programme. It was not just mutual admiration. Perhaps it was something to do with the feeling of instant friendship and relaxation that can occur almost magically between isolated and outwardly dissimilar individuals when they unexpectedly collide and fuse.

Spike was always quick to share his frequent exasperation with Robert – in the security of their affinity he would pour out his troubles:

> I've just arrived back from the theatre (I'm appearing in Oblomov) and it's going on for 1 A.M., everything is still, there is a lemon-slice moon low in the sky. I wonder what you are doing at this moment (I wonder what I am doing at this moment). Like you, I find life a great mathematical sum which no one can solve. I am particularly upset as the Income Tax people have almost cleaned me out of money. What miserable bloody stuff it is – I don't want any of it but all my tradesmen do. I offered to write short stories in exchange for food. But they weren't interested.

Robert was doubtless amused to receive this letter, and it is interesting to conjecture whether he had a fleeting memory of his own early approach to the same subject. Around fifty years before, as a young man, he had written a contribution for a diary-type of publication called *Focus*. In it he was discussing letters he had reluctantly written from his home in Majorca.

> . . . Two of the letters were to people who wanted to reproduce things of mine, of no value, in educational books, of no value.

I replied in the first case yes on consideration that they sent me a copy of Walpole's *Castle of Otranto* (which Laura* wanted) in any cheap edition, and to the other yes, on condition that they sent me a copy of Philostratus's *Life of Apollonius* (which I wanted) in the Loeb Library. No answer, as though I had offended the Educational publishing system by introducing the barter principle!

Spike, aware of Graves's erudition, frequently refers to his own lack of formal education. Graves, who in any case has often been extremely vocal in deriding conventional school and university training, managed in some way to mitigate Spike's hypersensitivity in these areas, and the tone of their friendship was set very early on by Graves's confident (and correct) assumption that in every way necessary he and Spike were on a par. 'Each one of us thinks most highly of the other,' he says in an early letter. Spike was always a little in awe of Graves, but the awe had nothing to do with diffidence, fear or hero-worship. Robert Graves had a curious aura, an aura at once magnificent and humble. It was a reflection of his greatness and humility, and hardly anyone with whom he came into contact failed to be moved by it. Spike was no exception, and so it was all the more interesting to see how Robert, in his turn, fell bewitched under Spike's charismatic spell. Their meeting was a matter of keen and constant delight to them both. 'And to think,' Robert wrote in a letter to Spike, 'that I nearly turned down that *Muses* TV show on the grounds that I needed neither fame, nor money, nor voice practice.'

Beryl Graves remembers her husband's reactions to Spike: 'He was mad about him. Absolutely entranced. Talked about him often and hailed him as a great genius. We were all longing to meet him but we never quite did – even though Robert was always asking him to come, they

* Laura Riding, the American poet who lived with Graves during the 'thirties.

never got it organized. But he always looked for Spike whenever he went to London and they always wrote to each other.'

In 1973 Robert Graves was the predominant figurehead in a move to ban traffic on the newly repaired Albert Bridge. He besieged the organizer of the appeal. 'Find my friend Spike Milligan. I don't know his number. No, I don't know his address. My wife would. But I promise you he is the man we want and he is a very good friend of mine. This is exactly the sort of thing he cares about. He is a splendid fellow, you know. And of course he's an artist, so he'll put something in the book. He cares a lot about this sort of thing.'

Alas, the organizers were short of time and did not get past the smokescreen that surrounded Milligan at that moment. Told about it years later, he looked sad.

Of course I would have come. Why didn't they get me? If he said it was right, that would have been good enough for me. I'd do anything for Graves. He's a marvellous man. Not another one of his calibre in this century, is there?

The idea that he has somehow missed out on a formal education is never far from Spike's mind. In essence, of course, it is true. In effect, it is irrelevant. Spike not only has a powerful intelligence, he has all the equipment of an intellectual. The speed at which his mind works, coupled with his almost legendary articulacy, makes him a formidable opponent in argument, and his unusually developed intuitive powers enable him to assess, absorb and retain vast amounts of material which is filed away in some sort of partitioned memory-bank. His capacity for total recall has already been demonstrated in his war memoirs.

It is not easy to hazard what paths Terence Milligan might have taken academically. He is a dedicated, meticulous researcher capable of sustained and painstaking effort, but his intolerance of human error and his horror of inefficiency would have rendered him a difficult faculty member. He would have been an irascible, unpredictable, feared and loved teacher. Students who could have kept up with his mercurial, racing mind would almost certainly have benefited from the constant and exhausting stimulation to which they would have been exposed. The less able would have pleaded for transfers or quietly and thankfully dropped out. Certainly his seminars would have been memorable, and his lectures would have passed into the college mythology: standing room only.

Measuring up to such an extraordinary man as Robert Graves gave Spike's career as a writer and poet fresh impetus. The long, traumatic years of writing the *Goon Shows* had made savage inroads in his creativity. The speed at which he had been required (and required himself) to work had left him with a sort of spiritual writer's cramp, and during these years he had turned despairingly to painting and effectively blotted out the agonies of the writer's deadlines. In any event, Spike had always felt himself to be something of a pretender to a writer's throne; he never lost the sense of inadequacy born of his unconventional education. He knew Robert as a great writer, a classicist and a scholar, and was consequently overwhelmed at his simplicity and casual, easy availability. He was intrigued by his disregard for formality, by his knotted neckties, his bulging pockets and his gnarled hands which bore the stamp of hard physical work. When they were in the company of others, Robert was quite capable of turning his head disdainfully on an important lettered personage and whispering, with a wicked little grin, 'Hah! We two know that he's an idiot, don't we, Spike?'

Spike's excessive sensitivity is acutely attuned towards the flattery that often comes his way from sycophants. Egotistical though he may be – and he is not immune to

flattery – he is allergic to patronage. Robert never needed
to patronize Spike, their stinging, sharp minds met head-
on in delighted recognition, and the instant, undeniable
mutual respect that ensued gave his confidence an enormous boost.

During the making of *Muses with Milligan* Spike was
suffering from mercurial mood swings, but making a creditable effort to keep everything together. He became friends
with the poets Dannie Abse and Laurie Lee and got on
well with most of the others. He was still appearing in
Oblomov; he was still struggling with Associated London
Scripts, and he was also in the throes of a massive correspondence with various authorities whose collaboration he
needed to achieve a determined ambition. He wanted to
restore a tree.

Milligan has been involved with many different conservation and ecological concerns over the last twenty years.
One of the least known and most successful was his long
struggle to restore and preserve the Elfin Oak, a wood
sculpture in Kensington Gardens which dates back to 1898.
Preliminary correspondence and work on the tree lasted for
over four years. Milligan has two boxes of correspondence
dating from 1964 until 1978, and volumes of photographs
showing every stage of the restoration. He was aided in
this enterprise by numerous interested people including
commercial wood-rot firms, paint suppliers, Ministers of
the Crown, MPs (who were obliged to alternate according
to elections), artists, actors, writers, passers-by, friends
and layabouts. These people came and went, but Milligan
stayed steadily at the helm for over four years. He
describes the work in a letter to Robert:

You may know of the 'Elfin Oak' in Kensington Gardens. It is
the stump of a once mighty oak that grew in Richmond Deer

Park for four or five hundred years. It was destroyed by
lightning; in 1898 a wood sculptor called Ivor Innes carved the
stump with about 70 pixies, fairies, elves, witches, all about
6″–8″ tall and using all the contours of the trunk to make
caves, tunnels, etc. He also carved about 150 forest creatures,
toads, rabbits, woodpeckers, it was a little masterpiece. Alas,
for the last twelve years I've watched the tree go to the point
of ruin. Finally I decided to do something. I wrote to the
Minister of Works in the Spring of 1962 – I asked permission
to restore the tree gratis. I received a reply in the Winter of
1962. Thus, owing to the weather, making it impossible to
start work as stripping the old paint off would have let the rain
and damp into the bare wood. The Minister agreed to let me
do it, so I said Spring 1963, when that arrived the Conserva-
tives were out and Labour in, so I had to start requesting all
over again. Anyhow I've started work on it this spring, and I
found such mental peace in the process, at first I was plagued
by autograph hunters so the M.O.W. had screens put all
around. Three other friends (and fellow neurotics) all meet
every Saturday, each armed with a bottle of Vin Rosé, cheese
and bread, and work on the tree till the light goes. It is a most
rewarding task. We have stripped all the figures, soaked them
in raw linseed (a lovely wood oil with a beautiful smell) and
remodelled lost limbs, legs, ears, etc. The tree itself we are
going to treat for all ailments it has, and will be subject to.
Then we have to pin the bark to the tree as it is falling off. We
are trying to finish the job before the cold glass hand of winter
lays us off. I'll send you a colour photo of the completed job –

Working on the tree was therapeutic for Milligan, who
always responds well to physical tasks, especially if they
are concerned with what is important to his sense of
values. His friend Graves, who spent hours attending to
the compost, the almond trees and the wood-gathering
between the long sessions of writing in Deya, would have
understood him exactly.

The tree became a symbol of life and achievement.
When the pressures at 9 Orme Court (now Milligan's
office) became too great he would thankfully disappear

behind the screens thoughtfully erected by the Ministry of Works. His secretary was happy. Twenty years later, she was to say with fervency: 'I used to dread the day that the tree would be finished. It was his refuge from the world. He always came back into the office so refreshed and happy, he just loved that tree.'

One day, when Milligan was hiding behind his screens, a newspaper feature writer managed to locate him. Spike, feeling wretched, refused an interview. The writer persisted. 'What is it about this tree that you like so much?' he asked. Milligan glared at him dourly. 'I love it,' he said, 'because I don't have to make it laugh.'

On 22 April 1965, HRH Princess Margaret arranged a dinner party at Kensington Palace to celebrate the Queen's birthday. Beforehand, the royal party, which included Peter Sellers and his wife Britt Ekland, visited the Comedy Theatre and saw a performance of *Son of Oblomov*. Not unexpectedly, there was some backchat between Sellers and Milligan during the play.

After the theatre, Spike drove Paddy to the Palace in his Mini. The dinner was informal and delightful. Paddy, looking very beautiful, wore a black full-length dress with a silver ribbon in her hair. Before she left for the theatre, Laura, Sean and Silé had given her the birthday presents they had been making for the Queen for several weeks.

At the dinner, Spike sat on the left hand of Princess Margaret. Prince Philip, on Princess Margaret's right, sat opposite. At the other end of the table Paddy sat on Lord Snowdon's right. It was the first occasion that Milligan had an opportunity to converse with Philip and the time was not wasted. They talked about ecological concerns, conservation matters and population control. Spike was gratified and a little surprised to find that the Queen's husband had a very clear grasp and a deep concern over these matters.

Joan Greenwood's dressing-room at the Comedy Theatre was the centre for band-aids and sympathy. One night a young actor appeared there, distraught and sobbing. Apparently Milligan had just watched a part of his performance in *Oblomov* and, as he left the stage, had said, sourly: 'I think that man must be the worst actor in the world.' Joan set off down the corridor to Spike's dressing-room in high dudgeon. 'I told him that I thought he had been dreadfully cruel and that the poor young man was beside himself with distress. I said "I will not have this cruelty in the theatre" – I said that he had been most unkind to that boy and it was not good enough.'

Spike accepted the onslaught gracefully, which must have been more a sign of his respect for Joan Greenwood than any belief that he might possibly have been in the wrong.

Well, it was his fault. He accosted me in Kensington Gardens when I was working on the tree one day and he told me that it was very nice for me to be well-known and always working, but that *he* was a great actor who'd never had a chance, so I said OK, here's your chance, you're in *Oblomov*, right? And he was absolute shit, I put him in the play and he couldn't act a line. I've never heard of him since, nor has anyone else. That's how great an actor he was.

When it was suggested to Spike that he might have been ill-advised to put an unknown young actor in a West End show without auditioning him first, he gave a belligerent glare. 'Well, I trusted him, didn't I?'

Paddy Milligan had settled down as well as could be expected. She was baffled and upset by Spike's frequent descents into depression. She found it difficult not to take a lot of his 'moods' personally. She had no experience in running a home and found it a lot to cope with. She was trying hard with the children – and to some extent succeeding, especially with Sean and Silé. Laura couldn't help but remember June with a wilful, hidden longing, and perhaps she rebuffed her would-be substitute mother – certainly Laura and Paddy did not forge the same loving relationship that was established between Paddy and the younger children. Paddy had little time to think of herself now, or of her career, which seemed to have somehow slipped away. In the late summer of 1965, she was overjoyed to discover that she was pregnant.

Everyone was excited about the idea of a new Milligan baby. Paddy was already enjoying being mother to Spike's children, and to have their own child seemed the ultimate blessing on the family. Spike hid his genuine joy even from himself; preoccupations with population control were beginning to obsess him, and although he loved his family more than anything else in his life, he still felt that four children were too many.

On the morning of 17 May 1966, Paddy Milligan sat up in bed and wrote in her diary:

> Today, at 5.30, Jane was born. She is 10lbs 11oz, bruised and battered and I love her.
> I have a baby and I love her.

The birth of Jane brought a great whirl of happiness to the whole family. Laura, Silé and Sean were thrilled with their new, beautiful little sister. Paddy was ecstatic and proud. Spike, whilst admitting he had wanted a boy, kept sneaking upstairs to have a look at Jane. He was thinking of a new vintage of fairy letters, and of a new audience for his marvellous stories. The work on the Elfin Oak was almost

completed. He felt that he could not wait to take Jane by
the hand and show her each little figure.

The following year, Robert Graves was persuaded to appear
at a poets' evening at the Royal Albert Hall, which was
being promoted by Jonathan Boulting. The fact that he
could look forward to more dinners with Spike, who was
also appearing, may well have influenced him. In any case,
he had responded to young Boulting's requests. Graves
was always inclined towards tolerance and generosity with
young people.

For the next night Robert and Spike were planning a
much less ambitious evening at the Mermaid for Bernard
Miles. Robert wrote to Spike and asked him to be particularly gentle with Isla Cameron, a folk-singer greatly
beloved by the Graves family, who was to take part. Spike
wrote:

> Don't worry about 'I', she could not be in more understanding
> hands than mine, believe me Robert I have settled on the
> floors of hell with mental trouble, so a cushion of deep
> understanding will be hers, I will be a pukka sahib. Lovely!
> Your son is appearing. I have promised to do the Albert Hall
> 'do' for young Boulting. I thought I'd read some Lear and
> Hood. I'm not quite sure what it's all in aid of (candidly I don't
> know what life is all in aid of!). Shall we sit together? I hope
> so, I don't know anybody there either!

The occasion was labelled *The New Moon Carnival of
Poetry* and a number of poets had been persuaded to
appear. To begin with, Milligan was feeling rather
uncertain:

> I think all the other poets seemed to resent me a bit, didn't
> like my ideas, thought it a bit preposterous that I should be
> mixed up in their show . . . All those Audens and Isherwoods
> and the rest. They kept going into a little complaining cabal

and muttering. They wanted it all heavily structured and kept saying things like, 'Well, this will take eight minutes, etc.' I was saying, 'Oh well, let's try it and see what happens, shall we?' They didn't like it at all, and they didn't know why I was there.

The evening appears to have been badly organized and eventually deteriorated into something of a fracas. Certainly Spike and Robert Graves made a hasty getaway and repaired to their favourite restaurant, 'Le Matelot', in Pimlico where they had a splendid evening. Later, there was some criticism in the press about the unsuitability of an Oxford Professor of Poetry's being involved in such an occasion. Robert became somewhat haughty now and added his bit to the correspondence columns of the *Daily Telegraph*. After a few acerbic comments his letter concludes:

What happened at the Albert Hall after Spike Milligan and I left I do not exactly know. Jonathan Boulting had never taken control of the show, has not yet thanked me for attending it, and still owes me 30s for a cab fare borrowed when he visited me here in Majorca.

Yours faithfully
Robert Graves

However, the following evening at the Mermaid more than made up for the ill-fated carnival. Bernard Miles and Spike had been in joyful liaison to try and raise badly-needed funds to keep the Mermaid afloat and an evening of poetry and music was loosely planned to take place on Sunday, 19 June. Graves had obviously been uncertain of exactly what would be expected of him:

I don't play the guitar. My son Tomás does – aged 13, he's very cool, has twice sung talking blues to huge audiences on his own – Lovely that Paddy will sing – what can *I* do? I have about 600 songs and a carrying voice. I can tell stories, recite crazy poems, my own included, hold an audience by my magnetic presence, pick up broken Q's BUT hate rehearsing or learning a part!

Spike replied:

I do hope you aren't worrying about June 19th. You ask 'What can I do?' Answer: Anything. Talk, read your own verse, sing any song you know or takes your fancy – read excerpts from your books, tell a joke or if you wish just sit there drinking Rose Hip Cordial '47. It's an evening of mutual enjoyment twix audience and us. Muggeridge, I'm still trying to get him. I'll let you know if I do. Really, anybody who wants to appear, let them. Most certainly we won't rehearse. Just turn up on the evening and see what happens! Paddy has had a baby girl. Jane Fionella. 10lbs 6oz. Both doing well. I did want a son, but that was primitive ego at work. *You're* broke! Everybody's broke. At least you're not taxed on your overdraft. I only need money to buy wine. All love, Spike.

The evening, in the end, was a magnificent success. Several years later, when Graves flew to London to appear in the Eamonn Andrews show *This is Your Life* for Spike, he talked almost exclusively about the Mermaid evening. He reminded Spike that the audience had refused to go home: 'D'you remember, Spike? They just sat tight. We had to give them another half hour, didn't we?'

After the first half of the show, which included Paddy singing and Tomás, Graves's youngest son, playing his guitar, a young boy from the audience went behind the scenes and found Milligan and Graves sharing a bottle of wine. He informed them that he was nine years old, that he too was a poet and could recite just as well as they could. Young Danny Black was treading fruitful ground; both Robert and Spike have unusual depths of respect for children. After the interval, Danny was called up from the audience. 'This young man,' said Graves importantly, 'is a poet, and is going to recite for us.' Milligan swung Danny up onto a chair and he recited. The *Daily Telegraph*, a little mystified by all this, gave Danny a respectful mention and referred to his poems as 'ironic'. The title of one of them was 'False Chemistry' and another one was 'Comments on God'.

Milligan kept in touch with Danny Black for years. He wrote words of comfort on various subjects that worried Danny. These included his asthma and his parents. He was angry that Danny's mother queried his name and business with her son when he tried to telephone him once: 'As soon as I said it was Spike Milligan she was all effusive and charming after having been suspicious and nasty. So because I'm a well-known name that's OK, is it? I could still be a sexual pervert, couldn't I?'

In August 1966 Milligan acquired a new secretary. This in itself wasn't unusual, but the outcome was. The girl he employed had worked for some years in the offices of Independent Television, so she was well-versed in show business. Her name was Norma Farnes; within months she had the hang of practically every aspect of his career. Intelligent and articulate, she could see what Spike needed. They got on like a house on fire, they sailed through calm seas and squalls, good days and bad days. She understood the miseries of his low days, and nurtured him along on his high ones. She was as fiercely protective of her boss as Florence Milligan was of her son, and in due course the two ladies became great friends. Norma became the most patient and loyal manager in the business. When Milligan engaged her, it was certainly his lucky day.

Within a few years Norma needed help in the office. Once again, Spike was lucky and Tanis Davies came to Orme Court to stand firmly next to Norma. The two ladies perfected the art of closing ranks to protect their vulnerable and often suffering employer. Sometimes, on a bad day, he will rage about them, often unfairly. If his 'phone isn't answered immediately he will say: 'That's my bloody office for you. Always at the hairdressers or sitting there not answering the 'phone. That's all they do.'

The words are largely unjust, and certainly unmeant. Milligan and his manager have a unique relationship, marvelled at by many and understood by few. The telephones are very frequently slapped down by both parties, nobody minds too much. Milligan's agitation is easily aroused and causes his manager a certain amount of stress, but permanent rifts do not occur. When Norma likewise shows a trait of North Country truculence, Spike raises his eyes to Heaven, vows that no man ever bore so much so patiently, and waits for the storm to pass.

By the end of 1966 Spike had formed his own production company, Spike Milligan Productions Ltd, which still exists in more or less the same form. He is allergic to the complications of income tax, accounts and contractual law. As with Associated London Scripts, the joy of creative work turns to dust when he is harassed with bureaucracy and his office does its best to protect him. He is not always as grateful as he should be:

> What are they doing in my office I'd like to know. They get me no work. All they do is VAT. They are marvellous at VAT, and meanwhile I have a big overdraft and no work.

In times of great need, when Milligan can seem almost beyond human help, Norma Farnes gets in her car and drives up to his home in Barnet: Monkenhurst. She will sit quietly with her ashen-faced employer, perhaps murmuring a few words from time to time. She will look almost as drawn and ill as Spike.

These occasions are mercifully rare now, but when they do occur her understanding and compassion are total.

* * *

How much does Milligan owe to his co-writers? There have been a few, and several of them have been gifted in their own right. Among them are John Antrobus, Eric Sykes, Jack Hobbs (a competent and sensitive editor and an early publisher), Neil Shand, and the late Larry Stephens, perhaps the most valuable of all. Stephens, as we know, dated back to the earliest *Goon Show* days; there seems to be no doubt that Milligan learnt a great deal from the collaboration of this disciplined and clever writer.

Roger Wilmut, in *The Goon Show Companion*, tells us: 'One of the collaborators working with Milligan in most recent times is Neil Shand. Perhaps his main function has been to kick-start Milligan when slightly below par and to rein him in gently when he is raring to go.'

Neil Shand, a scriptwriter and reviewer employed by the BBC on a permanent basis, has collaborated with Spike on several occasions. No doubt Wilmut's description of his role could be extended to other collaborators as well.

Collaborators have helped Spike with the more frivolous of his books and perhaps also with his comedy scriptwriting. Jack Hobbs and Neil Shand have both worked with him at his home. When one of them is closeted with Spike it is heartwarming to hear their combined peals of laughter echoing around the big Victorian house. Sometimes Spike and Jack will read to each other the poems of the great William McGonagall, the world's worst poet, and howl with mirth. Spike will end up prostrate, weeping helplessly; Jack will be bent double, shuddering and groaning with laughter. But Spike's more important writing is achieved without help or support.

Pressed to discuss the value of his co-writers Milligan will be purposely vague, although he is a generous man who finds no boost to his own success by dismissing the work of colleagues. He seems genuinely to struggle for objective honesty:

Well, I don't know how much they have all helped me. I suppose it was necessary to set them all up dotting i's and crossing t's for me but – well, I don't want to put any one of them down, but is it a fair answer to ask 'What has any one of them ever done on their own?'

In 1963 Roger Wilmut wrote a review in the *New Statesman* of a 'satiric' nonsense by John Antrobus which was playing at the Establishment.

Antrobus is highly gifted in his own right, apart from his share in *The Bedsitting Room*, but most of the sketches in this show are below his best, needing a Milligan to animate them.

Perhaps this is an important criticism which can be considered in reverse. It could be that sometimes the real high-flyers need a skilful hand to wind them in.

Milligan is a formidable author from the publisher's point of view. He seems to have developed an almost instant cognizance of every stage of publishing, and he has a growing confidence about exactly how his books must be produced. In some ways he is a publisher's nightmare because he involves himself deeply with the actual production of the book; frequently he insists on late changes in format. Where technical areas are concerned, publishers often feel (with some justification) that the author is better out of the way. Alan Samson was a young editor at Michael Joseph when he was put to work on the first volume of Spike's war memoirs. He remained closely concerned with the production of the next six or seven books, and ending his working relationship with Spike was a matter of considerable regret to him when he moved to another publishing house.

'He was a very agreeable author in my experience,' Samson recalls. 'Even though he almost always changed everything at the last moment – there were always late changes – he was an extremely nice man to work with. He had views about things which other authors would gloss over or would not have the experience to care about.'

Alan Samson, however, found him unsuggestible. At some stage in the production of the war memoirs, he wrote to Spike and suggested that perhaps there were too many Jewish jokes? Spike was not receptive to this idea. He replied, 'You must be Jewish.' (Alan, in fact, was not.) 'The Jewish jokes stay. I bet you tell Irish jokes.'

17
Milligan, Writer

The hypersensitives are out of harmony with themselves. These are the persons who, while they can prove so attractive because they are so out of the ordinary, can also prove so uncomfortable to live with because of their intolerance.

Edwin Pulay,
Allergic Man

One of the reviewers of *Adolf Hitler: My Part in His Downfall* remarked that the book was Gunner S. Milligan's Second World War version of *Goodbye to All That*. This was curiously apt, for Milligan, like Graves in his time, felt the need to expurgate, or perhaps regurgitate, some of the violence and destruction to which he had been exposed. Robert Graves suffered all his life from a degree of physical and nervous ill-health which had been his legacy from the trenches of the First World War. Stricken and shattered by shellshock and the human carnage he saw all about him, he struggled on, after the armistice, to fulfil his poetic and literary ambitions. He took up the threads of his young marriage and lived in relative obscurity in Oxford, where he lacked even the stability to graduate in the customary fashion. He found great solace in the love of his children and spent many hours domestically occupied in their care. But, eventually, in Graves's own words, 'everything that had simmered so long eventually came to the boil' and ten years after the armistice he wrote, at top speed and almost without corrections, the book that brought him his first fame – *Goodbye to All That*. It was a poignant memoir to Graves's wartime agonies, and his state of mind at the end of the war was recalled with painful clarity.

In much the same way, after Spike had emerged from the war and struggled frenetically through the *Goon Shows*, fatherhood, a broken marriage and mental breakdown, he also sat back and took stock of his life. Perhaps it is significant that when he decided to write his autobiography he plumped not for the colourful, Kiplingesque years of his Indian boyhood, nor for the important and riotous Goon period, but for the relative obscurity of his years in the army. *Adolf Hitler: My Part in His Downfall* was Milligan's second full-length prose work, after *Puckoon*. Following its publication he wrote to his friend Robert Graves:

> Since we last met, the only thing that is of literary note is that I wrote the 1st volume of a trilogy entitled *Adolf Hitler: My Part in His Downfall*. It is a light-hearted account of what befell me in H.M.'s Army from 1938 to 1947, well, beyond my wildest hopes it became a best-seller. The first thing I did was to 'phone my parents in Australia and in so doing I realized in fact I was a little boy of seven, running to his mum and dad to tell them that he had got a good conduct star at school. Anyway, it sold 30,000 copies and it had to reprint almost at once. I can't tell you how good it feels, for a person whose education ended at 14, to be a best-seller.

Robert replied within the week: 'How good to be a best-seller – Dearest Spike! I remember what it felt like in 1929 . . .'

Years later, when Graves came to London to appear in Milligan's *This is Your Life* he remarked, 'He is a poet with a fine sensitivity who has not been ruined by education.'

As Spike's poetic abilities developed, so also developed the protective Milligan mantle of near-disdain towards some of his sensitive or self-revealing poems. This seems to be synonymous with Spike's occasionally bizarre attitudes over matters which could be expected to cause him great personal anguish. Peter Sellers' death in July 1980 is a case in point – the loss of a friend with whom one had instant and constant rapport may seem almost threatening to people who are as isolated as Spike. In a television interview Michael Parkinson was discussing Peter's death with him.

'You were at the funeral, weren't you?'

'Yes – so was Peter,' answered Spike.

He does not easily suffer in public and this is one way of masking his anguish. Even privately he will machinate to deny his pain – not only to those close to him but to himself as well. This denial becomes acutely important and has led him, at times, into almost involuntary indiscretions which must reflect adversely on his generosity and loyalty. In a television interview almost immediately after Peter Sellers' death, he criticized his old friend sharply, relating a stinging anecdote about Sellers' known tendency to make unexpectedly generous gifts to his friends and, subsequently (and just as unexpectedly) to remove them.

The story concerned Alan Clare, a musician and mutual friend. He had accepted with delight the gift of a cumbersome electric organ, a new toy which (predictably) had soon palled on Peter. When it began to get in his way Sellers cast around for a recipient and Alan, though he lived in a small flat, found room for it in his bedroom and practised on it with enthusiasm for several hours each day.

'Then just as he was playing it one morning,' Spike remembered, 'the removal men arrived and took it away to Kensington Palace. Peter had given it to Princess Margaret – that's the sort of thing he did. He was like that.'

To speak with such obvious criticism of his late friend so soon after his death must have seemed questionable to many of Sellers' – or indeed of Milligan's – admirers. But Milligan was being painfully honest. Peter Sellers *was* 'like that'. Perhaps Spike was seeking refuge from a loss that left him feeling desolate by masking his pain with a harsh anecdote which would have been better left untold.

Sometimes roughly scribbled poems that are the outcome of his anguish and pain will lie in a box in his room for many months; only in a certain reflective mood will he look at them again. He is not good at reworking a draft. 'That's how it came out,' he will say, dispassionately. If it seems a good poem, he will be pleased, but not proud. An article or piece of prose that succeeds will fill him with a sense of achievement. Poetry is different. 'I can't take any credit for it,' he said once. 'Something just takes hold of me and it writes itself.'

Spike's experiences in Italy towards the end of the Second World War were important in his development. By then, at the age of twenty-five and building on the help he had received from army officers like Tony Goldsmith and a free run of the abandoned library at Bexhill, he was fast extending his curiously deprived literary background. Excerpts from his war diaries show the fluency with which he was beginning to use words. He wrote to his parents from Tunis:

> I believe they are shortly to issue Tropical Kit, or KD's (Khaki Drill) which will bring back memories of Poona. Clearest are memories of hearing the strident Bugle, and Drums of the Cheshire Regiment playing 'When we are marching to Georgia', and the Regiment swinging by, so impeccable, bayonets and brass buttons flashing light signals in all directions, the blinding white webbing, boots like polished basalt, trousers crackling with starch, the creases with razor edges, the marks of sweat appearing down the spines of the men, the Pariah dogs slinking from the path of the column, and the silent resentment of watching natives.[1]

Words were beginning to arrange themselves in his mind with an economy and clarity that would hallmark much of his future work. Yet there has been something in his hyperkinetic mind that has driven him relentlessly on; book after book has been churned out. Possibly he has, to some extent, been ill-advised. Almost certainly he would have benefited from a smaller output. Perhaps because the books have flowed from his pen with so little apparent effort he has cultivated an almost derisory attitude to them. There is a faintly mocking sound to most of his titles:

> *Silly Verse for Kids,*
> *A Dustbin of Milligan,*
> *The Little Pot Boiler,*
> *A Book of Bits,* etc.

Yet Milligan the poet is glad when his work is singled out for inclusion in anthologies. He was particularly pleased when no fewer than four of his poems were selected *by children* for the 1980 'Year of the Child' anthology edited by Kaye Webb for Penguin. Spike distributed signed copies to all his children, gleefully pointing out to them that his share of poems in the book was second only to William Shakespeare's.

The poems chosen were 'On the Ning Nang Nong', 'Silly Old Baboon', 'The ABC', and 'Granny'. All four show a skilful and disciplined approach. 'On the Ning Nang Nong' is inspired Milligan, by way of Lewis Carroll and Lear – two of Spike's favourite poets.

> On the Ning Nang Nong
> Where the Cows go Bong!
> And the Monkeys all say Boo!
> There's a Nong Nang Ning
> Where the trees go Ping!
> And the tea pots Jibber Jabber Joo.
> On the Nong Ning Nang
> All the mice go Clang!
> And you just can't catch 'em when they do!
> So it's Ning Nang Nong!

Cows go Bong!
Nong Nang Ning!
Trees go Ping!
Nong Ning Nang!
The mice go Clang!
What a noisy place to belong,
Is the Ning Nang Ning Nang Nong!!

'Silly Old Baboon' was written for one of Milligan's children. He can't, at this distance, remember which one, but he knows that he wrote most of these poems for them at a traumatic stage in his life when he felt that he was slipping into the role of an absent father. He is confused as to whether this absence was going to be the ultimate result of his parting from June, or a consequence of the destructive illness that he was battling with.

'All I know is that I wanted to give my kids some little thing, just to remind them of me, and to know that I loved them.'

There was a Baboon
Who, one afternoon,
Said, 'I think I will fly to the sun.'
So, with two great palms
Strapped to his arms,
He started his take-off run.

Mile after mile
He galloped in style
But never once left the ground.
'You're running too slow,'
Said a passing crow,
'Try reaching the speed of sound.'

So he put on a spurt —
By God how it hurt!
The soles of his feet caught fire.
There were great clouds of steam
As he raced through a stream
But he still didn't get any higher.

Racing on through the night,
Both his knees caught alight
And smoke billowed out from his rear.
Quick to his aid
Came a fire brigade
Who chased him for over a year.

Many moons passed by.
Did Baboon ever fly?
Did he ever get to the sun?
I've just heard today
That he's well on his way!
He'll be passing through Acton at one.

The child (Zoe Parker) who chose this for inclusion in the 'Year of the Child' book gives her reasons succinctly: '. . . because it is funny but is also sad in some ways. The Baboon would probably never be able to fly anyway: it's somehow like a wild dream.'

Baboon has delighted many readers: he is (as Zoe says) both funny and sad. We end up not being too sorry for Baboon, he was at least in charge of his own destiny. Milligan has obviously taken a delight in not allowing humans either to confuse the issue or to exploit the animals. For although we may deduce that the 'fire brigade' was human, and not, perhaps, a team of more stable Baboon contemporaries, so far as the Baboon was concerned man was ineffectual and foolish to spend a year on such a lost cause. Milligan's Baboon reflects the wry, disparaging mirth so often visible in his attitude to life.

Spike is not so much a doom sayer as a doom watcher. The mood swings which manipulate him with such merciless regularity sometimes render him agonized and silent when he observes what appears to him some fresh outrage against humanity. At the same time he finds it hard to look objectively at experiments on animals, and he is cynically persistent in his belief that the adult human animal is less acceptable than the domestic or wild one. His attitudes are uncompromising, intolerant and occasionally conflicting. In 1981 he heard Professor Nicholas Humphrey give his remarkable Bronowski Lecture on Nuclear Disarmament. Deeply impressed, he wrote to the lecturer:

> Dear Dr Humphrey,
> I listened with great interest to your lecture, what a wonderful lecture it was, it shone so brightly into the minds of men, what you said was so true. The tragedy is that not one word of it will survive (unlike the writing finger on the wall), it will be forgotten amongst the mere fact that we sent a nuclear submarine to get scrap iron merchants off the Argentine mainland. But what you said was all true, just as what Jesus said was true, but to be heeded on a mass scale has never happened. You cannot sell people the truth. Cat food is more easily sold than truth. People need cat food and they don't need truth. That's the awful part of it.

Professor Humphrey replied on a sheet of writing-paper headed 'Cambridge University, Sub. Dept. of Animal Behaviour'. Spike was stricken. He wrote again to Professor Humphrey; he could not accept his validity if the humanity of his lecture was coupled with the inhumanity of animal experiments. The Professor presumably felt unable to answer and so an acquaintance between two people who would probably have found great interest in each other's company foundered. When questioned about this Spike was low in spirit but vociferous.

> Well, it's too bad. When I heard his lecture I thought 'He's for me, brother,' but if he's one of the people who shut monkeys up in cages, and take a baby chimp from its mother and lock it up with a scrubbing-brush to see if it sucks the scrubbing-brush – well, what has a monkey done to deserve that from humans? What are we going to learn from it? That a baby chimp is unhappy and needs its mother and sometimes accepts a scrubbing-brush as a substitute? I could tell them that

without making the poor chimp and its mother miserable. These sort of humans are the rightful material for the bomb. Why protect them? Tell me that.

This is not untypical of the sort of incident that keeps Milligan a resigned, mentally-belligerent outcast from a society where his keen intelligence and acutely perceptive insight could make a sizeable contribution. It is to be regretted that his emotive, uninhibited gut-reactions can so frequently decimate the fundamental strength of his argument. It seems unlikely that he will change.

In August 1966 Spike decided his family needed a holiday. They went to Tunisia. Baby Jane had been left in London with a nanny. The holiday was not a great success. Spike wrote sadly to Robert Graves telling him that his idea of a holiday would be to put 'don't disturb' on his office door and hide behind it. 'I don't like doing nothing,' he wrote. 'I need something to do. I'd like to write and paint and potter with my window boxes and browse through my books.' After a few days, Paddy got unhappy about Jane and flew home. Spike, in the throes of a depression by this time, did his best but the younger children were distressed by Paddy's sudden departure and the holiday ended in tears and chaos.

Spike returned to London with the children, unrefreshed and harassed. The home situation was difficult, Paddy was not getting on any better with Laura. She had always managed the younger children with reasonable success but Laura seemed increasingly isolated and difficult; yet she loved Paddy and longed for her love and approval in return. One day she went to pick up her baby sister and cuddle her. This angered Paddy who ordered her never to touch the child again. Laura undoubtedly was approaching difficult adolescent years and the almost inevitable crime of an untidy bedroom and so forth drove Paddy into tirades of wrath. A decision was made to send Laura to boarding school which distressed Spike and left the rest of the family (including Laura) uncertain and confused. Eventually, a compromise was reached and Laura was allowed to be a weekly boarder. Things became calmer at home, but not any happier.

But later that year the Milligans had one great stroke of luck. Paddy advertised in the north country papers for a nanny/mother's help. Mrs Jean Reid, recently widowed, applied for the post. She had brought up her own family in Ayr and saw no reason to embrace an early retirement. She joined the Milligan household as Nanna when Jane was six months old and has remained there, a stalwart infusion of Scottish reliability and good sense, ever since.

As Jane grew up and became more aware of what was happening, Milligan went to enormous lengths to make sure that she never heard a word spoken in anger. Paddy, serene in her love for the child and her respect for the joys of a happy family, was able to collaborate in this area at least, and whenever Spike was at home and Jane was present the child undoubtedly felt herself to be the centre of a loving and secure family, which in effect she was. Paddy's influence on Sean and Silé was enormous. When Paddy died of cancer in 1978 Silé in particular suffered a severe and irreparable loss, whereas Jane, buttressed not only by her mother but also by the love and care of Nanna from the age of six months, was perhaps less vulnerable. There is no doubt that when Milligan fell in love with Patricia Ridgeway the emerging realization that she was going to make a loving and generous mother to his three little ones had a lot to do with his determination to marry her.

Paddy, however, had an artistic temperament to match her husband's and the tensions that grew in the marriage were inevitable. Milligan, for all time saddened by the failure of his marriage to June, was determined that Jane would never suffer as Laura, and to a lesser extent, Sean and Silé had. He applied the sort of creative talents to his hearth and home that he gives to his work and, with an instinctive foresight, designed a way of living that was acceptable to Paddy and himself.

His work demanded that he already spent a considerable amount of time out of the home. He established a permanent bolt-hole at Orme Court on the floor above the office. It served, virtually, as an extension to the office: an odd-shaped room, meagre in size and eccentrically furnished, it was nevertheless a sanctum of privacy and respite. As the years passed, the shelves and cupboards groaned under the accumulation of old bits and pieces – an ancient screwdriver or hammer would be placed lovingly next to an old pebble or bottle, a toy made by one of the children next to a Victorian snuffbox. The importance of the pieces was never dictated by their intrinsic value – only by their association with Milligan and those close to him, or by their antiquity. There was a narrow couch that served him as a bed, a couple of shaky basket chairs, some old filing cabinets, a table in the window with his typewriter. There was a window-box for flowers and ledges where he fed the birds. It was a refuge, and Paddy probably had the good sense to appreciate Spike's need for fairly frequent isolation from his family during the difficult times. In a rare magazine interview which she gave three years before her death she spoke with an instinctive insight and understanding of her husband's illness.

People always think of Spike as a funny man but I found he seemed to do more suffering than laughing. I watched depression engulf him and take him to the depths of despair. I'd never known that a human being could be in despair so absolute that nothing remained but mental agony. Occasionally he'll leave home and live in his office, to try and spare us the worst of it. When he does stay at home all you can give is loving and just being there. Over the years I've learned that usually you can't help at all.[2]

Nanna was close to Paddy for many years. She nursed her devotedly through the painful illness that ended her life. After the funeral, she managed the domestic arrangements at Monkenhurst calmly and lavished affection on the twelve-year-old Jane. When pressed, she would speak of Paddy with a subdued affection and a fierce Scottish pride. 'She was a really splendid person. A very special person. She was admirable – and always so loyal. I never heard her say a bad word against her husband, even though he gave her a hard time often enough. She was totally, totally loyal.'

Milligan now rehearsed a new production of *The Bedsitting Room*. It had a successful provincial tour before opening at the Saville Theatre in London on 3 May 1967 with a cast containing an unusually high proportion of Australian actors including Bill Kerr and David Nettheim. The tour opened at the old Edwardian Theatre in Wimbledon, which had been consistently threatened with demolition for years. When *The Bedsitting Room* played there it had just received its almost annual reprieve and it was gratifying for all parties that this 2,000-seat theatre broke all business records for the previous sixty years. Milligan had directed the play and was in his element. Touring seemed to suit him well, and his limited appearances at home were perhaps conducive to an easier relationship developing between Paddy and himself. When the play went to Dublin, Spike joined the students in a sit-in to preserve a Georgian building at the corner of Hume Street and St Stephen's Green. They had a triumphant success. Whilst in Dublin he was approached by Michael Mills of the

BBC, who suggested a series based on J. B. Morton's 'Beachcomber'. For many years Milligan had enjoyed his column in the *Daily Express*, and the series eventually took shape. During this year too Spike was making a film of *The Bedsitting Room* with the director Richard Lester.

After *The Bedsitting Room* opened in London, Flo wrote to Spike:

My Dearest Son
   With what delight and great pleasure we just received the lovely colour photo of the Saville Theatre with your name up in bright lights. We are so proud of you, my son, and your great achievements, for you have done it all by yourself and the greatest of credit is due to you. My! My! Fancy, we never thought in the days when Dad and I were going flat out with our concert parties in our stage days that one day our dear son Terence would have his name shining brightly in London. God bless you always and may you go on to success upon success, and Dad and I feel *quite* sure of that.

On the evening of 18 June *The Bedsitting Room* played to an especially receptive audience. It drew uproarious applause at the line-up, the curtain swinging up and down again and again. It was a standing ovation, the audience cheering, stamping; some even climbed on to their seats. The stage manager, whose responsibility it was to raise and lower the curtain, grew tired before the audience's enthusiasm had waned. The roars of applause continued. 'Take it up again,' yelled Spike, in a frenzy that was shared by the euphoric cast. 'Take it up,' he screamed as the clapping and shouting continued without pause. The stage manager declined. Milligan was not to be beaten. He grabbed the hand of the artist nearest to him, yelled 'Follow me,' and dragged a conga-like collection of the curtain call across the darkened stage, through the wings, past the incredulous stage-door keeper, into the side street and round the corner into Shaftesbury Avenue where the

line re-formed in the middle of the road and stood bowing
and smiling as an amazed and delighted audience emerged
from the theatre. The clapping and bowing became hysterical while bemused bus- and taxi-drivers attempted to
thread their way up and down the street. The cast were
now so far removed from reality that they needed no
encouragement from Milligan, who then led them up the
street to where the next theatre was disgorging its audience. They made their bows to this audience as well.
The aura of delight and euphoria was unabated as the
enthusiastic cast of *The Bedsitting Room* made a triumphant progress up Shaftesbury Avenue.

David Nettheim recalls the outcome of this unpre-
cedented event.

> Of course we were all on a massive high by this time – Milligan
> wasn't the only one – we were all in a state of near-delirium.
> We didn't begin to come down until eventually we wound our
> way back to the stage-door to find the theatre dark and locked
> up with all our possessions and clothes inside, and ourselves
> outside still in our extraordinary costumes and full stage make-
> ups. I don't even remember how we got sorted out and home,
> but it was a magic night, magic and unforgettable.[3]

When *The Bedsitting Room* ended, Spike paid a further
visit to Australia. Once again he became involved in
conservation and animal rights work, and it was on this
visit that he first started inspecting early aboriginal art. In
future years, he was to locate some previously undiscov-
ered cave drawings only a few miles from where his parents
were living. Australians were delighted with all this interest
and publicity and christened the place 'Milligan's Cave'.

His visit now coincided with the showing of the *Beachcomber* series, which he wrote, on ABC. Spike was also
anxious to negotiate the sale of *Q5*, which had been
successfully shown on BBC TV in England but there were

difficulties about this because its somewhat surreal humour meant that it could only be shown during limited late-evening hours. Nevertheless *Beachcomber* had been popular, and the Australians wanted to see more of Spike.

Dr Clement Semmler, then Director of the Australian Broadcasting Commission and an Australian literary critic of note, became a great friend and ally of Spike's. They shared a love for jazz, good wine and reading. 'Clem' was interested in Irish writers and had just completed a book on James Joyce when Spike and he met. During this visit, they dined together in Sydney on several occasions. One evening, Spike returned to Woy Woy (he was staying with his parents) and dashed off a letter to Clem. He was continuing the conversation that had gone on all evening:

My Dear Clem,
    I agree with Whitney Balliet. Peterson and Brubeck ARE cocktail pianists. Peterson has arpeggio-dysentery, in time it will be possible for a computer that has been fed jazz clichés to play like Peterson. Brubeck is advanced schmaltz whose contribution has been to compose in 5/4, but Tchaikovsky did it in 1880, neither can compare with the creative jazz of Tatum, Hines, Wilson, Zorbe, in fact GAINER is nearer true jazz than Peterson. I walk Miles (Davies)! to avoid him!

As ever,
Spike.

In London, Spike's publishers were on the point of producing *The Bedside Milligan*. Milligan included several poems, one of them 'Manic Depression' which he had written in hospital in 1953. The poem begins:

The pain is too much
A thousand grim winters
grow in my head

A few pages further on he includes a comic verse, untitled:

> I had a Dongee
> Who would not speak
> He wouldn't hop
> He wouldn't creep
> He wouldn't walk
> He wouldn't leap
> He wouldn't wake
> He wouldn't sleep
> He wouldn't shout
> He wouldn't squeak
> He wouldn't look
> He wouldn't peep
> He wouldn't wag
>   his Dongee tail
> I think this Dongee's
>   going to fail.

The Bedside Milligan also touches on his old favourites, bureaucracy and apartheid. 'The Sun Helmet' tells the story of Mr Oliver Thrigg:

The man booked aboard the Onion Castle and was handed £10 and an oar (Assisted Passage they call it). The ship headed south, and, so did Mr Thrigg and his enigma, which he used for colonic irrigation. During the whole trip the man appeared at all times in a sun helmet. Several or eightal times he was almost tempted to ask the man his secret. But no, as Thrigg was travelling steerage and the man 1st Class, plus the fact it was a special Non-fraternizing Apartheid Cruise, no contact was possible. On the 12th of Iptomber the ship docked at Cape Town. Even though Thrigg got through Customs and Bribes at speed, he just missed the Sun Helmet as he drove off in a taxi. Thrigg flagged down an old cripple Negro driver. 'Follow that Sun Helmet,' he said jumping on the nigger's back. (The change from Negro to nigger denotes change from UK to SA soil.) Several times Thrigg let the nigger stand in his bucket of portable UK soil so that he could be called Negro!

Milligan was born into a racist society, and spent the first fifteen years of his life being taught that he was superior because he was white. Eventually, however, his intellect developed ahead of his emotional indoctrination. He knew, but in some way he could not or would not recognize, the unacceptable face of racism, and from then on he has fought a losing battle with himself. He makes racist jokes that are fiendishly unfunny. He seems not to want to consider the implications of changed attitudes. He will justify the use of 'wog' and 'nigger' on the rather odd premise that if the words are said often enough they will become meaningless. Pushed into a corner in conversation, he will extricate himself with skill. Suddenly, the talk is about overpopulation or famine. Milligan is not happy to talk about racism. He is deeply anxious, defensive and both arrogant and perplexed. He finds it difficult to have been – or to be – in the wrong.

Yet if a black man or woman were to be run over outside his home, Milligan would be the first out there with intelligent help and true compassion for suffering. Touring in a racist society, such as South Africa, he will determinedly introduce black guests to a mortified white gathering expecting to lionize a white celebrity. He will do this in the certain knowledge that he will (a) embarrass his host and (b) not receive any future invitations, and will take a Machiavellian delight in both these circumstances.

On 13 August 1968, Leo and Flo's fifty-fourth wedding anniversary, a small celebration dinner was being enjoyed at Woy Woy when Leo, without speaking, suddenly laid his head down on the table. He had suffered a major stroke. He survived, and was admitted to hospital.

All seemed to be progressing well, and after extending his stay as long as possible Spike returned to England.

I went to say goodbye to my father. I never realized, I had no idea that it was for ever. No idea at all – he was progressing well, Desmond and Nadia were there with my mother for much of the time and I went back to England in October or November.

Spike spent Christmas at Holden Road with Paddy, Nanna and the children. In Australia, Desmond and Nadia and their young son Michael joined Flo at Leo's bedside. Shortly after Christmas, Leo's condition worsened and he sank into a coma. He was moved to an intensive care unit in Newcastle, New South Wales. Flo wrote firmly to Spike:

> I think it would be very unwise of you to start rushing over here. In the first place, Dad can linger for days (although we don't think so) and you must *not* jeopardize your work as you must think of your family. *Dad would not wish* you to do that. Please give Bill Ridgeway* the news, etc. We have all got to face it sometime my son and God has made me pretty strong in many ways. I've felt for a long time so has Des that this was going to be Dad's final bow. Please keep your chin up. We are a tough band, we Milligans.

Leo died peacefully on 14 January 1969. The doctors had told Florence, who was accompanied by a woman friend, that there was no hope for Leo and she must not allow herself to suffer. So, as she later wrote in a letter to Spike, she 'said fond farewells to Dad', and set off back on the three-hour journey to Woy Woy. As she arrived at the house, the telephone was ringing. It was the hospital to say that Leo had passed away.

Flo showed her usual courage and fortitude. She was now 75: after a few days with Desmond and Nadia she returned purposefully to her much loved home and settled in alone. 'Don't worry about me, my son,' she wrote to Spike. 'I thank God that I can always occupy myself with my garden and my fancy work.'

---

* Paddy's father.

Spike grieved for his father for a long time. He was comforted by the knowledge that they had shared some parts of their lives, and he was especially glad that for his father's last birthday he had managed to organize a long-planned present. He had Leo's interesting treatise on pistols *The Saga of the Six-Shooter* privately printed and bound in tooled leather. Leo had received four copies, beautifully packed and posted, on his birthday. He was overwhelmed with pride and delight.

Leo went to his grave largely unfulfilled. He was a man of great talent who had been effectively subdued by a system that made him a soldier in his teens and a responsible husband and father in his twenties. Yet his value in Spike's life was considerable. His capacity to move into a fantasy world was almost certainly a bonus of great value to his artistic and imaginative sons. And he, along with Flo, gave Terence and Desmond the immeasurable benefit that is denied to so many. He gave them security.

When, in 1969, Spike started to write his war memoirs, he embarked on a meticulous programme of research which, at first sight, might contrast oddly with the predominantly hilarious intention of the books. Milligan's war books do not presume, they are apolitical and they have no considered message. 'I wasn't trying to impress anyone about the war,' says Milligan. 'I just remembered a lot of the camaraderie and the fun which sometimes seemed to be lost when people talk of the pain and misery of war. I suppose I wanted to show people that it hadn't been all bad, and there had been good times and loyal friendships.' The books have drawn extensively on the experiences and memories of his Battery companions, notably the musician Alf Fildes who wrote up his diary punctiliously every day. Milligan was pained by a critic who referred to the 'unreliability' of his war books. He wrote an aggrieved foreword to the fourth volume, *Mussolini: His Part in My Downfall*:

> Clive James, in a review of one of my war books, quoted it as 'an unreliable history of the war'. Well, this makes him a thoroughly unreliable critic, because I spent more time on getting my dates and facts right than I did in actually writing. I admit the way I present it may seem as though my type of war was impossible and all a figment of a hyperthyroid imagination, but that's the way I write. But all that I wrote *did* happen, it happened on the days I mention, the people I mention are real people and the places are real. So I wish the reader to know that he is not reading a tissue of lies and fancies, it all *really happened*. I even got down to actually finding out what the weather was like, for every day of the campaign. I've spent a fortune on beers and dinners interviewing my old Battery mates, and phone calls to those members overseas ran into over a hundred pounds. Likewise I included a large number of photographs actually taken *in situ*, don't tell me I faked them all, so no more 'unreliable history of the war' chat.

Curiously, academics at the University of Sydney in Clive James' native Australia have recently set an essay question for their first-year humanities students:

> How helpful are the 'war memoirs' of Spike Milligan as a source of serious study of the social history of the British Army during the Second World War?

Primary sources list the first four volumes of Milligan's autobiography,* and a note says that 'students may, if they wish, concentrate on two of these rather than attempt to make a detailed study of all four volumes.'

Secondary sources for this question list a number of

---

* *Adolf Hitler: My Part in His Downfall*, 1971.
'*Rommel?*' '*Gunner Who?*', 1974.
Monty: My Part in His Victory, 1976.
Mussolini: His Part in My Downfall, 1978.

rather more conventional books, including Arthur Marwick's *Britain in the Century of Total War* and A. J. P. Taylor's *English History 1914–1945*.

Milligan was non-committal but secretly gratified when his works received this formal recognition. In his prologue to Volume I, *Adolf Hitler: My Part in His Downfall* he had emphasized that the accounts of his wartime experience were basically true, and he made this point again, rather differently, in '*Rommel?*' '*Gunner Who?*' The prologue reads:

> Of the events of war, I have not ventured to speak from any chance information, nor according to any notion of my own. I have described nothing but what I saw myself, or learned from others of whom I made the most careful and particular enquiry.
>
> Thucydides, Peloponnesian War

> I've just jazzed mine up a little.
>
> Milligan, World War II

Researching the details for his army books triggered the archivist in Spike to dig more deeply into the past of his family. He began a collection of large, red morocco guardbooks, folio-sized volumes which required a special shelf in the drawing-room at Monkenhurst. The books were ordered from Harrods stationery department. Over the next few years Spike frequently added to them or referred to them to check some detail of family history and they were admired and praised by practically everyone. The first volume covered over a century and ran from 1813 to 1917. To help him in his endeavour Spike needed constant recourse to his brother Desmond in Australia. He was an invaluable source of help as, like Spike, he was a methodical keeper of records and he had easy access to Mrs Milligan who, in her eighties by now, was still very alert and with a good – if selective –

memory. This large and still growing collection of anno-
tated photographs is a source of pride and pleasure to
Spike. Virtually deprived by his parents of any coherent or
documented family history, he has taken an almost obsessive pleasure and pride in arranging the material for these
volumes. They contain not only photographs dating back
to 1890, but many relevant papers, certificates and so
forth. There is the occasional disarming Milligan pride.
'Another good school report for Terence,' he notes, rather
fatuously, on one page. The report is, in fact, a good one –
but the need of the mature, famous, outwardly successful
man to remind himself (and others) of childish achievements seems curious.

Paradoxically, and unlike many famous contemporaries,
he is not very worried about present-day reviews, articles,
press notices and the like. Asked why he doesn't subscribe
to a press agency, he is vague:

> Well, it's all rubbish, isn't it? I don't know. Ask Norma. It
> costs the earth, anyway, and it's the ultimate in self-indulgence,
> isn't it? And they never get it right, do they?

Thus he will dismiss the achievements of his present,
while the need to bolster his childhood image, or more
properly the need to remember his childhood with confidence, is perhaps a further thread in the web of his basic
insecurity.

The more Spike probed into his family's past, the more
intrigued he became about his father. He formulated vague
plans for perhaps writing a book on Leo's life, and with
this end in view began to collate material, mostly dates
and records, in a green rexine ring-back file. He headed
the first page:

Chronology of the Life of Leo Alphonsus Milligan
Soldier. Artiste. Author.

He noted the date of his father's birth, the street in Sligo

where he was born and the fact that he was baptized in
Sligo Cathedral. He noted that Leo's mother, Elizabeth
Higgins, was six feet tall and a lady's maid by profession,
and that Leo's father, who became a wheelwright in
the Royal Artillery, was one William Milligan, a former
cabinetmaker.

The research, by reason of Spike's other commitments,
was sporadic but always thorough. He wrote off for baptism
certificates, school reports and army records. He took a
particular delight in establishing his own roots, and seemed
indifferent as to whether they were humble or exotic. He
just wanted the facts. The green file is kept in his bedroom.
There is an S-shaped tear in the fabric of the cover. At
some stage Spike has taken a pen and redesigned the tear
into an outline of a bird, possibly a heron standing.

In the latter half of 1969 an interesting project was suggested. Oscar Lowenstein wanted to present Spike Milligan and Marty Feldman in Samuel Beckett's *Waiting for
Godot* in London. Perhaps the idea had been fired by
Milligan's self-promoted dustbin image. When *A Dustbin
of Milligan* was published in 1961 the cover of the book
showed Milligan sitting cheerfully in a dustbin. The two
main characters in *Waiting for Godot* are tramps, Vladimir
and Estragon. Similarly *Endgame*, Beckett's next play,
features two derelicts, Clem and Lucky, who are depicted
on the cover of the book as living in dustbins. Marty
and Spike were both enthusiastic about the play and
arrangements soon went ahead. The venue was to be the
Roundhouse at Chalk Farm, and a tentative date in March
1970 was arrived at. Oscar Lowenstein, in a letter to
Spike's manager, Norma Farnes, was confident that there
would be no difficulties. Samuel Beckett's agent, he said,
was certain that Beckett would give his permission without
hesitation. In the event, Beckett did more than hesitate.

He categorically refused to license his play for performance in London at that time. Lowenstein was at pains to assure Spike that the proposed casting of the play had not in any way influenced the decision. 'There is an overall blanket refusal to allow productions of his work in London at this juncture,' he wrote to Norma.

It is difficult to speculate with any real accuracy why this was so. Beckett was an intensely private man who would have felt no need to justify his decisions. *Waiting for Godot* had been an immense success when it was first produced at a small theatre (Théâtre de Babylone) on the Boulevard Raspail in Paris but Beckett disapproved of the first London production, which opened at the Arts Theatre Club in 1955. This may have influenced his decision fifteen years later.

Oscar Lowenstein remembers the disappointment he felt when the project was shelved:

Beckett has always been very decisive about his work. When Billy Whitelaw did *Not I* at the Royal Court, they also did a revival of *Krapp's Last Tape* with Albert Finney. Now Beckett never liked that because Albert played it completely differently to the way that Beckett would have played it, the way that Pat McGee played it originally. There tends to be someone who plays one of his parts and then he wants it to be always done in somewhat that way. I mean, he's got many clear rhythms in his head, and if these rhythms aren't adhered to by the actor he doesn't find it works for him, so he's very loath to see any of his plays done in a new or different way. I'm not saying that the way he wants it done isn't right, but I think usually with a great play there are various ways you can do it and there is no one right way; whether Spike would have hit on the right way the Lord alone knows but he might have made it quite extraordinary. The best performance of Godot in the States was by the comedian Bert Lahr. I never saw it, but it was supposed to be brilliant. Bert Lahr was associated mainly with music-hall and vaudeville. Spike might have been wonderful as Godot, but he might have been dreadful. With Spike, it was taking a chance but I do believe he would have been memorable. Sam eventually said yes, but by then – some long time afterwards – everyone had dispersed. It's sad that he gave such a firm *no* when Marty and Spike were both available and enthusiastic.

One wonders whether Beckett would have felt differently about the Milligan–Feldman proposal if he had had the opportunity to know Spike. It is possible that the Englishman's unsuspected depths would have appealed to him. In many ways there are similarities. Beckett was frequently too low in spirit to get up until mid-afternoon; like Milligan, he laboured under an overall despair for humanity. Also like Milligan, he was prey to deep and constant anxiety. It seems likely, however, that Beckett's concept of Spike would be the conventional one of a zany comedian who might take liberties with his script. Perhaps he had heard of what happened to *Oblomov*. A first glance at the script of *Waiting for Godot* would impress only a trained Beckett aficionado with its importance, and Beckett – who wrote in French rather than in his mother tongue of English because 'The discipline of finding the right word or phrase in a second language is valuable' – would have been justified in having doubts about Milligan. Asked if he would have ad libbed or strayed from the script, Milligan was adamant that he would not.

Of course not. I couldn't have. I would have respected it as a superb representation of what our foolish lives are all about – the waiting, the talking and the saying nothing. I know I fooled around with *Oblomov*, but that was a dull, old-fashioned play and it was how the audience seemed to want it. They sent it up as much as we did. But Beckett was something else – you couldn't justify altering a word or a syllable of *Godot*. It was in itself a magnificent send-up of humanity. And I think I might have crossed the great divide between the stand-up comic, which I wasn't, to the area of the serious artist which I still haven't penetrated.

It was not until the 1970s that many able people became aware of the ecological crisis. Milligan, at some level, has been alert almost since childhood to such issues, and has tried to lend them his support. In recent years he has shown a massive distaste for the bureaucratic functioning of official bodies who control, to a greater or lesser extent, the manner of our survival. In practically everything he has written, it is possible to discern an underlying strain of despair or anger about the degradation of the environment and what he sees as the inhumanity of the human animal. Even in short humorous articles he lets slip the occasional reminder of future menace: as early as 1958 he wrote a short piece for the *Tatler and Bystander* called 'Gone Fishing'.

> Next morning, with the sun streaming through the holes in my underpants, I left the hotel and, armed with string, straw hat, a hook, a photo of Isaac Walton and the plans of a fish, made my way to the waterside. As I walked onto the oldddddddddd creaking wood jetty, the warm green waters spread out before me, still and calm, broken only by an occasional fish mouthing an O at the surface. All was peace, save for the roar of bulldozers starting work on the Australian end of the Cromwell Road extension and the crash of the mighty bauxite factory that discharges all its nuclear waste into the quiet green waters. Realizing I was not alone, I donned my trousers.

The overall public concern for nuclear waste had not really been alerted in 1958. It is interesting that Milligan, having touched on this point, reverts immediately to ribaldry.

The same article also manages to send up fishing. Milligan, although a fish-eating vegetarian, is not happy about the concept of fishing, although he accepts the killing of certain flesh foods like venison and fish because they have been 'caught in the wild'.

I continued fishing.

'What bait are you using?' he asked.

'Sausages.'

'You won't catch anything with them.'

'Well, they caught me, I paid a quid for 'em!'

'Here, let me fix you a bait.'

He threaded a prawn on my hook and ate the sausages.

The afternoon wore on, the novelty wore off, and then I felt a nibble at the bait! I pulled the prawn up – thank heaven, it was safe! To make sure no other fish got it, I threw rocks in the water. By keeping up this vigilance till dusk, I preserved the prawn intact.

This short article shows something of Milligan at his most typical, cloaking his sadness in an almost off-hand way, hiding a gnawing anxiety for the future under a shower of jokes. The clown, indeed, is sad today. He dangles the lowly prawn on his line in much the same way that the mediaeval jester would have shaken his miniature cap and bells. He is laughing but unamused. Years later, even though he had become jaundiced with what he sees as a collective failure of the majority ('people we laughingly call Human Beings'), he still had enough spirit to write to Sir Charles Curran, Director General of the BBC from 1969 to 1977, to question the necessity of keeping an earthworm pinned to a display board after an Open University physics lesson. 'Couldn't the worm – low creature though it is – be removed from the glare of the TV arc lights and placed in a box of damp earth?' he writes.

Milligan has espoused many causes. He has found it difficult, sometimes impossible, to ignore the humanitarian issues that are constantly in his mind. He listens to news programmes, reads the daily and weekly newspapers, watches current affairs and topical programmes almost as a background to his normal routine of writing, appearing and performing. His love for animals has drawn him towards anti-blood sports and anti-vivisection movements and he has been deeply involved with one specific cause – seal hunting. He has been associated for many years with wildlife concerns. Much of his writing has been inspired by his interest in these areas.

The fascination exerted over him by children and his uncomplicated love for them fired his interest and support for the movement to provide refuges for women and children. He dedicated one of his books to Erin Pizzey, who did so much to draw the attention of society to the plight of the battered wives and children of violent men.

He has been active in preservation and conservation. From time to time his single determination to preserve something (for example the Elfin Oak or the Regent's Park iron lanterns) has surmounted bureaucratic indifference with astonishing success.

Overriding all these concerns, however, is his passionate anxiety for population control. He believes that over-population is the cause of virtually every ill known to contemporary man. His belief goes back many years and seems to have stemmed from his childhood in India. 'Somehow,' he says, 'I just knew that there were too many people.' References to an overcrowded world have infiltrated all his writing, especially his poetry, for the last twenty years.

In his most recent children's anthology, *Unspun Socks from a Chicken's Laundry*, he has included a short poem called 'Standing Room Only'.

> 'This population explosion,'
> Said Peter to St Paul,
> 'Is really getting far too much,
> just look at that crowd in the hall.
> Even here in heaven
> There isn't any room,
> I think the world could do with less,
> Much less fruit in the womb.'

Thus heaven is overcrowded,
the numbers are starting to tell,
So when the next lot knock at the gates,
tell 'em to go to hell.

The signing sessions which Milligan is frequently called
upon to give are usually riotous. He will arrive in good
time, and will generally have made a small spate of
requests. He will stipulate that the crowd must form an
orderly queue and not develop into a mob, there must be
no piped music, no smoking, and that books must not be
put in paper bags unless it's raining. These requests are
not unreasonable and, whether they are adhered to or not,
Spike invariably gives extremely good value. He will sit
for double or even treble the advertised length of time
(usually an hour) if people are still waiting for their books
to be signed. The request that the volumes must not be
put in paper bags usually causes the most trouble; harassed
bookshop managers are hard put to handle the difficulty of
potential shoplifters if the sales staff are not allowed to
wrap the books after purchase. Drawn into argument on
this score, Spike is unshakeable. 'I would rather have the
trees,' he will say. 'Paper bags to put books in are a
monstrous waste. You can give people a receipt.'

At a signing session, it is possible to see several sides of
the public persona. Gentle and tender with small children,
he can be abrasive with a hapless parent who has done no
wrong save perhaps speak on the child's behalf. He is wary
when parents appear forceful or dictatorial.

Spike: 'And what's your name?' A small girl looks at him
with wide eyes, speechless. Child's mother pushes the
book forward. 'Her name's Amanda. And she'd like one
signing for her little brother as well, please. He's Toby.'
Unwisely, nervously perhaps, she gushes. 'They're both
great fans of yours.' Spike glances at the child, doesn't look

at the mother, signs the books. 'And I suppose Toby can't speak either? I've got two silent fans.' A slight uncertainty prevails. Who is saying what? What is being said? Spike disperses it as easily as he helped create it by a sudden, almost secret smile for Amanda. It is a smile of great sweetness and generosity. It is exclusively for her. It lights up his face and hers and for a moment, perhaps, he completely shares her world.

A love for children is fundamental and immediate in him and perhaps it is heightened by his own intuitive recognition of how children feel. This is a rare capacity, even among the most caring and loving of adult people. It is often to be seen in the rapport which is shared between clowns and children. And we know that the clown in Milligan is never far beneath the surface.

The unfortunate mother, however, has in some odd and undeserved way been snubbed. Or has she? And if so, why has Milligan, basically a kind man, felt it necessary implicitly to rebuke her? The nuances of this fan out like ripples on a pond. Any sort of indoctrination of innocence – even on this relatively mild sort of issue – causes Milligan a sort of helpless anger. To him, the children being gently pushed towards ingratiating themselves in this harmless situation are as potentially wronged by their manipulators as the small children being drilled by the Khmer Rouge.

Milligan was by now brooding seriously on the work he wanted to do. His autobiography covering the war years was churning in his head, and he had already published a handful of poems which he wanted to collect and add to. A little-known volume (*Values,* * 1969) was printed privately by the Offcut Press. Milligan was impressed by the hand-made paper and the dedication of Tony Savage who ran this small business.

* This volume is housed in the North Library of the British Library.

In years to come he met Tomás Graves again and was overjoyed to hear that he was restoring his father's old press imprint – the Seizin. Tomás went to Monkenhurst to have tea; the talk was all about the French Pedallo press which Tomás was in the process of restoring.

It is typical of Milligan to encourage what he sees as true commitment to old skills.

On another occasion Paul Joyce, a photographer, followed Milligan at a discreet distance for three days. Spike was in a particularly manic state at that time and emerged from his car only to race, head down, into his office. Joyce hung around for his entrances and exits to 9 Orme Court, but Milligan never paused for long enough for him to set up his antiquated camera. Eventually, they came face to face and Spike paused. Joyce was young and courteous and, if Milligan had noticed him, which is doubtful, he would have been seen to be serious. 'I apologize for dogging you. May I take your photograph?'

A transient irritation passed over Milligan's face. It wasn't a good moment for him (few moments are). Joyce hopefully produced his camera. Milligan, at the sight of the brown wooden camera box, relaxed visibly. A faint smile flitted across his face.

'All right. Don't take too long. And I'm only agreeing because you're using a beautiful old camera.'

The photograph of Spike Milligan hung in the National Portrait Gallery in an exhibition called *Elders*. Milligan, still in his fifties, was the youngest by far. Asked why he had included him in his exhibition, Joyce was explicit.

'I felt the photograph showed him in the pain of his life. He has lived through so much and it all shows, as in the photographs of the really old people. I had to use it. It belonged with the other photographs.'

18

The Other Spike

I have known no man of genius who had not to
pay, in some affliction or defect either physical or
spiritual, for what the gods had given him.

Max Beerbohm

Further incarceration in mental hospitals in the mid-sixties
had some strange spin-off benefits for Milligan. His poetic
abilities flared and some inhibitions began to dissipate; he
wrote several poems whilst in Bethlem Hospital in 1966.
He also started painting again, and in 1972 was given an
exhibition in the Whitechapel Art Gallery. Several of the
pictures sold for sums in the region of a hundred pounds.
A few were given to friends. A good number have simply
gone missing. Milligan put one or two inconspicuous
paintings in a cupboard at Orme Court and forgot about
them for years. Coming across them unexpectedly he
found one small watercolour which he had painted by a
curious experimental method of allowing drops of water to
fall on dry powder. This had been painted at his parents'
house during one of his visits to Woy Woy. On an off-
chance, Milligan entered it for the 1981 Summer Exhibition of the Royal Academy. He seemed surprised and
not particularly gratified when it was selected and hung.
The picture was called 'Infra-Pelvis'.

Subsequently he accepted an invitation to a special VIP
dinner at the Academy. Whichever RA had been detailed
to 'look after' this particular distinguished guest couldn't
find him. This is not altogether surprising, for Spike has a
way of effacing himself very adequately if the social furore
seems too great. When, the next day, he was asked if he

had enjoyed himself he said 'Oh, yes. I found some of the musicians playing in the band and I was able to talk to them.'

One of the poems that sprang from his time in hospital at Highgate was later included in *Small Dreams of a Scorpion*.

> Born screaming small into this world –
> Living I am
> Occupational therapy twixt birth and death –
> What was I before?
> What will I be next?
> What am I now?
> Cruel answer carried in the jesting mind
>   of a careless God.
> I will not bend and grovel
> When I die. If He says my sins are myriad
> I will ask why He made me so imperfect
> And He will say 'My chisels were blunt'.
> I will say *'Then why did you make so many of me?'*

In 1970, John Goldschmidt produced a powerful documentary for Granada TV on Milligan. It was called *The Other Spike*. Spike appeared both as himself and as the po-faced, pin-striped psychiatrist as he relived the agonies of the periods in isolation wards and mental hospitals. Subsequently, he talked freely in television interviews about his sufferings and the merciless pressures that torment him. The overall term 'manic depressive', frequently misused and misunderstood, became, as a consequence, more respectable, and a growing number of people began to develop an awareness of a condition which is at best a sad and heavy burden to carry and at worst an almost totally disabling illness. We owe a debt to Goldschmidt for his sensitive pursuit of Milligan's torment, and to Milligan who relived this torment with lucid honesty.

In 1972 *Small Dreams of a Scorpion* emerged. It was

Spike's first recognized volume of poems. It gave him a lot
of satisfaction – and some of his readers food for thought. In
the foreword, Spike as usual sends up everyone, including
himself:

> I do hope you enjoy them, but if you don't by the time you
> have found out it will be too late and the money will be in my
> Post Office Book.

There are forty-one poems. Most of them echo with a
despairing pain that Milligan does nothing to conceal. Only
two or three suggest any vestige of hope. Many reflect his
immediate concerns with ecology and conservation. He
includes 'Myxomatosis' which first appeared in *Milligan's
Ark*, the compilation of animal drawings which he and
other artists gathered together in aid of Prince Philip's
World Wildlife Fund.

> A baby rabbit
> With eyes full of pus
> Is the work of scientific
>
> US.

One or two poems are included which illustrate Milligan's
conflicting anxieties on population and abortion. The
volume is dedicated to Flo:

> This book is dedicated to my mother
> Who spent a lifetime dedicated to me.

It went into paperback the following year. The publishers
categorized it as 'humour'.

In the spring of 1973, Eamonn Andrews made one of his
famous 'This is Your Life' programmes about Spike. Flo,
Desmond and family were flown from Australia for the
occasion and Harry Edgington, now living in New Zealand,

was linked up by cable. But what delighted Spike most of all was Robert Graves's appearance. Graves was staying for a few days with friends in Chelsea. No lover of technology, he declined to go to the studios but sat firmly on a window-seat with his back to a garden. While he reminisced about the times he had spent with Spike, the light shone through his mass of fluffy silver hair, transforming it into a curious, shining halo. He concluded his completely unrehearsed words with an affectionate 'Well, Spike. Goodbye now – I love you and you know it.'

Whilst he had been speaking, the milkman walked up the path in shot to deliver the milk, passing the window closely. The desirability of a retake was discussed and stoutly vetoed by Graves.

'Nonsense. Certainly not,' he said. 'The milkman is part of life. Spike will have no objection to the milkman.'

About two weeks later, when Graves had returned to Majorca, Spike wrote him a letter.

> April 16 (my birthday)
> Orme Court,
> Bayswater W2

My Dear Robert,

How delighted I was to see that unexpected film of you on the 'This is Your Life' show, . . . yes, I know you love me – but it's mutual. I wish I had known you were in London recently, I would have loved to see you. When you come again, I will take you to where there is food, wine, music and friendship, who can refuse such an offer? I go on trying to make a living by my pen, but alas, I finished schooling at 14, and not until I was 35 did I become aware of Literature, since then by assiduous reading I have tried to teach myself, but it is in the green absorptive years that one should learn. I am instinctively drawn towards Victorianism – War – Nostalgia – Comedy – Nonsense – Children's Stories and Poetry. I am currently writing the second volume of my war memoirs, and going over war diaries (personal and Regimental). I find it very nostalgic, almost traumatic. At the end of a day, I find I am immersed in 1939–45, it takes hours for the aura to wear off, and for a period, even with my family around me, I feel very cut off. At night I can hear the guns going in my mind, the shouts of men under stress, the dramatic incidents that suddenly flash back into mind's eye, are all, well I feel as if I am 'possessed' and need exorcizing. Here is something very interesting. 4 years ago, on the Bayswater Road, I watched a handsome Early Victorian Home being 'Developed'. When it was razed to its foundations, the ground floors were exposed to the elements. I was drawn towards the place, why I don't know, it was like some strange magnetic pull from the past. I stood, in what must have been the front room, littered around amid the ruins were documents, letters, envelopes, newscuttings, snaps, photographs, albums, books, a few World War I medals. I don't know why, but I carefully collected all of these, under the suspicious gaze of the navvies. For 2 years these documents lay in a box in my office, on Nov 11 last (significant date) I started to collate the collection into chronological order. The story and photos go back to about 1848 and terminate in about 1931. And it was strangely exciting to have a family story, lasting nearly 150 years, on your hands, and it was like being an invisible relative, or am I a ghost? looking at them, and they not aware of me. There are major disasters in the family, 2 sons killed in World War I, the mother turning to Spiritualism for solace, one son remains, Capt C. Tate. If you come to London again, do let me know, and I will show you the documents. I must finish, London is closing on me!

Love from Spike

In the summer of 1973, Paddy Milligan noticed a small lump in her breast. She went into hospital, and within hours was thankfully telephoning Spike to tell him the good news – the growth was benign. Unhappily, this was not so. A short while later, she was given a more ominous report. Paddy rang her husband for the second time; she was now incoherent in her distress. The growth was malignant and her breast was to be removed.

Spike, far from well himself, and deeply anxious about his frequently precarious work and financial position, was shattered by Paddy's illness. Tragically, there was little he could do to help her through her trauma; his own anxious misery kept him in a state of agitation and despair much of the time. When Paddy was in hospital, he did the best he could to help at home and to comfort the children. One evening, he took Nanna, Jane, Silé and Sean to the Royal Tournament at Earl's Court, whilst Laura went to the hospital. Paddy in due course returned, and settled down with as much optimism as she could muster. She recovered from the operation and was able to take part in a charity concert at the Gatehouse Theatre in North London just before Christmas.

Milligan now fell deeply in love with a neglected old Victorian house called Monkenhurst on the outskirts of Barnet. It faced a common and had a magnificent stained glass window, making it look not unlike a church. There was a hundred-year-old tree in the garden which was going to be uprooted when the house was demolished and the intending developers got their plans passed for several small (but profitable) houses. Milligan was anguished at the idea of this. The end of the tree probably grieved him more than the thought of the houses. The outcome was that he bought Monkenhurst.

The piece of land on which the tree grew was still threatened by the developers. All the official ways of preserving the tree seemed to be blocked. Milligan had recently been searching his conscience as to the rightness of accepting work in South Africa. The thought of the magnificent tree being felled clinched matters. He gave his one-man show in South Africa and used the money he made to buy the land. The tree was saved, but Milligan received some bad publicity for appearing in South Africa. 'I don't mind too much,' he said. 'I let foreign fascism work to combat British bureaucracy. And just look at that tree! Isn't it marvellous?'

Paddy was thrilled with her lovely new home. There was a beautiful kitchen with a high picture window onto the garden, and a huge pine dresser gracing one wall. The wood panelling in the entrance hall was restored. A dining-room with Spike's favourite round table was arranged. Spike designed a film-star bedroom for Paddy, with a king-sized bed on a pale blue carpeted dais. Complicated but beautiful curtains with authentic Victorian pelmets were ordered for this room and the ground-floor drawing-room. Spike's own room shared the same beautiful view of the garden, but it was essentially spartan: he had it decorated entirely in white, with shelving all around the head of his bed. As the years passed, the shelves filled with all his favourite books. To begin with, he had double-glazing installed in an attempt to shut out noise. It didn't work. Eventually, he had triple-glazing. This didn't work either, but at least when a harsh winter came his room was beautifully warm. Milligan takes nothing for granted, however. 'I'm so grateful that I have a nice warm room to be in, and warm slippers to wear,' he said once, when the temperature went below zero. 'The slippers,' he added, 'were a Christmas present. I really am lucky.'

Over the next few months, the beautiful double-pleated pelmets in both Paddy's room and the drawing-room went back to the designers several times. Milligan, amidst the mounting pressures of his life, is indefatigable in his search for perfection in all areas.

In 1973 Richard Lester gave Milligan a chance to act in his new version of *The Three Musketeers*. Milligan took his chance and somehow survived the hazards of bedchamber scenes with Raquel Welch. The location work in Madrid was a particular success. Lester and Spike were happy to be working together again and Spike, on a personal level, was grateful for a break from the pressures of family life that were steadily mounting with the further decline in Paddy's health.

The screenplay stuck closely to Alexandre Dumas. Milligan, in his fifties, normally looked fifteen years less but as the innkeeper in *The Three Musketeers* he was immediately and memorably an old man. He had eight or nine short scenes, some of which would have been very promising material for 'sending up'. Lester had faith in his actor and rightly so; Milligan became the old innkeeper and under Lester's direction was not allowed to be (or nudged into being) Milligan. One scene towards the end of the film shows the old fellow babbling to his cronies about his young wife who is prominent in royal circles. 'Sometimes I come up at night just to see her through the windows, being part of it all.' His eyes shine with a sort of fanatical delight, yet there is a poignant glimpse of a sad, silly old man, frustrated and unwanted. Milligan's part is not large, his contribution to the film is that he plays a cameo part so well. Lester's astute direction and his faith in Milligan as an actor is part of the success story; the other part probably belongs to Spike. On this occasion the shadow of Alexandre Dumas has been felt.

With his historian's heart and soul Milligan was in his element. He read extensively on the period and looked with a keenly critical eye at the sets, locations, properties and costumes. Dick Lester remembers one particular scene. It was in the palace ballroom. No expense was spared; hundreds of beautifully dressed extras were wearing authentically designed costumes of the period. The figures swirled around the impressive pillars; the ballroom was a mass of flowers, liveried footmen and blazing chandeliers. Horse-drawn carriages were sweeping up a circular driveway to deposit the guests.

Milligan was watching from an adjacent terrace with

Lester. He was entranced. They had been standing silently for some minutes when he turned to the director.

'Can you imagine, Dick? It really was like this, wasn't it? This is how it actually looked in the past. We've brought back the past.'

'He was stunned by the whole scene,' remembers Richard Lester. 'I looked at him a few moments later and he had tears in his eyes. He was so moved by the whole thing that it brought him almost to weeping.'

Although Spike spent a lot of time at Orme Court, he tried very hard not to neglect his family. Weekends he always tried to be at home, and if he stayed in town during the week he would often try to arrange a dinner with Sean or Laura who were no longer living at home. One day in March 1974 he invited Sean to come and eat with him that evening. During the afternoon, a temporary extra typist was summoned from a secretarial agency to assist with the heavy workload. Spike was dictating letters at a very high rate of knots; Norma and Tanis must have been grateful to see help arrive. Shelagh Sinclair was twenty-eight years old, dark-haired, plump and very pretty. She had beautiful, mischievous eyes and an infectious laugh. Milligan asked her why she was working as a temporary typist and was genuinely upset when she explained that she already had a job as production assistant at the BBC but was working during her leave as she was short of money. 'Well, I'm having dinner tonight with my son,' he said. 'Please come and join us and I'll see that you get some good food.' He then proceeded to dictate at high speed. Fortunately, Shelagh was able to keep up. Work completed, she arranged to meet Spike and Sean later that evening, then she left Orme Court and walked through the Park to her home near Gloucester Road. 'I remember that I couldn't help smiling,' she says. 'I'd had such a nice afternoon. And

I remember that the first letter he dictated to me was to Robert Graves, then the next one was to the Pope. I thought he was the most interesting and fascinating man I'd ever met.'

Spike has spasms of feverish letter-writing. This is not so much to friends or relatives (here, the telephone is called into use), but he will join in – or just as often provoke – a controversy in the press. He will fire off letters in all directions, often showing a gratified surprise when one appears in a newspaper. He will write on topics that are important to him: when his susceptibilities are aroused, when he is hurt, angry or scathing. He is also capable of demonstrably wanting to know something. Quite often, no answer would satisfy him, but he will pursue, for instance, his distaste for piped music, or smoking, or dogs and their necessary excrements time and again. His views on all these areas are fierce and inflexible, and it will not cross his mind that he could be wrong. Not infrequently a letter will grow into an article. Some of his protests touch on matters which have been very close: should a person dying of cancer be denied the knowledge of their approaching death? Milligan believes that they should. He bases this belief on his understanding of what happened to Paddy.

In 1977, the cancer that had lain dormant for four years flared again. Constant and devoted care from the doctors, from Nanna and the family could not help. Paddy lay in her beautiful blue and white bedroom dying slowly. Spike was horrified at the suggestion that she should know the truth. He angrily dismissed the protestations of one adviser who said firmly that both Paddy and twelve-year-old Jane should be told. 'And Jane must share her mother's death experience,' he was told. Milligan was quite unable to accept this. He still exploded with anger about it five years after Paddy's death:

So what is supposed to happen? Is Paddy to break her heart every time Jane comes into her room and know that this is her daughter and she'll never see her grow up? And what about Jane? How can she live her little life and go to school and come home and do her lessons and say, oh yes, my mummy's going to die soon, soon I won't have her but now I must go downstairs and get on with my homework. How could she live her little life like that? I did it the right way. I waited till nearly the end and then I told Jane and she had twenty-four hours of awful grief knowing her mother was dying. That was enough for her to bear.

Many correspondence columns have been filled on this subject, many cogent arguments have been expressed for both sides, but nothing would ever convince Spike that his conduct of this matter was anything other than absolutely right.

Paddy Milligan died bravely, refusing almost to the end any drugs that she believed had become available after animal experimentation. The young Milligans were now bereft of their second mother. Silé wept piteously; Paddy had been the only mother she could remember. 'Why did Mum have to die?' she asked. 'She was just teaching me how to set my own hair, and I did love her.' Jane, distraught, not quite believing, was comforted by her Aunt Ann (Paddy's sister), by Nanna, by her older brother and sisters and by her despairing father.

By the time the blue and white pelmets were finally completed several years had passed. Jane had left school and started her first job in the theatre. Spike and Shelagh Sinclair had just become engaged. Nanna and Shelagh spent a morning supervising the final adjustments to the pelmets; that afternoon Shelagh confessed to a great sadness. 'It may sound rather odd,' she said. 'I just feel so sorry that Paddy never saw them finished. They look so lovely. It just doesn't seem fair.'

* * *

There are facets in Milligan's life which seem curiously unavailable for public scrutiny. He does not studiously avoid the interest of outsiders; were he to be faced with an interested questioner he would probably be prepared to discuss the matters patiently and at length. He just does not see certain areas as other than private, and in this he is, of course, fundamentally correct.

Diana Keys first wrote to Spike in the early seventies. She had seen him on television talking about his own experiences in mental hospitals. Diana was used to hospitals. She had been in one since the age of twelve, and at the time she started writing to Spike she knew no other life and, indeed, had no other home. Spike sent her a book or two and wrote her a few friendly lines. Diana wrote back immediately and a desultory correspondence ensued. She had rarely, if ever, received a letter from anyone. She was overjoyed.

For the next two years Spike wrote to her regularly and she remembers that when he was to be away in Australia for several months he made a special point of telling her.

'Don't worry if you don't hear from me for a few weeks,' he wrote. 'I'm going away to do a one-man show and earn my living and see my mother in Australia. When I come back I'll be writing to you again.'

The correspondence continued. When Spike was unable to write, Norma Farnes would often write in his place. Diana was happy.

Eventually things went adrift. Perhaps Spike was ill or overworked, perhaps Diana increased her output of letters; in any event the time came when Spike's entourage of harassed minders saw fit to divert some of her letters from his immediate notice. When he found out, he fell upon the small pile of letters in wrath.

'That poor girl, writing to me, begging me to do something. How cruel can people be! She should have had answers. Just another let-down in a miserable life of nobody caring.'

Spike (unfairly) castigated everyone around him, then wrote to Diana and to the hospital authorities. It was agreed that Diana should come to Monkenhurst for a weekend. The first visit was far from being a success. Diana was unused to the outside world and she was in turn withdrawn and demanding. Spike, free at the time he invited her, was heavily committed by the time the weekend arrived. The family had to bear the brunt of the strange visitor. Spike's daughters were kind, but, understandably, wary. Nanna sighed, put a draw-sheet on Diana's bed, and wondered whether all this sort of thing came to any good in the long run. Shelagh, vigilant only for Spike's happiness, was sympathetic. Diana alternately glowered and chattered, stared beseechingly or aggressively at the assembled company, but shone like a light whenever Spike came near. Her history was distressing. It was a long rigmarole of a rejected childhood, cruel step-parents, neglectful foster parents, clinics for 'difficult' children, and eventual confinement, at the age of twenty-seven, in a long-stay mental hospital. She was incontinent and depressed, she had no relatives and no friends, and was unco-operative with any of the social workers who had for so long formed the only background she knew. Spike put crayons and pencils in her room, and before she left, on that first rather painful visit, she drew scrawled pictures for them all. Spike's was executed with a great attention to detail. He was delighted with it and put it immediately on his bedroom wall. The girls praised Diana for her attempts and showed their pictures to friends who came for tea on the Sunday. Diana stared fiercely at the floor and almost smiled.

A pattern was established, and over the next year or so Diana made frequent visits to the Milligans. Jane and

Shelagh took her shopping so that she would have something other than hospital handouts to wear. Silé helped with shampoos and hair styles. Nanna talked good sense about learning to consider others in general and attending to one's own draw-sheet in particular. Sometimes Diana exploded and sulked but more often she smiled. Often, when it was time to go back to her hospital home she would get angry and Spike would take her in his arms.

'Diana, you'll come back. We all have to get on with our lives. Silé has to go to work, I'm working, Shelagh works, Jane has to go to school. Nanna has all the house to see to. You'll come again.'

The situation had pitfalls, of course.

'I'm afraid that she'll fall in love with Spike,' said Shelagh. 'Not exactly as a lover but as a sort of father figure that she's never had. He means so well but he can't take it, he can't take the sort of pressures that people like Diana put on him. He'll crack.'

Shelagh was right and for one rather exhausting period Diana developed an obsessive need for Spike's attention.

Somebody gave her his private phone number, used by relatively few people. The number had to be changed as Diana couldn't be persuaded not to call every five minutes. Eventually, however, everything settled down. Over a long period, the whole family spent many hours with Diana. She began to confide in them, and everyone was pleased with her progress. Spike was jubilant about her.

Well, it's just that she never had anyone who really cared about getting her out of that place. She didn't need to stay in a hospital for life. She wasn't ill. She was only in terrible need of love.

In due course Spike took up the cudgels on Diana's behalf with the appropriate authorities. There was a fairly slow but fierce exchange and the culmination was a happy one. Diana progressed from the hospital ward to a small home of her own under the auspices of 'sheltered' housing. Shelagh and Nanna went shopping with her and helped her to stretch a small grant over the necessary possessions. The Milligans undoubtedly subsidized Diana from time to time, but there was a significant understanding of her need for a growing independence. Shelagh scooped up unneeded items from her own bachelor days, Nanna combed the cupboards for spares. Even her frugal Scottish heart was affronted by the parsimony of the local council: 'Have you seen the list of things Diana's grant allows for? One pan, one kettle, one plate, one cup, one spoon – is the puir lass going to live like a hermit and never ask anyone in for a cup of tea, now?'

Diana now lives very differently. The draw-sheet has become a thing of the past. She is much more relaxed, and talks easily to people. She has become quite sociable, she is developing domestic skills and beginning to be in control of her own life. She is reserved and shy, perhaps, but no longer cowering and speechless. Obviously there are still frustrations and fears, and she is sometimes unhappy. But the Milligans were a powerful force for the good in a life which knew only stultifying apathy and loneliness. With a growing degree of self-sufficiency Diana now invites the Milligan girls and Shelagh to her own tea parties. She visits her old hospital simply as a day-patient, her prognosis is good and a future in which she will conceivably hold down a job is not unlikely. Her life is certainly a far cry from that of the incontinent girl incarcerated in a long-stay hospital who once wrote, in despair, to Spike Milligan.

19

The Black Hat

Reverence for life shows that sympathy for animals, which is so often represented as sentimentality, should be a duty which no thinking man can escape.

Albert Schweitzer

'If all my youth had been spent in Catford, there would have been no *Goon Show*,' Milligan says decisively. 'On the other hand, I'd have probably risen to being a foreman fitter at Woolwich Arsenal and it would have made my mother a lot happier. She'd have been prouder of me that way – I'd have succeeded by her standards. Being a success in something like the *Goon Show* has basically rattled her. She hasn't quite been able to say, "Why don't you get a decent job?" but that's how her mind really works.'

Milligan himself is fundamentally dissatisfied with his lingering aura of Goonery. Since he is capable of achievement in so many other areas, some of them far removed from show business, this is understandable, but he recognizes the importance of his first public success and acknowledges the relevance of the twists of fate which gave him his first impressionable fifteen years in the dying magnificence of the British Raj.

If I'd have been smothered in the drab grey of working-class misery from birth I'd probably never have emerged. But the way it happened, I had all these insights into the Imperial mish-mash of grandeur and a sort of moral decadence. I saw so much of the pretences, and the hollowness and the foolishness of people. You see, I saw it all as a child and as I grew older so much of it seemed ridiculous and hysterically funny. I found them all out there – Major Bloodnok, Osric Pureheart, all of them.

The capacity to see through the eyes of childhood has probably been Milligan's greatest continuing asset throughout his life. It is a childlike glee that allows him to make what society calls 'a fool' of himself – as when he once jumped on the revolving circular platform in an airport luggage retrieval area.

'Just once more round and then I promise I'll get off,' he reassured the startled and angry officials. 'I've always wanted to do this, all my life.'

This sort of episode is not a publicity stunt – there were no pressmen or photographers present when it happened. It was no especial plea for attention, but more like the action of a bored, inquisitive and uninhibited child.

Spike Milligan, curiously diffident about his fast developing multiple talents, really needed the roars of affectionate mirth that he inspired within the magic Goon circle. None of the Goons (with the possible exception of Bentine, in the beginning), were fundamentally self-assured, but neither Harry Secombe nor Peter Sellers had quite the same fragile, destructible ego. Sellers sprang from the proverbial theatrical background of variety tours and one-week engagements. Further to this he had the constant and unfailing encouragement of possibly the most dedicated, most dominating and most protective Jewish mother in the business. Harry Secombe had the richness of the Welsh valleys, the Eisteddfod prizes, the admiring, affectionate relatives behind him. Spike had only the confused memories of his highly talented father (who never even tried to make it professionally) and the doting love of his mother who set her sights for him no higher than a steady job at Woolwich Arsenal.

'We reverted to working-class status as soon as we

returned to England in the thirties. The important thing was to get a regular job, go to it every day, get a rise, give it to the Catholic church, go to mass on Sunday and go to bed early, preferably alone,' says Spike, dismally.

He jokes like this but there is a deep frustration beneath the surface. More than anything, he has wanted the approval of his parents; especially – and pathetically – he has longed for his mother's approval. The grown man is well aware of this foible. His first action on learning of the success of *Adolf Hitler* was to telephone Australia, like 'a seven-year-old boy, running home from school and wanting praise'. In the morass of loneliness, confusion and despairing anger that surrounded the break-up of his marriage to June, one of the children's poems that he wrote recalled Flo's dismal theme song:

> Look at all those monkeys
> Jumping in their cage
> Why don't they all go out to work
> And earn a decent wage?

Even so, he does not allow the monkeys' scenario to end disrespectfully.

> How can you say such silly things,
> And you a son of mine?
> Imagine monkeys travelling on
> The Morden–Edgware line!
>
> But what about the Pekinese
> They have an allocation.
> 'Don't travel during Peke hour'
> It says on every station.
>
> My Gosh, you're right, my clever boy,
> I never thought of that!
> And so they left the monkey-house
> While an elephant raised his hat. [1]

Milligan leaves the human adult looking both foolish and pompous whilst the child and the animals are vindicated.

Spike is unfortunate in his extreme vulnerability to noise. Walking round his garden at Monkenhurst one early spring day he remarked sadly that he regretted not having been able to afford more land at the time of purchase.

'I'd have liked more land, more privacy.'

'But you've got a big garden – ?'

'Yes, but look – ' He gestures towards the fences on the perimeter of his land.

'But you said you'd got good neighbours.'

'Yes, but – whirr, whirr, whirr – you know, mowers . . .'

With something between diffidence and irritation, Spike is at this moment sensitive to the point of appearing arrogant. It's not difficult, however, to appreciate the perpetual pain that normal, next-door noise must cause him when he is wanting to work or relax. This may be another instance of his having a 'skin short'. Most of us tolerate a next-door mower with resignation. For Spike, the irritation is very likely to become unbearable, deeply frustrating and finally exasperating. His possible 'boiling over' on this sort of occasion is not so much a display of temperament or anger as an imminent danger warning of 'malfunction'. A lot of the time he struggles gamely for what he will call 'the retention of my sanity'.

Every time he fails to keep an appointment or fulfil an engagement Spike is, in a sense, demonstrating his courage. Aware of this extreme vulnerability, he will hesitate for days, even weeks, before negotiating and agreeing a contract. His manager Norma Farnes says, 'You never know with Spike. He can be hopping with excitement about a new series or a special engagement only to crash down the next day saying "How did you let me in for this?"'

At the time of agreeing or accepting work or an appearance Spike can be confident and enthusiastic. Within hours, the mysterious changes which occur – some say within the body's chemistry – can reduce him to wretched despair and shuddering misery. This stage of hopelessness is further exacerbated by the mortification, self-blame and guilt that follow his failure. The saying that 'The manic can see no problem, the depressive can find no solution' is appropriate. Spike, however, has long periods of relative 'normality', and it is during these that his courage is enduring and consistent. At the back of his mind there is always the knowledge that his spirits may suddenly plummet downwards, yet he constantly agrees to enter into situations either working or social which he must know could end in failure. It is rare, but it is possible. He has had to build his career on this shaky premise, and it must be the ultimate tribute to his talent that he works as consistently as he does.

As a solo performer, Spike lacks the sort of egotistical security that has been the prerequisite of other artists, of profound importance to stars like Noel Coward and Marlene Dietrich who have extraordinary records of being able to hold an audience in transports of delight even when appearing on the back of a lorry. Yet, taken by surprise as it were, Spike can give a solo performance enhanced by the sort of unstructured, charismatic magnetism that was so much a part of Coward and Dietrich.

The great divide is that Coward and Dietrich simply knew that they could do it. Spike Milligan, anxious and uncertain, is never sure. There have been one-man shows in cabaret-type performances in Australia, in South Africa and in England, but Spike has been both hesitant and wary about setting these up and has been known to procrastinate, decimate, even virtually sabotage his act before a definite opening day has been fixed. It seems to be part and parcel of the fundamental lack of ego or self-confidence, and in the apparently self-assured celebrity of the 'eighties there still lurks the angry, distraught youth of the 'forties who smashed his trumpet.

There is a true story which still goes the rounds that on one occasion in Coventry Milligan raved and yelled at an unresponsive audience. 'You hate me, don't you?' he shouted. 'All right, I'm leaving.' He stamped on his trumpet, destroying it completely, and then locked himself in a dressing-room for many hours. The story then becomes embellished, and Milligan, supposedly, attempts to hang himself. He is indignant at the different versions of this incident that have been given.

> What, hang myself for Coventry? I wouldn't do that. The truth is, I'd bought a hangman's noose in some junk shop whilst we were touring around. I used to fool about with it. I'd hang it up on a beam – it was an evil-looking thing – and when anyone knocked at the door I'd jump on a chair and put it round my neck and call out 'Come in' or 'Don't come in' or something – anyway it was all a joke. Or my idea of a joke at that time. It was never serious.

Spike agrees, however, that the Coventry audience brought him to despair. 'Well, I never believed in myself, did I? You get crucified by people sometimes, don't you? People can be lethal.'

Norma Farnes was pressured by an impresario and by Spike himself to set up a one-man show for the Mayfair Theatre in 1979. In fact it never came off, not because the impresario changed his mind, or because terms could not be agreed or a time slot found. The reason, given with total seriousness by Spike, was simply that the soft black hat that he required as a 'prop' had been lost during a recent Australian tour and had not been replaced. 'Can't any fool get me a black hat?' he raged. 'How can I do my act without a hat?' 'It is his excuse,' said Norma patiently, with a familiar and dismal wisdom. 'I could get him a dozen hats tomorrow. He really doesn't want to do it. He does want to do it, but he doesn't if you see what I mean. He's worried about it. He's not convinced that he's going to be a great success.'

The black hat can assume significant proportions. It is as important to Milligan as the comic masks were to the actors in the Commedia dell' Arte. Milligan's apparent anger or despair, rage or petulance is not trivial, it is fundamental to his needs as a performer. The hat is not only one of his important props, he uses it as both a shield and a weapon. Dark to the eyes and soft to the touch, it has become a comforting place to hide, a place of escape. Its very foolishness supports him in his endeavours. It helps to convert his pain to laughter. In a sense, his hat braces him with strength towards his performances.

In November 1984 Milligan was to appear on *Loose Talk*, a chat show presented by Steve Taylor. On the evening planned, Spike was to be interviewed with Roger McGough and Tina Brown. A car was to pick him up at 8 P.M. The studio was at Deptford and transmission was to take place that evening. Spike had just returned from a gruelling tour of his one-man show. The tour would have been less gruelling if he had been able to sleep at nights, but the painful 'low frequency' noises which torment him had been particularly disturbing during the last few days and he arrived home shattered. He took to his bed and tossed restlessly, eschewing visitors, accepting little or nothing to eat, turning his telephone off for most of the time. A pile of unopened mail left on his pillow filled him with sullen rage. 'That's a nice thing to come home to,' he said fretfully. Another day he would have been irritated and frustrated if his mail was not waiting for him. This time, however, he was in a bad way, and Norma must have been alert to the possibility of cancellation. However, two days' relative rest and quiet were beneficial and on the late afternoon of the day Milligan had tea, Marmite toast, a bath, a shave and by 7.45 P.M. he had dressed carefully in a shirt and tie appropriate for the occasion and suitable for the TV cameras. He put on dark trousers and a midnight-blue velvet jacket. The depression was lifting gradually but he was by no means sanguine. He was not looking forward to the occasion but rather holding on, hoping (and knowing) that he could make it, if nothing went wrong. Perhaps this is the stage when his courage, in the long run, becomes his downfall. He is fit to work, but he has no reservoir for emergencies. He is drained, and the sort of setback which would not throw him when he is ebullient will today destroy him.

Spike was ready. He looked, and was, immaculate. His family and those close to him would detect the strain, but to his large and diverse public he would just be Milligan in one of his several moods – perhaps flitting mercurially from one to the other, now morose, now lively, revealing for a moment an abysmal sadness, rapidly outpacing this with a keen and cynical humour. On this occasion, there is no doubt that he could have got to the studio and reached an acceptably high standard of performance. He was not yet at the stage of recovery that would be coupled with a genuine lifting of the spirits followed by the desire to relax over a meal, a bottle of wine and then either an hour's good conversation or an hour spent listening to jazz at Ronnie Scott's. He would, however, have made the show and after a fairly tight-lipped goodnight rushed for the cover of his car. After a silent journey he would have thankfully sought the privacy of his own room. His predominant feeling would be relief that the evening was over. The next day, it is likely that his mood would have lightened and a near serenity would have consolidated the improvement, a direct consequence of the fact that on the previous evening he had not failed.

In the event, having been told that the studio car would collect him at 8 P.M., Milligan sat, waiting. He was ready on time and very tense. He would not be likely to make a telephone call or chat or pick up a newspaper. He would stalk around his room – perhaps straightening a few books on his shelves, breaking a dead leaf from a plant, and looking frequently at his watch. He might check that the time on his watch was correct. We know that eventually he telephoned the studios. It was then 8.15. He was told that there was a change in the arrangements. He would be picked up at 10 P.M. for transmission at 11.30. Spike trembled with frustration and anger. He swore. He threw off his clothes and collapsed into his bed in a rage of misery and despair. He probably swallowed a handful of sleeping pills. He threw the covers over his head and tried, no doubt without success, to sleep.

To an unaware observer, the scenario could suggest an unacceptable degree of self-indulgent, petulant tantrum. Over the years, Milligan has been accused of all this, and more. Yet on this occasion, he had pushed himself extremely hard to get to the point when he was ready to work. The frustration of preparing two hours too early would aggravate most of us. Spike, poised on a precarious threshold and ready to go, could only collapse. There is no way that he could maintain the fragile hold he exercised on 'normality' that night.

Reflecting on the comparative rarity of incidents like the one just described, one is led to consider the actual disability under which Milligan labours. Perhaps it is worth reflecting on the words of a thoughtful acquaintance who heard something of the above:

I never seem to hear anyone commenting on the colossal amount of work Spike gets through – his performing, his writing, his work for conservation – this seems to go on constantly even though he is battling most of the time with what is really a serious and debilitating illness. If he was on crutches, people would praise him for courage and effort. As it is – he just gets slanged for his failures.

The probably physical change in the body of the manic-depressive is often shrouded or confused by purely emotional or physical concerns; in many cases, reactions seem to be triggered by relatively minor occurrences. In Spike's case this is true, and those who are close to him are vigilant in their attempts to protect him from the frustrations and aggravations of the day. Concessions are made and arrangements are manipulated so that ideally he will suffer the minimum of stress. Not surprisingly, he cannot fail to know that he is being 'handled' in this fashion and it is possible that at some perhaps subconscious level he is humiliated and ashamed; consequently, in an effort to mitigate his vulnerability, he shrouds himself carefully, donning, as it were, a sort of protective cloak. It may be that this tautness becomes a part of him and this 'stress resistance' – self-perpetuating as it must be – contributes to his isolation. When efforts are made to give him the supportive help he needs these often fail dismally, for human beings are only human and quite often error, miscalculation and ordinary carelessness crop up. Everyone becomes exasperated, eventually, with making an effort – Spike becomes incensed at what can seem to him to be almost a deliberate campaign of 'leave it to him – he'll see to it'. His meticulously high standards make practically every area of his life impossible for him to delegate. The distressing thing is that in most cases Spike can bring in the logs, straighten up the filing cabinet, book tickets for an aeroplane or a concert with more speed, acumen and success than the majority of his associates, friends and family. Consequently, he takes upon himself a virtually unbearable load – in pursuit of the perfection that must always evade him.

On the day of the chat-show catastrophe Milligan was at the stage when he could almost cope. There is no doubt that if his schedule had not been rearranged at the last moment, he would have appeared in the show and most probably given an excellent interview. But there are days in his life, sometimes almost weeks, when his torment and despair effectively remove any possible hope of work or social life. In 1982 he was preparing to tour his one-man show in England, opening in London in November. He was in a state of some anxiety. As the opening night drew nearer Spike began to withdraw. He cancelled appointments and interviews and took to his room. If he emerged, it was only for the purpose of making fresh demands on his immediate associates. They were minimal, but trying. The blackboard he used needed varnishing. He needed a different type of chalk. He wanted a different type of tambourine. The famous black hat needed alteration. A minor affliction of his throat and chest began to trouble him. This was a cause for concern as it altered the timbre of his voice. The doctor came and gave comforting words but no exact diagnosis. From time to time, family pressures that needed Spike's attention would arise. Friends would telephone with invitations, requests and demands. Contract difficulties arose which were larger than usual. Norma Farnes handled the matter with scrupulous attention to detail and tried hard to maintain a harmonious working relationship with all concerned, but problems (which could not be resolved without reference to Milligan) seemed insurmountable.

Predictably, Spike now withdrew totally from the situation. He literally threw the blankets over his head and

refused to discuss the matter further. When he emerged
from time to time it would be only to make a brief, angry
request for what would appear to be an inconsequential
item or prop. He showed no great emotion and was not
prepared to discuss the larger issues.

'I don't know about all that business,' he said. 'That's
their problem. They own me, it seems. Let them argue
about me. I'll just try to do my act the best I can.'

Milligan by now was revelling in a sort of grandiose
melancholy. It was, in a sense, helpful to him that severe
and genuine problems had arisen. It took the edge away
from his own deep fear that his comedy was too far out,
that he might not succeed, and that the audience might
not laugh.

Spike spent five days locked in his room, surrounded by
the paraphernalia of his life. Files were scattered all over
the floor and the room was ankle-deep in papers, letters
and documents. During these days, he left his bed only to
use the lavatory. He did not bath, shave, or even wash. His
hair grew tousled and a fine quarter-inch beard speedily
covered his face. His eyes were cloudy and haunted.

From time to time he would telephone Norma Farnes
and dictate letters. These were not always letters which
those close to him would consider necessary or even
important. They were invariably lucid but would reflect
his deeply entrenched attitudes and occasional prejudices
with a blinding determination to be in the right. This
meant that while a letter on blood sports or animal exploi-
tation would be authoritative and incisively damning, a
letter on the infiltration of our life by taped music in lifts,
supermarkets and aeroplanes would be inappropriately
savage and carry overtones of an almost hysterical censure.
Norma Farnes, from her long experience with Milligan,
can sometimes 'lose' a paragraph, or even a whole letter, if
she feels its appearance will reflect damagingly on her

client, but she would need to exercise great caution in any such editing as his mind at these times is often as clear as a bell and his memory excellent. His capacity for being 'ten people' is often intensified at times of partial breakdown. This means that just leafing through a pile of magazines can initiate immediate and diverse responses to a dozen areas that are of interest to him. Almost anything can be grist to the mill of his mind; in fact his mind at this time is akin to a mill whirling in space, absorbing and discharging at a high rate of knots.

During this particular illness, he spent one whole night tape-recording a message to Harry Edgington in New Zealand. Harry has been an important friend of Spike's for many years but a series of inexplicable misunderstandings, accelerated no doubt by distance, have brought about a hiatus to this long and affectionate association and both parties are distressed. It was a long tape, anguished, angry and repetitive. It was full of pain, despair and paranoiac need to go over the confused sequence of non-events that seemed to have precipitated and then perpetuated the breakdown of their lifelong friendship.

He was driven to put this on tape for three reasons. Firstly, even the loyal Norma would call a halt to letter writing at 2 A.M. Secondly, he believed that Harry would throw a conventional letter aside unread, but would listen to the tape. Thirdly, he needed to pour out some of the accumulated distress and despair that the breakdown in the friendship caused him. But despite the long taped letter Harry remains out of reach. The misunderstandings survive – a block between two old friends who did a lot for each other. Perhaps the boys of Battery D are being little boys? One thing is certain; the yearly Battery Reunion (which has to be growing gradually smaller with the fullness of time) would raise a hearty cheer to see the matter resolved.

Active though he was in the nights, the days would bring Spike no respite. Sleep or relaxation was far away; the most he could hope for was a comatose few hours after swallowing a dose of sleeping pills and tranquillizers. This at least would alleviate his suffering for a few hours, but he would awaken doped and unrefreshed.

He would talk at length to one or two of his close friends who were solicitous and ready to listen. His speech would be distraught but lucid; he saw clearly what was going on, and if he raved it was only about his inability to surmount the almost self-inflicted torment of his environment. He requires everything to be done to a high standard, and when he is ill, his capacity for tolerating the bumbling attempts of those trying (usually ineffectually) to help him, drops to zero. Not surprisingly, those close to him, stung by his cryptic ingratitude, quite often give up and contract out. Invariably it is a short-lived desertion, for love of this irascible, difficult, unhappy tyrant brings them back.

Milligan frequently cancels dinners, social occasions, parties and various other commitments, sometimes with impunity, but more often with a sense of angry resignation. Sometimes the occasion that he misses is something that he dearly coveted. One year, for instance, he cancelled Christina Foyle's literary luncheon when the guest of honour was Sir Peter Scott, a man for whom he has a profound respect. Thus we learn that the cancellations in his life do not spring from laziness or tantrums. They are usually brought about by a combination of circumstances which, when he is already low, can feel like a series of savage blows.

When the Mermaid Theatre was due to reopen in 1981 Spike promised to appear in an all-star benefit scheduled for a Sunday in July. At lunchtime he was still in bed, ill and wretched. 'I don't want to let Bernard Miles down,' he said fretfully. 'He can't really be expecting me. It isn't today, is it?' Attempts were made to ring the theatre, to talk to Bernard Miles. Attempts were also made to lull Spike into the belief that his appearance need only be brief. He was reminded that the Mermaid had been the scene of an evening of spectacular success when he and Robert Graves had appeared together.

As Spike's contribution was to be a short poetry reading, someone suggested that he might like to include a poem of Graves's. As Graves was by now too frail to appear himself, this seemed a good idea. 'It would be a sort of tribute to him,' agreed Milligan.

Some hours later, Spike made one of the Herculean efforts which indicate that his depression could be at the point of lifting. Grey and anxious, he struggled to the theatre. The atmosphere was, of course, frenetic and the producer – Jane Asher – with clipboard in hand, showed a touching mixture of delighted joy that Spike was to appear after all and horror that her already overlong programme was now even longer. 'I shall be five minutes,' he said, 'at the most.'

In the event, he was on for three-quarters of an hour and the audience was reluctant to let him go. For those forty-five minutes, he held the audience intrigued and delighted with readings from his poetry. He included a poem by Robert Graves.

'I would like,' said Spike, 'to read a short poem by a dear friend with whom I once shared a marvellous evening at the Mermaid. I know he would like to have been here tonight.'

Milligan read *Postscript*.

> I'd die for you, or you for me,
> So furious is our jealousy –
> And if you doubt this to be true
> Kill me outright, lest I kill you.

The audience applauded heartily. The evening, if overlong, had gone very well. Only those close to Spike would have recognized the strain he was under. A few people must have been surprised that he did not join Bernard Miles's party after the show. Milligan was merely thankful that he had survived the evening, that he had not let the Mermaid down, and that he could slide quietly away, back to the temporary refuge of his sickbed.

As a live 'stand-up' comic Milligan rarely, if ever, fails. His rapport with the audience is immediate and constant. He occasionally loses a joke from indistinct delivery (he is an extremely rapid speaker) but his basic capacity to delight and enchant seem to insulate him against the sort of audience disapproval that can overwhelm less fortunate performers. Yet the comic in Milligan stands a long way behind the clown. Milligan is a natural, superb clown. It is his clowning that invariably captivates the audience. His clowning, back in the Bexhill days, was at the core of all the laughter that sprang from the Battery Band. It was the clowning that shone through his first forays into satire when he produced *Black Baggage* and *Men in Gitis*. It was the clowning that consolidated the brilliance of the jazz-playing Bill Hall Trio.

In Milligan's most recent one-man show he made great use of one prop – a white wooden hand with a pointing finger. It was mounted on the end of a long stick. No text could adequately reproduce the movements of the hand and the expressions on Milligan's face that would nightly keep the audiences convulsed. Another prop for this show was a life-size dummy of Margaret Thatcher. At one point, Milligan suddenly notices the dummy. Then he looks at his white hand, then he looks at the unfortunate Mrs Thatcher, then at the audience. The expressions of mischievous intent, of questioning, of doubt and then guilty delight flee across his face in quick succession. We know that he is on the point of sticking the white finger in her ear. In a three-minute sequence he does not utter a word.

Milligan can be very articulate when he is willing to discuss his stance on comedy. But it is not easy for him, because he is hampered by the pain barriers of frustrated ideas and diminishing hopes.

All my life I've tried to write comedy. Now, I write for the BBC and I've never been successful in television, and the reason for that has been this – when you write, when I write a book and it's been successful I know that I've controlled all the characters exactly as I want to, but in television I've always wanted to be like – say that there's a big army: to find out what's up front you send a searching patrol forward, and I've always had to fight through the Benny Hills in the wilderness. They are like the main bunch of the army, they know the obvious, and what they think the audience wants – bums, knickers, tits, funny double-entendre jokes, things like that. But in the long term, to live on a diet of that becomes boring, so what I try to do is to do what the patrols do, I try to go out into enemy territory where nothing has happened before, and of course you get shot at like mad out there, but I would rather be up there, trying to make or to do something different than is here already.

So what happens is this – when I do these experimental shows, first of all it has to go through a set of actors who might not think like I do, therefore they perform the part differently. Likewise it goes through a producer and a director who think differently from me and see it from a different camera angle – the sound guys – the sound effects might not be what I want – they might be. So overall what happens is if about 60% of the jokes even could get through, well I think I'm pretty successful. If 100% got through I'd be much more popular, I think. That's how this sort of show goes. But it's very difficult to do things which are very far out. When you try to explain to a producer you say to him, for instance, 'Look, this is my idea. I want a – just a chap walking through a piece of paper,' and he says 'This looks like a good place for it,' and the other bloke says 'Yes, it does.' He says 'Well, let's try it here, then, right?'

Then you realize they are not grasping what you want to try to do. Or because it hasn't been done before they don't want to risk their jobs doing it now. Or sometimes they are willing to try but can't get it right.

I need freedom to work in. I never get enough. I got it for the *Running, Jumping and Standing Still Film*, which was the only film I've made. The only one I've ever directed. Runs for seven minutes, cost £50, and won all the awards in the world. But I'd like to add that the *Running, Jumping and Standing Still Film* did owe something to Dick Lester who gave me mostly first-class advice and then help with all the cutting. What I would like to do is to prove implicitly that you can do funny things without having the odd millions. Anyway, if you make a film for seven millions it must make a winner or else you're an idiot – in fact you can spend seven million and still make a flop.

The occasion was one of the first location shoots for Milligan's most recent television series, *There's a Lot of It About*. The evening was cold and damp; the last few visitors were being gently ushered out by the attendants and the BBC film crew were at work setting up the lights and cameras. The venue was the entrance hall to the Natural History Museum and the project was to shoot a few feet of Spike Milligan prowling inside the massive bony chest of a dinosaur.

Milligan has often had a reputation for being 'difficult' to work with, but on this particular evening there was certainly no sign of it. There was a small preliminary hitch when he discarded the dinosaur chosen by the film team in favour of another, but this seemed reasonable enough as it was he who had to play a complete scene from the place formerly occupied by the monster's entrails. He settled on the skeleton he wanted and climbed inside it; the cameras were resited and the rehearsals began. One small scene was played again and again. The producer, Alan Bell, was as keen on perfection as Milligan himself and they went assiduously through and through this short scene until both were satisfied. Milligan was positioned inside the skeleton, speaking through a space in the dinosaur's ribs. This looked vaguely like a face peering through prison bars. Alan pointed out that Spike was not consistently speaking through the same rib-slot. As he had to pace up and down inside the rib-cage this wasn't surprising. Aggravated, Spike produced a piece of chalk from his pocket and triumphantly marked the inside ribs. The Senior Uniformed Guard on duty was already showing anxiety about the rules which were not being adhered to. The exhibits were on no account allowed to be handled, much less chalked on. Milligan saw what was coming, and as the responsible gentleman cleared his throat, stepping purposefully forward, Spike appealed to him with an angelic, heart-warming smile. 'All right, Mr Martin?' (He had taken care to learn the official's name.) 'OK, is it?' He held the chalk up for everyone to see. 'It's only chalk, Mr Martin – and only on the *inside*.' He was the picture of blue-eyed innocence.

Milligan's television showing rarely seems to justify his talent. Alan Bell came near to producing moments of real brilliance, but sometimes, inevitably, really superb moments were lost for ever in the retakes or even on the cutting-room floor. Yet Spike got a lot of rope from Alan, who was sensitive to his artistic needs.

Milligan is a unique artist deserving of very special treatment. I like working with him, he gives you a lot. Of course, I'm a fan, basically. I genuinely find him marvellously funny. And I don't find him difficult. He's always on time. He knows his lines. But he's a spontaneous artist and doesn't react well to several retakes. Something magic gets lost and that's a tragedy.

The next stage of the production was the shooting of some indoor scenes at Ealing Studios, now used exclusively for BBC television work. Running to schedule becomes even more vital; the technical staffs work on a firm 9 A.M. to 5.30 P.M. basis with strictly-adhered-to breaks. Overtime can become a crippling financial disaster. This adds a good deal of strain to a long day's filming, and no doubt both Alan Bell and his leading actor had their fair share of apprehension. However, shooting on Monday and Tuesday went so well that one or two scenes scheduled for Wednesday were brought forward and shot on the Tuesday afternoon. This was just as well, for Wednesday's quota could have moved into disaster areas of delay and re-arrangements.

The first scene was sited in an undertaker's funeral parlour. There were half a dozen extras wandering about wearing shrouds and funny hats. Milligan would have left Monkenhurst by 7.00 A.M. to be on the set and made up by 9 o'clock. For this occasion he was dressed as Hitler/Liberace with a rather half-hearted forelock and moustache. He didn't look very like Hitler. He was wearing a rather tatty golden brocade coat with spangled revers. He didn't look very like Liberace either, but he did sound extremely funny when he snatched up a banjo and sang his introductory verse to the tune of *Congratulations*:

Stand by Funerals, oh Stand by Funerals,
Stand by Funerals are good enough for me.

David Adams was playing the part of a reluctant corpse in this scene, which culminated in his having to climb into a coffin and be nailed in by Milligan. The coffin was wrongly sited, an inflatable doll which had to be pushed into the coffin with him was too fully inflated and various other matters had to be seen to. Milligan is never able to relinquish a feeling of responsibility when it is his show and his script (let alone his scene), and he seized the opportunity to lead his six shroud-clad extras onto an adjacent stage to give them a quick preliminary coaching: 'You've all got to look pleased and happy, jumping about in your shrouds. You are all excited, and waiting impatiently for your funerals,' he told them.

The little team were obedient and interested and Milligan instructed them patiently for ten minutes. They were required to sing in chorus, with various arm raisings and so forth. Eventually the work on the first stage was reset and shooting recommenced. This time Spike grumbled about the hammer he had been given. 'This is a very heavy hammer,' he moaned. No one reacted. He nailed the coffin down for another two takes and finally got exasperated. 'Can't anyone get me a lighter hammer?' He was growing more truculent. Someone went off to get a lighter hammer. Spike was mollified, perhaps slightly apologetic. He tapped away rather more happily at the coffin, saying by way of an (unlikely) excuse, defensively, 'Well, I was afraid of damaging the coffin.'

Now it was David's turn. He tripped over his shroud whilst trying to climb into the coffin.

'My shroud's too long. I can't help tripping over it.'

Spike was sympathetic with another actor's difficulties.

'His shroud's too long,' he joined in. 'He'll break his neck. Bring some scissors.'

A good twelve inches were cut off David's shroud, and the filming recommenced.

Watching Milligan hard at work in the TV studios, seeing his dedication and his effort, it is difficult to understand why he has not achieved greater success in this medium. Perhaps, as when the *Goon Show* was making its first appearance, he is still too far in advance of his time.

Michael Parkinson has invited Spike onto his television chat-show many times, both in England and Australia. As an impromptu guest, Milligan strikes fear into the hearts of many seasoned interviewing hosts, but not, apparently, into Michael Parkinson's.

> I love having him on the show. He's danger, that's why. Real danger. You never know how he'll be to handle, but I'll take the risk every time. I think Milligan is a genius. When you look back over the history of comedy over the last thirty years everything – *Python, Not the Nine O'clock News* – all that – well, their father was Spike Milligan. He was the man. Look at the Goons – Spike was the creator of that marvellous programme. Well, the rest put voices to it and contributed but Spike was the founder member.

Parkinson has made several memorable programmes with Spike. Probably the most famous took place in Australia. Spike entered the studio wearing a hat adorned with swinging corks and held the whole show in a sort of limbo for a full ten minutes whilst the studio audience, other guests and Parkinson himself rocked helplessly with mirth.

Michael Parkinson has ideas as to why Spike has never received real recognition for his television work in England.

> The awful business with Milligan is that he has never been rewarded. If Spike were a Russian he'd get a free flat and car and be exempted from all taxes. He'd be given the status of an important creative artist, which he is: it's impossible to expect Milligan to cope with income-tax forms and all that. He's an extraordinary man. And the reason that he should be rewarded is because he gives such joy to all of us, and if you could put a tax on that and pay it to him he'd be a millionaire. He shouldn't be burdened, especially someone like him that has such a problem. I haven't a quarter of his talent, and all the bureaucratic bit drives me nearly insane. If I had his talent and got the sort of shit he gets I'd feel like getting a gun and going out to shoot someone, most probably myself.

The kittens arrived on the Milligan doorstep in a basket early one Sunday morning. Spike had already left for a filming commitment, and it was only after a routine call to check on his family's well-being that he heard the news.

'Oh Christ, a day old, Jane says. Why do they do it? Why don't they give me the poor mother as well, or keep the kittens for a week?'

Dressed as Al Jolson with a blackened face and big white lips, Spike was almost comically dismayed. Agitated messages about filler-feeders, vets, linen cupboards and warmth were filtered through between takes of his new TV series. Shelagh, capable, calm and understanding, was stationed in a phone booth. When Spike was out of earshot her exasperation showed.

'We could,' she said succinctly, 'have done without this performance this morning. Why are people so stupid? The kittens are bound to die and Spike will be terrible. He'll be distraught if we can't save them.'

Whoever had dumped the kittens had left a large tin of Kit-e-Kat next to them on the doorstep.

'A token that they wanted them to be looked after,' said Spike dismally. 'It was probably kids whose parents were insisting on drowning them.'

The filming finished on schedule that day and Spike drove home at speed. The kittens had been installed in a basket of warm rags in a large walk-in airing cupboard. There were four of them. One was particularly fragile and weak.

'Oh God, it's going to die,' said Shelagh despairingly. 'This is going to be a disaster.'

The first kitten died overnight, and next morning special feeding pumps were procured from the vet.

Spike was, at this time (1982), just beginning on *There's a Lot of It About*. He and Neil Shand had been closeted together at Monkenhurst collaborating on the writing for some weeks. Then came the lengthy and taxing filming and recording sessions. He had very little free time, and every night he needed to learn his lines for the following day's schedule. This did not stop his becoming totally involved with the care of the unfortunate kittens, which could barely suck and were fast losing their hair. The vet demonstrated the use of small syringes, and the kittens were fed every two hours. They appeared singularly indifferent to the attempts of the Milligan family to rear them, but Spike was fierce in his determination to keep them alive. He was deeply critical of the syringes.

'Why can't some idiot invent a sort of soft frame or something round the syringe to encourage the kittens to suck – something like the mother's tits? When you think of all the torturous instruments like bombs and computers that they are inventing all the time you'd think that they could invent something simple and life-giving. I don't suppose the kittens feel very encouraged to feed when they only get milk squirted down their throats. They need the comfort of the mother.'

Possibly everybody in the house except Spike knew that the kittens wouldn't live. Possibly he knew too, but if he did he pushed the thought far from his mind as he drew up rosters for their feeding and care. Shelagh and Nanna bore the brunt of the night shifts, one of them getting up every two hours to cope. The kittens lived, but did not thrive. Spike called in the vet again. He got vitamins and medicines for them. He got ointment to treat their eyes, and made case history sheets to pin up on the wall of the airing cupboard so that the kittens' feeding, medication and bowel movements could be charted. During breaks on the film set, he would telephone home to hear how the kittens were. A second one died. Spike became frenzied in his attempts to keep the others alive.

'Oh God,' said Shelagh. 'If only one of them would live. It means so much to him. He'll be destroyed if they all die.'

The kittens' arrival had coincided with the war in the Falkland Islands. 'I suppose,' said Milligan bitterly, 'I must seem crazy. Am I crazy to be struggling to save the lives of these unwanted creatures when supposedly sane adults are sending young boys straight out there to their deaths? That's the real lunacy, isn't it?'

The kittens were almost the only topic of conversation now. Spike never gave up hope. He hugged the kittens close after feeding them and stroked their faces gently with small balls of moist cotton-wool.

'It's like their mother licking them,' he said hopefully. 'It replaces the mother. It will make them feel more like living.'

Finally only one kitten was left. 'And that one's bound to die soon,' said Jane miserably.

The last kitten died one Saturday afternoon, at the end of the first recording session for the new series. Nanna, Jane and Shelagh had come up to the studio in time for the last bits of recording. Dinner out with his family was planned for later, a treat that Spike would have been looking forward to all day.

'I shan't tell him about the kitten,' said Shelagh. 'I can't bear to spoil his evening.'

In fact, she had no option, as Spike demanded the news from her. He sat for a long time, staring at the floor. Finally he said, 'I want a post-mortem. I want to know how they died. Maybe we've force-fed them and caused their deaths. Perhaps we can learn something. I just want to know.'

In due course, the vet gave his report. The kittens had died from a form of gastric inflammation, possibly accelerated by the only form of feeding them that was available. There is a file on the kittens now, at Monkenhurst. Spike collated all the details and case histories along with the vet's report.

'That file makes me feel so sad,' said Jane several months later. 'It says on the front, day-old kittens, born on this date and then died, May something or other. They only lived about a fortnight. It wasn't really worth it, was it? They had such a suffering life. It just makes me sad.'

Spike and Shelagh were married very quietly in July 1983 at the Roman Catholic Church just off Barnet High Street. It was during a fantastic heat-wave; Spike climbed on a pew before his bride arrived and opened a piece of the roof. Great attempts at secrecy had been made; consequently the church, usually deserted at the hour chosen for the wedding, had not been closed to the public. Just before Shelagh was due to arrive, a stranger, an elderly lady, trotted into the church. She made her way to the front and sat down next to Spike. Spike, unperturbed, smiled at her and said, 'Oh dear – have you come to marry me as well?' A few minutes later Shelagh arrived, radiant and very pretty in a cream-coloured dress and hat. Milligan was wearing a white suit and a boldly striped shirt. He looked up at Shelagh and smiled. 'Gosh,' he said. 'I *am* glad that you turned up!'

Afterwards, whilst champagne was being opened at Monkenhurst, Sean, who had been his father's best man, said, 'You know, I'd never have believed it. Dad was as nervous as a kitten.'

20

Conservationist

Men! The only animal in the world to fear!

D. H. Lawrence

Milligan has had this feeling in his heart for many years. One of the lines in the *Goon Show* 'Robin's Post' broadcast in December 1955 comes from Wallace Greenslade, the announcer. Following a cacophony of noise, Wallace's line is: 'That was the sound of the Human Race – resignation forms are now available.'

How serious is Milligan about this? He is very serious, and it is part of his frustration that he cannot, in fact, make any impact on the enormous areas that he sees as signs of our deterioration as a species. He is not usually impressed by the achievements that stir most of us to excitement and hope (Why walk on the moon? Wreck that with garbage and greed and over-population? We are wrecking the Earth fast enough.) He will work tirelessly for the causes that come close to his heart, at the same time voicing his despair that, however great the effort to combat the particular ill, it can never be enough: Save it today, they'll knock it down tomorrow – lock them up or treat them today, they'll beat the child again tomorrow. Fatalistic and disheartening though his attitudes are, they are genuine and deeply entrenched. If his incredible capacity to care had not been twinned with the acutely sensitive perception of ultimate futility, what a massive achiever he would have been.

Norma Farnes has compiled two books of Spike's letters; they reflect his changing moods and the diversity of his interests. Unlike the more usual collections, these have been interspersed with scribbled notes and photographs; they make interesting reading for aficionados and suggest areas of importance in Milligan's life that have been hitherto unrecognized. One important point emerges – Milligan has great tenacity, and is not easily defeated; when something is on his mind he will pursue it to a final conclusion. The letters give a perspective on Milligan's deep commitment to environmental concerns. One letter, in 1968, to Anthony Greenwood, MP, grieves for the demolition of Brent Lodge which, as President of the Finchley Society, Spike had tried so hard to preserve.

Milligan has gained some pleasure over the years as a direct result of his involvement with movements like Greenpeace, Friends of the Earth and the World Wildlife Fund. The inevitable frustrations that he encounters during his attempts to help in these areas dishearten him if he is already low in spirit. At his worst, he will disparage any past successes he has had a part in and look towards a bleak and hopeless future. An attempt to chivvy him out of despair is pointless. Told not to be a pessimist, he will give a sharp look with steely grey eyes and say quietly, 'I'm not a pessimist. I'm a realist.'

When he is on good form, his enthusiasm and energy are contagious, and he will work non-stop for the things he believes in.

Milligan is loyal to his friends, loyal and extremely generous. When a dear friend of his collapsed into a sudden and seemingly bottomless depression, he first spent hours on the telephone with him, persuading him that it would lift. He sent cars to collect the friend (a famous but impecunious musician) and had him to stay at his house. When all this couldn't help, he insisted on providing private medical care. The bill eventually ran into several thousands of pounds. Milligan had to double his overdraft at that moment to pay it. 'I dare say the hospital cheated me with the bill,' said Spike glumly. 'But I'm just thankful he's OK now. He couldn't have stood an NHS hospital, could he, poor man? It would have killed him. He's a great artist and look at the pleasure he brings to people. He was too good to lose.'

Fiercely independent, Spike values his privacy and he often shows a smouldering anger for strangers who might recognize him enthusiastically and clamour for his autograph. He will willingly comply with the demands of fans at TV appearances, book-signing sessions and the like, but he bitterly resents the intrusion of outsiders when he is on a private visit or mission. Such an occasion cropped up recently when he drove a few miles from his Hertfordshire home to photograph an old house scheduled for demolition.

'About the last house ever that has pantiles,' he said morosely, 'and the vandals are pulling it down. I've tried every way to save it.'

Apparently he parked his car and started taking photographs of the house. A woman approached him and asked for his autograph.

'Why do you want my autograph?' he asked truculently. 'It's only by chance that I'm here and I came just to take photographs and didn't expect to be signing autographs.'

To begin with she was unabashed, and only started to show resentment when Spike continued to question (and criticize) her action in approaching him.

'When have you ever wanted my autograph unless you actually had me in sight? If you wanted it, why haven't you approached me by letter, for instance? Why do you only demand my autograph when you just happen, accidentally, to run into me? You didn't want it until you saw me. If you hadn't seen me today, you wouldn't have thought of it or wanted it. It's just a mugging. Just an autograph mugging.'

Spike had lashed himself into a fine fury about this incident, but there is no doubt he felt badly done by. As always in this sort of circumstance, he was anxious to justify his action.

'Of course, she started to get very angry and I said to her, Listen, you're getting angry. Well, I've got angry for this sort of occasion many times in the last thirty years. You've only had to get angry once. Think how lucky you are.'

It wasn't surprising that the unfortunate lady eventually took off in an offended condition, leaving Spike rattled but certainly not contrite.

'Well, that's one fan less,' someone said.

'Fan,' said Spike angrily. 'She wasn't a fan. She was just an autograph mugger.'

Milligan is grateful when he is able to put aside his clown's role for an hour or two. This is infrequent; people expect him to be funny and being funny is natural to him; humour erupts and pours out like lava from a volcano. But there is a strong intellectual need for something with which his mind can grapple. He has been a voracious reader and applies his mind to concepts and problems in wide-ranging areas. He likes to meet people who share his interests in conservation and wildlife and his concern for animals. Fenner Brockway was 94 years old and still going very strong when Spike was introduced to him in the summer of 1983.

Fenner Brockway has long been involved in humanist areas of political sensitivity such as unilateral disarmament, population control, racism and prison reform. His parents were Christian missionaries in Calcutta at the time of his birth in 1888, and he received a firm, Christian upbringing. Spike, born thirty years later, also in India, was brought up within devout Roman Catholic principles. Both men discussed their departure from the religious convictions of their parents with an objective moderation. 'My parents, grandparents, uncles and aunts and my sister were all Christian missionaries,' said Fenner. 'But I am not a Christian. I'm a Humanist.'

'Well, I became very confused,' said Spike. 'I was born an Irish Catholic, brought up indoctrinated, then bit by bit realized the frailties of this Catholic vision of Jesus going up to Heaven in the clouds, with the Devil in Hell, twisting a fork. But I did have a great liking for Jesus as a Prophet; everything he said seemed right. The Sermon on the Mount was beautiful. I decided I'd settle for him – I don't know what that makes me. A Jesuit, I suppose, in that sense.'

Conversation ranged over many topics. After they had parted, Spike was elated. 'What a wonderful human being,' he said. 'I am so lucky to have been able to talk with him. When I talk with someone of his calibre it almost gives me hope for the future.'

Milligan became a vegetarian in the sixties. It is not an easy regime for an actor: available rehearsal snacks are often of the hamburger variety only, and most celebrity lunches tend to be very carnivorous. Doing without meat is a sacrifice he makes as a matter of principle. Most vegetarians seem to dislike meat; Spike will glance longingly at his neighbour's plate while applying himself to his spaghetti Neapolitan. He rarely eats eggs; but for those of his household who do he insists that free-range ones are ordered.

When venison is in season, Shelagh will go to some lengths to buy venison steak or sausage. The meat has come from culled herds, and Spike finds eating this flesh morally acceptable. He feels the same about fish. 'It has a free life,' he says firmly. 'It isn't reared under cruel conditions. It just takes its chance and gets caught occasionally – as happens in nature.'

Of recent years, he has spent many months in the Londolozzi Game Reserve in South Africa, where he spends hours watching the wild animals and sometimes collaborating in the making of documentary films of wild life. During one of these visits, Shelagh also turned vegetarian. 'It was the animals that convinced me,' she says, 'not Spike. I always respected his views but they weren't mine, and I wouldn't have made the break from meat-eating just to please him. It had to come from me, from within myself. And after that last month at the Londolozzi, that's what happened.'

Spike receives enormous solace from the ordinary manifestations of nature – winter passing into spring enthrals him, and he has the sort of profound reverence for growing and living things that would seem credible if he had just arrived back in this world after ten years in a prison cell, or on the moon. He will occasionally allow friends or even strangers a glimpse at his delight, willing them to participate in it and share it with him if they can. He has a low tolerance of the sort of environmental degradation which the majority of people take for granted, and he can become incensed or dejected (according to his present mood) by what he interprets as slovenly or destructive attitudes. One day, after an outing, he returned home in a state of despairing chagrin.

'Do you know what I've just seen – a crush of cars, all stationary – and a man sitting in the driving seat reading a paper – he just put a dog out of the car, held on to its lead and sat there giving the dog its walk *from the car* – expecting it to do its piss and shit right there.' His voice sank to an angry whisper. 'And they'll go mad when there's no petrol for private cars – and yet they are adding now to fuel wastage, and pollution without thought, without any thought I tell you. They can't think . . .'

On another occasion, he was walking with Jane on the common near his house.

'This young chap was in the distance, running – I praised him to Jane and said see, that's good – someone looking after his health, and his body, out running and breathing the good air, listening to the birds – that's great. But then we came nearer to him and what do you think I saw – *what do you think I saw?* He had earphones on and a radio strapped to his back. Can you believe it – can you really believe it?'

This offender must have been in the advance guard. Within a few months of this incident, it seemed that practically all the people under forty on the common (including Spike's daughters) were wearing earphones whilst they jogged. Milligan never referred to it again. Almost certainly he silently marked it down in his mind as another sign of the degradation of humanity.

Jimmy Grafton makes a surprising and controversial point when he maintains that the Goon character Eccles 'is closest to the real Spike – his *id* or *alter ego*; a simple, happy soul content for the world to regard him as an idiot, provided that it does not make too many demands upon him'.

Spike is far from simple, and he is rarely happy. He is not content to be regarded as an idiot and he actually *needs* demands, his system benefits from some stress. This is proven by the fact that if no one is immediately making demands on him – and sometimes even if they are – he will manufacture a genuine and often immediate task that will absent him from his telephones, his house or his office. 'I had to go out for a while,' he has been heard to growl into the telephone. 'I was just taking all the bits of logs and stones off the daffodils that are trying to come up in the garden – somebody has to do it.'

It seems possible that at the same time this is Spike's safety-mechanism working well at a subconscious level, to protect him. He will temporarily abandon the demands that may seem to threaten his sanguinity for less destructive self-imposed tasks that give him a brief respite of tranquillity.

Far from being happy to be regarded as an idiot he is often bitterly frustrated when he is not taken seriously. Recently, he agreed to speak for a population control group at a private meeting at the House of Lords. The meeting was a success but Spike was not enamoured by the cocktail-sipping supporters who tended to giggle nervously when he warmed to his theme that copulation takes only a few seconds, whereas the care and support of a child demands years of energy and effort.

He reminded the gathering of the words of their president at the close of the World Food Conference in November 1974, words which had outlined their target for the next ten years, 'By the end of the decade we must be able to say that no child shall ever go to bed hungry.' 'Well, we've failed in that endeavour,' said Spike. He made a thoughtful, articulate speech and stayed to talk to some of the group afterwards, but he left the meeting without the conviction that he had made any impact. 'I don't know what they are all about – are they really *doing* anything?' he demanded. 'They were really only waiting for me to say something funny, weren't they?'

Milligan has, in fact, been deeply concerned with population issues for many years. In his own rather embittered and cynical way he has tried, inadequately, to reach a public that largely doesn't want to know.

His third book, scathingly titled *The Little Pot Boiler*, opens with a cryptic and despairing short story:

Once upon an unfortunate time, there was a hairy thing called man. Along with him was a hairier thing called animal. Man had a larger brain which made him think he was superior to animals.

Some men thought they were superior to men. They became leader men. Leader men said, 'We have no need to work, we will kill animals to eat.' So they did.

Man increased, animals decreased. Eventually leader men said, 'There are not enough animals left to eat. We must grow our own food.' So man grew food.

Now, the only animals man had not destroyed were tiny ones, like rabbits and mices, and these little animals were caught eating some of man's crops. 'These animals are a menace. They must die.'

In China they killed all the sparrows. In Australia they killed all the rabbits. Everywhere man killed all wild life. Soon there was none, and all the birds were poisoned. Leader man said, 'At last! We are free of pests.'

Man's numbers increased. The world became crowded with men. They all had to sleep standing up. One day a leader man saw a new creature eating his crops. This creature's name was starving people.

'This creature is a menace!' said leader man . . .

The Little Pot Boiler was published in 1963. The *Blue Print For Survival*, which was published in *The Ecologist* in 1966, was for many intelligent and able people the first real intimation of an approaching ecological crisis. Not only as an innovator of comedy is Milligan a man far in advance of his time.

In 1984 Spike realized a long-held ambition: he appeared in a pantomime. Asked why he had waited so long, he is indignant:

I always wanted to be in pantomime. I love children and I get on well with them. I wanted a clean panto with no blue jokes but just a lot of fun. It's just that nobody ever offered me a job. In the end they did and I was delighted. I met Willis Hall who is a lovely writer and he suggested it.

The pantomime was *Babes in the Wood* and was for the Chichester Festival Theatre in Sussex. Milligan likes this part of England and during the previous winter he had spent a week in Southsea with his one-man show. There his pleasure had been equally divided between the delightful little Victorian theatre where he was appearing and the Elizabethan sailing-ship *Mary Rose* which had now been raised and was open for inspection. He spent hours there, poring over the artifacts and cogitating on the sort of lives that the sailors must have lived. On the whole, it had been a happy visit and he liked the simple and secluded 'digs' that Shelagh had managed to find in nearby South Harting.

The summer of 1984 took Spike once again to Australia. At one stage in his tour, whilst he was staying in the Hunter Valley at the home of his Australian manager, he received a telephone call from Norma Farnes in London who informed him that his new TV series planned for the autumn had been axed by the BBC. Spike brushed this information aside with disdain. 'I see. But what about Chichester? Is *that* contract signed?' The pantomime was the thing which he was looking forward to. Financially and professionally, a national TV series must be of greater importance than a four-week pantomime engagement in a provincial theatre, but Milligan's mind runs on wayward tracks; for the moment the pantomime was a matter of much greater importance to him. He was looking forward to the fun he was going to have with the children.

The pantomime did materialize, and Spike played the part of the 'good' robber to Bill Pertwee's 'bad' one. A character emerged during the rehearsals and Milligan developed his part assiduously – he was an over-anxious, timid, childlike clown of a robber, hanging on nervously to the bad robber's shirt-tail for much of the time. The audiences loved it, the press were kind, the children were in raptures of joy and Chichester did record business for the season. Spike and Shelagh stayed at the same quiet old house as before, and during the hard snows of January they drove ecstatically through the almost snow-bound lanes to get to the theatre and back again. As the snow-laden branches shone in the moonlight, Spike would sigh with delight. 'I'm so lucky to be able to see all this. Isn't it a wonderful sight?' London, his office and all his anxieties were, for the moment, a thousand miles away.

Milligan will continue to write. Writing for him is not an arduous chore, it is an enjoyable task. He finds research stimulating and exciting. It seems to harness his intellect in an unexpected way, and rather untypically he seems to resist the pitfalls of side-tracking as he applies himself to whatever is in hand with dedication and a firm discipline. His low threshold of frustration is less vulnerable, possibly because when he is writing, he is invariably alone. Whilst he is writing, he is a happy man. His sense of achievement is solid and unshakeable. He is fortunate inasmuch as he does not suffer from the enforced loneliness of writing. He actually needs to spend a good deal of time alone, and consciously or unconsciously it must assuage his easily triggered (but often denied) feelings of guilt that when he is withholding himself from his wife, family and friends he is not merely indulging himself with a book or a TV programme but is actually working.

Poetry, unlike prose, he does not consider work. Poetry to him is instinctive, intuitive and immediate. His reluctance to edit his poetry seems almost superstitious:

> If a poem is born deformed you can only change it and give it an artificial limb, that's the only way I can see it. Then you have to graft it on. It must come in one go I think, one beautiful running go, like a javelin throw. That's how it seems to me. Some people may be better mechanics – poetic mechanics – they can write lines and then they have a good

enough mechanical, well, imagery, to sort of put the bits on and weld them on again so that you can't notice the joins. I haven't got that sort of gift.

Writing enables Milligan to pace his rapid, whirling imagination. Out of the blue he will say, 'I'd like to write a book about Victorian mangles.' Even before the idea transmits to his listeners' minds, he is away hot-footed, chasing his idea, filling in details, making it feasible. Once when he was confined to his bed for a week with diverticulitis he decided to write a hundred limericks. *101 Best Limericks* was duly published. Most of them broke all the rules; several were exquisitely funny:

> A man who was asked out to dinner
> Came back looking hungry and thinner.
> He said 'Don't look baffled,
> The dinner was raffled,
> And somebody else was the winner.'

A few were terrible:

> A sailor who sailed round Cape Hope
> Pulled ashore to borrow some soap.
> He used it for hours
> In the bath and the showers,
> But did he return it? Nope!

Spike didn't mind. The week in bed had passed quickly.

At the Edinburgh Festival in 1981 Pauline Reese and Malcolm Jones, young drama Graduates, formed the Witsend Theatre Company and put on a show called *Milligan Again*. The text was all Milligan, prose and poetry. Many people found a new vision of Spike's work; the forty-minute performance provoked laughter and an unexpected sadness. A year later, the same company produced a play for children, once again using Milligan's work. *Around the Bend, or Journey to the Centre of the Bathplug!* shows a young boy trespassing in the Under Bath World, searching for the monster who is destroying the environment.[1] A lot of the marvellous Milligan animals (the vegetarian lion, the sardine, the now defunct dodo) join in the search. The menace, of course, is man, and the play invariably ended with tumultuous enthusiasm as the children promise to save their environment. Milligan allowed the company to use a poem destined for his next collection.

> The sky is burning
>   the birds have flown.
> I had so much bread
>   why didn't I feed them
>   when there was time.
>
> The wind has changed
>   I smell burning feathers
> Where are the birds
>   are they hiding somewhere –
>   naked?
>
> The seas are boiling
>   The gulls can't fish
> they stand on the shore
>   watching the horizon
>   Like all of us.[2]

He also agreed to write a letter, copies of which were given to the children.

A Letter to the Children from Spike Milligan

Dear Children,

Animals are our brothers and sisters, they belong to us and we need to love them and guard them. I do hope you will all enjoy this show, which has a lot of fun in it, but I think you will learn things from it about being kind to animals – and maybe you can go home and help some of the grown-ups to understand.

Love Light & Peace
Spike

The play toured London schools with success for a year.

Many people must have been mystified of late over the curiously persistent matter of Milligan's nationality. In 1960, Spike went along to renew his existing British passport and was told that, following changes in the law, he was no longer British. He was vociferously indignant but received no sympathy from the official. 'What am I, then, if I'm not British?' he demanded. 'I fought for Britain in the war, I live here, I work here, I pay my taxes and I do a lot of conservation work, all for free.' The official was not impressed. 'Actually,' he said, 'you are stateless, but you can fill up a form and reapply.'

Milligan was both enraged and deeply hurt. He marched out of the office and subsequently took out Irish nationality, which was available to him without any form-filling. 'I think,' he said mournfully, 'they were delighted to have me. They said that they are short of people and they welcomed those with talent, which was a nice thing to say.'

Matters rested for a number of years but Spike smouldered gently. He felt he had been ill-used, and that at the very least he should have been officially notified that his British status was no longer automatic. In 1983 Zola Budd, the young athlete from South Africa, was given British nationality almost overnight so that she could compete for Britain in forthcoming Olympic trials. Spike exploded. He put on a track suit and was photographed running up Whitehall, past No. 10 Downing Street. Pictures and funny stories appeared in the press. Understandably it was the media Milligan who was to be seen, but hidden from public view was the man, brooding on the remembered angry humiliation of the Passport Office in the sixties, still mortified and saddened by what he has always interpreted as an undeserved rebuff. The matter of the form-filling has been resolved, but Milligan was then told he must pay £55 and swear loyalty to the Queen. This outraged him even more than the form-filling. 'Don't they *know* I'm loyal to the Queen?' he asks. 'Didn't I get a war disability pension fighting for this country? Am I to stand in a Hall full of foreigners waving my arms about and shouting, "I'm loyal, I'm loyal"?'

This is not Milligan in tantrum. It is a Milligan who is hurt, sad and growing embittered over a situation which ought never to have arisen in the first place. It is to be hoped that someone, somewhere along the line, has the perspicacity to realize that Milligan, more of a giver than a taker, needs to be appreciated for his contributions, and welcomed back into his rightful British nationality.

* * *

> Someone left the mirror running
> I pulled the plug out
> It emptied my face
> And drowned my reflection
> I tried mouth to mouth resuscitation
> But the glass broke
> My reflection died
> Leaving me alone
> How will I brush my hair tomorrow?
> If only I were bald.

This poem, 'The Mirror Running', written when Milligan was in his sixty-fourth year, shows the poet struggling with the futility he feels when he is at a particularly low ebb. His poetry often reminds us that he is a Celt and a poet of rare, discordant sympathy and humour. He writes with a strange, oblique vision and many of his poems reflect a depth of frustrated pain above which he constantly strives to surface.

There is a powerful death-wish here, but Milligan, somehow, is a survivor. Courage, ultimately, does not desert him. The lines:

> How will I brush my hair tomorrow?
> If only I were bald.

are not so much an attempt to trivialize the poem in the occasional Milliganesque fashion but rather the despairing reflection that he is required to go on, to continue in a life which is sporadically so painful as to be almost unendurable. Milligan, implicitly demanding (but overtly rejecting) pity, is truly the clown poet here. Baldness he equates with comedy; the last lines mask the profound loneliness and isolation that the poem reveals.

Spike Milligan is a man marooned, out on an island, on his own, speaking a language that most people can't understand, asking questions and then answering them himself with replies that he can't accept.

In another world he might have been a prophet or a visionary or a monk or a court jester.

He is a man lost in our world, painfully aware of so much that passes us by – lacerated by the pollutants of noise and dirt that infiltrate into all our lives, burdened by bureaucracy and by the stupidity, ignorance and indifference that most of us take for granted.

He is angered by the massive inhumanity in the world. Every new example of man's inhumanity to man and to animals causes him rage and despair. His anger at his own inadequacy to right so many wrongs contributes to the pain that is the pattern of his life.

Perhaps this is a good moment to leave Milligan – still working, still trying, still grieving, still loving and still hoping. He is a fortunate man inasmuch as he has immeasurable gifts and talents; he has four attractive, intelligent and affectionate children; he has a young wife with an endless depth of compassion, love and admiration for him. He has good and genuine friends, and as long as he works (for he is not a rich man) he can enjoy the comforts of privacy, warmth, quiet and the solitude he often needs. He copes with the misfortune of his precarious health, struggling on gamely with his battles against depression. He bears with conflicting feelings of failure and achievement a world in which his value and his great potential value are recognized only by a curious cross-section of people who know no barriers of class or generation. In so many ways, he is a voice crying in the wilderness. We could all do to listen to him carefully. He will get it wrong occasionally, but insight, wisdom and true humanity seem to spring from him as though from an eternal font. And as well as all that, at the end of an awful day (his, ours or both) he can still make us laugh.

APPENDIX I
Books by Spike Milligan

AUTOBIOGRAPHY
1971 Adolf Hitler: My Part in His Downfall
1974 'Rommel?' 'Gunner Who?'
1976 Monty: His Part in My Victory
1978 Mussolini: His Part in My Downfall
1985 Where Have All the Bullets Gone?

FICTION
1963 Puckoon

DRAMA
1970 The Bedsitting Room (with John Antrobus)

POETRY
1959 Values
1972 Small Dreams of a Scorpion
1979 Open Heart University

MISCELLANEOUS PROSE
1977 The Spike Milligan Letters (edited by Norma Farnes)
1981 Indefinite Articles and Scunthorpe
1984 The Spike Milligan Letters, vol. 2 (edited by Norma Farnes)

CHILDREN'S BOOKS
1959 Silly Verse for Kids
1968 Milliganimals and the Bald-Twit Lion
1973 Badjelly the Witch
1974 Dip the Puppy
1981 Unspun Socks from a Chicken's Laundry
1982 Sir Nobonk and the Dragon

HUMOUR
1961 A Dustbin of Milligan
1963 The Little Pot Boiler
1965 A Book of Bits, or a Bit of a Book
1969 The Bedside Milligan
1971 Milligan's Ark
1972 Goon Show Scripts
1973 More Goon Show Scripts
1974 Book of the Goons
1974 Transports of Delight
1975 The Great McGonagall Scrapbook
1975 The Milligan Book of Records
1976 William McGonagall: The Truth at Last
1978 Goblins
1979 The Q Annual
1980 Get in the Q Annual
1982 101 Best and Only Limericks
1982 Goon Show Cartoons
1983 There's a Lot of it About
1983 More Goon Cartoons
1983 The Melting Pot

APPENDIX II

Films in which Spike Milligan Appeared

Let's Go Crazy, 1951
Penny Points to Paradise, 1951
London Entertains, 1951
Down Among the Z Men, 1952
Super Secret Service, 1953
The Case of the Mukkinese
    Battlehorn, 1956
The Running, Jumping and
    Standing Still Film, 1960
Watch Your Stern, 1960
Suspect, 1960
Invasion Quartet, 1961
What a Whopper, 1961
Postman's Knock, 1962
The Bedsitting Room, 1969
The Undertaker, 1969
The Magic Christian, 1970
The Magnificent Seven Deadly
    Sins, 1971

Rentadick, 1972
Alice's Adventures in Wonderland,
    1972
The Cherry Picker, 1972
Adolf Hitler: My Part in His
    Downfall, 1973
Digby the Biggest Dog in the
    World, 1973
Man About the House, 1974
The Great McGonagall, 1974
The Three Musketeers, 1974
The Last Remake of Beau Geste,
    1977
The Hound of the Baskervilles,
    1978
The Life of Brian, 1979
Monty Python and the Holy Grail,
    1980

APPENDIX III
The Records of Spike Milligan

Protest Song. Spike.
Warner Bros. K 16240.

1973 Ying Tong Song/I'm
Walking Backwards for
Christmas. The Goons.
Decca. Re-issue. F 13414.

1974 Cheese/Shipmates. Spike
and Others. From the LP
'Treasure Island'
Starline. PSR 367

1974 On the Ning Nang Nong/
The Silly Old Baboon.
Spike. From the LP
'Badjelly the Witch',
Polydor. 2058 524.

1974 Wormwood Scrubs Tango/
The Little Grey Hole in My
Vest. Spike and others.
BBC Records. Stereo.
RESL 18/2.

1976 Remember You're a
Womble/Die Wombles
Sind im Kommen. Eccles
and Bluebottle. Sung by Sir
Winston Eccles and Adolf
Von Bluebottle.
Reprise Records. Stereo.
K 14422.

1976 The Snow Goose/Goose
Walk. Spike and LSO.
From the LP 'The Snow
Goose'.
RCA Victor. RCA 2752.

1978 The Raspberry Song/
Rhymes. The Goons.
Decca. Stereo. F 13769.

1979 One Sunny Day/Woe Is
Me. Milligan and Welch.
From the LP 'Sing Songs
from Q.8'.
United Artists. Stereo.
UP 36489.

LPs
1959 Best of the Goon Shows.
The Goons.
Parlophone. PMC 1108.

1960 Best of the Goon Shows.
No. 2. The Goons.
Parlophone. PMC 1129

1961 Milligan Preserved. Spike.
Parlophone. Mono
PMC 1148. Stereo
PCS 3018.

1962 The Bridge on the River
Wye. Spike and Others.
Parlophone. Mono
PMC 1190. Stereo
PCS 3036.

1964 The Goons Unchained
Melodies. (10″ disc) The
Goons.
Decca. Mono only.
LF 1332.

1964 How to Win an Election.
The Goons.
Philips. Mono only.
AL 3464.

1964 Best of Milligan's Wake.
Spike. From the ATV
Production 'Milligan's
Wake'.
Pye. Mono only.
NPL 18104.

1965 Rhymes and Rhythm. Spike
and Others. Boxed set of
two LPs and four books of
children's rhymes, etc.
Argo. RG 414/5.

1965 Muses with Milligan. Spike.
From the BBC2 TV Series.
Decca. Mono only.
LK 4701.

1967 Goon – But Not Forgotten.
The Goons.
Parlophone. PMC 7037.

1968 World of Beachcomber.
Spike. Based on J. B.
Morton's *Daily Express*
column and the BBC TV
series.
Pye. Mono only.
NPL 18271.

1968 Goon Again – Goon Shows.
The Goons.
Parlophone. Mono only.
PMC 7062.

1969 World of British Comedy.
Spike and The Goons.
Decca. Mono only. PA 39.

1969 No One's Gonna Change
Our World. Spike and
Others.
Regal. Stereo. SRS 5013.

1971 A Record Load of Rubbish.
Spike. Radio London
Broadcast of 26 December
1970.
BBC. Mono only.
RED 98M.

1971 First Men on the Goon. The
Goons.
Parlophone. Mono only.
PMC 7132.

1972 The Last Goon Show of All.
The Goons.
BBC. Stereo REB 142S.

1972 Alice's Adventures in
Wonderland. Spike and
Others. Film soundtrack.
Warner Bros. Stereo.
K 56009.

1973 Michael Parkinson Meets
The Goons. Parkinson and
The Goons. From the TV
show of 28 October 1972.
BBC. Mono only.
REB 165M.

1973 World of Children. Spike
and Others. Children's
poems and verse.
Argo. Stereo. SPA 200

1974 He's Innocent of
Watergate. Sellers and
Spike.
Decca. Stereo. SKL 5194.

1974 Goon Show Classics. The
Goons.
BBC. REB 177.

1974 Treasure Island. Spike and
Others. From the Mermaid
Theatre Production.
Starline. Stereo. SRS 5191.

1974 Badjelly the Witch. Spike.
Polydor Select. Stereo.
2460 235.

1974 Very Best of the Goons. The
Goons.
EMI. EMC 3062.

1974 Live at Cambridge
University. Taylor and
Spike. Recorded at the
Lady Mitchell Hall, 2
December 1973.
Spark. Double Album.
Stereo. SRLO 3001.

1975 Goon Show Classics. Vol. 2.
The Goons.
BBC. REB 213

1975 Golden Hour of Comedy.
Spike and Others. Has
quarter of World of
Beachcomber.
Golden Hour. GH 530

1976 Goon Show Classics. Vol. 3.
The Goons.
BBC. REB 246

1976 Twenty Golden Giggles.
Spike and Others.
EMI. NTS 125

1976 The Snow Goose. Milligan
and LSO. From Paul
Gallico's book. A musical
setting adapted and
narrated by Spike Milligan
with the LSO, conducted
by Ed Welch.
RCA. Stereo RS 1088.

1976 Forty Years of Television:
The Comedians Sing. Spike
and Others. Spike sings
Sewers of the Strand.
BBC. REB 249.

1977 Goon Show Classics. Vol. 4.
The Goons.
BBC. REB 291

1978 Goon Show Classics. Vol. 5.
The Goons.
BBC. REB 339.

1979 Sing Songs from Q.8.
Welch and Spike.
United Artists. Stereo.
UAG 30223.

1979 Cavalcade of London
Theatre. Spike and Others.
Spike is in Poetry and Jazz
250 and sings Carrington
Briggs/I've Never Felt
Finer/Bazonka!
Decca. D 140D/1–4.

1979 Goon Show Classics. Vol. 6.
The Goons.
BBC. REB 366.

1980 World of the Goons. The
Goons.
Decca. SPA 569.

1980 Goon Show Classics. Vol. 7.
The Goons.
BBC. REB 392.

1980 Puckoon. Spike. Spike
reading from his book of the
same name.
EMI. Stereo. SCX 6630.

1981 Adolf Hitler: My Part in His
Downfall. Spike. Adapted
from the book of the same
name.
Columbia. Stereo.
SCX 6636.

1981 Goon Show Classics. Vol. 8.
The Goons
BBC. REB 422

1981 Voice Behind the Mask.
Sellers and The Goons.
Boxed set of four discs as a
tribute to Peter Sellers.
Guild. 62002A to D.

1981 We Are Most Amused.
Double album for Prince
Charles.
Ronco. RTD 2067A & B.

1982 The Snow Goose. Re-issue
of 1975 disc.
RCA. INTS 5224.

1982 Goon Show Classics. Vol. 9.
The Goons
BBC REB 444

1982 Unspun Socks from a
Chicken's Laundry. Spike.
From his book of the same
name.
Ridedrop. Spike L 1.

1984 Wolves, Witches and
Giants. Welch and Spike.
Children's music and story
adaptations by Ed Welch.
Narrated by Spike.
Impression. Double
Album. MIL 2.

APPENDIX IV
TV and Radio

TELEVISION

1947	Paging You (Bill Hall Trio)	1969	The World of Beachcomber
1948	Rooftop Rendezvous (Bill Hall Trio)		Q5
			Curry and Chips (LWT)
1952	Goonreel (A Television Newsreel)	1970	Oh in Colour
	Don't Spare the Horses		The Other Spike (John Goldschmidt documentary)
1953	Frankie Howerd Show	1971	Q6
1954	Right at the Top	1972	Marty Feldman's Comedy
1955	The Lid Off the BBC (A 'behind the scenes' documentary about the BBC)		Machine (awarded Golden Rose and Special Comedy Award, Montreux) (ITV)
			The Last Goon Show of All
1956	Idiot Weekly		(As part of the BBC 50th
	A Show Called Fred (Associated Rediffusion. TV Writer of the Year Award)		birthday celebrations)
			A Milligan for all Seasons
		1975	The Melting Pot
	Son of Fred (Associated Rediffusion)	1977	Q7
			The Best of British
	Off the Record		The Best of Fred
1963	The Telegoons	1978	Q8
	Milligan at Large	1980	Q9
	Milligan's Wake	1982	There's a Lot of It About
1965	Muses with Milligan		

NB: Programmes made by the BBC unless otherwise stated.

RADIO

To list Milligan's hundreds of radio appearances would be a daunting task. I decided that the most appropriate course would be to outline the early years that preceded the *Goon Show*, and then take a random year at a later period, which would give an indication of Spike's varying radio work.

Establishing the facts has not always been easy. For instance, in a pre-Goon programme *Listen My Children*, Robert Beatty believes that Spike was in it and remembers him at the microphone along with Harry Secombe and himself. BBC records show no mention of Milligan. Taxed with this, Spike has a simple explanation: 'Well, of course I was there. I was TRYING to get in, wasn't I?'

Radio programmes in which Spike Milligan appeared in early years

25 Feb. 1949	BBC Light Programme: *Opportunity Knocks*.	Produced by Dennis Main Wilson
5 Aug. 1949	BBC Home Service: The Bowery Bar.	Produced by Charles Chilton
Sept.–Dec. 1949	BBC Third Programme: 13 Weekly instalments of *Hip Hip Hoo Roy*.	Produced by Leslie Bridgemont and starring Derek Roy
May–July 1951	BBC Home Service: 6 programmes of *Junior Crazy Gang*.*	Produced by Dennis Main Wilson
Aug.–Sept. 1951	BBC Home Service: 5 programmes of *Junior Crazy Gang*.	Produced by Dennis Main Wilson
19 Nov. 1951	BBC Home Service: *Bumblethorpe*.	Produced by Peter Eton
26 Dec. 1951	BBC Home Service: *Cinderella* (Pantomime) with Lizbeth Webb as Cinderella, Graham Stark as Prince Charming, The Goons, The Stargazers, the Ray Ellington Quartet, Max Geldray and the BBC Dance Orchestra conducted by Stanley Black.	

* This was, in fact, the start of the *Goon Show*. The BBC archives show the titles as above for the first six programmes. Next, the title became 'Those Crazy People, The Goons'. Neither title satisfied the artistes, and by the beginning of the second series they were billed as they had always wished, simply as 'The Goon Show'.

Sample year of Spike's radio broadcasts

11. 1.75 R4: Interview by Howard Rogers with Spike Milligan on writing film of Wm. McGonagall.

11. 1.75 R2: Michael Parkinson. Guests included Spike Milligan.

17. 1.75 R4: Encore the Goons (repeat series). (1) The Lost Emperor. Script by Spike Milligan.

24. 1.75 R4: Encore the Goons. (2) Fear of Wages. Script by Spike Milligan and Larry Stephens.

31. 1.75 R4: Encore the Goons. (3) Drums Along the Mersey. Script by Spike Milligan.

7. 2.75 R4: Encore the Goons. (4) King Solomon's Mines. Script by Spike Milligan and Larry Stephens.

14. 2.75 R4: Encore the Goons. (5) The Childe Harolde Rewarde. Script by Spike Milligan.

7. 3.75 R4: Encore the Goons. (8) The Silver Doubloons. Script by Spike Milligan.

14. 3.75 R4: Encore the Goons. (9) The Phantom Head Shaver. Script by Spike Milligan.

14. 3.75 R4: Plain Tales from the Raj. (2) Lances and Rifles. Speakers included Spike Milligan.

21. 3.75 R4: Pick of the Week. Face Your Image. David Dimbleby interviewed Jimmy Grant and Spike Milligan.

20. 5.75 R2: Pause for Thought. Bernard Jackson interviewed Spike Milligan.

21. 5.75 R2: Pause for Thought. Bernard Jackson interviewed Spike Milligan.

22. 5.75 R2: Pause for Thought. Bernard Jackson interviewed Spike Milligan.

23. 5.75 R2: Pause for Thought. Bernard Jackson interviewed Spike Milligan.

3. 6.75 R4: Dateline. Spike Milligan. Keith Davie interviewed Spike Milligan.

5. 7.75 R4: PM Reports. Pete Van Den Bergh feature on Harrods first day of Summer Sale being petitioned by Friends of the Earth Conservation Committee, including Twiggy, John Pardoe, MP, Spike Milligan and shoppers.

17.10.75 R4: Pick of the Week. The Goon Show – Fear of Wages. Written by Spike Milligan and Larry Stephens.

31.10.75 R4: Pick of the Week. The Goon Show – King Solomon's Mines. Written by Spike Milligan and Larry Stephens.

9.11.75 R4: More Plain Tales from the Raj. (5) Milligan Chota Sahib: An Indian Childhood. Speaker Spike Milligan.

5.12.75 R4: Pick of the Week. The Goon Show. Written by Spike Milligan.

Notes

CHAPTER 1

1 Letter: Leo Milligan to SM, 20.3.67.
2 Letter: Leo Milligan to SM.
3 Tape: Harry Secombe/PS, 17.3.82, Cheam, Surrey.

CHAPTER 3

1 Work in Progress by SM on Leo Milligan.

CHAPTER 4

1 'Catford', *Open Heart University*.
2 'Spring Song', 18 March 1972. *Small Dreams of a Scorpion*.
3 *Goon Show* script, 28.5.51.
4 Tape: Ronnie Scott/PS, 7.3.84, Frith Street, W1.

CHAPTER 5

1 Article by SM, *The Countryman*, September 1981.
2 *Adolf Hitler: My Part in His Downfall*, Part 2, Dunkirk.
3 Tape: D Battery 56th Heavy Regiment Royal Artillery Reunion, Bexhill-on-Sea, 2.4.81.
4 *Adolf Hitler: My Part in His Downfall*, Part 2, Summer 1940.
5 *Adolf Hitler: My Part in His Downfall*, Part 3.

CHAPTER 6

1 *Adolf Hitler: My Part in His Downfall*, Part 3.
2 Ibid.
3 *'Rommel?' 'Gunner Who?'*, Jan: Feb.
4 Ibid.

5 *'Rommel?' 'Gunner Who?'*, April.
6 *Monty: His Part in My Victory*, Carthage.

CHAPTER 7

1 *Mussolini: His Part in My Downfall*, Salerno.
2 *Mussolini: His Part in My Downfall*, 25 September 1943.
3 *Mussolini: His Part in My Downfall*, 28 December 1943.
4 *Puckoon*, Chapter 2.

CHAPTER 8

1 Tape: Antoinette Pontani/PS, 14.3.84, Paris.

CHAPTER 12

1 Article by Philip Oakes, *Books and Authors*, December 1957.

CHAPTER 13

1 Tape: Michael Foot/PS, 7.10.84, Westminster.

CHAPTER 14

1 Tape: Bernard Miles/PS, 19.6.85, Islington.

CHAPTER 15

1 *Puckoon*, Chapter I.
2 Tape: Joan Greenwood/PS, 28.9.82, Chelsea.

CHAPTER 17

1 *Monty: His Part in My Victory*.
2 Feature Interview with Patricia Milligan, *Woman's Realm*, 24 April 1975.

3 Tape: David Nettheim/PS, 5.7.84, Sydney.

CHAPTER 19

1 'Look at All Those Monkeys', *Silly Verse for Kids*, 1959.

CHAPTER 20

1 'Around the Bend' and 'Milligan Again', both compiled by Keith Gray.

2 'Inferno'. Poem to be included in Milligan's forthcoming collection, *The Mirror Running*.

Index